The Sword of the Crown

The New Model Army: Cromwell at Dunbar

The Sword of the Crown
A History of the British Army to 1914

Eric W. Shepherd

The Sword of the Crown: a History of the British Army to 1914
by Eric W. Shepherd

First published under the title
A Short History of the British Army to 1914

Published by Leonaur Ltd

Text in this form copyright © 2008 Leonaur Ltd

ISBN: 978-1-84677-510-9 (hardcover)
ISBN: 978-1-84677-509-3 (softcover)

http://www.leonaur.com

Publisher's Notes

The opinions expressed in this book are those of the author and are not necessarily those of the publisher.

Contents

British Military History   11

The Beginnings of the British Army
  1. The Early and Medieval Armies 55 B.C. to A.D. 1642   15
  2. The First Civil War 1642-1646   20
  3. The New Model Army   22
  4. How the New Model Army Lived and Fought   23
  5. Cromwell's Career of Victory 1645-1660   28

The Duke of Marlborough and the Contest with Louis XIV
  1. The Army Before and After the Glorious Revolution 1660-1701   32
  2. Marlborough's Career of Victory 1702-1713   39
  3. Marlborough's Chef-d'oeuvre: Oudenarde July 11, 1708   51
  4. The Character of a Great Captain   55

The Struggle With France for Overseas Empire
  1. The First Round: the War of the Austrian Succession 1714-1748   59
  2. The Early Stages of the Seven Years' War 1749-1757   68
  3. The Conquest of Canada 1758-1760   74
  4. The Subsidiary Operations in Europe and the Indies 1758-1762   80
  5. William Pitt as a War Minister   89

The Period of Anglo-French Rivalry in India
  1. The French Initiative under Dupleix 1740-1755   96
  2. The Extinction of French Power in India 1755-1761   104
  3. Our Early Indian Wars   110

The Loss of America
  1. The Conflict with Colonial Revolution 1764-1777   113
  2. The World War 1778-1783   119

The British Conquest of India: 1
1. The British Conquest of Bengal 1760-1767 — 130
2. The Fight with Hyder Ali for Southern India 1767-1782 — 134
3. The Overthrow of Mysore 1783-1800 — 139

The Fight With Revolutionary France
1. The Outbreak of the Conflict, 1783-1793 — 148
2. The Campaign in the Low Countries 1793-1795 — 152
3. The Campaign in the West Indies 1793-1800 — 156
4. Minor Operations and Expeditions, 1793-1798 — 162
5. The North Holland Expedition 1799 — 166
6. The Campaign in Egypt 1799-1800 — 168

England Against Napoleon: the Last War With France
1. Six Indecisive Years 1803-1808 — 175
2. The Peninsular War: the Defence of Portugal 1808-1810 — 183
3. The Peninsular War: the Period of Tension 1811-1812 — 194
4. The Peninsular War: the British Counter-Offensive 1813-1814 — 203
5. The Battle in Wellington's Day — 213
6. Minor Operations in Europe and Elsewhere 1809-1814 — 216

The American War and the Waterloo Campaign
1. The War with the United States 1812-1815 — 219
2. The Waterloo Campaign 1815 — 224
3. Wellington and His Campaigns — 228

The British Conquest of India: 2
1. The Second Mahratta War 1803-1806 — 243
2. The Nepal Campaign and the Overthrow of the Mahratta Confederacy 1807-1825 — 251
3. The Conquest of Lower Burma 1824-1826 — 260

The British Conquest of India: 3
1. The First Invasion of Afghanistan 1838-1842 — 265
2. The Subjugation of Sind 1843 — 272
3. The Sikh Wars 1845-1849 — 273
4. The Second War with Burma 1852-1853 — 280
5. The English in India — 282

From Waterloo to the Boer War
1. The Army During the Long Peace 1816-1853 — 286
2. Minor Campaigns 1816-1853 — 288

3. The War with Russia 1854-1856	292
4. The Birth of the Modern Army 1855-1882	298

The Mutiny and Our Later Indian Wars

1. The Sepoy Revolt 1857-1859	307
2. The Second War with Afghanistan 1878-1881	320
3. The Conquest of Upper Burma and the Subsequent Campaigns on the North-East Frontier 1885-1898	325
4. The North-West Frontier Campaigns 1852-1913	330
5. Other Minor Expeditions in India and the Reorganisation of the Indian Army 1861-1914	339

Half a Century of Small Wars

1. Minor Campaigns in Asia 1856-1901	343
2. Minor Campaigns in East and Central Africa 1868-1904	347
3. Operations in West Africa 1873-1906	350
4. Campaigns in South Africa 1877-1896	353
5. The British Army in Egypt and the Sudan 1882-1898	358
6. A Minor Campaign in Canada: the Red River Expedition 1870	367
7. The Maori Wars in New Zealand 1863-1870	368
8. The Imperial Policeman	371

The South African War and After

1. The Early British Reverses October-December 1899	382
2. The Restoration of the Position in Natal and the Occupation of Bloemfontein January-March 1900	386
3. The Clearing of Natal and the Orange Free State, and the Capture of Pretoria April-July 1900	390
4. The Guerrilla Warfare to the End of Roberts' Period of Command June-November 1900	394
5. Kitchener's Operations to the Conclusion of Peace December 1900-May 1902	398
6. Towards Armageddon 1902-1914	403
Epilogue	407

To my wife, Peter

Chapter 1
British Military History

The military history of Great Britain may be divided into two parts, the campaigns fought by British troops in Europe, India or America against the armies of Continental powers, and the small wars within the British Empire which have recurred at given intervals since that empire was first won. Of necessity such a narrative as this must deal mainly with the former of these two categories of operations, the latter being but briefly touched on.

With regard to those wars in which the British army has been matched against civilised and regularly organised foes it may be pointed out that on no occasion has it appeared in the field except as part, and seldom the principal part, of an allied force. Marlborough's command comprised Dutchmen, Austrians, Germans and Danes, besides his own countrymen. Germans, Spaniards and Portuguese served in the Peninsula under Wellington. In the Crimea our former hereditary foes, the French, and also the Italians, fought beside us against the Russians, who again, in the Great War, allied themselves with their enemies of sixty years ago against this country's age-long friend Germany. We shall do well before embarking on the story of these Continental campaigns of ours to remember that such glory as may accrue from them is not solely our own, but must be shared in greater or less degree with practically every nation in Europe.

It may also be pointed out for the better understanding of the narrative that these campaigns were none of them waged solely, or even mainly, by the regular standing army of Great Britain. Our settled military policy throughout our history has invariably been to reduce our establishments well below any reasonable margin of safety in time of peace, and then on the outbreak of war, as a kind of forlorn hope, to send overseas the tiny striking force available. By this means we have gained time for the hasty raising and training of the raw recruits, inspired by the imminence and urgency of the crisis to come forward for the defence of their country. The first campaigns have usually seen the shattering and complete disappearance of the regular troops, leaving behind them nothing but a trained cadre and a tradition of valour; indeed both have been heritages invaluable to their heirs and successors and yet, perhaps, too dearly purchased at the price of so much blood and treasure. The regular troops of Great Britain have throughout their history given of their best to their country; yet it has usually been their task to perish, gathering into their hearts the spears of the enemy's first and fiercest onset; and our great British victories have been won mainly by amateur soldiers, who came from peaceful pursuits to save their menaced motherland, and returned whence they came when their heroic task was accomplished.

One may sum up the historical role of our army by saying that it was a projectile fired by the British fleet. Particularly appropriate would this text be if hung in a prominent place in the Cabinet room in 10 Downing Street. It suggests that if the projectile is to take full effect it must be well manufactured and carefully preserved; and that the gunner who is to discharge it must be competent to find and keep his eyes fixed on the most suitable target and to direct his shot straight and truly towards it. These things are the province of the statesmen who conduct our wars, and throughout our history not one has been found whose policy and actions in this respect do not lie open to criticism and condemnation. Even the most arresting of these statesmen, William Pitt the elder, turns out on close investigation to have been mainly an inspirer of men, a dynamic force more suited to whip up energy than to direct it; a man who could call armies from the soil but had only vague and unpractical ideas as to how to use them when he had raised them. And yet the conduct of war by the statesmen seems so easy when an ordinary politician like Lord Liverpool could make good a claim to the eternal gratitude of his country simply by allowing Wellington to go on beating her enemies and by refraining from withdrawing his army from the scene of its victories as long as it was not defeated.

Nevertheless, despite the tendency inherent in the political leaders of Britain to avoid, if and whenever humanly possible, getting the best value out of the British army, the record of that army in Continental wars may well be a matter for our legitimate pride. It is, however, as much eclipsed by the tale of our smaller campaigns as the ordinary Academy painting is eclipsed by a masterpiece of Da Vinci or Turner. The history of our Colonial and Indian operations, fought in every quarter of the globe against every conceivable variety of enemy, and in face of the greatest difficulties of climate and terrain, is a long and unbroken catalogue of successes. So rarely has it been chequered by anything that could be termed a defeat or even a check that the rare occurrence of such a phenomenon causes as much surprise to the present-day student as it once aroused consternation in the minds of contemporaries. Continental armies, trained year in and year out for service against one particular sort of enemy and in one particular theatre of war, have often broken down badly under the searching test of battle. The British army may be called on at any moment to proceed to the uttermost end of the earth, go into action against an enemy of which it knows little or nothing, and march and fight in a climate where a white man can with difficulty live, and over ground practically impassable to any one but a trained mountaineer or woodsman, yet it is expected as part of its normal routine of service to prove itself equal to the emergency, and has so proved itself for the past 100 years. When we tell, as in these following pages we shall have to do, of English victories in France and Belgium, in Germany and Spain, we are dealing with matters that can be closely paralleled from the military history of any of our Continental allies and enemies. But the long record of British triumphs in the plains and mountains of India, in the swamps and deserts of Africa, in the deadly West Indian islands, and amid the depths of the American forests, constitutes in sum an achievement unlike any other recorded in history, and yet one which, in great part because of the very monotony of its tale of success, usually passes unrecognised and unacclaimed.

Chapter 2

The Beginnings of the British Army
55 B.C. to A.D. 1660

1. The Early and Medieval Armies
55 B.C. to A.D. 1642

For the purposes of this book it seems needless to touch at any great length upon the earliest armed forces in these islands. It would serve no useful end to dwell upon the fortunes of the Celtic warriors who, half armed and undisciplined as they were, none the less put up no discreditable opposition to the trained veterans of Rome, led by the first of Roman generals, or upon the Anglo-Saxon pirates who, after the departure of the legions from the shores of the province of Britain, set foot on and gradually overran the whole island, carving out a new heritage for themselves with spear and sword. Later, in the ninth century the Norsemen descended like a plague of locusts upon the north-west of Europe, menacing with pillage and massacre every human habitation and being within striking distance of the coast or of the course of the great rivers. Our British kings were therefore compelled to secure the safety of their dominions by some more reliable means than the spasmodic and unorganized efforts of local populations mustered hurriedly in arms at the first news of danger. Accordingly they raised a force of heavy armed feudal infantry liable for service on the basis of land tenure; and this force supplied the bulk of the armies which, under Alfred the Great, threw back in decisive defeat the hosts of the Danes. The peril, however, was averted only for a century, when the enemy returned in greater force and better organised than ever before, and so successful was he that in a few years a Danish king, Canute, ascended the throne of England, and his house held it for a generation. Canute's house carles, a personal bodyguard of trained mercenaries, may be regarded as the first germ of our standing army; they formed the kernel and mainstay of those armies which consolidated his rule from Forth to Channel; they were maintained after the extinction of the Danish line by the succeeding Saxon monarchs, and in 1066, on the ridge at Hastings, they found a glorious death around the corpse of the last of the English kings.

That battle marked the temporary supersession of the foot soldier by the mailed cavalryman as the decisive arm. Both in England and on the Continent the armoured knight on his huge steed ruled the battle-field for 300 years, during which period infantry suffered a complete eclipse, serving on the few occasions of its appearance merely as lance and sword fodder. In England the Norman and Plantagenet kings, ruling over an alien and conquered people, were engaged in continual fighting, both within and on the borders of the country, and also on the frontiers of their Continental possessions. They gradually, in the course of their major military undertakings, replaced the comparatively inefficient feudal host (which still remained based on land tenure, though the land had entirely changed hands after the Conquest) by bodies of foreign mercenaries who were found to be in every way more useful and more reliable. These mercenaries formed the backbone of the royal armies which in the time of Henry II., Richard I. And John strove to make head against the unceasing efforts of the French kings to regain the west and south of France, and also of those which in the reigns of John and Henry III. combated with alternating fortunes the baronial rebels, called into being by the tyranny or weakness of the Crown.

Edward I., the royal power having been consolidated in England, set to work to unify the island by a series of expeditions into Wales and Scotland. In the course of these campaigns, which necessitated the adoption of strategic and tactical methods very different from those which had hitherto served well enough in previous wars, Edward developed a new system of fighting which was in a few years to revolutionise the military art, restore to infantry its former place of the battlefield, and deal the death-blow to the supremacy of the heavy horseman. The discovery of the long bow gave the English foot soldier a weapon equally useful for preparing the attack of his own cavalry and for repulsing that of the enemy at long range; and the English men-at-arms, hitherto the main fighting force of the army, by degrees became little more than an escort and a stiffening for the archers.

The new tactics, first experimented with by Edward I. In Wales and Scotland, were put to a searching test by his grandson in the early part of the Hundred Years' War with France.

Edward III.'s method of making war was a combination of offensive strategy with defensive tactics. His men-at-arms, experienced in Border wars, were as good as those of his adversaries; his foot, consisting partly of pressed men and partly of volunteers enlisted in "free companies" under some wealthy and popular leader, were far superior to anything brought against them. The English army proved everywhere victorious against the French knights, whether these assailed it on horseback as at Cressy or on foot as at Poitiers, and a large part of France was rapidly overrun. The riposte to the English tactics, however, was eventually found, and once the French had adopted the policy of firmly declining to oblige Edward by attacking him in his chosen defensive positions, he realised that a continuance of the war could hardly give him greater advantages than could be gained by the conclusion of a prompt peace. For some time, however, English leaders and troops found plenty of scope for their energy and skill in the various intestine struggles of France, Spain and Italy, in all of which countries they won for themselves a reputation as the finest soldiers in Europe.

The second period of the Hundred Years' War, which opened by a crushing French defeat at Agincourt in 1415, raised the military fame of the English army to a pinnacle never reached before. France, torn by civil dissension and demoralised by the irresistible pressure of her foes, was helpless before the skilful strategy and methodical tactics of Henry V. and his school of generals. Paris and half the land fell into the hands of our armies; Henry VI. of England was crowned in Paris, and the rightful heir to the throne fled beyond the Loire. From this desperate situation the hapless band was rescued by what can only be described as a miracle in the form of an unlettered country maiden, who fired with her own white-hot enthusiasm King, army and people, shattered in a few whirlwind strokes the veteran English hosts, together with their reputation for invincibility, and ending her own meteoric career with a martyr's crown, left as her legacy to her country a stainless name and a talisman of victory which in a few short years swept the invaders clean out of France.

Then England's weapons were turned into her own vitals. The bands of armed men flooded back home from overseas, where for years they had lived by fighting, plunder and licence, and found congenial employment in the hosts raised in support of the claim of one or the other aspirant to the English throne. From 1455 to 1485 the dynastic conflict known as the Wars of the Roses raged spasmodically throughout the land. The middle and lower classes took no active part in the war, which was waged entirely by the great nobles and their hired levies. Despite the fact that the invention of gunpowder had rendered possible the devising of weapons of new and terrible power, the battles were still fought mainly with bows and bills, with axe and sword, as in the time of Cressy and Agincourt, and the strategical and tactical methods had also changed but little since those days. The war produced a considerable number of good leaders of troops, at least one strategist of real ability in Edward IV., one legendary hero in Warwick the Kingmaker, and the greatest battle ever fought in England, that of Towton, in which close on 70,000 men were engaged. At the end of it the noblesse had been decimated, the armies had torn each other to pieces, and the country, weary of battle and bloodshed, settled down thankfully to a long period of economy, peace and prosperity under the Tudors.

Meanwhile the firearm was gradually taking its place on the battlefield and ousting the long bow as the missile weapon of the infantry. Cannon had from the fourteenth century been a useful and effective auxiliary weapon, but the hand-gun took longer to perfect. The first and most curious effect of its general adoption was to restore to cavalry, which had gained in mobility by discarding its defensive armour, the ascendency which it had lost in the heyday of the long bow. Meanwhile the cost of the new armament was so great as to be prohibitive for everyone except the King, who had all the resources of England at his back; and hence a force which would have seemed ridiculously small to Edward III. and Henry V. proved sufficient to keep the peace in a country exhausted by civil strife and united in whole-hearted support of the monarchy.

Apart, therefore, from certain isolated military episodes such as Flodden, the period of close on 200 years, from 1485 to 1642, must from the point of view of military history be regarded as a fallow one. In theory the defence of the country was in time of crisis the function of the militia, the units of which were heterogeneous in their armament and alike only in their complete lack of any sort of training. At the time of the danger of the Spanish invasion Elizabeth raised an army which, though formidable enough on paper, by the mercy of God and the British fleet, never had the opportunity of putting its military virtues to the test against Parma's veterans. Thus, though individual Englishmen were gaining experience in the armies of foreign powers and proving in Holland, France and Germany that the warlike virtues of the race had not been lost, the national forces of England were practically a negligible quantity. The disgraceful episodes of the Rochelle expedition of 1625 and the Scottish wars of 1637-1640 were clear evidence of the lamentable inefficiency of what had once been the proudest army of Europe.

Such was the state of affairs in 1642, on the eve of the outbreak of that Civil War which was destined to raise England from a position of complete military impotence to one of comparative respectability, and to see the formation of the force from which our standing army of today is directly descended.

2. The First Civil War
1642-1646

By 1642 the ever-widening breach between the absolutist and Anglican King Charles I. and the propertied and Nonconformist middle classes had grown so great as to render inevitable a resort to the arbitrament of arms, and the so-called Great Civil War commenced. To go into details of the military movements on either side would be tedious. Neither party had any very definite ideas of its aims or of the means necessary for victory. The numbers enrolled by the contending parties were, in proportion to the available man power of the country and the importance of the constitutional principles at stake, surprisingly small; it is doubtful if out of a population of close on five millions there were at any time more than 150,000 men under arms, and of these a great proportion were militia levies, locally raised by various districts for purposes of self-defence, and ill-equipped, even had they been willing, for service far from their homes. Other bodies again, amounting in the aggregate to a considerable total, were employed in leisurely and genteel garrison service in the various castles and manor houses, held for one side or the other by prominent partisans up and down the land. For these reasons it long proved impossible for either Royalists or Parliamentarians to assemble a field army of respectable size, to keep it together for any length of time, or to replace the losses incurred by battle, sickness and desertion. The host under the King's personal command fell from 14,000 at Edgehill in 1642 to under 9000 at Naseby in 1645. The main Parliamentary army under Essex had between 1642 and the end of 1644 been reduced from close on 20,000 to under 5000 of all arms; while in three months of not over strenuous campaigning in 1643 it lost 66 per cent of its effectives from one cause or another. For the greatest battle of the war, Marston Moor, neither side could concentrate as many as 25,000 men.

So far as it is possible to generalise in such a planless and haphazard war as this, it may be said that the country gentlemen and aristocracy who controlled most of the west and south-west of England and formed the bulk of the Royalist horse, in the early part of the war the queen of the battlefield, were aligned against the richer and more populous east and south, whose main stronghold was the capital. To the assistance of the King there came in the early part of the war a certain number of troops from Ireland, but these were more than counterbalanced by the accession to the popular cause of the well-organised and well-disciplined Scottish army, 21,000 strong. Charles appears to have had some shadowy and vague plan for uniting to his own army, stationed about Oxford, those of Newcastle from the north and Hopton from the south-west, with the ultimate purpose of a general advance on London, but was not competent enough to carry it out. Hopton, after overrunning Wessex, was checked at Cheriton, and Newcastle's army was broken at Marston Moor in Yorkshire. Meanwhile, after three years of war, the conduct of operations on the Parliament side was falling more and more into the hands of a body of resolute and determined men, led by Oliver Cromwell, who realised that decisive military victory, the sole solution of the contest, could be achieved only by the provision of a disciplined and reliable fighting force. This he set to work to secure, and by the spring of 1645 the "New Model" army had come into being. This body of troops, little stronger than a present-day division, in less than a year of campaigning crushed the Royalist resistance everywhere and made itself master of England.

3. THE NEW MODEL ARMY

The New Model, when first raised, had as nucleus three of the original Parliamentary armies, and was made up to its regulation strength of 7600 cavalry and 14,400 infantry by in recruits compulsorily enrolled. This method of filling its ranks was not abandoned till 1651; that is, after the victorious termination of the Civil Wars and the complete establishment of the supremacy of the Parliament throughout the British Isles. Once this had been achieved, the New Model, which originally had been only one of several forces at the disposal of the Parliament, and had gradually absorbed the others as the years passed, could safely rely on voluntary recruiting. At this date its strength had been increased more than threefold, so that it numbered close on 70,000 of all arms.

Its first Commander-in-Chief was Sir Thomas Fairfax, who led it to complete victory in the First Civil War, and only resigned his post before the Scotch campaign of 1650, in which year Oliver Cromwell succeeded him, retaining his position until his death eight years later. On the Headquarters Staff of the army were the lieutenant-general in command of the Horse and the major-general in command of the Foot, and various other heads of services and departments in charge of artillery, engineers, intelligence and commissariat. These high officers upon occasion formed the council of war, which was frequently summoned to assist the commander-in-chief.

The New Model infantry were recruited mainly from the lower classes of the agricultural or urban population, but the cavalry consisted largely of men of education and means. The officers, many of whom had won promotion from the ranks, and were for the most part drawn from the new squirearchy or the monied business classes, had learned their soldiering in the best of all possible schools—that of war—and their advancement depended mainly, if not entirely, on good and faithful service in the field which might bring them to the favourable notice of the commander-in-chief.

The New Model was distinguished from all other British armies that preceded it by the strictness of its discipline, which was enforced by severe and often ferocious punishment, and included in the catalogue of things forbidden many offences usually regarded as contrary to the moral and the social rather than the military code. This must be attributed mainly to the deeply religious spirit of the army. This spirit made of every trooper and pikeman a crusader in the cause of liberty of conscience, which caused the army's camp-fires on the night before a battle to echo with the sonorous voices of preaching captains and Bible-reading corporals, and made the field of victory resound with thundering psalms of thanksgiving to the Lord of Hosts. No British army of history has ever marched forth to war with such a firm, fanatic and vocal conviction that the cause of truth and righteousness was entrusted to its sole keeping.

4. How the New Model Army Lived and Fought

Let us imagine ourselves for a few moments carried back for close on 300 years of time and watching this first of our great national armies at work. In the peaceful leafy lanes and tortuous rutted streets of an English village the regiments of Fairfax's host are assembling for the day's march. Musketeers, red-coated and knee-breeched, with felt hat on head and knapsack on back, bandolier and powder-horn on shoulder, and each bearing his four-foot-long matchlock or firelock, are mingling in the ranks with other foot soldiers armed with a sword and a sixteen-foot-long pike, and equipped with crested and combed helmet and back and breast-plate. Heavy cavalrymen, similarly armoured over their buff coats, are leading their horses from the stables and yards, buckling on their long straight swords, seeing to the priming of their big pistols, or loading up their haversacks with the seven days' rations brought up last night by the train, and carried on the men now that an action is expected. Close by a company of dragoons, unarmoured men on light horses, with sword and firelock as their weapon, are trotting forward up a by-street to take their place in the van of the advance. Artillery teams of six or four horses, and one or two teams of oxen, are being harnessed to the clumsy long-trailed guns of various calibres from twelve to three pounds, on which their detachments of three men are loading round-shot and barrels of powder. In the rear of all, country carts and pack-horses are collecting on the village green, where have been dumped the army's heavy baggage, the bread and cheese requisitioned from the reluctant inhabitants of the district, and the variety of other foodstuffs purchased locally in open market by the regimental sutlers and followers.

An hour later, when the sun is already high in the heavens and clouds of swirling dust have begun to render wearisome the march of the heavily laden infantry, a mounted officer at full gallop is seen descending a crest in front of the vanguard of the army. Urging his horse past the sweating ranks of the "forlorn hope" of musketeers at the head of the column, he draws up and salutes beside a knot of mounted officers, who bend forward eagerly in their saddles to hear his news. Scarcely is it delivered than it spreads like a ripple down the ranks of the following cavalry regiment, and from there to the toiling infantry of the main body. The enemy is at hand! The horsemen look carefully to sword and pistol; the Foot shake themselves up and step out more vigorously; and all eyes are eagerly bent towards the ridge in front, over the crest of which the commander-in-chief and his headquarters staff, with their escort of heavy cavalry, are just disappearing at the gallop.

As the "forlorn" of musketeers top the rise they see in front of them undulating stretches of open unfenced country, and beyond a few small copses, a thicker wood, and in the distance the tapering spire of a village church nestling among the trees. Clouds of billowing dust and the glint of uniforms and arms between the copses give unmistakable evidence of the presence of the enemy. As each regiment passes over the crest the lieutenant-general or the major-general rides forward from his position by the roadside and enters into brief conversation with its colonel, telling him his place in the line, the word of the day—"God is with us"—and the field sign—in this case a leafy branch affixed to the hat or helmet—which every officer and soldier must wear to distinguish him from the enemy in the forthcoming battle. Then slowly and by degrees the army arrays itself for action. The infantry form the centre and mainstay of the line; each regiment drawn up in dense clumps, six deep, pikemen interspersed with musketeers, the regiments of the second line covering off and closing up the intervals between those of the first line; the cavalry, also in two lines of regiments, each regiment in line three deep, on the wings of the infantry. The heavier guns unlimber and come into position in the intervals between the regiments of infantry, while the lighter guns, two of which are attached to each of these regiments, are also brought forward; the round shot and barrels of powder are placed behind the guns, and the crews prepare for action. About a hundred yards in front of the centre of the army is stationed the "forlorn" of musketeers which we saw leading the march. Behind hedges and ditches, and in among the copses and broken ground on the flanks of the line, lurk the companies of Dragoons who have dismounted for action and sent their horses and horse-holders to the rear. Well behind the centre of the line the trains and baggage-wagons are filing slowly and laboriously into the shelter of a large farm and its enclosures.

All this arraying and ordering of the line takes up much time, for there being no intermediate echelon of command between Army Headquarters and the regiments, all details of interval, distances, dressing and so forth have to be personally supervised by the commanders of the Horse and Foot. The enemy, however, 1200 yards off across the plain, is engaged in a similar and equally lengthy process, so the operation can be completed at leisure.

At long last all is ready, and one by one the guns open on the dark lines of the enemy, firing steadily and regularly at the rate of one round every four to five minutes. To the dull boom of the pieces is added the intermittent rattle of musketry-fire from the "forlorn", then suddenly there rings out a deep fierce shout from thousands of throats, and the whole battle-line of the New Model sways and begins to roll steadily and resolutely forward, muskets at the ready, pikes levelled, swords and pistols drawn. So it goes until within 150 to 100 yards of the motionless array of the enemy. Then in a moment that array comes to life. Cavalry dart forward from its wings; clouds of smoke veil the lines of its infantry and there breaks out the thunder of a fierce volley. The New Model infantry halt for a moment, not because of the enemy's fire but in order to deliver its own. Its six-deep array has, by a process known as doubling the ranks, now become three deep, the front rank men drop to their knees, the second stoop, the rear stand upright; the muskets are levelled—one shattering volley and then another—then down come the pikes, and with a run and a cheer the Foot close with the enemy hand to hand.

Meanwhile on the wings the heavy cavalry have broken into a good round trot which has brought them face to face with the foremost ranks of the hostile Horse. Their array has already felt the effects of the galling fire of the Parliamentary Dragoons from the flanks, and as they came within effective range further gaps are caused by the independent fire of the pistols of the Cuirassiers. None the less they bear themselves gallantly enough, and the opposing ranks, throwing their empty weapons in each other's faces, meet sword to sword, and, halting, engage in fierce individual fencing matches. For some time the issue, both in the centre and on the wings, is doubtful. One of the Parliamentary Cavalry regiments on the left, indeed, disordered in its advance by getting entangled in a field of haycocks, is caught in flank by a strong body of the King's Horse, and scattered, its component parts still fighting sternly with individual Royalist troopers. Fortunately for it the main body of the latter, espying the teams and wagons of the New Model's train still slowly filing into the yard of the farm in the rear, ride off hell for leather in that direction and are for the moment lost to the battle. Moreover, the right wing has now gained the advantage over its immediate adversaries. A gap has been made in the ranks of the Royalist Horse by a group of vigorous and skilful swordsmen, their comrades near them have pressed in and widened it, and in a few minutes the mass of the King's Cavalry, shivering, breaking and falling asunder, is scattered into flying fragments, seeking refuge and a rallying point in the woods to their rear.

During all this time the infantry battle in the centre has been practically stationary. King's men and Parliament men have locked pikes all along the front and are swaying backwards and forwards like a rugby scrum, their ranks still unbroken and with no advantage as yet to either side. Suddenly there breaks out on the left of the Royalist line a rattling volley of pistols; the right-hand regiment of Foot finds its ranks swept by whistling bullets, and then is heavily struck and sent staggering and reeling sidelong by the impact of heavy men and heavy horses charging full on its flank. In an instant its ordered ranks are hustled, jostled, broken and dissolved; and their disorder communicates itself to the regiment next on the right. The red-coated infantry seize their chance and press vigorously home with fierce pike-thrusts, and gradually the steady Royalist array begins to sag and give. Here and there a crack corps, or one favoured by a rise in the ground or a ditch in its front, continues to fight with undaunted resolution; but these bodies rapidly become ever-diminishing islets in a flood of disordered and broken men, and, surrounded on all sides by hacking horsemen and stabbing pikemen, are borne down and crushed out of existence. In less than an hour from the beginning of the fight the Royal army is in flight, and the soldiers of the Parliament are falling in on their standards. More than one is laden with the spoil of some fallen Amalekite, and all are telling each other in fiercely exultant tones of their own share in the great deliverance God has this day wrought for His poor servants, or thundering forth some deep-toned chant of praise to the Lord of battles, Who alone can break the bow of the wicked and bring victory to His chosen warriors.

5. Cromwell's Career of Victory
1645-1660

At Naseby field, on June 14, 1645, the King's main army, despite a gallant resistance to an adversary more than twice its size, was completely defeated and dispersed, and the New Model, turning its arms southward and westward, was left with the comparatively easy task of putting an end to the ill-organised resistance of the local Royalist forces. By the summer of 1646, after various sharp encounters and one or two tedious sieges, this had been successfully accomplished, and

shortly afterwards Charles himself signalised his realisation of the hopelessness of further struggle by surrendering in person to the Scottish army.

The long negotiations following on the close of the war were broken off sharp in July of 1648 by the appearance on the Border of a new Royalist host raised in Scotland, which had fallen out with England over the future form of government for the two kingdoms. This force marched south through Lancashire, receiving recruits from the local gentry who were Royalist at heart, but Hamilton, its old and incapable commander, let himself be surprised by Cromwell, who, hurrying from Wales into Yorkshire, crossed the Pennines and fell on his flank while his army was spread out over a depth of some forty miles. In a series of small encounters the Scots were completely defeated, and hardly a man of them escaped back to his own country. This catastrophe was the prelude to the execution of Charles I. and the rise of Cromwell, the head of the army, to supreme power in England.

Scotland and Ireland still remained recalcitrant, and while the new ruler was engaged in subduing the latter country with fire and sword, he was suddenly summoned home by the news that Charles II., the son of the Martyr King, had arrived in Scotland and was preparing a new invasion of England. In July 1650 he advanced on Edinburgh along the coast at the head of 16,000 men, but was brought up before the walls of the city by a Scottish force, his inferior in everything but numbers and leadership. In the manoeuvres that followed he was outwitted and forced to fall back, but the unrivalled battlefield qualities of the New Model asserted themselves to good effect at Dunbar, and the Scots, severely defeated, retired northwards beyond the Forth. In this area both armies went into winter quarters, Cromwell concerning himself with the subjugation of the Lowlands, and active operations were not resumed till late in the summer of 1651. Then the Scots gave the English the slip and, taking young Charles with them, made for the Border; they pressed southwards on the west side of the Pennines and reached the Severn valley before their opponents, hurrying after them through Yorkshire, could come up with them. On September 3, 1651, the New Model, attacking from east and south on either bank of the river, enveloped and destroyed the Scotch army at Worcester. From now on till 1660 the army was the government, and Cromwell, its chief, the recognised head of the State.

Supreme at home, the New Model during these nine years sent a contingent to fight in the Low Countries against Spain, which at the Battle of the Dunes in 1658 aroused by its efficiency and valour the admiration both of its foes and of its French allies, and in 1655 undertook in cooperation with the fleet a joint expedition against the Spanish colony of St. Domingo, in the West Indies. The enterprise miscarried, mainly owing to dissensions between the military and naval commanders, but the occupation of Jamaica served in some sense as a consolation prize for the failure of the larger undertaking. Meanwhile, however, England was chafing under the regime of Cromwell and his army chiefs, which, though just and efficient, was narrow and unimaginative, and began to turn Royalist once more. The great soldier's death in 1658, while the army he had made was still fighting victoriously in Flanders, marked the beginning of the end of that army's rule; its leaders soon had no choice but to accept the inevitable, and in May 1660 the red coats of the New Model were arrayed on Blackheath to do honour to the monarch whom nine years before it had hunted into exile. A few months later, setting an example which has since been followed by all the great armies of England, it had laid down its arms and passed silently and peacefully into the pursuits of peace, leaving behind it, in the minds of the governing class and the people, besides a deservedly high military reputation, a legacy of hatred and distrust of all standing armies which has endured to our own day.

A few words must be said on the stern figure which, of

all the able generals who led the New Model to victory, typifies in history the Puritan soldier and statesman. Efforts have been made in recent years, by both soldiers and civilians, to endow Cromwell with a transcendent genius for war to which he seems to have no real claim. Admittedly he was a first-rate cavalry leader, equal to any, and superior to most, of his comrades or adversaries; admittedly also he was an organiser of a high order, an administrator of industry and competence, and a stern but just disciplinarian. But as a strategist he was more than once outmanoeuvred and caught napping by adversaries of greater experience and ability than himself, and as a tactician he owed much to the weakness or incompetence of the Royalist and Scotch generals, and still more to the incomparable fighting qualities of his own army. The New Model was in every way the finest military machine of its day, and throughout its history never found an adversary who could stand against it on a fair field. It seems that Cromwell's military reputation would be more surely founded on his predominant share in the fashioning of this terrible instrument of war than on his methods of conducting a campaign or a battle. Even so his place among the three greatest names in the history of the British army is secure enough, though he should appear to be the prototype of Moltke rather than of Napoleon.

CHAPTER 3

The Duke of Marlborough and the Contest with Louis XIV
1660-1714

1. THE ARMY BEFORE AND AFTER THE GLORIOUS REVOLUTION
1660-1701

Despite the distrust of all standing armies deeply borne in upon the minds of Englishmen by their experience of military supremacy under Cromwell, and the natural reluctance of Charles II. and his advisers to acquiesce in the continued existence of the regiments of the New Model, there was an evident necessity for some sort of permanent armed force to secure the King's person and maintain order in the country. The trend of British foreign policy, which tended to embroilment both with France and with Holland, gave additional force to this point of view; and accordingly Charles II. very soon after his accession decided to maintain four regiments of Foot and three of Horse, consisting partly of former units of the New Model army, and partly of specially raised troops. By the end of his reign, these 5000 men had been increased to eight regiments of Foot and four of Horse, some 16,000 in all. Apart from the fact of this definite establishment of a permanent peace time army in the pay and at the disposal of the Crown, there was during the period from 1660 to 1685 little of military importance to record. The possession of Tangier on the northern coast of Africa, which formed part of the dowry brought to the King by his Portuguese wife, gave our army its first experience of warfare against an uncivilised enemy, and the earliest battle honour borne on its colours. Some units also saw service against the Dutch both on sea and on land; in the former case with the British fleet, in the latter as part of the French army commanded by Turenne, under whom young John Churchill, then a colonel, had his first taste of regular warfare.

The first year of James II.'s reign was marked by an unsuccessful attempt on the part of the Duke of Monmouth, an illegitimate son of Charles II., to seize the throne by an armed rising in the west, which was completely crushed in the last battle ever fought on English soil, at Sedgemoor. Ostensibly as a consequence of this insurrection, the army was increased to 30,000 men by the addition to it of eleven new regiments of Foot and eight of Horse; but this measure in reality served to cloak other and more sinister designs on the part of the King, who, himself a devout Catholic, hoped by the aid of the army to secure, if not supremacy, at least toleration in England for his faith. In this matter he was completely at variance with the opinion not only of the mass of the English people but even of the troops upon whom he relied. When he endeavoured to secure their adhesion to his designs by recruiting Irish Catholics into the more violently Protestant regiments, he quickly lost what little hold he had upon the affections of his soldiers. Thus when in 1688 William of Orange, the Stadtholder of Holland, landed in the west and marched on the capital, the higher officers went over to him almost in a body, the regiments sent to oppose his advance deserted or refused to fight, and James fled the country, leaving the throne to his rival.

Although the fall of the last of the Stuart kings had been largely, if not mainly, effected by the adhesion of the standing army to the popular cause, the main legacy left by him, as far as concerned the military policy of the country, was a considerable increase in the fear of all permanent forces as actual or potential instruments of tyranny, which had been widespread throughout the nation ever since Cromwell's days. Consequently the new king, William III., whose main motive in life was an implacable hostility to France, and who regarded his newly acquired kingdom in the first place as an additional asset in the conflict against that country, found Parliament determined upon strictly limiting and defining his powers as regards the raising and the control of the armed forces of the Crown. In three Acts, the Bill of Rights, the Act of Settlement and the Mutiny Act, the Houses, by taking under civil control all questions of finance, administration and supply, and leaving only the actual command to the King, secured a preponderating voice in all military matters save the actual conduct of war. Further, by making the Mutiny Act valid from year to year, they ensured for themselves a means of averting any possibility of using troops for the purposes of a *coup d'état*. This system of control, by which the army from a royal force became a constitutional one, remained in being for over 150 years from the date of its first introduction.

Even at the very moment, however, when these Acts were passed, the state of England, at war with France and faced with Jacobite rebellion in Scotland and Ireland, imperatively demanded an immediate large increase in military strength. William was therefore authorised to proceed at once with the raising of twelve additional infantry and ten cavalry regiments for the purpose of putting down the risings throughout the realm, and assisting in the defence of the Low Countries against French invasion.

The insurrection in Scotland collapsed with the death of Dundee in the moment of victory at Killiecrankie, but that in Ireland was a far more formidable affair. James II. had proceeded thither in person to take command of the Irish forces, and a respectable French contingent had come with him. Moreover, the operations undertaken in 1689 by Schomberg at the head of a hastily raised force of some 19,000 untrained men, practically destitute of transport and inadequately supplied, came to an ignominious conclusion barely a month after their inception; and this fiasco brought sharply home to the authorities in England the necessity for taking serious steps to put an end to James' adventure. Accordingly a seasoned army of some 37,000 English, Dutch and Danish regiments were despatched to Ulster, which had remained loyal throughout to William III., and that monarch himself shortly followed them to assume personal control of the forthcoming operations. In June 1690 the army advanced from its position of assembly about Newry upon Dublin and encountered James' adherents in position behind the line of the Boyne. The battle that followed was decisive in as far as it put an end to all James' hopes of maintaining himself in the country or making it a jumping-off ground for an attempt to recover the throne of England, but it by no means put an end to active operations. The Irish army, abandoning Dublin, fell back southward and westward and continued to put up a stubborn resistance. Limerick and Athlone held out successfully against determined attempts on the part of the English to reduce them, and the completion of the conquest of the country had to be postponed till 1691. William had returned home at the close of the previous year's campaign, taking with him a large proportion of the army for service in the Netherlands, Ginkel being left in command in Ireland. With the 20,000 men remaining at his disposal the new general-in-chief advanced on and captured Athlone, completely routed the Irish field army at Aghrim, and then set down to invest Limerick, the last stronghold remaining to James. The town capitulated after a heroic defence of six weeks; and the subjugation of the country being thus completed, the British army was free to give its undivided energies to the war against the French in Flanders.

The position in that theatre at the beginning of that year had been that the French, with about 67,000 men, were holding the line of fortresses from Dunkirk on the coast by way of Menin, Valenciennes and Maubeuge to Dinant on the Meuse, opposed to a heterogeneous Allied army, comprising contingents of British, Dutch, Spanish, Danish, Imperial and German troops, which was slowly and belatedly assembling under William's command around Brussels. Luxemburg, the French *generalissimo*, and no unworthy successor of the great Condé and Turenne, was, thanks to the slowness of the Allied concentration, able to assemble at his leisure close on two-thirds of his army for a blow at Mons, which capitulated after a discreditably short siege, just as William, who had at last managed to get his army together, was advancing to relieve it. A series of intricate manoeuvres followed, and William's failure to pursue a momentary advantage enabled the French to draw off and close the campaign with the honours of war.

For the campaign of 1692 the Allies collected 40,000 men, of whom 23,000 were British, around Brussels, but again too late to anticipate the French in the field. Before William was ready to move, Luxemburg had invested and secured Namur, and then moved rapidly north-westwards as if to menace the capital. His opponent, who had arrived before the fortress just too late to relieve it, followed hard after, came up with the French in position near Steenkirk, and resolved to attack them by surprise in the early dawn. This bold move was almost crowned with success; the English in first line broke clean through the French position only to find themselves checked and driven out again by a fierce counter-attack before the rest of the Allied army, which was too far back and ill commanded, had arrived to their support. William therefore had to draw off his troops and admit a defeat, though a by no means discreditable one.

The next year saw yet larger forces in the field on both sides, 60,000 Allies as against 80,000 French. Once more Luxemburg opened operations, this time with an advance direct on Brussels; then swinging off to his right, he made rapidly for Liège. William, moving parallel with him, took up a defensive position to cover that city in the neighbourhood of Neerwinden, where his opponent attacked him, concentrating his forces against the Allied right; that wing was driven off the field in disorder after several hours of fierce fighting, and this compelled the retreat of the whole army, much of which had not come into action at all. Before the end of the campaign Luxemburg had exploited his victory by securing the whole of the line of the Sambre.

The remainder of the operations of this so-called War of the League of Augsburg need not detain us longer. 1694, a year of manoeuvres in the Low Countries, in which Luxemburg once more gave evidence of his superiority to William, was also marked by an ill-fated British raid on Brest, of which Marlborough, now in disgrace with his sovereign, owing to secret correspondence with the Jacobites, seems, in defiance of honour and military duty, to have given information beforehand to the French.[1] In the course of the year 1695, which saw the death of the able Luxemburg, William seized the opportunity, when the French, exhausted by years of warfare, were confined to the defensive, to restore his military reputation somewhat by storming the strong fortress of Namur. Neither side was now capable of any real further exertion; and desultory and abortive operations were terminated in 1697 by the inconclusive Peace of Ryswick.

The review of these campaigns shows that in them the British army had acquitted itself respectably, if not with any especial brilliance. The fighting qualities of all ranks remained as high as in the palmiest days of British military achievement, but command and administration were always mediocre and often lamentable. Under a first-rate leader and

---

1. Mr. Winston Churchill in his *Life of Marlborough* has satisfactorily proved the falsity of this accusation.

a capable organiser, however, results might be expected very different from the splendid failures of Steenkirk and Neerwinden, and, as it happened, the man who was to achieve these results, and to exalt the quality of British generalship to a height never reached before or since, was already on the point of making his first bow. Meanwhile the immediate need of a large standing army having disappeared on the conclusion of peace, Parliament, despite the protests of the King, at once proceeded to reduce the existing regiments practically to cadres. The forces in the British Isles were ruthlessly cut down to thirty-three weak regiments of Foot and nineteen of Horse—in all some 30,000 men; and the disbandment of the surplus units and personnel was attended by flagrant and scandalous abuses which bade fair to arouse something more serious than mere discontent.

Fortunately, as on more than one occasion before and after, the blundering of England's enemies averted from her the just consequences of her own folly. In 1701 the throne of Spain, falling vacant, was left in testament to Philip, the grandson of Louis XIV. of France. Such an immense accretion of power to one who already all but dominated Europe could not be borne, and the whole Continent rose up in arms to forbid it. Sweden, Prussia, Denmark, Holland and the Empire formed a grand anti-French alliance, to which England gave her enthusiastic adherence after Louis, by a second act of incredible unwisdom, had, on the death of William III., openly recognised the claim of the Jacobite pretender to the throne. Steps were at once taken to increase the army to 40,000 men; twenty-one newly raised regiments of Foot and eight of Horse, some 18,000 of all ranks, were allotted for service in Flanders, where the French had opened active operations by securing at one fell swoop all the fortresses on the southern frontier, complete with garrisons; and, most important measure of all, John Churchill, Duke of Marlborough, was sent to that country in chief command.

2. Marlborough's Career of Victory
1702-1713

The position of affairs, when the Duke arrived in the Low Countries in May 1702, had already taken a turn unfavourable to the Allies; the French held in their grasp the whole of the Spanish Netherlands with its fortresses, and had wiped out with one blow the flower of the Dutch army, and their host of 60,000 men under Boufflers, assembling near Cleve in the angle between the Lippe and the Meuse, was at the gates of Holland. Moreover, the Allied army was not yet half concentrated. Boufflers therefore, vigorously assailing the weak Dutch forces in his front, drove them to a hurried retreat behind the line of the Waal. But by this time Marlborough had collected some 60,000 men, of whom 12,000 were British, and with these he suddenly issued out from behind the Waal, about Grave, and marched rapidly due southward past the French left. The latter, falling back hastily on Ruremonde to secure their menaced line of retreat, exposed themselves to the chances of battle at a complete disadvantage, and Marlborough made all preparations to seize this favourable opportunity. Unhappily, though theoretically in supreme command of the Allies as well as of the British contingents, he was not a free agent, the Dutch having attached to their army certain civilian "field deputies" whose duty it was to secure the safety and special interests of their national troops, and who now intervened with a complete veto on the proposed battle. The chance of a decisive blow was let slip, and Boufflers found safety behind the line of the Demer, west of Maastricht. Marlborough skilfully lured him out by the pretence of exposing a large convoy to capture, and once more took post across his line of retreat, forcing him to prepare to fight in a position where defeat must have meant disaster; and for the second time the Dutch deputies, by their obstructionist attitude, fatally tied the Duke's hands. Boufflers was not again to be enticed into open country, and sat tight behind his lines while his adversaries besieged and captured in turn Venlo, Ruremonde and Liège—no inconsiderable fruits of a year's campaigning despite the failure to defeat and destroy the French field army. The results achieved in this theatre were the more important as elsewhere things had not gone well for the Allies: the French, with the assistance of the Bavarians, had driven the Imperialists from all the line of the middle and upper Rhine, and a combined expedition against Cadiz, mismanaged by Rooke and Ormonde, ended in a discreditable fiasco.

The next year, 1703, was also destined to be a disappointing one. Marlborough's design, ambitious enough for these days, was to pursue his advantage of the previous campaign and counterbalance the French successes on the Rhine by invading Flanders and Brabant; but he was, as might have been expected, unable to induce his timorous and pedantic Allies to agree to a project so seemingly hazardous, and had to content himself with sitting down to the siege of Bonn. This fortress having fallen into his hands, he conceived a new combined operation by which the Dutch were to seize Antwerp while he himself contained the main French army under Villeroi on the middle Meuse, and a secondary Dutch force carried out a diversion against Ostend. The scheme, which promised important results, was ruined by the disobedience and incompetence of the Dutch generals who had perforce been entrusted with the execution of the operations in Flanders; Villeroi managed to arrive in time to rescue Antwerp, and though Marlborough, following him up, managed to entice him from the shelter of the fortress, the field deputies once more intervened to forbid a battle. The Duke thereupon made a rapid countermarch to the Meuse, captured Huy, and was even prepared to assault the incomplete hostile lines north of Namur but for the unwillingness of his colleagues to enter upon so risky an operation. Accordingly the campaign was tamely concluded by the capture of the petty fortress of Limburg. The lack of decisive success in the Netherlands was all the more regrettable because the situation elsewhere had turned decisively to the disadvantage of the Alliance. A French and Bavarian force united on the Danube had defeated the Imperialist army opposed to it and secured an open road to Vienna and an assured base on the Rhine, while the adhesion of Portugal and Savoy to the Alliance seemed likely to prove a remote rather than a present advantage.

To Marlborough it was clear at the opening of the campaign of 1704 that the menace to the heart of the Empire and to the continued existence of the Alliance afforded by the rapid hostile progress in south Germany called for a more heroic remedy than a continuance of the tedious operations in Flanders. Accordingly he resolved on a bold measure, nothing less than the transport of his own army to the rescue of the Imperialists in Bavaria. In undertaking this design he was fully aware that he would have first to persuade his own Government of its feasibility and then to hoodwink his reluctant and timorous allies as to its true extent. The perils inherent in such a flank march across the front of the whole array of the French armies from Flanders to the upper Danube, and the intricacy and difficulty of the necessary supply and administrative arrangements, were indeed great, but not, as the event proved, insuperable.

At the time when Marlborough, after having wrung from the British Government a consent to his proposals, arrived in Holland, there were 50,000 French and Bavarian troops on the Danube, with additional reinforcements on the upper Rhine, preparing to overwhelm the 30,000 Imperialists under the Prince of Baden, covering the road to Vienna. The need was therefore urgent. To the Dutch the Duke imparted only a scheme for the transfer of the army to the Moselle, for he believed, and rightly, that to persuade them even to this would tax all his powers. However, he at length gained his point, and set out early in May with the British contingent, 14,000 strong, skilfully eluding Villeroi, who was observing the Flemish frontier. On the Moselle the Allied army, over 50,000 of all ranks, completed its concentration, and then, to the amazement of foes and friends alike, suddenly struck off south-eastwards into Germany. Moving at a steady twelve to fourteen miles a day, by way of Coblenz, Mayence and east of Stuttgart, Marlborough's men in less than six weeks covered the 250 miles to the Danube, and by the middle of June were assembled near Ulm, fresh, in good order and in better heart. The march had been a triumph of organisation, and the sudden appearance on their flank and rear of this new and formidable host put an immediate end to the Franco-Bavarian designs on Vienna. The junction of Marlborough's army with the Imperialists under the Prince of Baden brought the total of the Allied forces to close on 100,000, and thus outnumbered, the French and Bavarians fell back to the south of the Danube. Determined to bring them to action before they could be reinforced from the upper Rhine, Marlborough marched on Donauwörth to turn their right, and became hotly engaged on the evening of June 21 with a detachment hurried up by the defenders to secure that town, and strongly posted on a fortified hill known as the Schellenberg. After an hour and a half's fierce fighting the position was won, and the beaten enemy drew off southwards to Augsburg, where they were compelled to remain impotently watching the Allied armies systematically and methodically laying waste the fertile fields of Bavaria.

Marlborough's hopes of bringing the Elector of Bavaria to terms by these forcible means, however, were falsified by the arrival on the scene of a new French army of 20,000 men under Tallard from the Rhine, which, despite the simultaneous advent of 4000 Imperialists from the same area, restored the numerical advantage to his adversaries and placed them in a position to resume the offensive. Moreover at this very moment the Prince of Baden had gone off with 20,000 men to invest Ingolstadt. But the newly arrived Imperialists were led by the best of Austria's generals, Prince Eugene of Savoy, a man whose military talents were only second to those of Marlborough himself, and who was to prove himself an ideal colleague for the great Englishman. The French and Bavarian commanders, determined to seize the opportunity and fall on their weakened enemy, crossed the Danube and moved against Eugene on the left bank; Marlborough, hurrying his army across the river east of Donauwörth, effected the junction in ample time, and the combined forces advancing westwards came on their adversaries on the morning of August 11 in the act of taking up position at Blenheim.

In the ensuing battle the 60,000 French and Bavarians with 120 guns under Tallard, Marsin and the Elector, were opposed by the 50,000 men and sixty-odd guns of Marlborough and Eugene. The former held a position behind the marshy Nebel brook, between Blenheim and Lutzingen, their right resting on the Danube and their left secured by hilly and wooded country. Marlborough's plan was to break in the hostile centre, which was held only by cavalry, while delivering holding attacks on the wings. Shortly after noon, when the approach march and deployment had been completed, the British commenced a series of strong but unsuccessful assaults on Blenheim, garrisoned by the flower of the French infantry; and Eugene's attacking troops on the left were also checked and severely handled. By 4 p.m., however, the Duke's cavalry stiffened by infantry had completed their passage of the Nebel, and a grand charge burst asunder the centre of the enemy line. The Franco-Bavarian army was split into two fragments; the left wing managed to get away, but the whole of the right was herded together and captured in Blenheim village. Their losses were very heavy, 40,000 men of whom 13,000 were prisoners, against the Allied total of 12,500; of these latter the 11,000 British troops had over 2000 casualties.

The remnant of the beaten army fell back in disorder to the west; Bavaria sought and obtained peace from the Allies, who, following up their routed enemy, secured the fortresses of Landau and Trarbach and thus obtained good positions and comfortable quarters west of the Rhine, and a favourable jumping-off ground for the next year's operations. To add to the glories of the year 1704 there came the news from the Mediterranean of the capture of Gibraltar. The whole situation had thus undergone a startling change in favour of the Allies; yet great as were the material fruits of the victory of Blenheim, perhaps the most important results were the shattering of the French reputation for invincibility, the restoration of the moral ascendancy to their enemies, and the mighty enhancement of the fame of British arms throughout Europe.

The year 1705, however, was destined to be a disappointing one. The British commander had planned an advance from the Moselle into Lorraine, which would turn the French positions both in Flanders and in Alsace; but the ill-will of the Dutch and the dilatoriness and half-heartedness of the Germans brought this promising scheme to naught. By the middle of May only 50,000 men out of the 80,000 hoped for had been assembled, and the Duke felt himself too weak to deliver battle against the strongly posted army opposing him under the able leadership of Villars. Then suddenly a dash by Villeroi on Liège summoned him in haste to Flanders; Villeroi sought refuge behind his strongly fortified lines along the Geete and prepared there to deliver a defensive battle. But the Duke passed the lines with ease and forced him to fall back in haste to the Dyle. Once again he broke through the French defences, but this time the Dutch came to the rescue of Villeroi and caused the loss of the advantage gained. For the third time the persevering English general outwitted his adversary, moving round his right and catching him with his army only half assembled in an unfavourable position near Waterloo. It was all in vain; the Dutch deputies were too blind to see the opportunity or too timorous to take it; and in deep disgust Marlborough retired to winter quarters. Matters elsewhere, however, had gone better for the Allies; the French fleet besieging Gibraltar had been caught unawares and dispersed, and a small British force under an eccentric but brilliant commander, the Earl of Peterborough, had set foot on the eastern coast of Spain, captured Barcelona and Tarragona, and rallied the provinces of Catalonia and Valencia to the side of Charles, the Imperialist claimant to the throne of Spain.

A French success on the Rhine early in 1706 compelled Marlborough to abandon a cherished project for the transfer of himself and his army to Italy and an invasion of the south of France, and left him no choice but to continue the difficult operations in Flanders. But the very first weeks of the campaign gave him an unhoped-for chance for a decisive strike at Villeroi. The French marshal, hoping to catch the Allies while their concentration at Tongres was still incomplete, left his lines behind the Dyle and moved eastward with 60,000 men, only to find Marlborough with an approximately equal force ready and anxious to give him battle. On May 23 the French, in position around Ramillies, were attacked and completely overthrown after four hours' fighting. Marlborough, masking his real intentions by a partial attack on the hostile left, assailed their right centre in force, and with the aid of his reserves and additional troops rapidly and skilfully transferred from his right, broke through and drove the enemy in rout from the field. So vigorous was the pursuit that the beaten army was given no chance to rally; Villeroi was forced to abandon Louvain and Brussels, and to seek refuge to the west of the Scheldt under the guns of Lille. The fruits of this great victory, apart from the 15,000 casualties inflicted on the enemy, were the surrender to the Allies of the fortresses of Brussels, Ghent, Bruges, Antwerp, Ostend, Menin and Ath; and these sweeping gains were cheaply bought at the price of their own 4000 casualties. By the end of the campaign they had secured the whole of Brabant and Flanders, and had carried their arms in less than four months from the Meuse to the sea.

The operations of 1706 in Spain had also made good initial progress, and an army advancing from Portugal had even penetrated to and occupied Madrid. While awaiting the arrival of the second British column from Catalonia, however, it was assailed by the French under Berwick and forced to evacuate the city; joining up with its comrades from the east, it then retired unmolested into Valencia.

One other result of the disastrous issue of the campaign of 1706 in Flanders was the replacement of Villeroi in command of the French armies by the more capable Vendôme, whose instructions were to avoid battle and confine himself strictly to the defensive. Marlborough also, at the opening of the 1707 operations, was inclined to adopt a waiting policy in view of a large-scale offensive to be undertaken by Eugene against Toulon, and when the news of the latter's advance gave the signal for a renewal of activity on the part of the Allied armies in Flanders, the break up of the weather made it impossible to come to grips with the French. All Marlborough's attempts to entice Vendôme to stand his ground proved in vain, and at length the incessant rain and the exhaustion of both armies brought the campaign to an early and unsatisfactory conclusion. Elsewhere, too, things had gone badly for the Allies; the enterprise against Toulon miscarried completely, and a rash incursion into Spain from Valencia led to a severe defeat at Almanza, where the gallant conduct of the British contingent could not avail to counterbalance the timorousness or treachery of the Portuguese. In 1708, therefore, it seemed to the French Government, who had assembled on the Netherlands frontier a strong army of 100,000 men under Burgundy and Vendôme as joint commanders, that a more enterprising policy might be possible. French gold undermined the loyalty of the authorities of Ghent and Bruges, and when Burgundy and Vendôme, leaving their position about Mons and marching northwards, appeared before the gates of these cities, they were at once opened to receive them. Marlborough, calling up Eugene from the Meuse and marching westward, struck at his adversaries' line of retreat by the valley of the Scheldt, and, seizing the crossings of that river before they could double back to save them, brought them to battle at Oudenarde. This, the most skilfully conducted of all Marlborough's tactical triumphs, will be described in detail later in this chapter; it is sufficient to say here that the defeated French were forced to seek refuge behind the Ghent-Bruges canal and for the time being put entirely out of action. The way lay open before the Allies to the heart of France, and the Duke was only too anxious to utilise the opportunity thus offered for a decisive advance direct on Paris. But the scheme was too bold and unprecedented even for Eugene, and it was finally agreed that the latter should undertake the siege of Lille while Marlborough covered him against interference either from the beaten French army of the north or from Berwick, who had hurried up from the Rhine to its rescue. All the repeated and ingenious French efforts to raise the investment were foiled by the cool adroitness of Marlborough. An attack on a large convoy coming from Ostend, where the English had opened a second base of operations, was beaten off at Wynendael; a raid on Brussels by way of diversion was also satisfactorily dealt with; and after a siege of two months the city of Lille was surrendered, the garrison retiring to the citadel. Seven weeks later this last stronghold was likewise reduced, and the campaign was ended triumphantly by the recapture of Ghent and Bruges. The Allied victories in the north were fittingly complemented in the Mediterranean by the capture of Sardinia and Minorca by a combined naval and military force.

Indeed so evil was the case of France at the end of this year that the proud Louis XIV. so far humbled himself as to sue for peace. The negotiations, however, broke down over the exorbitant demands of the Allies; the French King appealed to his people, and by dint of their self-sacrificing exertions a formidable host of 100,000 men was once more got together and placed under the command of Louis' best general, Villars. Well aware that his was the last army of France, the marshal entrenched himself to the teeth in fortified lines between the Scarpe and the Lys and awaited the Allied attack. Marlborough and Eugene, whose combined forces totalled some 120,000 of all ranks, moved forward and made elaborate preparations for an assault on the French centre; thus having induced Villars to assemble all his army in front of them, they suddenly wheeled off to the east and proceeded to beleaguer Tournai. On the capitulation of this fortress after a two months' siege, Marlborough once more feinted against Villars' centre near Douai and then counter-marched rapidly towards the right of his lines at Mons, which he invested before his adversary could come up to save it. The latter, however, determined not to lose this place also without an attempt at rescue, assembled his army in the gap between two woods just east of Malplaquet village. Here he entrenched himself, and here on September 11 the Allies attacked him. Hours of ferocious and confused fighting followed; the original plan of enveloping the French left by a frontal and flank attack combined with a holding attack against their centre and right, broke down in the stress of the combat; and only after heavy losses was sufficient ground gained to allow the main body of the Allied army to debouch from the woods and push the enemy off the battlefield. So weakened were the victors in this sanguinary struggle—their total losses came to over 20,000 men, of whom 14,000 were British—that there could be no question of a pursuit, and they had to be content with the capture of Mons as the sole fruit of their success.

When operations reopened in the early spring of 1710, Villars, engaged in the completion of his formidable entrenched position from the Channel by way of Arras, Valenciennes and Charleroi to the Meuse, left the Allies free to work their will in all the area to the north of that line. Accordingly Marlborough settled down to the investment of Douai, with the idea, once this place had been taken, of capturing Arras, establishing a base at the Channel ports, and invading the heart of France. Villars, fearful of risking the last army of his country, dared not venture a battle for the rescue of Douai, which fell at the end of June, whereupon he drew back to cover Arras. Marlborough finding his enemy too strongly posted to be assailed without disproportionate loss, which the increasingly difficult political situation in England made him loath to incur, therefore moved to his right and invested and captured in rapid succession the fortresses of Bethune, St. Venant and Aire. At this moment, when the military position seemed full of the fairest promise, with the Allies face to face with the last fortified barrier covering the heart of France, a political crisis broke out in England which ended in the fall of the Whig party, Marlborough's constant supporters, and the accession to power of the Tories, whose avowed intention was to put an early end to hostilities. For the moment the Duke's personal position remained unaltered, but he was all too well aware that he could no longer reckon with certainty on the whole-hearted cooperation of the home Government in his conduct of the war.

Meanwhile, in Spain, the Allied cause had received a ruinous set-back. In July the new commander, Stahremberg, again assumed the offensive westwards from Catalonia and pushed forward to Madrid. Here, while his forces were widely dispersed, he was suddenly attacked by Vendôme at the head of a new French army, and forced to a hasty retreat. Pursuing vigorously, the French cut off the British contingent under Stanhope, which was acting as rear-guard, at Brihuega and forced it to lay down its arms. Next day the Allied main body was brought to battle a little to the east of that place; it succeeded in maintaining itself in the field till nightfall and drawing off under cover of darkness; but the Spanish population at once turned against the Allies, and rapidly rendered their position so hopeless that they had no alternative but to withdraw their troops and evacuate the country.

Under these depressing circumstances Marlborough entered upon what was to prove his last campaign. He found the Allied army weak in numbers and rent by internal dissensions, and his enemies strongly posted behind an immense belt of powerful entrenchments which Villars proudly nicknamed the *ne plus ultra* (thus far and no further) lines. But he rose superior to all these obstacles. By July he was ready for action and, after a close examination of the position, resolved to distract Villars' attention by feints against the west end of his lines, and then by a swift counter-march to cross them at their eastern end and consolidate his success by the capture of Bouchain. The scheme worked to perfection. The Allied army, assembled in the plains of Lens, made extensive and obvious preparations for a direct assault on the lines in that sector, and then by a rapid move eastwards secured the passage of the Sensee at Arleux and broke through the weakly held fortifications without striking a blow. Villars, baffled and outwitted, fell back sullenly on Cambrai, leaving Marlborough to besiege and reduce Bouchain at his leisure.

There the campaign ended and with it the war, as far as concerns the British army. Before the end of the year 1714 the great leader, whose unbroken career of victory had shattered one after the other the best armies of France and raised his own military fame and that of his country to a height never surpassed in all her history, had been arraigned on a trumped-up charge of financial corruption and ignominiously dismissed from his command. Early in 1712 negotiations were opened at Utrecht for the conclusion of a general peace and dragged on their weary length throughout the whole of that year. The British regiments under a new leader, Ormonde, were condemned by the orders of their Government to stand idly by while the French, whom they had beaten in countless combats in the last ten years, wrested back from Eugene, the former colleague of their great chief, the fruits of their last victories. Finally, in July, a definite armistice was signed, and in March 1713 there took place the ratification of a general peace. It cannot be denied that this country secured under its terms great advantages, though perhaps not as great as might have been hoped for or obtained; and the acquirement of large areas of land in America and the West Indies, and the leasing from France and Spain of valuable trading and commercial fights in their Western colonies, were some of the tangible fruits of Marlborough's talent for command and the courage and energy of his armies.

3. Marlborough's Chef-d'oeuvre: Oudenarde July 11, 1708

Let us now devote a few minutes to a glimpse of Marlborough and his army at work on the battle-field before passing on to estimate the Duke's position as a general.

It is an early hour on a gloriously warm July morning, and the roads leading north-west from Lessines towards the valley of the Scheldt are thickly veiled in the dust thrown up by the marching columns of the Allies. Many and various are the races and nationalities, equally variegated the uniforms, of this advancing army; but for us the main interest lies with those red-coated and cocked-hatted infantry, with their white cross-belts and gaiters, who, firelock on shoulder, are striding vigorously and fiercely along in rear of bodies of heavy cavalry, similarly uniformed and accoutred, armed with sword, pistol and carbine, and mounted on heavy, sturdy chargers. For these are the British regiments, the flower of Marlborough's command; and as they press steadily forward, their faces, beneath the dust that covers them, their uniforms and their boots in one all-pervading white cloud, betoken confidence in themselves, pride in their past achievements, and unbounded trust in their great leader.

Shortly after eleven a rumour comes down the ranks that far to the front the Allied advance-guard under Cadogan, sent forward earlier this morning before sun-up, has managed by hard marching to steal a march on the enemy and secure a footing beyond the Scheldt; and that the French themselves are still in the act of crossing the river, and may, if all haste is made, be taken at a disadvantage. Instantly, and almost before the order can be given, the step is quickened all down the long column; but as the infantry, with whatever haste they move, cannot hope to reach the scene of action for some hours yet, let us precede them and go forward to see what we can see.

As we pass the crest south of the little village of Eename, with its abbey, we gain our first view of the battle-field. Below us meanders the marshy and sluggish Scheldt, with the walled town of Oudenarde to our left front, and to the right of it the pontoon bridges thrown by our advance-guard this morning, and now guarded by infantry. Beyond the river rises a long low ridge on which is to be espied the gleam of scarlet and blue, the glitter of steel and clouds of smoke, all betokening a strong force hotly engaged. It is Cadogan's command, which, since midday, has been in action with the leading troops of the enemy. From our present position we can gather but little of what is going on. Marlborough and Eugene are up on the far ridge, whither they have ridden to join Cadogan, and where they can go so can we. A glance back, as we move forward up the slope of the ridge, will show us the leading files of the main body passing the crest above Eename, on the far bank of the river, and swinging down into the valley to relieve the battalions left on guard at the pontoons and now mustering to reinforce the battle-line of the advance-guard. That battle-line now comes into view as we reach the crest of the long ridge for which we have been making; it seems to consist mainly of mounted men with here and there a stiffening of solid infantry and a cluster of guns. In front of us the ground sinks to a valley and a sluggish stream, the Norken, which to our right runs through open rolling meadow land, affording good going for all arms; more to the left and nearer its source, however, the country, enclosed and wooded and diversified with isolated farms, hedges and ditches, is passable only by infantry. Finally, well to our left rises a broad open plateau known as the Boser Couter, which commands all the ground on which we stand and the whole course of the Norken. Beyond that stream again the ground rises to a long and well-defined spur, sloping down to the valley of the Scheldt. On the lower slopes of this spur are to be descried dark masses of troops in battle array—the enemy's main army under the Dukes of Burgundy and Vendôme, joint commanders, who, if gossip is to be credited, are at the moment not on too good terms with one another.

It is close on 3 p.m., and the combat between the advanced troops, we hear, has just turned in our favour. The French Horse and Foot who, for some reason unknown, have been pushed forward unsupported to a little village, Eyne, nestling on the Scheldt banks to the right of the ridge on which we now stand, and nearly two miles in front of the main hostile army, have been attacked by a superior force of cavalry and infantry launched at them by Cadogan; most of the infantry have been rounded up and captured in the village, and their supporting cavalry sent flying back in rout, chased right across the Norken by the victorious Allied horsemen. But we have little time to consider even this brilliant success, for as we watch the French main army is seen to be on the move. Heavy masses of troops—cavalry in the van, infantry following in support—detach themselves and move down into the valley; guns galloping forward unlimber on the banks of the stream and begin to thunder against our lines, and while some of the assaulting columns push forward frontally against our ridge and the villages below, which are garrisoned and fortified by Allied infantry, others, pissing more to our left along the higher and more enclosed ground, are evidently engaged in an attempt to turn and envelop our line on that flank.

Fortunately the passing hours have brought the leading infantry of our main body on to the scene of action. In rapid succession the units file swiftly across the pontoon bridges, breast the slope, and prolong the already existing line of battle on both wings. As they come up, one and all become hotly engaged. Below us, amid the copses and farms, in the tangle of hedgerows and ditches and woods, can be distinguished here and there formed bodies of Foot advancing, retiring, engaging in fierce fire fights at short range, pressing in upon their adversaries with lowered bayonets, while at still wider intervals little knots of mounted men dart rapidly forward, as favourable chances offer themselves, to the attack of hostile troops or guns. Gradually as the time passes the whole battlefield becomes veiled in dense clouds of billowing smoke, so that little or nothing can be seen in all the valley below; but as we turn our eyes to the far left we suddenly see, on the flat top of the Boser Couter, a large and powerful column of all arms moving rapidly and steadily northwards. Even as we gaze it halts, its centre and rear still on the plateau, its van well forward and out of sight over the further edges. There is a long pause, and then the whole mass of men, which has evidently faced to the right and formed line, sweeps majestically and with imposing steadiness down the slope towards the battle raging in the valley below.

The purport of the move is now clear: a detachment sent by Marlborough to outflank the French right is about to envelop that end of their line, throw it back in disorder on the centre, and club their whole army together in inextricable and disastrous confusion in the valley of the Norken. But it is already after 8 p.m., and darkness is falling and a fine rain. The fighting is still raging fiercely, as the flashing of muskets in the gloom clearly shows, but the course of the battle can no longer be distinguished, and the danger of friends firing on friends in mistake for foes becomes one to be reckoned with. Shouts and cries and a confused clamour gradually receding show that our flanking movement is still making progress and that the foe is trying to draw off; trumpet calls, rolling of drums, and other signals show that the Allied regiments have received orders to rally and collect their men. At length it is pitch dark, and rain begins to come down in torrents, drowning with its hissing and splashing the few last scattered shots of the battle. The day has been won and the enemy beaten from his ground; no doubt, we think, as we retrace our steps to try and find some shelter in the town of Oudenarde, tomorrow's dawn will show him to have acknowledged his defeat by his abandonment of the field of battle.

4. The Character of a Great Captain

When we consider the character and career of the great soldier whose deeds we have just briefly recounted, it appears astonishing that his place in the history of the army which he led so often to victory, and of the country whose fame he raised to such a pinnacle of glory, stands so far below what seems fitting. It is impossible satisfactorily to account for this, save by the unhappy fact that Marlborough was not only a soldier but also a politician, and therefore could hardly help being touched by the brush of corruption which few politicians of his time escaped. But such corruption, common and therefore venal in the game of politics, sits but ill upon a soldier; and on this count Marlborough has been tried and harshly, if not unjustly, condemned. It has been laid to his charge that he used petticoat and backstairs influences to help him to and keep him in office; that he took money to which he had no right; that he betrayed secret military plans to the enemies of his country; that he turned his coat to suit his own purposes; and that as between Jacobites and Hanoverians, as between William of Orange and James II., he pursued a policy of running with the hare and hunting with the hounds. It is no purpose of ours in exculpate him from these accusations, or even to defend him save by remarking that these were the faults—if faults they were—of Marlborough the politician rather than of Marlborough the soldier, and that these same things which in other politicians are found pardonable and even at times commendable are irrelevant when brought forward in an endeavour to belittle the great Duke's military achievements in the field.

A second reason for the general lack of appreciation of Marlborough among his countrymen may perhaps be found in the fact that up till a few years ago he had found not merely no worthy but even no competent biographers; and that he has hitherto been presented to posterity only in the distorted mirrors of those who detested his politics and could therefore only with difficulty appreciate him as a soldier. It is a luminous commentary on the statement that the pen is mightier than the sword, that Macaulay's jaundiced pen was able for three generations to obscure the fame of the greatest commander in British history, so that the glory of Blenheim and Ramillies could be more than counterbalanced in the eyes of posterity by John Churchill's unfortunate omission to profess with adequate loudness and frequency his theoretical adhesion to the shibboleths of Whiggism.

For the man was beyond comparison great—the greatest captain by head and shoulders that ever donned a red coat, and the only commander in modern times whose name it is not an impertinence to mention in the same breath as that of Napoleon. He was the incarnation of the spirit of eighteenth-century warfare; a warfare which it is the fashion today to condemn as pedantic, antiquated and formal, merely because in this epoch when armies are nations, and have in time of war all the national resources actual and potential at their beck and call; when the supply of cannon and all that cannon need is only equalled by the supply of cannon fodder; when economy of means is usually labelled false economy; when manoeuvre and stratagem have become atrophied by long disuse, and when the successful commander's outstanding qualities are those of character rather than of intellect, eighteenth-century war is no longer even comprehensible to our minds. Yet that war demanded in the leaders who conducted it no common or despicable talents. It called for high powers of organisation, for intimate knowledge of the working of all arms, for a good for country, for quick decision, for prudence, for adaptability of mind, and, last but not least, for personal courage. And Marlborough in all these qualities was pre-eminent, the master of his time and of all the men of his time. Frederick II. of Prussia, whom English hero-worshippers and German propagandists have contrived to deck with the title of Great, bears in the annals of eighteenth-century generalship a higher fame than our own Duke; yet both as man and as commander he was as much his inferior as was Moltke to Napoleon. Frederick, the supreme ruler of his country, the supreme commander of its armies, with no allies to fetter his movements, with no home government to hamper and thwart him, was as often defeated as victorious, and more than once trod the brink of disaster. Marlborough, the leader of the host of a coalition, dragging with him at every move a suspicious and disaffected crowd of jealous colleagues and ignorant civilians, any one of whom had the power to obstruct and to veto, and compelled always to have one eye watching not one but many political superiors in many lands, each tortuously pursuing divergent and selfish purposes, conducted successful campaign after successful campaign, and never suffered even a check either in battle or siege.

 And yet it may be this is not the Duke's chief title to greatness. For, like the other few outstanding figures which throughout the centuries tower conspicuous in the annals of war, he was not merely the first general of his time, but was also above and in advance of his time. Though eighteenth-century war from its very nature made little call on the qualities of energy, singleness of purpose, vision and personality, Marlborough's career displays all these virtues in luxurious profusion. Where other leaders saw only as far as the next fortress or the nearest strong position, Marlborough's wide ranging glance embraced the main strength of the hostile army, and the whole theatre of war. Where lesser men would have shunned battle he eagerly sought it; where more timid or more sluggish minds would have let slip an opportunity, he in an instant saw and seized it. No man of his day save Marlborough only would have dared even to dream of the invasion of Lorraine from the Moselle in 1705, or the march upon Paris after Oudenarde. None would have carried out, even had he dreamed of it, that astonishing march from Brabant to Bavaria, which changed the whole face of the war in a twinkling of an eye, and which recalls in its rapidity and unexpectedness the lightning strokes of a Hannibal or a Napoleon. None could have so departed from all the tactical rules of the day as to fight such an action as Oudenarde, which might serve for all time as a classic exposition of the basic principles of war as applied to the encounter battle. And, finally, none would have had the vision and energy to carry out the thundering pursuit after Ramillies, which proved once for all that the great Englishman, unlike the great Carthaginian, knew not only how to gain a victory but also how to use it to the full. All these things establish the Duke of Marlborough's claim to a place beyond *les bons généraux urdinaires,* beyond the galaxy of talented and brilliant commanders who are the legitimate pride of many lands and times, amid the few, the very few, gods of war who are above all lands and all times, and who, to quote the words used by a chivalrous Englishman about his country's greatest foe, Napoleon, "Have made past glory doubtful and future renown impossible".

CHAPTER 4

The Struggle With France for Overseas Empire
1714-1763

1. THE FIRST ROUND:
THE WAR OF THE AUSTRIAN SUCCESSION
1714-1748

In accordance with invariable British practice after a war, the army, at the earliest possible moment after the conclusion of hostilities with France in 1713, was drastically reduced. The established strength, which under Marlborough had attained a maximum figure of 200,000, fell in 1714 to 30,000; which, after a temporary increase of 6000 owing to the Jacobite rising next year, further declined till, in 1719, it touched the hopelessly inadequate level of 12,000. Not till the accession to office of Walpole was the figure permanently fixed at 18,000 men—few enough in all conscience to ensure the security of the realm against internal disorder and invasion by Jacobite or foreign troops; nor can it be said that what the army lacked in numbers was compensated for by exceptional military quality. The officers were insubordinate, slack and corrupt; the men, recruited largely from the dregs of the people, could only be controlled by the most ferocious and brutal punishments; desertion and fraudulent enlistment were crimes common to the point of scandal; and the ill-feeling between the undisciplined troops and their overbearing officers on the one hand, and the war-weary and suspicious civil population on the other, was so bitter as to form a serious menace to public order. The system—or lack of system—by which the garrisons in Britain's outlying possessions were maintained involved the unfortunate units concerned in interminable exile in unhealthy foreign lands, without hope of relief for many years, if at all; and short-sighted economy was the order of the day in all offices concerned with military equipment and administration. It is doubtful if at any period of our history the lot of the average soldier has been as pitiable, or the level of efficiency and morale as low throughout the army, as in the twenty-five years of peace between the Wars of the Spanish and Austrian Successions. Yet even this dreary period has its redeeming features, for from it date the introduction of a regimental organisation for the artillery, the earliest appointments of permanent engineer officers, and the raising of the first two regiments from the Highlands of Scotland.

Apart from the participation of a few regiments in the putting down of the above-mentioned Jacobite rising of 1715, and a raid on Vigo, the only noteworthy incident in a war with Spain which dragged on its desultory and uneventful course from 1718 to 1720, the British army saw no active service under the first two kings of the Hanoverian line until a trade dispute with Spain led to the outbreak in 1739 of what is commonly known as "the War of Jenkins' Ear". For this there were at once raised ten regiments of Marines and seven new regular regiments of Foot. Enthusiasm for the war was widespread among all classes who had grown weary of Walpole's uninspiring and pacific leadership, and was further inflamed by early successes at sea. Under the stress of this emotion there was planned a combined expedition against Cartagena, a Spanish port on the shore of New Granada, in South America. Blundering and incompetence combined with a malign fate to overwhelm it in a crushing disaster. Delayed for four months in sailing, the armament only arrived off the port at the opening of the sickly season in March 1742; dissensions between Admiral Vernon and General Wentworth, together with the helplessness and incapacity of the latter, clogged all its operations. The assault on the fortifications, delivered by night, resulted in a bloody repulse; and to crown all, yellow fever set in and did its fatal work so well as to lay low no less than nine-tenths of the force. The pitiful remnant returned to Jamaica in May 1742, having accomplished nothing but the strewing of the Spanish Main with English corpses.

Fortunately perhaps for the politicians, to whom must be attributed the chief share of the responsibility for this ghastly fiasco, the eyes of all England were now directed on military operations nearer home. The death of the Emperor Charles VI., and the accession to the throne of the young and inexperienced Maria Teresa, gave the enemies of the House of Hapsburg an opportunity for a war with a view to the partition between them of the Austrian provinces. The first to move in April 1741 was Frederick II. of Prussia, notable in history as the first inventor of those Prussian "receipts for victory" which made so unfortunate a last appearance in France in the late summer of 1914, and also as the first statesman to admit and glory in the selfishness of his own motives and the unscrupulousness of his methods. His invasion of Silesia set the spark to the powder magazine; France and Bavaria, whose ruler had a shadowy claim on the Imperial crown, fell on Austria; England and Holland took the opposite side. The British Government decided to raise 62,000 men for the new war and ordered the despatch of 16,000, under the command of Lord Stair, an experienced veteran of Marlborough's wars, to form part of an Allied army of 50,000 men assembling for the defence of the Austrian Netherlands. Here they remained inactive all that year, while Stair was vainly endeavouring to rouse the Dutch to a sense of their responsibilities as belligerents, and to secure the consent of half-hearted and timorous colleagues to a bold design of his own—no less than to seize the opportunity afforded by Frederick's conclusion of peace with Austria to invade France, open up a new line of communication by the capture of Dunkirk, and push direct on Paris. Such a move was too alien to all existing military ideas to find favour with the Dutch or the Austrians, or even with Stair's own political superiors, and as no one else had any other plan, nothing was decided on and nothing done in 1742.

The coming of suitable campaigning weather heralding the opening of operations in 1743, saw the Allied army of 40,000 men on the march eastwards from Flanders to the valley of the Main, with a vague idea of interposing between France and Bavaria and preventing the cooperation of their armies. Another and probably more potent motive for the move was the, anxiety of King George II. to ensure the security of his Electorate of Hanover. All through this war, and all through the Seven Years' War as well, there may be traced this preoccupation of the British King with his Continental dominions, and also a predilection for Hanoverian troops and generals, excusable enough in truth, but hardly calculated to enhance the popularity of the Crown in the British army or in England. Stair not only found himself ere long opposed by a formidable French army of 70,000 under Noailles, but also gravely hampered in his operations by interference on the part of George II., who was at Hanover on his way to join his troops in the field. By the time he arrived Stair had been completely outmanoeuvred by his opponent, and cut off from his base, and saw himself reduced to a perilous retreat along the north bank of the Main, through a defile between the river and wooded hills, exposed to flanking fire from French artillery all along its length. When Noailles passed troops across both in front and in rear of the Allies, the latter seemed irretrievably lost, but the commander of the detachment of 30,000 men sent to head them off rashly assumed the offensive instead of awaiting attack in a good defensive position, and thus threw away the advantage gained. In the ensuing battle of Dettingen, the French detachment was routed and partly driven into the Main, suffering severe losses, and the Allies were enabled to effect their withdrawal to Hanau and their supplies. It was a Pyrrhic victory, for George II. made no attempt to follow up his success; the army remained inactive at Hanau till the close of the campaign, its leaders spending the time contending with each other instead of the enemy. The end of it all was that Stair in disgust laid down his command, being replaced by the aged Wade, a great road-maker but no general.

The new commander's task was not rendered easier by the recession to supreme command of the French army in the Netherlands of Maurice de Saxe. Saxe's reputation as a soldier stood and still stands high, based as it is on a series of brilliant and unbrokenly successful campaigns; in view of the fact, however, that throughout his operations he enjoyed a numerical superiority over his opponents, in the proportion always of three to two, and more often of two to one, his achievements hardly form a true criterion of his talents. In 1744 at least he had an easy task. Assembling an army of 80,000 men at Lille, he rapidly overran all West Flanders, and his progress was only checked by the necessity of detaching a large force to oppose an Austrian army, which, liberated by the cessation of operations against the Prussians, was advancing on the Rhine. The Allies, having at length mustered a respectable force of 65,000 around Brussels, felt their way slowly southward, and finally came to a standstill before Courtrai, where Saxe had entrenched himself and was awaiting them. Here they dallied until the return of the French detachment from the Rhine rendered the prospects of a successful attack hopeless, and then fell back to Ghent, where they took up quarters for the winter. Wade was recalled, being superseded by the young Duke of Cumberland. The new commander possessed no inconsiderable military talents, but throughout his career was the victim of such ill-fortune as entirely to nullify them. His solitary victory loaded his name with more opprobrium than any of his defeats, and his last act as a general was to append his name to a capitulation in the open field. Like another unlucky royal commander, the Duke of York, however, his work as an administrator and an organiser was of great and lasting benefit to the British army, of which he was for many years an able and hard-working commander-in-chief.

For the campaign of 1745 Cumberland concentrated around Brussels an army of 47,000 men, of whom 23,000 were British, and with these troops at the end of April he set out to relieve Tournai, which Saxe, who as usual was first in the field and had skilfully masked his designs against that fortress until the actual trenches were opened before it, held invested with 20,000 men while another 60,000 covered the siege. Moving southward and westward by a somewhat circuitous route, the Allies on May 10 came face to face with the French holding a strong and well-fortified position on the east bank of the Scheldt at Fontenoy. The battle on the following day was all but won, despite the complete miscarriage of the attack on both wings, by the magnificent assault of the British in the centre, who broke through and shattered the French first line, held their ground unsupported for three hours, and only retired slowly and in good order before the desperate counter-attacks of the whole of the hostile reserves against their front and flanks. None the less Saxe gained his victory and secured himself leisure to carry out to its conclusion the siege of Tournai, which fell at the end of June. Inferior in numbers and disunited, the Allies were now in no position to guard the whole wide extent of country between the Meuse and the sea, and their vain attempts to do so only frittered away their forces, already too few for the task in hand. Eventually Cumberland saw himself compelled to abandon to the French all Austrian Flanders west of the Scheldt; but before the end of the campaign he and practically the whole of the British contingent had been hurriedly called home to meet a new danger which was menacing the heart of England.

This peril was caused by the southward advance of the force of Charles Edward, the "Young Pretender" to the throne, and the last male descendant of the Stuart line of kings. Landing in the western isles of Scotland in July 1745, he had rallied to himself a small but formidable Highland army, which Cope, the British commander, who had marched north from Edinburgh on receiving news of the rising, hesitated to encounter in the open field. Prince Charles then advanced by way of Stirling on Edinburgh, where he was received with enthusiasm, while Cope, who had swung north to Inverness and then east to Aberdeen, took ship to Dunbar so as to be once more in a position to oppose any march southward. At Prestonpans his army fled in panic rout before the first charge of the Highlanders, and the latter, pushing forward in triumph across the Border via Carlisle, advanced at speed in the direction of London. No British recruits, however, materialised, and the Government took instant steps to put a term to the bold incursion of the Prince's 5000 men by hastily assembling 10,000 men in Staffordshire under Cumberland, and an equal force under Wade around Newcastle, while a third force was arrayed for the direct defence of the capital. Charles succeeded in evading Cumberland and reaching Derby; but realising all too clearly that his enterprise was hopeless, he halted at this point, and at length turned back to the Border, hoping at least to secure Scotland. A certain respite was allowed him. Cumberland was summoned south by rumours of invasion preparations at Dunkirk; and Hawley, to whom was entrusted control of the operations, found at Falkirk, as Cope had found, that his troops were insufficiently steady to withstand the impetus of a Highland rush. Cumberland, therefore, had once more to be called on. By dint of vigorous disciplinary measures he succeeded in restoring the shaken morale of the British troops, and in organising a reliable force of some 10,000 men with which he set methodically to work to restore order in the eastern part of Scotland. At length, wheeling westwards, he encountered the Jacobite army of 5000 weakened and dispirited men at Culloden Moor, east of Inverness, on April 16, 1746, and scattered it to the winds. The rising was at an end. While Charles Edward was engaged in the romantic Odyssey which finally ended in his safe escape from the country, his adherents were relentlessly hunted down and rounded up, and just a year after the first landing of the Pretender, Cumberland was able to report that his mission was accomplished and Scotland once more pacified.

Meanwhile the war elsewhere had been running its course. In India, the able and ambitious French representatives, Dupleix and La Bourdonnais, had been endeavouring in a series of campaigns, to which we shall later have to devote attention, to found a French empire on the ruins of the British East India Company, which in September 1746 had to surrender its chief settlement Madras. In America a hastily raised citizen force, assisted by good fortune, and dissensions and indiscipline among its enemies, and backed up by a British squadron, had succeeded in reducing the strong French defended port of Louisburg on Cape Breton Island. In the Low Countries Saxe was still pursuing his career of conquest, securing Brussels and Antwerp, and then turning south-eastward against the fortresses on the Sambre and the Meuse. The Allies, slow as ever in mustering their forces, were unable until the autumn to oppose him with approximately equal numbers, and even when at length the armies engaged in battle at Rocoux, outside Liège, Saxe had 120,000 men to pit against their 80,000. Masking their right and falling in force on their left and centre, he forced them after several hours of fierce fighting to relinquish their ground and retire in good order to the east of the Meuse. The tale of the year's disappointments was closed by a futile and unsuccessful British incursion against the coast of Brittany.

All this only spurred the Allies, and especially the British, to further efforts. An army of close on 100,000 men was collected early in 1747 at Breda under Cumberland's command, in face of the French force of 120,000 on the Lower Scheldt. After a futile advance against Antwerp, which he found too strong to be attacked, Cumberland fell back to the east of Brussels, whence he was hurriedly summoned by a report that Saxe was moving on the Meuse and menacing Maastricht. After a week of intricate manoeuvring, the contending armies clashed at Laffeld. Saxe succeeded after repeated efforts in piercing the Allied centre and compelling them to fall back, heroically covered by self-sacrificing cavalry charges. Though tactically defeated, Cumberland may fairly be said to have foiled his adversary's main strategic design and saved Maastricht; the latter had to be content with the capture of the less important fortress of Bergen-op-Zoom and the occupation of Dutch Brabant as the final fruit of the campaign.

By 1748 both sides were heartily sick of the war and quite ready to talk peace. The triumphant career of Saxe in the Netherlands continued uninterruptedly, and the Allies, who could only muster some 35,000 men against his 100,000, had no choice but to look on helplessly while he invested and took Maastricht. As against this, however, the supremacy of the British at sea and the depredations of their privateers more than compensated for the French victories on land, and by April the preliminaries of peace had been signed, to be expanded in October into the definitive Treaty of Aix-la-Chapelle. Frederick II. of Prussia, who retained Silesia, alone emerged with any positive gain to his credit; as far as concerned England, the position reverted to what it had been before the outbreak of war. Louisburg was restored to France in exchange for Madras; the commercial treaty with Spain was renewed; and the Hanoverian kings were reorganised as the rightful occupants of the English throne. In a word, the treaty was avowedly a truce in the contest between France and England for the possession of overseas empire.

During the period of hostilities just closed the army had shown itself possessed of the same high qualities which had at the beginning of the century made it the most formidable in Europe, and lacked only leadership to maintain it in that pre-eminence. On the conclusion of peace it was promptly reduced, as usual, its strength at the end of 1748 being seventeen cavalry and fifty-two infantry regiments. Nor might the process have stopped there, had it not been for the fact, patent to all intelligent observers, that a settlement of the great matters of dispute between France and England was only postponed. This view received striking and signal justification, while the ink of the signatures on the treaty was barely dry, by events in the distant American continent, where the first seeds of a new conflict were fast sprouting

2. The Early Stages of the Seven Years' War 1749-1757

The situation in America was that in the north the French held all Canada from the Atlantic seaboard along the St. Lawrence as far as the Great Lakes, and in the south the territory on the Lower Mississippi known as Louisiana; the English, their rivals, were in possession of all the coastal lands from the St. Lawrence estuary to Florida, as far inland as the foothills of the Alleghanies. New France enjoyed the advantage of being unified under a single Governor with a definite and consistent policy, which was pursued with far-sighted prudence and commendable energy. This policy involved an expansion southwards and westwards from the region of the Great Lakes into the Ohio valley and an eventual junction of territory with that of Louisiana in the south, with the idea of cutting off the British colonies from the virgin lands west of the Alleghanies. These colonies, for their part preoccupied with petty squabbles between themselves and bickering with their Governors, and cursed with a lamentable lack of any sort of public spirit or even any sense of enlightened self-interest, seemed likely to fall helpless victims to the ambitious designs of their neighbours. It was not till 1754 that some of the provincial governments, their attention having been drawn to their peril from New France by reason of a quarrel about Acadia, the French province west of Nova Scotia, took tardy and inadequate measures to check French expansion into their rear. The small expedition sent out under Washington was defeated and forced to capitulate and the colonies at once sent an appeal for help to the mother country.

Early in 1755, therefore, Braddock and two weak regiments set sail for Virginia to cooperate with the colonial forces in repelling French aggression and forcing them back within their own borders. The general plan of campaign did not fail in ambition. Braddock's instructions enjoined him to carry out operations simultaneously in the Ohio valley, against Niagara, up the Hudson and against Acadia. Rightly judging that the first of these theatres was the most important, Braddock decided to move with his British troops against Fort Duquesne, the French headquarters on the Monongahela, a tributary of the Ohio. Difficulties of supply and transport combined with the personal friction inevitable in a mixed body of regular and irregular troops to delay the start of the little force of 2000 men till the middle of June. After a slow and painful progress through the dense virgin forest which lined the banks of the river the British arrived within a day's march of the fort, only to be ambushed, cut to pieces, and compelled to retreat in disorder, carrying with them their mortally stricken commander, but leaving behind all their guns, baggage and stores, together with half their strength dead or wounded. The expeditions against Niagara and on the Hudson fared but little better, and only on the Acadian isthmus did success crown the British arms. Here the French frontier forts were reduced and the country occupied and pacified by the ruthless expulsion of all recalcitrant or doubtful elements, which in this case comprised the bulk of the population. Meanwhile the Indians in French pay burst in upon the western borders of the British colonies, laying waste the land far and wide with fire and sword.

The menacing situation in America was accompanied and intensified by a growing tension between England and France in Europe. The latter, following the example of her neighbour, had decided at the beginning of 1755 to send to Canada a considerable force under a capable leader, Montcalm. The attempt of the British fleet to intercept the convoy *en route* led to the first shots being fired at sea; and, though a declaration of open war was still delayed, the inevitability of ultimate conflict was everywhere recognised. The British Government, under the incapable leadership of the Duke of Newcastle, resolved therefore on the raising of ten new regiments of Foot, bringing the total of the army up to sixty, and of four foreign battalions for service in America; but for the moment the forces available were so weak, and the general situation appeared so menacing, that it was deemed necessary to bring over to England a number of German troops to secure the country in the event of a possible French invasion. Instead of this, however, the French struck at and captured Minorca in the Mediterranean; and in May 1756 war was declared against France. Shortly afterwards there took place on the Continent a diplomatic revolution which resulted in a complete change of allies all round; England found herself opposed to her traditional friend Austria, now united to France in an attempt to recover her old province of Silesia, for which she had never ceased to scheme since its occupation by Frederick the Great in 1742. The latter, knowing that he must soon be ringed round on three sides by superior enemies, concluded an alliance with England, and in October commenced the war on the Continent by an invasion of Saxony.

The operations of 1756 in America did nothing to better the parlous position of the British colonies. In the course of the summer there arrived from England a new commander, Loudoun, and two battalions, and a force was collected at Albany on the Hudson River, for an advance against the French outpost fort of Ticonderoga on Lake Champlain. The colonial levies assembled but slowly, and proved themselves ill-organised and ill-disciplined; and their jealousy of the British combined with the latter's arrogance and want of tact to wreck the whole enterprise. Loudoun felt himself too weak to attack the French in their strong post; they in their turn were quite content, to remain on the defensive, for Montcalm, their commander, had offensive designs elsewhere. In August he suddenly swooped down on the British fort at Oswego, on the shores of Lake Ontario, compelled it to surrender, razed it to the ground, and was back at Ticonderoga before Loudoun had realised his absence. The campaign thus closed in gloom and defeat for the British and with the French star in the ascendant everywhere throughout the theatre of war.

Meanwhile at home a change had come over the spirit of the scene. The aged and inefficient Newcastle had been compelled to resign the premiership, and the direction of the war had been taken over by the brilliant and energetic William Pitt. Fifteen new battalions of infantry were at once raised, and two more were recruited from the Highlands of Scotland, which had only ten years earlier been in insurrection against the House of Hanover. The artillery, engineers and marines were also increased, and the total armed forces available for service in 1757 were estimated at over 50,000 men. In addition to this increase in the regular forces the militia too was placed on a better footing, 32,000 men being enrolled by ballot for a term of service of three years. By these means not only were the needs of home defence adequately met and the army liberated for foreign service, but the latter was provided with a reservoir of partially trained men from which it drew a number of useful recruits.

The task which Pitt had to accomplish was no easy one. With the naval and military resources at his disposal he had at one and the same time to ensure the safety of the home country, to defend the Electorate of Hanover against French invasion, and to restore the situation in America. He quickly came to the decision that to the last of these tasks, where alone a decisive advantage could be gained over the enemy, he would devote the maximum force available. Thus the American theatre of war became for England the main theatre, and the Continent merely a secondary one. It was a revolution in British war policy, and, as might have been expected, Pitt met with considerable opposition in carrying it through. Indeed, early in 1757 there took place in England a first-class political crisis which culminated in his temporary fall from power ; the popular indignation and the logic of events, however, proved too much for his adversaries, and by July he was once more, and this time more firmly, in the saddle. His five years' premiership was destined to be one of the most glorious epochs in our history.

Of this splendour, however, the year 1757, thanks no doubt to the preoccupation of Government and country with domestic affairs, gave little promise. The defence of Hanover, where Cumberland at the head of a small and heterogeneous army was striving throughout the summer to make head against a much superior French force, ended in a disastrous defeat at Hastenbeck; the greater part of the Electorate was overrun, and the unfortunate Duke was compelled to conclude a convention at Kloster Zeven, by which he agreed to disband his troops and leave the French in undisputed possession of their conquest. The operations in America went no more favourably for British arms. Loudoun, the Commander-in-Chief, concentrated his contingent from the colonies and reinforcements from home at Halifax for an expedition against Louisburg, the French fortress which commanded the mouth of the St. Lawrence. The latter were late in arriving and it was not till well on in the summer that Loudoun had all his 11,000 men ready for action. Here he dallied for six weeks, unable to make up his mind to move against the strong works of Louisburg, defended as they were by a garrison of 7000 good troops and a formidable squadron. Finally the enterprise was abandoned and he returned to New York, to hear that Montcalm had taken advantage of his absence to capture and destroy Fort William Henry on Lake George, and that part of the garrison after the surrender had been massacred by the Indians in French pay. The tale sent a shudder of horror throughout the whole of the British colonies. Never had the prestige of our arms sunk lower, or our prospects everywhere seemed blacker, than in this disastrous summer of 1757. To crown all, a combined expedition sent out by Pitt in September against Rochefort, on the coast of Brittany, ended, thanks to dissensions between army and fleet, and the lack of energy and enterprise of the military leaders, in a discreditable fiasco.

Thus terminated this unhappy year of unbroken failure. It was to prove for England the darkest hour before the dawn. For once in a way, she had now at the head of her destinies a man who was to prove himself not unworthy to be entrusted with the handling of her army and fleet. Pitt was at length in a position to wage war according to his own ideas, and to follow out a policy the broad lines of which he had already laid down in his own mind. Cumberland, who had resigned all his offices after the catastrophe of Hastenbeck, was replaced as commander-in-chief by the wise and experienced Ligonier; large additional forces were sanctioned, which should bring the army in 1758 to a strength of close on 100,000 men; and the control of these forces was removed from the hands of aged incapables to be entrusted to brilliant young men of the new school who had already distinguished themselves in the war. Events on the Continent had, even before the end of 1757, taken a turn for the better. A French breach of the Kloster Zeven convention gave Pitt an opportunity for denouncing that agreement, keeping the Hanoverian army in being and placing it under the command of one of Frederick the Great's best subordinates, Ferdinand of Brunswick, who at once began offensive operations against Richelieu. The fortunes of Prussia had been restored after a series of defeats by the brilliant victories of Rosbach and Leuthen, and Pitt was therefore in a position to devote, without anxiety, all his attention to the operations against Canada, which in three years were to end triumphantly in the complete conquest of that country.

3. THE CONQUEST OF CANADA
1758-1760

For the forthcoming campaign of 1758 Abercromby was placed in chief command in America vice Loudoun—a nomination which reflects ill on Pitt's reputation for a judicious choice of his subordinates. A threefold advance was to be made against the French territory; 14,000 men, under Amherst, were to besiege and take Louisburg, and subsequently advance up the St. Lawrence against Quebec; 15,000 men under Abercromby's personal command were to strike northwards against the middle course of that river from Albany; and a column of 6000 men under Forbes on the left had as its objective Fort Duquesne.

Amherst's army was delayed in its passage across the Atlantic by calms and storms, and was not assembled at Halifax till June. The flotilla at once set sail for Cape Breton Island, to invest the "Dunkirk of America", strongly held by 4000 good troops and several ships of war. A landing was boldly effected by one of the British brigades under Wolfe, west of Louisburg, on June 8, in face of determined hostile resistance; the rest of the force was quickly got ashore, and by the 26th the investment of the fortress was completed, and the bombardment begun. Harbour, forts, town and ships were quickly reduced to ruins by the fierce and effective fire of the British guns, and on July 27, seven weeks after the first landing of the besiegers, the white flag was raised. At the surrender of the fortress there passed into British hands 5,600 prisoners, naval and military, 240 guns and much ammunition and stores, together with the whole of the territory of Cape Breton and Prince Edward Islands. The season was still young and many of Amherst's subordinates advocated an immediate advance up river; but the necessity of consolidating his conquest, and still more the arrival of bad news from the Hudson, induced the British commander to content himself with what had already been achieved. Small columns were sent out far and wide to destroy the French settlements on the coast, and Amherst himself, with five battalions, set off by sea to reinforce Abercromby.

That incompetent commander had met with a serious disaster. After assembling 15,000 men at Albany by the end of June, and transferring them by water to the head of Lake George, he had encountered the French under Montcalm in person entrenched in front of Ticonderoga. His adversary had under 4000 men available, but they took fearful toll of the British advancing frontally and in mass against their position, and Abercromby, having ruined the morale and sacrificed the flower of his army, fell back disheartened to his starting-point. Here Amherst found him on his arrival with the victorious battalions from Louisburg, but too late to renew the advance against Montcalm, who had himself received reinforcements. Some compensation for this set-back was afforded by the brilliant little raid of Bradstreet along the Mohawk valley against Fort Frontenac on Lake Ontario—a success which served to some extent to restore British prestige among the Indians, and also severed the communications between Duquesne and Montreal at the moment when the former place was menaced by Forbes' advance from Pennsylvania.

The third British column, setting out in July, was meanwhile pressing slowly and with much toilsome labour through the ninety miles of dense forest which separated it from Fort Duquesne. The patience and perseverance of its commander, himself sick to death, had its reward when in November the fort was reached and found abandoned. A garrison was left behind to restore and occupy it, and the rest of the force made its way back to Pennsylvania, carrying with it its dying leader, who was not destined to survive long enough to receive the thanks of his country for his services.

Thus the commencement of 1759 saw the French in Canada pressed hard on both their flanks, their communications with the home country by sea and with the south and west severed and their territory confined within the area of the middle St. Lawrence. Pitt's plan of operations for the ensuing summer was the logical consequence and continuation of that for 1758. Amherst replaced the unfortunate Abercromby in chief in command and was also entrusted with the advance by the central line of operations from Albany against Lakes George and Champlain; he was also directed to despatch a subsidiary expedition westwards to restore Oswego and capture the French fort at Niagara. Meanwhile Wolfe, with a semi-independent command of 12,000 men, was to advance up the St. Lawrence against Quebec.

In the actual event, only 8,000 men could be mustered for Wolfe's force, and with these he had to invest a strongly defended city, held by 16,000 troops, some among the best in the French army, and led by the capable and prudent Montcalm. His task, none too easy at the best, was rendered still more difficult by the negligence of the naval commander, who allowed French reinforcements to slip up the St. Lawrence as soon as the ice broke up, and by the fact that on one of the transports was Bougainville, one of Montcalm's subordinates, bearing an intercepted letter from Pitt to Amherst, which revealed the whole British plan of campaign for the year. None the less, Wolfe and Saunders, the admiral of the squadron detailed to cooperate against Quebec, entered on their operations with high hopes. Ships of war and transports were piloted with skill and daring up the tortuous course of the St. Lawrence, and arrived opposite Quebec on June 26. The French were found encamped to the east of the city on the north bank, their left on the Montmorency River; and Wolfe, setting his troops ashore on the opposite side of the St. Lawrence, passed a detachment across to the east of the Montmorency, and opened his batteries against the town. The dispersion of the British forces failed to entice Montcalm into a false move which might give his adversary an opening to attack him; and on July 31, therefore, Wolfe took the bull by the horns and, under cover of the guns of the ships, landed a detachment on the north bank in full face of the French lines; the reckless impetuosity of the covering party, however, led to a premature and futile attack from which he was glad to be able to draw off without a disaster. Other means, therefore, had to be tried. First a detachment under Murray was passed up the river to a position above the city from which it could harry Montcalm's communications with Montreal, and this was followed gradually by the bulk of the army. Wolfe, meanwhile, searching diligently for a place where he might gain a footing on the north bank and offer the French battle on equal terms, found a possible landing place and a practicable passage up the cliffs some two miles west of the city. On the night of September 12 the pick of his army, some 5,000 men in all, were ferried silently down to this spot and set on shore, and next morning Montcalm, looking out from the walls of Quebec, saw to his amazement the British army drawn up for battle astride his communication's on the Plains of Abraham.

In the ensuing battle his 7,500 men, despite their numerical superiority, were swept in disorder from the field by the deadly volleys of the British. He himself was mortally wounded and Wolfe killed in the moment of victory; the remnant of the French abandoned Quebec in disorder, and on September 18 the city surrendered on terms.

While Wolfe was still preparing for his ascent of the St. Lawrence, Amherst and his 11,000 men had set forth from Fort Edward. They moved but slowly; on their arrival at the foot of Lake George, a prolonged halt was made for the purpose of rebuilding the fort of the same name, and only at the end of July did they embark on the flotilla for Ticonderoga. The French garrison, seeing resistance to be hopeless, blew up their works and retired, and the British, pushing steadily forward after them, occupied Crown Point, on Lake Champlain, on August 4. Here another lengthy and inexplicable pause ensued, ostensibly for the purpose of consolidating the ground gained and constructing gunboats to wrest the command of the lake from the French. These were not ready till the end of October, when the hostile craft were rapidly put out of action; but Amherst considered that the lateness of the season forbade any further prosecution of the advance, and the campaign in this quarter came to an end.

The subsidiary attack on Niagara proved completely successful. Oswego was reoccupied and rebuilt without opposition, and in July the garrison of the fort was forced to capitulate after an attempt at relief had been beaten off.

The position of French Canada at the commencement of 1760 was critical but by no means hopeless. The zone of operations of the defence was rapidly contracting, but Levis, who had succeeded Montcalm in command of the army, believed he might still retrieve the situation by a bold counter-stroke. He decided to assume the offensive against the army of Wolfe, now under Murray, which was still halted at Quebec and had been reduced by cold and sickness to a paltry 3,000 men. Levis began to descend the river from Montreal in April, with a force more than threefold superior to Murray's; the latter was defeated in the open field at St. Foy and forced to seek refuge within the walls of the city, which was closely invested. He managed, however, to hold out until the arrival of the British fleet with the break-up of the ice in May rendered the besiegers' lines untenable; and Levis fell back to concentrate his forces for the last stand around Montreal.

Meanwhile Amherst, left by Pitt with a free hand to decide for himself the plan of operations for 1760, had decided on a convergent advance on the French capital with two strong wings under himself and Murray from Niagara and Quebec respectively, and a weak centre under Haviland from Lake Champlain. These movements, which were impeded more by natural obstacles than by the enemy, were carried out with a precision and accuracy that rendered resistance hopeless, and punctually to the minute on September 6 the three columns made a simultaneous appearance before the walls of Montreal. Two days later the city surrendered, French Canada passed once for all under the British flag, and the victorious commander, Amherst, proceeded to organise and set up a government for the newly conquered province.

Thus ended in a blaze of glory England's contest with France for supremacy in the New World. It was a triumph won entirely by British troops and British generals, for the colonial levies had proved at least as much hindrance as help to their comrades; no colonial leader had shown any ability beyond what was demanded by petty war, and the colonial governments had contributed nothing to the common cause. Of the victorious British commanders, the name of Wolfe has remained green in the memories of his countrymen, to the exclusion of that of the supreme commander of the armies and the real victor of the campaign, Jeffrey Amherst. The victory at Quebec was no more decisive of the fate of New France than was Nelson's at Trafalgar decisive of that of Napoleon; and in each case the work, though well begun, had to be clinched and completed by other hands. Yet the circumstances of the drama, the rapid and overwhelming *dénouement* and the fitting exit of the protagonist at the very climax of the catastrophe, have invested Quebec and Trafalgar alike with a human and romantic interest which has rendered their memory a national and immortal possession. And in truth, if an early death and a posthumous fame be preferable to long life and honour, then was Wolfe fortunate above his comrade and chief, even to the extent of having his own dead brow adorned with the laurels that of right belonged to the other. History, however, must recognise the real conqueror of Canada in that cautious, thorough and painstaking commander who never moved before he was prepared, who left nothing to chance nor ever put his cause to avoidable hazard, and who by a perfectly organised and perfectly executed operation of war crowned his life's work by reducing a vast hostile province and a gallant enemy army to an end so inevitable that not even the satisfaction of a final death struggle was left them.

4. THE SUBSIDIARY OPERATIONS IN EUROPE AND THE INDIES 1758-1762

It has been stated that Pitt's war policy aimed first and foremost at the conquest of the overseas possessions of France by means of combined operations by the British army and fleet. How successfully this policy—which was an entirely novel one in the military history of Great Britain—was carried into effect in the case of Canada we have just seen; but it had another side, less interesting and spectacular but not the less vital, which must now be dealt with.

Pitt was not free at any time during the war to direct all the military resources of his country against the French colonies; there were important interests nearer home which could not be left to take care of themselves. The security of the British Isles was the first and most vital, but there had also to be considered the safety of the Hanoverian territories of King George II., while honour also joined with interest in the demand that some assistance should be given to Frederick II. of Prussia in his struggle against the overwhelmingly superior forces of Austria, France and Russia. How to satisfy these various and often conflicting demands with the minimum possible expenditure of military effort was Pitt's problem in what he all along considered as the subsidiary theatres of the war.

His first attempt at a solution, in 1758, consisted merely in a repetition of the attacks on the coast of France, which had hitherto given little useful result for the expenditure and loss involved. The first of these, carried out in June by 13,000 men under Marlborough, proved a complete failure; the force landed on the coast of Normandy, marched up to and looked at St. Malo and Cherbourg, and then withdrew, unmolested indeed but with nothing accomplished. The second enterprise, carried out two months later by a corps of 10,000 men led by Bligh, was both more and less fortunate; it landed, captured and destroyed Cherbourg, and re-embarked in safety, but being once more set on shore to attack St. Malo, was driven back to its ships by a superior hostile force with the loss of practically the whole of its rearguard.

As some slight set-off to these mishaps the French trading stations of Senegal and Goree on the west coast of Africa were taken by small British forces, the one in April, the other in October. Perhaps the most important event of the year, however, was the determination of Pitt, suddenly arrived at in the middle of the summer, to embark upon operations in another theatre of war by, the despatch of a British contingent to Germany as part of the army under Ferdinand of Brunswick. No doubt he was influenced in this decision, to some extent at least, by the striking successes achieved in 1758 by that prince, who in a brilliant campaign had forced his French adversaries to evacuate Hanover and Hesse and fall back west of the Rhine. A corps of 10,000 men was despatched to Emden under Marlborough, who died soon after landing in Germany and was succeeded by Sackville; it reached the main army late in August, but took no part in active operations until the opening of the campaign of 1759.

Meanwhile, at the latter end of 1758, an armament was being prepared in the British ports for employment against the French West Indian islands, and in November 6,000 troops under Hopson were despatched to Barbados, which was to serve as a base for further operations. The first attempt against Martinique miscarried, despite some initial success; and the force was then directed against Guadeloupe. The western half of the island was secured without great difficulty, but the eastern half gave more trouble; and it was not till a large proportion of the men had fallen victims to disease, and Hopson had been succeeded in command by the younger and more energetic Barrington, that a vigorous and successful offensive completed the conquest, a few days before the arrival of French reinforcements, who sailed off in haste on finding that they had come just too late. The capture of Mariegalante effectively rounded off a highly successful little campaign.

From these minor operations we must turn to the German theatre of war. Here Ferdinand at the commencement of 1759 found himself with 45,000 men, cantoned from the area around Munster to the Diemel, opposed by two hostile armies, the one under Contades on the lower Rhine, the other under Broglie on the lower Main. As the combined strength of these forces was something like twice his own, Ferdinand struck at Broglie, who was nearest to him, before his colleague could unite with him, only to be repulsed and compelled to fall back northwards. Contades, advancing eastwards, came into touch with Broglie, and the combined forces, constantly menacing the Allied right, overran Hesse and the territories of Waldeck and Paderborn, and forced their adversaries back to the lower Weser. Contades, who was in chief command of the French, took up a position around Minden to cover the investment of Munster, Hameln and Lippstadt. On August 1, Ferdinand, advancing to meet him, induced him to expose himself to battle by the device of leaving a corps apparently exposed and unsupported within striking distance of his front. The ensuing fight was decided by the remarkable feat of a British infantry brigade, which, owing to a misconception of orders, advanced against and completely wrecked the French centre, mainly composed of cavalry; the fruits of victory were lost owing to the behaviour of Sackville, who held back the British cavalry from pursuit. Contades, abandoning in haste all the territory he had previously gained and raising the various sieges he had undertaken, fell back hurriedly by way of Cassel to a position behind the Lahn; Ferdinand followed him up, but, owing to the necessity of detaching strong forces to assist Frederick, for whom 1759 had been a year of disaster, was unable to push on beyond the positions he had occupied at the opening of the campaign.

Great and extensive preparations were made by Pitt for the year 1760. 1759 had been a year of triumph throughout the whole theatre of hostilities; in America, Quebec and Duquesne; in the West Indies, Guadeloupe; in Germany, Minden; at sea, Quiberon Bay, had shed a blaze of glory on British arms. The ultimate fate of Canada seemed to the popular mind to be decided; fears of invasion had vanished; Ferdinand had held busy and repulsed the greater part of the armies of France in Germany; and Frederick the Great still stood, though in the past year he had more than once staggered. All this only spurred Pitt to demand further exertions of the country. 132,000 men, regulars and militia, were voted for the army, and 55,000 German troops were taken into British pay, making in all close on 190,000 men. 10,000 additional troops sailed for Germany, and Granby, who had succeeded Sackville on the latter's recall after Minden, found himself by the middle of the summer at the head of some 25,000 men, about a third of the whole Allied army. Operations opened in much the same manner as in the previous year; St. Germain, who had replaced Contades, united with Broglie, who had advanced from the Main and surprised the passage of the Ohm, in the plain north of the Diemel, an attempt to prevent their junction being repelled with loss. Strong in the possession of a numerical superiority of over two to one, the French pursued their northward advance undeterred by a brilliant little fight at Emsdorf, where the British cavalry were mainly instrumental in completely destroying an isolated hostile detachment, capturing about five times their own number of prisoners. While siege was being laid to Cassel, however, another and more serious misfortune befell the French in the overwhelming of their left wing at Warburg. Here again the British Horse decided the day, arriving on the field with their horse artillery after a rapid advance of five miles, and driving the enemy in disorder across the Diemel. Still the tide flowed on; Cassel fell, and French detachments, crossing to the east of the Weser, carried terror and pillage into Brunswick and Upper Hanover, which had hitherto been untouched by war. Ferdinand, in sheer desperation, attempted a diversion by despatching a force under the Hereditary Prince of Brunswick to operate on the enemy's communications with the lower Rhine; that commander, having laid siege to Wesel, hearing that a retiring column under Castries was being hurried to the rescue, determined to surprise and disperse it by a night attack on its position at Kloster Kampen. The attempt miscarried, largely owing to the indiscipline and impetuosity of the British contingent, and the defeated army was with difficulty got back to the east bank of the Rhine and so to Westphalia. With this unhappy episode the campaign terminated.

Elsewhere throughout the area of subsidiary operations no event of importance had taken place in 1760, apart from a small and unsuccessful French raid on Ireland. But in October there had occurred in England an event which was to have a profound influence on the future course of the war. George II., whose former mistrust and dislike of Pitt had long given place to admiration of his achievements and complete confidence in his genius, suddenly died, to be succeeded by his son George III., a self-confident, self-willed young man who held very decided views on national policy and the royal prerogative, and was determined to be something more than a mere figurehead in his own council.

For the moment, however, Pitt's ascendancy remained unimpaired. The forces in British pay in 1761 were raised to 200,000 men—113,000 regulars, 27,000 militia and 60,000 foreign auxiliaries. Operations were early resumed in Germany. In February Ferdinand moved forward from his cantonments north of the Diemel, and in a few weeks rapidly overran all Hesse. Broglie fell back before him, leaving behind garrisons which the Allies perforce had to mask, denuding the country of supplies as he retired, and gathering with every day's march rearward successive reinforcements which soon swelled his army to 80,000 men, while Ferdinand's, drained by the necessity of detaching troops to secure its communications and watching the French garrisons, sank rapidly to a strength of little more than 20,000. Before March was out the Allies were back in their old lines behind the Diemel, and might count themselves fortunate to get there without disaster.

A pause now ensued for three months while each side refitted and recruited its forces, and it was June before the French Army of the Rhine, 100,000 men under the incompetent Soubise, and that of the Main, 60,000 under Broglie, commenced their advance against the 90,000 of Ferdinand. The Allied commander moved westwards to meet Soubise near Dortmund, and, completely outmanoeuvring him, marched round his left flank and took up a strong position facing east near Vellinghausen. Here he was attacked by the combined

French forces who had effected their junction; but owing to dissensions between Soubise and Broglie, coordination between the various columns was conspicuous by its absence; only the British contingent was seriously engaged, and beat off its assailants with ease. The French armies drew off and separated, Soubise falling back to the Rhine, where he spent the rest of the summer in inglorious and inexplicable inactivity, and Broglie, pursued by Ferdinand, to the Weser, and thence to the south into Hesse. Here he halted, and, while Soubise undertook a futile diversion against Emden, sought to recover the initiative by an incursion into Brunswick. This Ferdinand easily repelled and then took up his winter quarters along the northern banks of the Lippe and the Diemel, with his left wing astride the Weser.

Meanwhile British ships and troops had been active in other theatres besides Germany. The submission of Canada had liberated the army of Amherst for service elsewhere. That commander early in the year received orders to despatch a force to reduce the remaining French islands in the West Indies. The greater part of the troops from Canada were gradually concentrated at Guadeloupe, whence in June a small expedition was despatched to secure Dominica, which was effected with little loss. Nearer home a brilliant exploit had been carried out by a combined force under Keppel and Hodgson, who, sailing for Belleisle, off the Basque roads, with 7,000 men, landed successfully, and persisting in their enterprise, despite initial setbacks, compelled the capitulation of the island and its garrison in June after a two months' siege.

Once more, however, as in the previous year, there took place a domestic event of pre-eminent importance. Early in 1761 Pitt had begun to suspect with all too good reason that France was utilising the peace conversations into which she had entered as a cloak for further vigorous offensive designs with the aid of a new ally, Spain. He had evidence that an offensive and defensive alliance known as the Family Compact had already been signed between these powers, and that only the backward state of Spain's preparations was postponing her declaration of war against Great Britain. True to his policy of a vigorous offensive as a solution for all difficulties and perplexities of war, Pitt advocated in council that such a declaration should be anticipated by the inception of immediate hostilities by England. Jealousy and dislike on the part of the King and his supporters, war-weariness and financial exhaustion on that of the nation at large, combined to forbid the adoption of any such bold course of action ; and Pitt, faced with the impossibility of maintaining in the Cabinet and in the Commons that ascendancy which had alone enabled him to carry on the war with such brilliance and success, resigned office in October, being succeeded by Bute, one of George III.'s personal adherents. In less than three months from Pitt's fall, it became evident that his judgement in the matter of Spain's intentions had been only too correct, and by 1762 England found herself with an additional enemy on her hands.

Yet though the master hand was no longer at the helm the conduct of affairs remained vigorous, resolute and appropriate. The accession of Spain to the side of England's enemies seemed but to afford the island power more opportunity of evincing the wide reach of her outstretched arm. 215,000 troops were arrayed under arms for the campaign of 1762, and of these part were at once set aboard ship for the attack of the overseas possessions of Spain. 12,000 men under Pocock and Albemarle were directed against Havana. The siege was difficult and toilsome in the extreme; disease ravaged the British ranks, laying low close on fifty per cent of their effective strength; but after two months' investment the white flag was hoisted and Havana was ours, and with it the whole of Cuba. A smaller force sent from India in a short and sharp siege of ten days compelled the surrender of Manila and the Philippines. The operations against the French islands proceeded simultaneously and apace. Monckton led an expedition of 8,000 of his American veterans against Martinique; in a month of arduous campaigning he reduced it to submission, and quickly followed up his success by the capture of St. Lucia, Grenada and St. Vincent. A French counter offensive against Newfoundland surprised and gained temporary possession of the island, but the victorious troops, after being left in undisturbed occupation for three months, were then invested by sea and land and compelled to lay down their arms. Even on the continent of Europe the influence of British sea power and British aims made itself felt in new spheres of activity, and 7,000 troops assisted the Portuguese army on its eastern frontier in bidding defiance to the Spanish threats of invasion.

Meanwhile the French in Germany were reduced for the first time to the defensive. Soubise and d'Estrées with 70,000 men had received orders to confine themselves to maintaining their gains, while 30,000 more under Condé were held back to safeguard the lower Rhine. Ferdinand, detaching a force to observe the latter, advanced in May with 50,000 men on both banks of the Weser, and, arriving on the Diemel, found the French in position facing him at Wilhelmstal. On June 24 he attempted to carry out an ambitious scheme for enveloping both their flanks and forcing them to a decisive battle at a disadvantage, but they succeeded, though not without difficulty and loss, in escaping the embrace of the Allied wings, owing to the faulty co-ordination of the latter's movements. Ferdinand, pushing the pursuit, forced his foes steadily out of Hesse and back as far as the Main, where, being joined by Condé from the Rhine, they faced about, enveloped his right, and compelled him in turn to fall back behind the Ohm. Here their further progress was stayed in a fierce little action, and the capture of Cassel by the Allies ended the campaign, and the war in Germany, on a note of victory.

During the greater part of the summer of 1762 conversations had been going on between the representatives of the belligerent powers which eventuated on November 21 in the signature of definite preliminaries of peace. The decision of George III. and his minister, Bute, to put an end to the war, and still more the terms to which they finally consented, were both at the time and since subjected to fierce and bitter criticism. The conditions of the definite Peace of Paris, however, signed in February 1763, were favourable enough, including as they did the cession to England by France of the whole of Canada and Nova Scotia, of all French India but two insignificant factories, of Grenada, Tobago, St. Vincent and Dominica in the West Indies, and of Florida by Spain. This treaty, indeed, may be said to have sealed the results of the first and most successful of our Imperial wars, by the establishment on a sure foundation, both in the Eastern and the Western Hemispheres, of the beginnings of the greatest Empire in the history of the world.

5. William Pitt as a War Minister

No military historian can conclude a narrative of the Seven Years' War without an attempt to appraise the man whom common opinion, both contemporary and subsequent, has elevated to the position of the hero of that world-wide drama. William Pitt, Earl of Chatham, is universally accepted as the greatest war minister of our history, and while it is hardly possible seriously to put forward any other candidate for that position, one is irresistibly reminded, even in the act of concurrence in the common verdict, of the saying that among the blind a one-eyed man is king. For William Pitt, though he may have been our greatest, was far from being an ideal war minister. His title to fame is commonly based on his recognition of the necessity for Great Britain of concentrating her effort mainly on the winning of territory overseas; on his able direction of her available forces to that end ; on his uncanny power of searching out and promoting youthful ability to high commands; and on his immense influence in army, fleet and nation as an inspiring and uplifting force. As for the last-named claim, it may be pointed out that wars, though they may be lost by politicians, can only be won by sailors and soldiers, and that the idea that the courage and constancy of the men who hacked their way to victory through the trackless forests of the Ohio, or who served their pitching guns amid the howling of the wind and the lashing of the rain in Quiberon Bay, were appreciably raised, or indeed that their actions and behaviour at these or any other times were in the least influenced by the attitude or words of a posing minister in the safety and comfort of Downing Street, is entirely divorced from reality. As regards Pitt's skill in recognising and rewarding rising young talent, it must be remembered that the allotment of fleet commands rested almost entirely in the capable hands of the First Lord of the Admiralty, Anson, and that as regards the army Ligonier must share with the Prime Minister whatever credit may accrue from the selection of Mordaunt and Bligh to lead raids against the French coast, of Abercromby to the chief control of the operations in America, and of Sackville to the command of the British contingent in Germany. Finally, the legend of Pitt's recognition of the importance of and concentration of the British effort on the conquest of overseas empire rests largely on the erroneous idea that he was largely responsible for the conduct of our successful operations in India, with which he had in actual fact nothing whatever to do, and on the hypothesis that Wolfe and Amherst in Canada owed anything more to his direction of the campaign than the imposition of an essentially vicious plan of operations and the provision of hopelessly inadequate means to carry it out. It is a desolating commentary on Pitt's facility for recognising the decisive theatre, that while the total strength of the forces in British pay numbered in 1760—the last year of the Canadian campaign —close on 200,000 men, the regular forces under Amherst's command for the decisive advance against Montreal were a beggarly 10,000 all told. Our war minister could always find as many or more men for a petty and purposeless raid on an unimportant French coast town than he ever did for the conquest of New France, and his statement that he conquered Canada in Germany is borne out at least by the fact that the ratio of the number of troops sent by this country to the two campaigns was on the average two to one in favour of the theatre of war in Europe. If we add to these considerations the fact that Pitt was by general admission an administrator who too often exercised a criminal parsimony in such vital matters as the provision of winter clothing, hospital necessities and artillery ammunition, it will be realised that the giant was less stupendous and awe-inspiring than many of his biographers would have us believe. With all this, however, it is impossible to deny a high place in the annals of our military fame to the man who first realised, however hesitatingly and half-heartedly, that England's future was on the water, and who first set the British army on board ship, and sent it to conquer the vast and fruitful worlds that lay beyond the seas.

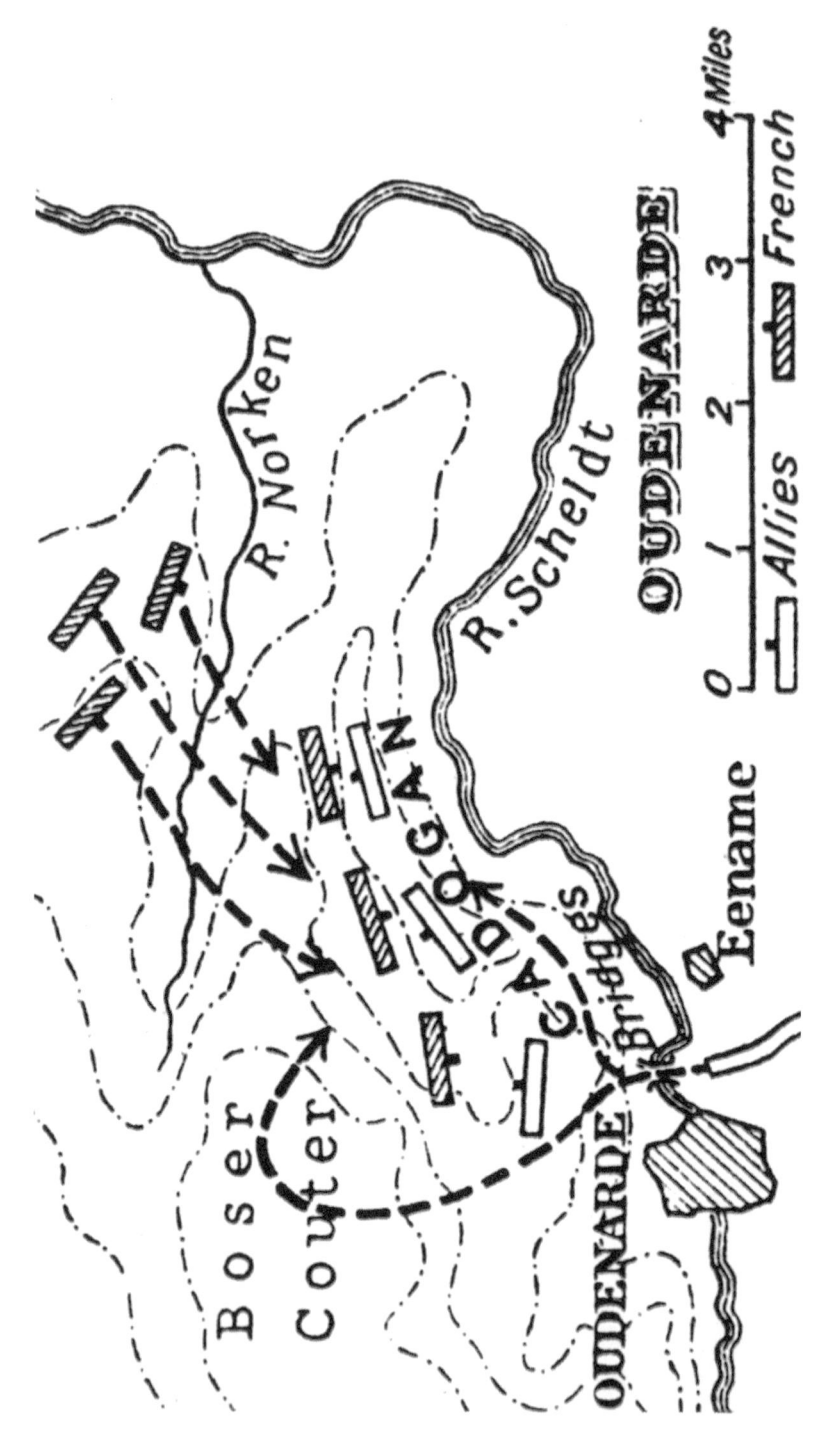

Duke of Marlborough signing a despatch, 1704

CHAPTER 5

The Period of Anglo-French Rivalry in India
1740-1760

1. THE FRENCH INITIATIVE UNDER DUPLEIX
1740-1755

Simultaneously with the conquest of Canada, Great Britain had won, at the opposite edge of the world, a series of victories, an earnest of others yet greater and more famous to come, which were to affix to her Imperial crown the brightest of its jewels. The course of her contest with France for supremacy in India, as in America, passes from initial incompetence and disaster through effort and crisis to victory ; but whereas the winning of New France was the result of a policy deliberately adopted and consistently pursued by the British Government, and of regular operations carried out by British soldiers and sailors, the rise of British dominion in India affords the most striking proof of the statement that we conquered our Empire in a fit of absence of mind. It is necessary to remember when telling or reading of our Indian wars, that they were in the beginning nothing but a series of private or semi-private adventures, conducted by men on the spot, dependent almost entirely on local forces and resources, in pursuit of purposes primarily if not entirely commercial. The great British trading interests in the East of course exercised considerable influence on the British Government of the day, even, as we shall see, to the extent of securing from it ships and troops for the defence of their commerce and property; but the main burden of the struggle with France for domination in India, which raged unbroken for over twenty years, contemporaneously with, but almost entirely independent of, the Austrian Succession and the Seven Years' Wars, and the armed truce intervening between them, was borne by levies locally raised, and paid, officered by amateurs with little military experience, and controlled from home by boards of civilian directors, whose aims were mainly directed towards profit-making for themselves and their shareholders.

It seems, therefore, necessary in this chapter to treat as a complete whole the story of our early wars in South and East India, regarding them as a series of independent private enterprises in which the British army, as such, played only an auxiliary, though creditable, part.

The first trading stations of the British East India Company were established in the first half of the seventeenth century at various points on the western, south-eastern and eastern coasts of India. The French, who were to be its most formidable rivals, did not appear on the scene till 1664, and the first beginnings of their enterprise were unpromising; it was not till the second quarter of the eighteenth century that they began to pursue a forward policy apparently aimed at securing for them a position as the dominant European power in India. The time chosen was favourable for such an attempt. The decline of the Mogul dynasty, which had ruled India for two centuries, had given rise to chaos throughout the country, with the usual accompaniments of secession and independence in the provinces, a crop of disputed successions, and the rise of innumerable pretenders to the various thrones and offices. The opportunity of fishing in these troubled waters was quickly seen and grasped by the men who controlled the policy of the French East India Company, and Dupleix, on his accession in 1741 to power at Pondicherry, the chief factory and headquarters of the company, situated on the Coromandel coast, some seventy miles south of Madras, set to work to secure a controlling influence with the semi-independent rulers of South India. His methods were the elimination as political factors of the other European trading companies, and the promotion to and maintenance in high places of such native rulers or ministers as would support French interests.

The outbreak of war between England and France in 1742 gave him the needed pretext for an open attack on the British, whom he had early recognised as likely to prove the most serious opponents to the fulfilment of his schemes. The presence of a French fleet at Mauritius, under the command of La Bourdonnais, afforded an opportunity for a combined attack on Madras by sea and by land; but before this design could mature, a British squadron appeared off the Carnatic coast, and Pondicherry seemed in danger. Dupleix, however, had already made himself *persona grata* at the Court of the Nabob of the province, who issued an order forbidding the British to attack the French stations within his territory; and La Bourdonnais' fleet arriving most opportunely at this juncture, the British ships were compelled after an indecisive action to retire to Ceylon. Dupleix, having thus secured command of the seas, proceeded to treat his adversaries as they had planned to treat him; Madras, invested by land and water, ill-fortified and weakly defended, fell in September 1746, only a few of the garrison making their escape to Fort St. David, just south of Pondicherry. The ultimate fate of the captured city became the subject of an acrimonious dispute between Dupleix and La Bourdonnais, and in the midst of it an army sent by the Nabob of the Carnatic, furious that the very people whom he had protected should now themselves disturb his peace, appeared before its walls. It was successfully beaten off by the French, who were now free to turn their attention to Fort St. David, the last British possession of importance in South India. An unaccountable delay of a few weeks in opening the siege gave time for the arrival of a relieving squadron, and Dupleix was compelled to fall back and assume a defensive attitude, to cover his own territory. An attempted diversion against Cuddalore was defeated by a skilful stratagem of the commander of the place, Major Stringer Lawrence, and the arrival of Admiral Boscawen early in 1748 with a powerful fleet and a force of some 4,000 regular troops seemed to have sealed the fate of the French and their schemes of domination. Siege was laid to Pondicherry, but the defence was stubborn and fertile in resource. Boscawen, to whom had been entrusted the supreme control of operations both on sea and on land, was entirely inexperienced in military matters, and after three months the coming of the rains obliged him to abandon his lines and draw off in discredit. The Treaty of Aix-la-Chapelle, therefore, found the French in the ascendancy in South India, and though the restoration of Madras to the British did something to restore the material balance, the moral gains of the period of direct hostilities just closed remained decidedly with Dupleix.

The prestige thus acquired was to stand him in good stead in the period that followed the conclusion of peace. Both sides found their rivalry too sharp and irreconcilable to be terminated by the mere signature of an inconclusive treaty by distant diplomats but little concerned with the interests at stake in India; and though open hostilities between them were hardly possible, they found ample opportunity for indirect warfare in the quarrels of various native princes or pretenders. The British were the first to embark on this promising yet perilous policy; and in 1749 their support was bought by one of the claimants to the throne of Tanjore. Dupleix meanwhile was flying at higher game. Disputes had opportunely arisen over the succession to the rule both of the Deccan, the wide territory between the Vindhia mountains and the Kistna, and of the Carnatic, and he threw himself ardently into support of the cause of Murzafa Jung, who was aiming at the Vice-royalty of the former province, and of Chanda Sahib, who was aspiring to become Nabob of the latter. The British were forced in self-defence to espouse the cause of Mohammed Ali, a rival of Chanda; but their measures were less vigorous and well-conceived than those of Dupleix, who succeeded in spurring on his two puppets to raise an army and march on Trichinopoly, the capital of the Carnatic. Unfortunately for him, their corrupt prodigality exhausted the funds which he had supplied—largely from his own private fortune—for the expedition before it had well set out, and they found it necessary to seek first to replenish their empty treasure chests by laying siege to Tanjore. Before they could force an entry, Nasir Jung, Murzafa's rival in the Deccan, marched to the relief of the city at the head of a large army and compelled them to fall back on Pondicherry, which he proceeded to invest. He was repulsed from before the walls, and fell a few days later by the hand of a traitor, whereupon Murzafa was proclaimed by the French undisputed sovereign of the Deccan. This title he was not to enjoy for long, for on his way to assume his new dignity he was slain in battle with two petty princelings who had taken upon themselves to oppose his advance. His successor, Salabat Jung, however, was so much in the hands of the French that he appointed Dupleix Governor of the whole of Southern India, from the Kistna to Cape Comorin, and confirmed the French East India Company and its officials in various privileges which had been promised them by his unhappy predecessor.

Thus by 1751, less than three years after the signature of the Treaty of Aix-la-Chapelle, Dupleix had attained more than he could at the outset have hoped from his policy of intervention in the dynastic disputes of the native kingdoms. His name and fame, and that of his country, were held in respect and awe from the Carnatic shore to Malabar, and from

Hyderabad to Tanjore; throughout that wide area the British had been outmanoeuvred and outwitted; their prestige rent from them, their designs checkmated, their very position imperilled. It only remained for him to establish himself beyond possibility of mischance by the capture or death of Mohammed Ali, who was still in possession of Trichinopoly; and Chanda Sahib, with a large army, was set in motion against his rival.

The British could not tamely stand by and watch their candidate to the throne of the Carnatic thus eliminated, but their first efforts to check the progress of Chanda's host were unsuccessful, and the greater part of their available forces were shut up in the invested city. They had no choice but to have recourse to a diversion, and a little column of 300 men, under the command of a civilian, Robert Clive, destined to become the first and most famous of the makers of British India, was despatched to attempt the surprise of Chanda's capital, Arcot. The little band successfully secured the town, held it for close on two months against the flower of Chanda's army, hurried back in haste to besiege it, beat off a desperate assault, and following up their foes whom the arrival of a Mahratta army had forced to raise the siege, completely defeated them at Arnee, with the loss of all their guns and many men. The tables were thus completely turned, and the French ascendancy had received a rude shock; but the contest was by no means over. While the British were concerting measures for the direct relief of Trichinopoly, which was still invested, the enemy raised fresh forces and advanced on Madras. Clive, hurrying out to meet them at the head of some 1,700 men, fell into an ambush at Covrepauk, but his fine battle-field skill extricated him successfully from a situation momentarily critical, and a bold turning movement against the enemy's rear drove them from the field in rout. Of all Clive's battles this little-known engagement most redounds to his credit, and shows his military qualities at their best.

Meanwhile the siege of Trichinopoly was being feebly and ineffectively conducted by the French commander, Law, and in March 1752 a force of 1500 men under Stringer Lawrence set out for its relief. Law allowed himself to be outmanoeuvred in his efforts to prevent its entry, withdrew from his lines, and shut himself up in an island to the north of the city, the approaches to which were swiftly closed by his adversaries. A relief column sent in haste by Dupleix succeeded under cover of darkness in breaking into Clive's camp, but was driven out again after some hours of fierce and confused fighting, in which the British commander once more gave striking proof of his personal courage and military talent. A second attempt proved even more disastrous, and the relief column, defeated and hotly pursued, was compelled to lay down its arms. Thus convinced of the hopelessness of further resistance, Law, in June 1752, signed the terms of a capitulation which, among other discreditable conditions, left Chanda Sahib to be done to death by his enemies.

The edifice of power so laboriously erected by Dupleix seemed thus to have tumbled about his ears; but he was not the man thus easily to admit defeat, and with admirable courage and resource set to work to retrieve his fortunes and those of his country. The native princes who had allied themselves with Mohammed Ali, and the British, fell to quarrelling in the moment of victory; Dupleix was quick to play upon their jealousies, and the opportune arrival of reinforcements by sea from Europe enabled him to back up his diplomatic endeavours by force of arms. A British detachment sent from Madras to capture the strong fortress of Gingee was cut off from its base and heavily defeated, but a move by the victorious French against Fort St. David was in its turn repulsed by Lawrence, and meanwhile Clive, in command of a body of untrained recruits just arrived from England, and a few newly raised sepoys, welded this unpromising material in an army formidable enough to overrun the country west of Madras and inflict a complete defeat on the French near Covelong. Dupleix, however, built his main hope on his endeavours to raise up fresh foes to the British around Trichinopoly; these endeavours were successful, and early in January 1753 the Mahratta and Mysorean troops, who had co-operated with the British in the campaign against Law, suddenly declared themselves our enemies, and invested the city, which was held only by a weak detachment. Lawrence at once marched thither in haste, and his arrival brought the garrison up to a strength of 5,500 men; but the besieging forces swelled in even greater proportion, and by July the British estimated that they had no fewer than 29,000 enemies of varying degrees of efficiency and military value on their hands. There now ensued a series of combats under the walls of the city which should alone have been sufficient to rescue the name of Stringer Lawrence from the obscurity into which it has undeservedly fallen. On July 7, and again on August 20, he completely outmanoeuvred and checked the overwhelmingly superior forces of the enemy, led and directed as they were by the ablest officers of France. Finally, on October 2 the British were completely victorious in a final battle, which opened with a skilfully planned and boldly led night attack against the besiegers' lines, and drove them once more to seek safety by a flight to their island stronghold. Lawrence, conceiving his task accomplished, went into winter quarters near by; but the garrison which he left behind had soon after to deal with a surprise night assault against the walls, which came within an ace of being successful and only failed by reason of the indiscipline of part of the attacking force. This attempt showed that the morale of the enemy was on the mend, and a British set-back in the surprise and loss of an important convoy still further encouraged them; so that Lawrence could hardly yet regard his difficulties as at an end. Fortunately, an, attempt to repeat the exploit a few months later was beaten off with loss by the escort; the decision of the ruler of Tanjore, after a period of indecision due to the blandishments of Dupleix, to adhere to the British alliance, eased the political situation; and the arrival of reinforcements enabled Lawrence once more to confine the French and their auxiliaries in their island.

Affairs in South India had thus taken a decided turn in favour of the British when, in August 1755, France dealt her own prospects of securing predominance in the East a mortal blow by recalling Dupleix. With the departure of that commanding personality, the only one on either side who can be said to have possessed and pursued a vision at once splendid and practicable, there disappeared the greatest and most formidable of our enemies—the one who, by his example, had done most to promote, and by his actions, most to hinder, the first beginnings of our rule in India. His successor made haste to conclude an agreement for the cessation of hostilities which was signed in June 1755. The period of French initiative thus ended with the casting away of the fruits of fifteen years of courageous and incessant effort. The coming decade was to see the British making better use of their opportunities.

2. THE EXTINCTION OF FRENCH POWER IN INDIA
1755-1761

Despite the recall of Dupleix and the conclusion of the truce of 1755, the power of the French in India was still so great that few prophets would have ventured to foretell its complete disappearance within the next decade. Their prestige stood as high as ever throughout the greater part of South India ; and the whole of the Deccan, governed nominally by Salabat Jung, was for all practical purposes ruled by Bussy, their able resident at his Court. None the less, the loss of the genius who had all but given to France the pre-eminence in the East was not to be compensated for by mere ability, of which there was as much if not more among the British; and the latter had the advantage in the contest that was to come of receiving support and encouragement from home in a greater degree and at more opportune moments than their rivals.

The agreement concluded in 1755 was avowedly only a temporary measure, and both sides had on several occasions infringed it before it was finally terminated, once and for all, by the outbreak of the Seven Years' War in 1756. About the same time the French cause underwent a serious set-back by reason of the quarrel between Salabat Jung and Bussy, which led, to the latter's dismissal from Hyderabad, and an appeal by the former for British assistance. While an armed force was being prepared for this purpose, however, a serious crisis arose in Bengal, which necessitated the instant employment of all available troops to avert it. The fortification of the British factory at Calcutta, undertaken in view of the outbreak of war with France, gave umbrage to the new Nabob of Bengal, Surajah Dowlah, who was already fearful and mistrustful of the spread of foreign influence within his borders; marching on Cosimbazar and Calcutta with an overwhelming army, he seized both settlements, cruelly exterminated the garrison of the latter and razed the fortifications to the ground. The insult was one not to be borne, and an armament was instantly fitted out in Madras under Clive and Watson, for despatch to the Ganges delta. The force, some 3,000 men and ten ships, concentrated there by the end of December 1756, and moving northward, re-occupied Calcutta successfully, after beating off an attempt to check its advance near Budge Budge. Here Clive was invested by a large army under the Nabob in person; and considering now, as throughout his life, that audacity was the best passport to success against Eastern armies, he moved out to beat up Surajah's camp at dawn. The material success achieved was but partial, but the moral victory was complete ; the Nabob in panic withdrew his troops, and in a hurriedly concluded treaty agreed to the restoration of all British property and privileges within his dominions.

Clive, however, not content with this, determined to seize the opportunity offered him to put an end to the French possessions and French influence in Bengal. He believed their machinations to be at least a contributory cause of the recent disaster; he had taken the measure of Surajah Dowlah's resolution and courage, and he had an army and a fleet ready at hand for the work. A sudden attack on the chief French factory at Chandernagore placed him in possession of it with little difficulty, but also brought the Nabob back on his hands. This appears at first to have caused him little anxiety; Surajah Dowlah's generals were known to be disaffected and to be already engaged in a conspiracy to overthrow their prince, and Clive believed that the mere advance of his little army would be sufficient to give them an occasion for carrying out their design. But Meer Jaffier, the leader of the malcontents, was too timid to move, and Clive, marching on Moorshedabad, his enemy's capital, suddenly found himself at Plassey, with only 3,500 men under his command, opposed to an army of 50,000 enemies. Desultory firing took place throughout the forenoon and afternoon, and in the early evening the Bengalese army melted away like snow before the resolute advance of the handful of British. Surajah Dowlah, a helpless and solitary fugitive, met a violent death at the hands of his enemies; Meer Jaffier, a mere puppet in the hands of the conquerors, was set up in his stead; and Clive, who had fought and won his last and most famous victory, found ample employment for the next twelve months in settling the complicated internal affairs of Bengal.

The French meanwhile, fortunately for their enemies, were in no position to take advantage of the diversion of hostile ships and troops to the Ganges, being themselves engaged in endeavouring to recover their lost position in the Deccan, and in the Northern Circars, a dependency of that province. Their only enterprise against the British, an attempt on Trichinopoly, undertaken at a time when the

Council at Madras had scattered its forces in petty undertakings to north and south, was brought to naught by the arrival of a relieving force led back in hot haste by Caillaud. By 1758, however, the French East India Company were in a position to embark on more serious operations. Their affairs in Central India had been re-established; and there had arrived from France a strong fleet and a body of troops, including some units of the Royal army, and a new Commander-in-Chief of high reputation, Lally. Unhappily for them, delays on the voyage, some accidental, some avoidable, had given time for a British fleet to make its appearance off the Carnatic coast, and of the two newly arrived commanders the admiral was luckless and incompetent, and the general headstrong, tactless and inexperienced in Indian ways and warfare. None the less, the prospects of a successful campaign seemed rosy, nor did the opening of it belie this promise. Lally swiftly reduced first Cuddalore and then Fort St. David, and planned to clinch these conquests by the capture of Madras itself. For this he had indeed the necessary forces, but not the wherewithal to pay and maintain them ; and he was compelled, as Chanda Sahib had been compelled before him, to seek to replenish his treasure chest with the plunder of the rich city of Tanjore. History repeated itself before its walls, and Lally at the point of success was compelled by the news of the defeat of the French fleet, and the resultant danger, not only to his own base at Carical, but to Pondicherry itself, to raise the siege and fall back to cover the latter town. From there, having managed to raise funds, he moved on Madras with 7,500 men. Stringer Lawrence, the commandant of Madras, could oppose to these only 4,000, but his defence was so resolute and skilful that after two months' siege Lally found himself at the end of funds, supplies and ammunition, and without the least prospect of being able either to replenish them or to force an entry into the city; the return of the British fleet completed his discomfiture, and in February 1759 he abandoned his trenches and his wounded and fell back in despair on Pondicherry.

Farther to the north in the Circars another disaster, even more spectacular and complete, had befallen French arms. Conflans, their commander, was assailed in October 1758 by a force of 2,500 men from Bengal under Forde. The latter though inferior in numbers defeated his adversary in a skilfully conducted engagement at Condore, capturing all his guns, chased him hot foot from his province, and shut him up within the walls of Masulipatam, which was at once invested. Here news reached Forde that a large army under Salabat Jung was advancing to Conflans' relief, and that a French corps had also appeared in his rear. His position, thus taken between three fires, was critical in the extreme; but he escaped from it as only a great commander would have dared to do, namely, by storming the strong fortress before which he stood and compelling its instant surrender and that of its garrison. The political results of this achievement equalled the military, for Salabat Jung, thunderstruck with its dramatic completeness, made haste to conclude an agreement with the British, which put an end once for all to French influence in the Deccan.

In the Carnatic, during the remainder of 1759, operations languished. Brereton, the British commander, who took the place of Lawrence, sent home sick, and later Eyre Coote, who arrived with reinforcements from England, succeeded in recovering a considerable part of the territory overrun by the French in the previous year, and a diversion undertaken by the latter against Trichinopoly failed of effect. Meanwhile in Bengal there had occurred an incident which at one time threatened to assume serious proportions; the Dutch East India Company, without, and indeed contrary to, the orders of their home Government, fitted out an armament, landed at the mouth of the Ganges and picked a quarrel with the British. These new enemies were completely defeated and destroyed by Forde in two engagements at Chinsura and Badara; the Dutch company sued for peace on British terms, which Clive took care to make such as to exclude the possibility of future trouble from that quarter.

By the opening of 1760 Lally was once more ready for the field, and with a force of some 5,000 men marched north from Pondicherry to open the siege of Wandewash, which had fallen into British hands the year before. Here there took place on January 22 a battle with Coote's army, approximately equal in strength, which, as an unusually far-sighted eye-witness put it, "gave us India". Lally was already outmanoeuvred and his army outfought before an unlucky accident, the blowing up of an ammunition wagon, threw his men into disorder and decided the day. The French fell back to make their preparations for a last stand at Pondicherry, but it was three months ere Coote, after carefully and methodically reducing the hostile posts one by one, appeared before the walls of the doomed city, and five more ere the siege was opened in regular form. The jealousy and corruption that raged unchecked among the leaders, civil and military, of the garrison were hardly such as to improve the prospects of a successful defence; and on January 16, 1761, terms of capitulation were signed, and the British entered into possession of the headquarters of French power in India. When it was restored two years later at the Peace of Paris, it was on such conditions as to render it no longer a menace to British supremacy, and it remained to France a mere trading centre, the chief factory of a commercial company, destined to survive only by the short space of sixteen years the ruin of these hopes which Dupleix had once fondly entertained, and which he had so nearly translated into reality. That heritage had been wrested from it in arms by an adversary quicker to seize opportunities and more resolute to sink selfish aims in a common purpose.

3. Our Early Indian Wars

The student of these campaigns, in which the influence of France in India was destroyed, root and branch, and the foundations were laid of a great British Empire in the East, must feel that if the vital importance of their results be left out of consideration, they seem to savour almost of comic opera. A close investigation of the numbers engaged and the methods of warfare employed only tends to bear out this resemblance. If it seems to us absurd that the destinies of Canada could be decided by a clash between two armies which together did not total 12,000 men, these Indian scuffles between gangs of a few hundred white men and sepoys must appear even more insignificant and purposeless, and it is hardly a matter for surprise that at the time they aroused little attention in England, and that Pitt's interest in our fortunes in India, and his active part in the first founding of our Eastern Empire, was confined to the despatch of a fleet, or of two regiments, and the loan to the East India Company of a few comparatively junior regimental officers. The extraordinary facility with which large and imposing native armies were put to flight by handfuls of Europeans might, one would think, have induced him to experiment with what could be done by larger forces; but no doubt the first effect of this factor on his mind must have been to increase doubt as to the seriousness of these petty wars—or to discount the tales of these astonishing achievements. The East India Company was therefore left largely to its own devices, and, it must be admitted, did wonderfully well considering the resources at its disposal and its natural tendency to aim at increase rather of trade than of territory.

An Indian Rajah, who had had personal, if painful, opportunities of witnessing the prowess of British soldiers in battle, is reported to have said that if they had been in his service he would have taken such care of them, and so indulged them, on the line of march and in quarters, with every luxury and material benefit (even to having them carried on palanquins into battle), that with them he would conquer the world. But, as a matter of fact, these early Indian campaigns left little to be desired in the way of luxurious soldiering. Traders, merchants, sutlers and camp followers of every kind—even to bevies of dancing girls—accompanied and ministered (no doubt at a price) to all the army's needs; baggage of all kinds was carried either by boat or by wagon, and so far at any rate as Europeans were concerned there was little or no limit to the quantity allowed each individual. Officers were carried in litters by their bearers, and a host of personal servants, a mass of personal belongings, followed behind them. Comfortable quarters for the night were always to be had; and most of the arduous work of the army, off the battlefield, was done by the native soldiery. In very truth these were gentlemanly wars enough, and in that respect may well challenge comparison with the French campaigns which the *Roi Soleil* deigned to favour with his personal attendance, and that of the greater part of the Court of Versailles, in the days before Marlborough brought war back to its stark reality.

Yet these early wars of John Company gave to British military history a galaxy of brilliant names who deserve a better fate than to be forgotten by posterity. Of them all only one, Clive, has lived in general remembrance; and one cannot resist the thought that he was lucky in thus being singled out for pre-eminence. Part of his fame, no doubt, is due to the fact that he was something more than a soldier; that in him were combined both great military virtues and high qualities of statesmanship in a degree hitherto unequalled; and that he found in India opportunities of exercising them such as arise only once or twice in a century. He was also fortunate in being the first commander to assert the pre-eminence of British arms against Asiatic hosts, however superior in numbers and armament; and Plassey is a household word because it is not the most astonishing but the earliest of our great Indian victories. Yet more than once in his career Clive had to extricate himself from a situation which only his own carelessness or want of vigilance had rendered perilous; and though his soldierly virtues were certainly great, they were less conspicuous off than on the field of battle.

Of his colleagues and comrades, Lawrence, Forde and Coote, it is probably true to say that their services to England, as soldiers, were as great as those of Clive; their deeds as meritorious; their qualities no less admirable. Lawrence, the cool-headed, stubborn defender of Trichinopoly and Madras; Forde, the bold exponent of the offensive at Condore and Badara and the audacious stormer of Masulipatam; Coote, the careful victor of Wandewash, the patient captor of Pondicherry—to these was due in as great a degree as to Clive the firm foundation of our Indian Empire. And when we see the mighty growth of the seed they sowed; when we realise how widespread has been the influence of their work on the history of two continents and two peoples, we see these little campaigns and fights of theirs in their true perspective—no longer as affairs of *opéra bouffe,* but as portents of the great things to be, far transcending in importance many of those gallant but barren battles in the Low Countries and in Germany which are borne with pride in many a tattered colour and have given rise to many a regimental tradition.

CHAPTER 6

The Loss of America
1764-1783

1. THE CONFLICT WITH COLONIAL REVOLUTION
1764-1777

The inevitable reduction of the British army to seventy regiments of Foot and seventeen of Cavalry—-about 17,000 men at home and 28,000 abroad—could hardly be justified by the extension of our overseas territories under the terms of the Peace of Paris or by the general political situation. The magnitude of the task of keeping order in the vast new lands of America was evidenced by the outbreak in 1763 of Pontiac's rising, which in a few weeks spread to all the territory south of the Great Lakes of Canada and was only suppressed a year later by the skill and energy of Bouquet at the head of a small column of British troops, with little or no assistance from the colonists.

Indeed, less than a decade after the conclusion of peace with France, England was once again to have need of her army in a great war in the New World, but this time not against her hereditary foreign enemy, but against her own subjects in rebellion under arms. It is no part of our task to decide the responsibility for the lamentable dispute which arose immediately on the termination of the Seven Years'

War between men of one blood on both sides of the Atlantic, who had so recently fought and been victorious side by side. The quarrel was primarily caused by the endeavours of Great Britain to induce her American colonies to contribute something towards the cost of the increasing burden of Imperial defence, which the latter, now that immediate danger to their existence had passed away, with the expulsion of the French from Canada, considered unreasonable. The questions in dispute were further complicated by the fractious spirit of the colonists, who fiercely resented the attempts of the mother country to tighten her control on their rights of trade and self-government; and by a lamentable lack of wisdom in the councils of the home Government, whose insistence on its legal rights and enforcement of petty taxes and levies served only to increase American irritation. When after a series of acts of violence a colonial congress assembled in the winter of 1774 and proceeded to raise armed forces, it was clear that war could hardly be averted; but the first shots were not actually fired till April 1775, when a detachment sent out by Gage, the British commander at Boston, to seize stores destined for the rebels, was forced to retire by the resistance of the Massachusetts militia at Lexington. The country at once rose, and in a few days the 3,500 British troops composing the Boston garrison were closely invested by some 20,000 enemies; while farther to the north a force under Benedict Arnold attacked and carried one by one the British posts on Lakes George and Champlain, the most direct route into Canada.

Both parties were thus definitely committed to war; and the military problem before each of them was of peculiar difficulty. For Great Britain it was a question of reducing by armed force the resistance of 3,000,000 revolted colonists occupying a semi-developed and difficult country 1,300 miles long by 300 wide, 3,000 miles—over a month's sail—distant across the sea. The colonies, on the other hand, themselves without disciplined forces, stores, supplies or money, divided in their sympathies,[1] and racked by mutual jealousy and mistrust, had to devise means for resisting the attack of trained troops under experienced leaders, backed by a navy with complete command of the sea.

Congress proceeded, therefore, to raise its new army on a term of short enlistment which rendered its numerical strength liable to violent fluctuation and constant though gradual diminution, but which at present placed some 20,000 men under arms; and chose for the supreme command a Virginian squire named George Washington. Great Britain on her side took measures to increase her army to a strength of 44,000 men, and, in addition, purchased the services of some 30,000 German mercenary troops; but these forces could, of course, only be recruited gradually. Reinforcements arriving at Boston soon enabled Gage to adopt a more aggressive attitude, and an opportunity for the offensive soon offered itself when an American detachment seized the position of Bunker's Hill, north of the city. The attack though ill-managed was conducted with splendid bravery by the troops, who, after suffering losses amounting to 40 per cent, carried the hill at the third attempt; but the Americans were none the less encouraged by the result of the day's fighting and pressed the siege with renewed vigour, at the same time pushing forward the organisation and armament of their troops. In Boston, then, Howe, who had replaced Gage after Bunker's Hill, spent a dreary and inactive winter, until, with the coming of the spring and the renewal of active operations, Washington seized by surprise the heights commanding the entrance to the harbour, and compelled him to withdraw by sea to Halifax.

This American success was somewhat offset by the disastrous failure of the offensive led by Montgomery and Arnold

---

1. It is doubtful if at any time during the war those who were wholeheartedly with the revolution were more than an important minority of the population.

against Canada. Despite supply difficulties and the rigours of a Canadian winter, the expedition pushed rapidly forward by way of Montreal and the St. Lawrence to the outskirts of Quebec, but was beaten off with loss in an attempt to storm the walls of the city. With the coming of spring and of reinforcements, Carleton, the British Governor, in his turn assumed the offensive, and, falling vigorously on the besiegers, drove them in flight up the river, recovering Montreal, clearing the whole of Canada, and pressing the pursuit along the shores of Lake Champlain to within sight of Ticonderoga. Of the American troops engaged in this operation less than half ever got back to their own country.

The British army, 25,000 strong, was now concentrated, and in a position to enter upon serious offensive operations. The plan of campaign, in so far as one can be said to have been definitely formulated, aimed at the isolation and reduction of New England, at once the most populous area of America and the main focus of the rebellion, by a concentric advance from north to south in the Hudson valley and a westward thrust from Rhode Island ; this was to be combined with minor diversions in the Southern States, the main source of supplies for the north, and strong centres of loyalism. In accordance with this scheme, while a subsidiary operation, which ended in a serious set-back, was undertaken against Charleston, Howe, whose sailing from Halifax had been unduly delayed by the lengthy process of concentration, landed in August 1776 over against New York, where Washington had for two months been busily fortifying his positions and erecting batteries and works. After thorough reconnaissances a British force was sent across to the east of the Hudson, inflicted a crushing defeat on the American detachment which endeavoured to check its advance, and compelled Washington to withdraw his troops on the west bank of the river, which he did with great skill in a single night. Howe now sent a second column across the East River beyond the American left wing—a move which gave him possession of New York, the defenders retiring in considerable disorder to the hills north of the city. Once more the British general extended his right, followed by Washington, until at length the colonial army was extended on a front far too wide for its numbers in a vain endeavour to cover the heart of New England, the Hudson valley and New Jersey; then rapidly counter-marching his main body, he fell on and captured the hostile forts on either bank of the river above New York and compelled his adversary to fall back hurriedly to re-unite his forces behind the Delaware in Pennsylvania. New Jersey and the lower Hudson having been thus cleared, he sent a detachment to occupy Rhode Island and went into winter quarters around New York. Everything seemed ready for a decisive campaign next year, when these fair prospects were rudely marred by a daring and successful American counter offensive. A Hessian detachment was surprised and overwhelmed on Christmas Day at Trenton, and Washington, skilfully refusing to let himself be brought to battle by the main British army, succeeded by a series of rapid marches in driving in its covering forces and re-occupying practically the whole of New Jersey before the opening of the campaigning season of 1777.

Howe now chose as his objective the city of Philadelphia, which he designed to capture by transferring the bulk of his army by sea to the mouth of the Delaware, leaving a small force under Clinton to hold New York. But, meanwhile, the Secretary of War in London, that same Lord George Sackville, now Germaine, who had been cashiered for his conduct at Minden, had been persuaded by Burgoyne, now commander of the British forces in the Lake Champlain area *vice* Carleton, to sanction, a year too late, an advance by the latter down the Hudson valley in cooperation with the main army at New York. Instead, however, of sending Howe definite instructions for such cooperation, Germaine at first allowed him to believe that he approved of the proposed move against Philadelphia and neglected to send him fresh orders till too late. Thus, while the British main army was operating eccentrically in New Jersey, Burgoyne was launched in an isolated and perilous advance down the Hudson, while the Americans, holding interior lines, could concentrate a greatly superior force to oppose him.

Howe with 14,000 men then, landing at the head of Chesapeake Bay late in August, once more found the indefatigable Washington with a force slightly inferior numerically, in front of him and covering Philadelphia. In a skilful little action on the Brandywine he succeeded in outflanking his opponent's right and driving him northward. The city thus uncovered fell into his hands; Washington some few weeks later was repulsed at Germantown in an attempt to recover it, and by the end of the campaigning season the British army was established in comfortable quarters in Philadelphia with a secure line of communication down the Delaware, while Washington's army, reduced by sickness and desertion to barely 3000 men, was shivering and starving in the miserable camp at Valley Forge.

This successful campaign, which had seemingly reduced the American fortunes to the lowest point they had yet reached, was, however, more than offset by the disastrous issue of Burgoyne's operations in the upper Hudson valley. He had at his disposal barely 8,000 men when he commenced his advance late in June. His plan was to push down Lake Champlain to Albany, where he would be joined by a detached force under St. Leger, operating from Oswego down the Mohawk, and where he hoped to hear news of the expected cooperation from New York. St. Leger was soon checked and forced back to his starting-point with heavy loss, but Burgoyne's operations opened well. He secured Ticonderoga with little difficulty, cleared the forts covering the approach from Lake Champlain to the upper Hudson and, despite the increasing length of his line of communications and serious shortage of supplies, pressed on to within twenty miles of Albany. Here he was opposed by a superior hostile force under Gates, with Arnold as his second in command, and was compelled to halt. An attempt to relieve the shortage of supplies, now becoming acute, by the despatch of a detachment to capture a hostile store depot at Bennington failed with heavy loss; and a frontal assault on Gates' entrenched positions, though carried out with the greatest gallantry, met with the like result. Meanwhile local militia and partisans were swarming around Burgoyne on every side, and though in actual fact Clinton had at this very time moved northward from his positions around New York and by a brilliant little *coup de main* carried the forts blocking the Hudson 50 miles above that city, his army was too far distant to exert any direct influence on the situation in Burgoyne's front; nor did any news of his success reach that General. Finally, at the beginning of October, Arnold was allowed by Gates to take the offensive; the British, forced back into the river valley at Saratoga, were surrounded on every side, and Burgoyne, without hope of succour, capitulated on October 16 with his whole force of 5,700 men.

With this disaster ended the first phase of the War of American Independence; and when the campaign of 1778 opened Great Britain was faced, not merely with the forces of her revolted colonies, but with a formidable array of hereditary foes and unfriendly neutrals eager for revenge for past defeats and slighted rights.

2. The World War
1778-1783

Considered as a purely military event, the surrender at Saratoga was a trifling affair enough, but its immediate consequences were such as fully to entitle it to a place among the decisive battles of the world. It brought France into the war on the side of the colonies, and her accession in turn brought other allies; and the task of Great Britain—to reconquer America while at the same time holding her own in every part of the world against an overwhelming force of enemies—quickly became too complex and enormous for successful accomplishment.

The spring of 1778 saw the conclusion of the French treaty of alliance with the United States and the throwing into the scale of the weight of French fleets and armies. None the less, the military strength of Great Britain was but little increased in the estimates for the coming year, and her forces in America, now under Clinton, remained at some 33,000 as against the 15,000 under Washington's command. The British general's instructions were to send an expedition against the French island of St. Lucia, in the West Indies, and reinforcements to the British garrisons in Florida; the rest of the army was to withdraw to New York. Accordingly in June the army fell back from Philadelphia, followed closely by Washington. The latter, thanks largely to the admirable work of Greene, who had reorganised the quartermaster-general's department, and a foreign officer, Steuben, who had taken in hand the discipline and training of the troops, was now at the head of a formidable force of considerable military value; but, thanks to incompetence or treachery among his subordinates, his attempt to interfere with the British withdrawal in the action at Monmouth proved costly and unprofitable, and Clinton arrived safely at New York. Meanwhile the first French assistance in the form of a fleet and 4,000 troops had arrived at the mouth of the Delaware, and a joint enterprise was concerted against the British detachment occupying Rhode Island. The French, however, failed to get on shore at Newport, and then sailed away to the West Indies, leaving the American co-operating force in a precarious position, from which it was with difficulty extricated. This concluded the year's operations; and from now onwards the main scene of interest in America lay in the Southern States, though for over two years the main armies and their respective commanders-in-chief remained in the vicinity of New York, closely observing each other, but largely inactive.

We must now turn our attention to the West Indies, whither, as we have seen, both the British and the French had sent armed forces. The fate of these islands, the possession of which was shared between France, Spain, Holland and Great Britain, was bound to depend on the command of the sea; and the belligerent which possessed this was in a position to concentrate and move a striking force which must speedily and in quick succession overwhelm the scattered little garrisons of its enemies. Hence the command of the sea was throughout the whole course of the war vigorously disputed, and more than once changed hands. During the summer of 1778 the British held it and used it to possess themselves, by a brilliant and well-combined joint expedition, of the French island of St. Lucia, but the arrival of the French fleet at the end of the year changed matters in this respect, and the result was the loss of St. Vincent and Grenada in the summer of 1779—though the prestige of British arms was well maintained by the courageous defence put up by the garrison of the latter island.

This year saw the inception of the British offensive against the Southern colonies, in which the main strength of our forces in America were for the rest of the war to be engaged. An expedition sent by sea to Georgia opened its campaign brilliantly with the storming of Savannah; in six weeks the whole of that State was in British hands, and the inhabitants, among whom loyalist feeling was known to be strong, flocked in considerable numbers to enrol themselves in our service. Throughout the whole of the Southern States the loyalists, or Tories, as they were then termed, were believed by the British high command to be in a majority, and the hope of utilising their services had been one of the main reasons for undertaking operations in this theatre ; but the strength of feeling on either side caused the struggle to take the form of an embittered partisan warfare in which the advantages were all on the side of the revolutionists.

The ill-success of an attempted British *coup de main* against Charleston was counterbalanced in the latter months of 1779 by the disastrous failure of an Allied counter offensive, supported by the French fleet from the West Indies, which was heavily repulsed by Prevost, the British commander, before the walls of Savannah. French assistance had, up to the present, brought little profit to the American cause, and the departure of the fleet for France brought ill-feeling between the Allies to a high pitch.

Nearer home affairs for a period became critical for England owing to the accession of Spain to the number of her enemies. Her fleet united with a French squadron and for several months cruised in the Channel unopposed, keeping the whole of the south coast of Great Britain in perpetual dread of an invasion which never materialised. Internal dissensions, both at home and in Ireland, added to the difficulties of the situation; but the crisis passed, the Allied armada dispersed without accomplishing anything, and the only visible fruits of Spain's entry into the war during this year were the close blockade of Gibraltar and a series of small and indecisive operations in Honduras.

The successes gained by the British in the South in the previous year encouraged Clinton in the further prosecution of the campaign with increased forces, and accordingly an expedition of 12,000 men under his personal command landed in February 1780 near Charleston and proceeded to invest that city. After six weeks' siege it capitulated together with its garrison of 5,500 men; whereupon Clinton, leaving Cornwallis with 4,000 men to complete the conquest of the Carolinas as soon as the end of the hot weather rendered possible a resumption of active operations, hurried back with the remainder of his troops to New York. The task of his successor was no easy one: guerilla bands under able and active partisan leaders sprang up on every side of him; and a regular force of 3000 men under Gates was despatched by Washington to recover the lost territory. This army Cornwallis, as soon as it came within his reach, struck at and completely dispersed at the combat of Camden; but the guerillas were not so easily dealt with, and in the operations of the few weeks after Camden proved themselves capable of giving and receiving shrewd blows without losing either activity or cohesion. Meanwhile in Greene, the newly appointed commander of the revolutionary forces in the South, Cornwallis was to find an adversary in every way worthy of his steel.

In the North the situation remained unchanged throughout the year. Washington's army, destitute, half-starved and mutinous, was in no condition to take advantage of Clinton's temporary absence at Charleston, while French help proved once more a broken reed. A squadron with 6,000 troops arrived during the summer at Rhode Island, which had been evacuated by the British some months before, only to be blockaded there by a superior British fleet.

In the West Indies, also, the position throughout 1780 remained one of stalemate. A French attack on St. Lucia was successfully beaten off, but British weakness, first in troops and then in ships, prevented any counter offensive. Meanwhile an ambitious expedition, launched with the idea of cutting in two the Spanish possessions in Central America by the occupation of the isthmus of Nicaragua, had been compelled to retire with its work half done owing to the great mortality caused by disease among the troops, and the Spaniards in their turn besieged and took Mobile and Pensacola, which gave them possession of the whole of Florida.

In October 1780 the Powers of Northern Europe, irked by damage caused to their overseas trade by British sea power, formed themselves into an armed neutrality which was obviously directed against this country. The latter at once, by way of counter offensive, declared war on Holland, which was known not merely to be rendering covert assistance to our enemies by every means in her power, but to be actually on the point of concluding a treaty with the revolted colonies. Early in 1781 there took place an unsuccessful French attack on Jersey, and in April the siege of Gibraltar was begun in earnest by a bombardment which was to continue practically without cessation for over a year.

In the West Indies the year 1781 opened favourably for Great Britain. The capture of the Dutch possessions of St. Eustatius, a vast depot of stores and the headquarters of the contraband traffic to America, and of Demerara and Essequibo, were the first fruits of the declaration of war against Holland, and were followed by the repulse of a second French attack on St. Lucia; against this, however, had to be set the loss of Tobago.

In the Southern colonies Cornwallis, who at the beginning of 1781 found himself in complete if somewhat precarious occupation of South Carolina and Georgia, resolved to pursue his advantage and extend his gains into North Carolina. Accordingly, detaching forces on either flank to deal with the partisan leaders who might attempt to harry his advance, he pushed forward with his main column against Greene. The latter, declining battle, retired before him to a depth of close on 250 miles in six weeks, leaving the whole of North Carolina to fall into British hands; but by the time the latter had arrived at the Roanoke they had shot their bolt. Their troops were exhausted and short of supplies; their left flanking force under Tarleton had been badly defeated at Cowpens; and Greene had now received reinforcements which gave him a twofold superiority over his adversaries. Nevertheless, this did not avail him when he offered battle at Guilford, for, after a fierce frontal assault and a desperate battle lasting over four hours, Cornwallis forced his opponent from the field. The victory, dearly bought by casualties amounting to close on thirty per cent of the British strength, was a barren one: immediately after it Cornwallis fell back southwards to Wilmington, whence, after reorganising his army, he set off along the coast to effect a junction with a detachment from Clinton's army, which had established itself at the entrance to Chesapeake Bay.

Greene at once determined to seize the opportunity of falling in superior numbers on Lord Rawdon, who had been left with some 8,000 troops—mostly scattered in small posts— to hold South Carolina and Georgia in the absence of his chief. Sending his partisans forward on either flank to deal with these hostile posts, Greene himself moved direct upon his enemy's headquarters at Camden. Here he was outmanoeuvred and checked; but Rawdon's position in face of the guerilla activity on all sides of him was untenable, and he was compelled to fall back southwards, leaving his garrisons to be captured one by one by the enemy. In August, Greene himself resumed his advance, and encountered Stuart, Rawdon's successor, at Eutaw; once again the British held their ground during the battle and then fell back, leaving Greene to reap the fruits of his strategic skill at his leisure. By the end of the year their area of occupation in the South was confined to Charleston and Savannah and the coastal strip between them.

Meanwhile Cornwallis effected his junction with the Chesapeake detachment, drove away a small French force, under Lafayette, which was observing that area, and after displaying a certain amount of activity in Virginia, established himself at Yorktown. From this point Clinton apparently intended to withdraw him to New York, but he was not left the leisure to do so; for, simultaneously, a French fleet, under De Grasse, put in an appearance and blockaded Yorktown by sea, while the main American army, under Washington, arriving from the North, invested the place on the land side. Cornwallis, with his 7,000 men thus shut in by 16,000, capitulated in a few days, and it would seem with somewhat unnecessary precipitation, for, five days later, Clinton arrived from New York by sea to relieve him. The blow put an instant end to the British prospects of victory in America ; and from this date to the conclusion of peace in 1783 Clinton attempted nothing beyond the maintenance of his positions at New York, Savannah and Charleston, although the condition of the American army was by no means such as to discourage all hopes of a successful offensive on his part.

The course of the war in the West Indies in 1782 was almost equally unfavourable to our arms. In quick succession Essequibo, Demerara and St. Eustatius were recaptured by the Allies; St. Kitts, Nevis, Montserrat and the Bahamas were also lost. The only gleams of success to set off against all these disasters were the recovery of Honduras and Rodney's great naval victory at the Saints, which bade fair to restore to us our lost sea supremacy.

In the Mediterranean, Minorca fell after a most gallant defence of six months, which ended only when the garrison had been reduced by losses and disease to under 600 men, but all the Allied efforts to reduce Gibraltar by attack, both by land and by sea, failed before the resolute and resourceful defence of Heathfield and his garrison of 7,000 men. In the grand attack on September 13, 1782, no less than 40,000 enemy troops, 200 guns, 47 ships of the line and many smaller craft took part, but made little or no impression on the fortress; and with the arrival of British reinforcements and supplies in October the Allied pressure slackened and gradually died away. When the news of the conclusion of hostilities arrived in February 1783, the siege had lasted over three and a half years. It is perhaps the one episode throughout the war on which we can look back to-day with unalloyed satisfaction.

The terms of the Peace of Versailles, though harsh enough, were less severe than might have been expected. Besides the American colonies and some territory which had hitherto been regarded as part of Canada, we lost only Tobago to

France and Minorca and Florida to Spain. Apart from this there was a mutual restitution of conquests, and it is probable that in the long run our foes, by the crippling of their finances, the revelation of governmental corruption and incapacity, and the effect of the hardships of the war on their people, suffered through their victory more serious and lasting consequences than did Great Britain through her defeat.

The War of American Independence is hardly a chapter in our history on which we can look back with any great satisfaction, but the army, at all events, has no particular reason to be ashamed of it. The men proved at Bunker's Hill and at Guilford—to cite two examples only—that they had lost none of their fighting qualities; Howe and Clinton, Burgoyne and Carleton all gave evidence on occasion of considerable powers of leadership; and among their subordinates Tarleton, Cornwallis and Rawdon deservedly gained high reputations, which the two latter were destined fully to maintain in wider spheres. In truth the British army in America was faced with a task of unexampled difficulty, for a parallel to which we must go to the South African War of 1899-1902; and in both cases it gave proof of a readiness of resource and power of adaptability which has hardly been appreciated as it deserved. If the same can hardly be said of the conduct of the war from the higher standpoint, the fault lay largely with the Government of the day, which permitted itself in the early stages, at all events, an undue interference with its chosen commanders in matters which properly lay within the latter's sphere. Later on, when the war, from being a mere attempt to suppress a domestic revolt, became a struggle for existence against the superior forces of a powerful coalition, there came about a decided improvement in this respect, and there is little to criticise in the general lines on which Great Britain conducted the contest, or to find fault with in the military and naval measures taken to safeguard the country and its world-wide interests.

Indeed a closer examination of the course of the war will

probably lead the student to wonder, not so much how it was that Great Britain failed to reduce her rebellious colonies to submission, as why American independence took such a long time to achieve. The truth is that the revolution, like all other revolutions known to history, was the work of an energetic and self-assertive minority of the colonists, the majority of whom were apathetic, and a considerable proportion hostile to the cause. Thus it came about that the armies at the disposal of the revolutionary generals were always inferior numerically, as in every other way, to those opposed to them; that Washington found his main difficulties usually lay behind rather than in front of his lines; and that from the first shot of the war to the last the British were practically never beaten on the field of battle. All the greater credit is due, therefore, to that galaxy of undaunted men, Arnold, Steuben, Lafayette and others, who defended for so long and under such thankless and trying conditions the cause of American independence, and finally led it through to triumph. Greatest praise of all must be given to the two outstanding figures of the war—Greene, the organiser of victory and the conqueror of the South, and Washington, the soul of the whole contest, the man who through constant defeats and incessant difficulties remained unconquerable and unbroken ; the hero who, to a degree unsurpassed in history, merited the honourable title by which he is known to posterity—"The Father of his Country".

CHAPTER 7

The British Conquest of India: 1
1760-1800

We must now turn our attention for a space to the most wonderful and romantic portion of our history—the conquest of our Indian Empire. This story has hitherto received somewhat less than the appreciation it deserves, partly, it seems, owing to the habit among military historians of treating it as a sort of appendage to the narrative of campaigns in other parts of the world which chanced to be contemporaneous with it. This method of treatment seems both mistaken and regrettable. Admittedly Indian affairs were in many respects closely bound up with, and at times considerably influenced by, the course of events in Europe and elsewhere, and this is as true of military and naval as of political matters; but this interdependence has often been greatly exaggerated, and by the undue emphasis usually laid upon it the continuity of the whole story has been frequently lost sight of. The British conquest of India was mainly accomplished after all by forces locally raised, paid and controlled by the East India Company, and should therefore be primarily regarded as one complete and independent episode in the history of the British army, which later absorbed these forces! This story may be roughly divided into four phases: (1) The expulsion of the French from India between 1741 and 1761, which has already been told in

Chapter 5.; (2) the acquisition of Bengal and the long struggle with Mysore for the control of Southern India between 1760 and 1800, now about to be described; (3) the contest with the Mahratta Confederacy, the conquest of Central India and the first war with Burma between 1802 and 1839; and (4) the extension of the British frontiers eastward and westward to their present limits from 1839 to 1857, which will form the subject of subsequent chapters.

1. THE BRITISH CONQUEST OF BENGAL
1760-1767

We left Bengal in the year 1758, with the puppet Meer Jaffier as its nominal ruler, subject in theory to the overlordship of the *fainéant* Mogul Emperor in Delhi, in practice to the dictates of Clive and the East India Company's representatives at Calcutta. But in the nature of things this state of affairs could only be of short duration; and it now remains to tell how the land became in the next seven years an acknowledged portion of British territory—the first province of British India.

The Mogul Emperor, Shah Alam, unwilling tamely to reconcile himself to seeing Bengal slip from his control, enlisted the help of Shuja ud Dowlah, the ruler of Oude, the province bordering its western frontier, and early in 1760 marched to recover his lost possession. The British contingent, serving as an auxiliary force to Meer Jaffier's army, numbered only some 1,500 men, under the command of Caillaud; but it was entirely thanks to it that the first advance of the Allies against Patna met with a decided repulse at Seerpore, the part played by the Bengalis themselves being inglorious in the extreme. The Emperor in actual fact reaped all the fruits of the battle ; moving round his adversaries' left, he effected a vigorous foray which compelled them to fall back hastily in order to cover Moorshedabad, their capital, and then, returning on his tracks, invested Patna, weakly garrisoned and already menaced by a French auxiliary corps under Law. At the last moment his prey was snatched from his grasp by the arrival of a small British column under Knox, which had marched 300 miles in the space of thirteen days to the rescue of the beleaguered city; the siege was raised and the Allies retired southwards, leaving Knox free to deal at his leisure with the Nawab of Purneah, who, advancing on the north bank of the Ganges to complete the investment, was vigorously assailed and routed in a hotly contested action at Beerpore. Meanwhile the main British army, under a new commander, Carnac, had reached Patna, and, following up Shah Alam and his confederate in their retirement towards Behar, inflicted on him a smart defeat which forced him to sue for terms. One of the conditions laid upon him was that he should install Meer Kossim as Nawab of Bengal in place of the aged and incapable Meer Jaffier, who went into reluctant retirement at Calcutta.

The energy and ability of the new ruler, however advantageous to his subjects, who for the first time for many years found themselves well and justly governed, soon brought him into open conflict with the East India Company and its servants, who regarded Bengal only as a sponge to be squeezed and its ruler as a convenient tool to effect such squeezing. Here, fortunately, we are concerned only with the military phase of this, perhaps the most discreditable chapter in the history of British India. Early in 1763, Meer Kossim, who had at his disposal a well-organised and trained force of some 45,000 men, and had obtained the assistance of the Emperor in his quarrel, was at open war with the Company, whose available troops numbered barely 11,500 in all. Hostilities opened with a serious disaster to the British. A treacherous and unprovoked attack made by them on Patna miscarried owing to the indiscipline of the troops, and while endeavouring to retreat they were overtaken and surrounded in open country and compelled to lay down their arms to the number of 3,000 men. It was under these unfavourable auspices that Adams, at the head of a little force of 2,500 men, commenced his advance up the Ganges from Calcutta. Meer Kossim's advance guard was heavily defeated in an attempt to cover Moorshedabad, and Adams, his troops doubled in numbers soon after the occupation of that city, found himself face to face with 40,000 enemy troops in a strong position at Sooty. After a desperate day's fighting the defence was broken through and fell back to the defile of Oondwa, where a marsh and powerful entrenchments closed the narrow gap between river and hills. For a whole month the British force was held up before this formidable obstacle; then in a daring and skilfully conducted night operation a path through the marsh was threaded, the fortifications were stormed and the troops of Meer Kossim were driven out with the loss of all their guns and several thousand men. Four weeks later trenches were opened before the walls of Patna, the storming of which put an end to the operations. Meer Kossim, defeated and desperate, sought refuge in Oude, and Carnac replaced Adams, who retired to Calcutta, sick to death, after a campaign which, for audacity and brilliance, will bear comparison with any recorded in the military history of India.

The new British General, who was made of less heroic stuff than his predecessor, found himself, at the opening of the campaign of 1764, faced with the forces not only of the two princes who had gone down before Adams, but also with those of the Nawab of Oude, while the European portion of his own army was discontented and inclined to be mutinous. Compelled to a hasty and somewhat undignified withdrawal within the walls of Patna, he nevertheless succeeded in maintaining himself there long enough to allow time for discord to arise among his adversaries, who, following the failure of their first assault on the city, retired to Buxar. Here Meer Kossim, broken and disgraced, finally disappeared from the scene, and his former allies sat down to fortify their lines and await the attack of the British army, now once more under a worthy leader, Hector Munro.

The latter, after repressing an outbreak of serious disaffection among his native troops, moved on Buxar with 7,000 men to encounter the overwhelmingly superior forces of the Emperor and the Nawab, variously estimated at from 40,000 to 60,000. On October 23, 1764, he found them drawn up outside their entrenchments to give him battle. In the ensuing encounter Munro both outmanoeuvred and outfought his opponents; their left wing, after fierce fighting, was driven in on their centre, broken into fragments and hurled back with fearful carnage into the muddy bed of a stream, which was only passed by the survivors over a bridge of their comrades' corpses. 847 British casualties were the price of this decisive victory; 2,000 enemy dead and 167 captured guns its trophies. The conquerors pushed forward rapidly to Benares and beyond it to Allahabad, and here, well within the territory of Oude, dictated their terms of peace, which included the recognition by the Emperor of the full practical sovereignty of the East India Company over Bengal, Behar and Orissa, and an offensive and defensive alliance of the late belligerents.

From whatever point of view it be regarded, Buxar has an undeniable claim to rank as a decisive battle in the history of India, of Great Britain and of the world; yet its name is unknown to the average educated man, so true is it that personalities rank in popular estimation more highly than achievements. It is because Clive was one of the greatest Englishmen of his day, and Munro merely an able soldier, that the military promenade of Plassey is remembered and the hard-fought victory of Buxar forgotten; yet the results of the latter, marking as they do the first definite stepping-stone to the achievement of British supremacy in India, far surpassed those of the former, and Hector Munro well merits at least a niche in the Pantheon of our Empire-builders.

The heroic deeds of the Bengal army in the field were followed by a curious anti-climax in the shape of a strike among the commissioned ranks, secretly backed up by certain malcontent civilian elements, for the maintenance in peace time of their none too munificent war-time rates of pay. Clive, who had returned from England, after having well feathered his own nest, with full powers to deal drastically with corruption in Bengal wherever found, repressed this movement with the energy of a poacher turned gamekeeper; and having successfully accomplished this task, turned to the more fruitful one of reorganising the army, which was now redistributed into three brigades, each of one European and seven sepoy battalions, with a total establishment of 17,000 of all ranks.

With the exception of the Rohilla War, where a force co-operated with the troops of Oude and distinguished itself greatly at the action of Babul, no military operations of any importance took place in Bengal for the next forty years.

2. The Fight with Hyder Ali for Southern India
1767-1782

We must now turn to Southern India, where the forces of the Madras and Bombay Presidencies were for the space of over thirty years to be engaged in an intermittent but, at times, life-and-death struggle with the most formidable of the native powers, the state of Mysore.

The ruler of this kingdom in 1767, when our narrative begins, was Hyder Ali, a soldier of fortune, who had risen by his own ability from a lowly position in the army to the throne itself, and a man whom the British would have done wisely not to antagonise. But though Warren Hastings, the first and perhaps the greatest of our governor-generals, was in nominal control at Calcutta, his power over the other Presidencies was but slight; moreover, he was preoccupied by the internal squabbles of his own Council. The Madras Government therefore foolishly let itself be induced by the bribe of a cession of the Northern Circars to cooperate with the other great ruler of Southern India, the Nizam of Hyderabad, in a joint aggression against Mysore. Before the operations had even opened, the British commander, Smith, realised that his Government had been duped, and that Mysore and Hyderabad were secretly planning an attack on Madras; he swiftly withdrew his force, succeeded in effecting a junction with a second column then on the point of invading Baramahal, on the eastern border of Hyder's territory, and found himself at the head of just over 10,000 men wherewith to make head against an adversary more than seven times his own numbers.

Smith's conduct of his campaign was in every respect admirable. Twice he checked the overwhelming masses of his foes in the neighbourhood of Trincomalee, but his army was short of everything that enabled it to live and move, and exploitation of his success was out of the question. But he had held off his enemy for a considerable period, and when he finally went into quarters he had the satisfaction of knowing that a series of vigorous operations in the Northern Circars had frightened the Nizam into abandoning his ally, and that the incursion of a British force from Bombay on the Malabar coast was raising trouble for Hyder in his rear. Thus, in 1768, he was able to commence an invasion of Mysore itself from the north-east, while a column under Wood, operating in Baramahal and to the south of it, secured his left.

But Hyder soon showed that he was no unworthy adversary. Moving rapidly across to the Malabar coast he restored the situation there, and then, returning in haste, while Smith, his progress delayed by the corruption of contractors and the meddling of politicians, was slowly struggling towards Bangalore, occupied that place in force and compelled him to call in Wood. As soon as the latter assumed control of operations consequent on the recall of Smith to Madras, Hyder resumed the offensive, recovered all the ground lost in Baramahal, and ended the campaign in a position of decided advantage. This he clinched early in 1769 by a rapid raid which carried him to the gates of Madras, and induced the alarmed Council to conclude a peace on the basis of the restitution of the *status quo* and a treaty of mutual alliance.

The agreement was but a truce, and its effects in no way lasting. The enmity of Hyder was relentless, and when in 1771 he appealed for British assistance against the Mahrattas and it was refused him, he resolved on revenge at the earliest possible moment.

The ensuing British campaigns against this race form, as it were, an interlude and a side issue to the main struggle with Mysore, and may here be briefly dealt with. The Mahrattas formed a loose confederacy occupying the whole of Central India from the frontiers of Oude in the north to those of Mysore and Hyderabad in the south, and from the mouth of the Mahanadi in the east to that of the Nerbudda in the west. Their various chieftains, Holkar of Indore, Scindia of Gwalior, the Bhonsla of Berar and the Gaekwar of Baroda, were all nominally subject to one supreme head, the Peshwa of Poona; but at this time the succession to the latter office was in dispute.

The Bombay Government in 1775 unwisely embroiled itself in the internal quarrels of the Mahrattas by supporting the claims of one pretender, Ragoba, in return for the cession of Salsette and Bassein. Their forces occupied these places and later marched into Baroda, and in alliance with Ragoba's troops gained a creditable success at Arass. The alliance, however, was speedily dissolved, and hostilities brought to an end by order of the Council of Bengal, which possessed a controlling authority in external matters over the other Presidencies. But the Board of Directors at home disapproved of this desertion and the alliance was renewed in 1778.

The war with the Mahratta Confederacy was therefore resumed, and while a detachment from Bengal, under Goddard, was despatched right across Central India to the assistance of the Bombay Government, the latter again sent a force to set up their client at Poona. It was checked with heavy loss, but the disgraceful convention which its leaders were induced to sign was disavowed, and the war continued. Goddard arrived in time to turn the tide of affairs in Baroda, while Popham from the side of Oude effected a division by his brilliant capture of the fortress of Gwalior, hitherto considered impregnable, and Camac defeated Scindia in the open field near Ujjein. Hence, despite the failure of Goddard's renewed advance on Poona, the Mahrattas by 1782 were quite ready for peace on the basis of a restoration of conquests and the abandonment by the British of Ragoba's cause. So ended this ill-managed and unsatisfactory interlude in the main story of the contest with Mysore, to which we must now return.

The news of the outbreak of war between Britain and France in 1778 was the signal for the immediate occupation of all the French factories in India, both on the Carnatic and Malabar coasts; these latter, however, were regarded by Hyder Ali as being under his protection, and he seized upon the British action as a *casus belli*. Still he delayed opening hostilities till 1780, when he suddenly burst into the Carnatic at the head of an army of close on 100,000 men and swept, pillaging and burning everything in his path, up to the suburbs of Madras. The British forces, who numbered barely 11,000, under Munro, the victor of Buxar, were scattered from the Kistna to Trichinopoly, and their commander rashly attempted to concentrate them at Conjeveram in the heart of the territory occupied by his adversary. The error was severely punished; the northernmost detachment was surrounded at Pollilore and overwhelmed by the main body of the Mysore army before it could reach the appointed place of assembly; and Munro had no alternative but to retire hurriedly under the walls of Madras, where he was replaced in his command by the veteran Sir Eyre Coote.

The latter now found himself the head of an army of some 7,500 men, demoralised, short of cavalry and almost entirely devoid of transport, with a formidable enemy in front of him and the constant risk of a threat to his rear by the arrival of a French fleet off the coast. Nevertheless, early in 1781, he assumed the offensive in order to relieve the gallant garrison of Wandewash, which had made head for six months against the whole of the main Mysore army; but so great were his supply difficulties that once this had been accomplished he was compelled to remain inactive for five months at Cuddalore. At the end of this period Hyder, with 150,000 men, suddenly moved against him and placed himself at Porto Novo across his line of retreat to Madras; Coote, however, skilfully passed his columns across his enemy's front, enveloped his left, drove him off in disorder westwards, and recovered his communications, not only with his base, but with a column which Warren Hastings had sent from Bengal to his assistance. Thus strengthened he once more encountered and defeated Hyder on the fateful field of Pollilore, only to be compelled by lack of cavalry and supplies to give up all hope of utilising his success and to retire to Madras. From here he once more moved out a few weeks later and relieved Vellore, sweeping Hyder out of his path at the stubbornly fought battle of Sholinghur, and then again withdrew to his base, with his army victorious indeed, but in the last stage of destitution. Meanwhile, as a result of the outbreak of war with Holland, a successful expedition against their possessions of Nagore and Negapatam had afforded Munro an opportunity of redeeming his damaged reputation; Trincomalee in Ceylon was also occupied, but lost again early in 1782.

Elsewhere, too, the new year opened badly for the British, and a serious disaster to a detachment at Negapatam and the arrival of a French fleet under Suffren jeopardised their command of the sea. At Arnee, for the last time ere he laid down his command, Coote foiled Hyder's renewed offensive in the

Carnatic, while the latter's son, Tippoo, was summoned westwards to deal with an expedition from Bombay which had landed south of Calicut. Suddenly, at the end of the year, news was received that Hyder was dead. With him there passed from the scene perhaps the greatest and ablest of all the enemies India has ever raised up against us. He bequeathed to his son Tippoo his formidable power and his hatred of the British, but, fortunately for us, not the full measure of his military and political ability.

Barely six months after Hyder's death his great antagonist, Coote, also passed away as he was about to resume command of the Madras army. A survival of the heroic period of the Seven Years' War, he had first helped to found and then to save our empire in the South. His last two campaigns in particular had been masterpieces of their kind, especially in view of the colossal difficulties under which they had been conducted, and conclusively proved him to possess military qualities of the first order.

3. The Overthrow of Mysore
1783-1800

With the departure of the two great protagonists in the drama the Second Mysore War rapidly lost in interest. Stuart, the new British commander, found himself faced not only with the forces of Tippoo, but with an auxiliary French contingent under the aged Bussy. Fortunately the former was once again called away to the Malabar coast, where a force from Bombay had possessed itself of Bednore and Mangalore, and Stuart therefore succeeded in shutting Bussy up in Cuddalore. His position, however, was no easy one, and it was perhaps fortunate for all sides when news was received that peace had been signed between France and Britain. Hostilities with Tippoo were brought to an end soon after, on the basis of the restoration of all conquests on either side, but not before Bednore and Mangalore—the latter only after a superb defence—had been retaken from us. The truce was to last but six years.

Before the Third Mysore War broke out the great Warren Hastings had handed over the reins of office to a new Governor-General, the Lord Cornwallis whom we last saw surrendering his sword to Washington at Yorktown. He came with strict orders to refrain from all aggression or conquest during his tenure of the appointment, unless driven into war by unavoidable circumstances. Tippoo was not slow to force a new war upon the British. Despite repeated warnings, he at the end of 1789 invaded the territory of Travancore which was under our protection and forced us to take up arms in its defence. The plan of campaign was for the main army of 15,000, under Medows, to advance from the south into Mysore while a force of Bengal troops operating in Baramahal guarded its right flank; the cooperation of the Nizam of Hyderabad and the Mahrattas from the north and of a Bombay contingent from the west was also secured. Medows moved forward in May and took possession of the Coimbatore district with little opposition, but his progress was checked on the upper Cauvery by the main army of Tippoo, who then seized the opportunity to strike against his enemy's communications, and moving south-east along the river valley overran the whole country as far as Pondicherry. Medows, receiving no news of the advance of the other columns which were to have co-operated with him, was compelled to follow in order to cover Madras, and the campaign thus ended decidedly to the disadvantage of the British.

Cornwallis now determined to take over the conduct of operations in person, and in 1791 moved his main army into Mysore by the north-eastern passes, his objectives being first Bangalore and then Seringapatam, Tippoo's capital. The former place was invested and stormed in two successive operations before the Mysore army could arrive to its rescue, and the Nizam's contingent of 10,000 cavalry having joined Cornwallis, the latter decided to make a dash for Seringapatam, where he found Tippoo awaiting him in a strong position. His attempts to cut off his enemy from the city failed; supply difficulties increased alarmingly and the army began to run short both of food and of ammunition. No news was to be had of either the Bombay column or of the Mahrattas, and Cornwallis reluctantly found himself compelled to destroy his siege artillery and fall back to Bangalore. Taught by bitter experience that only a regular and methodical advance could enable him to operate against Seringapatam with any hope of success, he devoted the rest of the year to making thorough preparations for a renewed offensive in 1792. These preparations included the capture of the strong series of posts known as the Droogs, north and west of Bangalore, which were stormed one after the other in a series of brilliant *coups de main*. Tippoo meanwhile was utilising the respite thus granted in recovering his lost province of Coimbatore, which was, however, lost to him again early next year.

By the beginning of February 1792 Cornwallis, with 22,000 of his own troops and 18,000 of the Nizam's contingent, was once more before the entrenched camp to the north of Seringapatam. This was assaulted on the night of February 6 in three columns; the left attack failed to make much headway, but by the next morning the centre and right had forced their way over the entrenchments into the heart of the city, and driven Tippoo to seek refuge within the walls of the citadel. The arrival of the Bombay division completed the circle of investment, and in less than two months from the commencement of operations Tippoo saw himself reduced to ask for terms. They were severe enough, involving as they did the loss of half his dominions to the various members of the alliance, the British share being a wide stretch of territory on the western, southern and eastern frontiers of Mysore. The power of that formidable State was clearly on the decline; yet

Tippoo's hostility remained unassuaged, and his hatred of the British and desire for vengeance on them was increased, if anything, by his disasters.

The outbreak of the French Revolution, soon to be described, and the entry of England into the Coalition against it, involved the Madras army first in the operation—by now almost standardised—for the capture of Pondicherry, and later, when Holland was absorbed into the new Republic, in expeditions for the conquest of Ceylon, and the Dutch possessions in the East Indies. Once these had been successfully accomplished, the whole of the East India Company's armies underwent its first complete remodelling. The native troops, about 57,000 in all, were reduced in numbers, and redistributed, as were the battalions of white troops, into two-battalion regiments; the establishment of British officers was increased, and the first artillery units were created. This reorganisation was only gradually carried out, commencing in 1796 and not being completed till 1804. Before the latter date the doom of Mysore had fallen.

Tippoo, as soon as the news of the outbreak of the European War reached him, set to work to use it for his own purposes. He coquetted with French convoys, remodelled his army with the aid of French instructors, and appealed for the assistance of French arms. When in 1798 Bonaparte's expedition to Egypt seemed to menace a direct overland attack on India, the authorities, both at home and at Calcutta, became alarmed; reinforcements were sent post haste to India, and the new Governor-General, Lord Wellesley, took steps to avert at least one source of peril—the presence of large numbers of French officers as advisers in the armies of various native princes. British officers were substituted for these in many cases, particularly that of the Nizam of Hyderabad, whose alliance was thus secured for the projected war with Tippoo. For it had become clear by now that the latter was bent on lighting again at the earliest possible moment, and putting his new army to the decisive test of battle.

Nevertheless, the initiative was left to the British, who early in 1799 had assembled an army of 21,000 men, under Harris, around Vellore, and on being joined by the Nizam's contingent of 16,000, at once proceeded to invade Mysore from the east, while a force of 6000 under Stuart co-operated by an advance from the Malabar coast on the west. Tippoo, who had some 50,000 men available, resolved on a bold stroke at Stuart before Harris's menace to his capital had fully developed, but it failed of its object, as did a second and somewhat half-hearted attempt to check the advance of the latter at Malavelly. After a march, therefore, which was rendered slow and toilsome mainly owing to the difficulty of feeding and handling the enormous mass of his transport, Harris arrived before Seringapatam, effected his junction with Stuart, and commenced a regular attack on the western face of the city. A practicable breach was soon made, and on May 4 the British assaulting columns forded the Cauvery and entered the place, which by nightfall was completely in their hands. Tippoo himself was among the dead, and the house of Hyder Ali had ceased to reign.

The territory of Mysore was partitioned between the British, the Nizam and the Mahrattas, and over the poor remnant of the land a puppet king, belonging to the old dynasty dethroned by Hyder, was set up. There was still work remaining to do for the Madras army in reducing to order the lawless tribes and elements that from time to time within the next few months disturbed the peace of Southern India, but a description of the operations would be out of place in a brief narrative such as this. From the date of the final fall of Seringapatam the paramount power of the Company was firmly established and fully recognised from Malabar east to Coromandel, and from the Kistna south to Cape Comorin.

WILLIAM PITT

CLIVE AT PLASSEY

Eyre Coote

WARREN HASTINGS

CHAPTER 8
The Fight With Revolutionary France
1793-1802

1. The Outbreak of the Conflict, 1783-1793

Within six short years of the triumph of France over Great Britain in the world contest arising out of the American rebellion, Nemesis had overtaken her incompetent and bankrupt monarchy, and the whole country was plunged into the throes of revolution. The course of that Revolution, wherein were laid the foundations of modern France and modern Europe, followed the usual road—from a limitation of the absolute powers of the Crown to the abolition first of these powers, then of the Crown itself; from government by elected assembly to mob rule, and thence to the unfettered power of a self-appointed oligarchy—a road as old as Greece, as new as Russia. From the military point of view, with which alone we are concerned, the Revolution heralded the first appearance of a new phenomenon—the nation in arms, and the complete supersession of eighteenth-century warfare by the strategic and tactical methods of our own day. The Revolutionary and Napoleonic epochs mark the beginning of modern military history. For the British army, in fine, they form the last and most bitterly contested of the long series of conflicts with France, which cover more than five centuries of our country's story, and the establishment of our national independence and the acquisition of our overseas empire. In these twenty odd years, from 1793 to 1815, the army underwent its sternest and most searching test in a struggle which, until a yet greater war came in our own time to rob it of the title, was justly termed the Great War.

That war was not entered upon lightly or easily. For a period of ten years, subsequent to the Peace of Versailles, England, under the prudent leadership of William Pitt, the son of the great Chatham, held aloof from all European entanglements, and devoted her energies to the restoration of her stability and economic prosperity. She held aloof from the Royalist crusade which in 1792, on the news of the dethronement of the House of Bourbon in France, set forth under the leadership of Austria and Prussia to repress the Revolution by armed force, and impassively watched the defeat of the invaders. Neither the Government nor the people, however, could see unmoved the violent course of the dominant faction in Paris, the tyranny and blood-lust of the Jacobins, or the doctrines, subversive alike of liberty and order, which French arms were to propagate wherever their career of conquest should carry them, imposing them by force on unwilling peoples. None the less, it was only when the Revolutionary armies, gathering in strength on their northern frontier, menaced the independence of the Low Countries, ever England's predominant Continental interest, that the latter felt herself compelled to have recourse to arms, and ally with Austria, Russia, the lesser states of Germany, Spain and Holland against the common enemy of Europe.

Thus the British army in the first months of 1793 found itself once more preparing for active service. Its constitution and government had been considerably remodelled during the previous ten years of peace; by the provisions of Burke's Act of 1783, all matters of recruitment and finance, hitherto the concern only of the regimental commanders, had been taken over by the Government, which had also reorganised the command and administration of the army under two newly appointed heads, the secretary of state for war and the commander-in-chief. The peace strength had now sunk to its normal level of 17,000 men, and steps were at once taken to increase it, first by the method adopted during the American War, of purchasing from Hanover and Hesse the services of 20,000 mercenaries, and then by the raising of a number of new regiments of Horse and Foot (some 37,000 in all). By these measures an adequate field army would be provided, while for purposes of home defence the militia was largely increased, recruiting by ballot being instituted in 1794, and two additional forces, known respectively as Fencibles and Volunteers, were also raised for the same purpose. As the result of these measures the establishments by the end of 1794 showed a sum total of 75,000 British regulars and mercenaries, and 90,000 home defence troops, in all 165,000 men under arms. Imposing as these figures were, they might have been largely increased by the elimination of competition for eligible men between the various arms and forces, and the institution of one regular, economical and efficient recruiting system for the whole of the armed forces of the Crown. Moreover, the physical and military qualities of both officers and men left much to be desired; training and fighting methods were out of date; armament, clothing and equipment were inadequate; and the system of transport and supply, only recently reorganised on a sound basis, was, as yet, inelastic and uncertain in its working. Altogether the British fighting machine was well below the standard even of the Continental armies of its day, and as yet by no means fit for the arduous tasks which the coming campaigns were to impose upon it.

Such being the weapon at his disposal, Pitt had now to consider how to use it. His main idea was to employ the army in cooperation with the navy against the overseas trade and possessions of France; such had been its role in recent wars, and in this case the historical argument was fortified by what appeared to be common sense. Pitt believed that Revolutionary France financially and economically was at her last gasp, and that sheer exhaustion must shortly compel her to lay down her arms; the capture of her few remaining colonies must tend to hasten this desirable consummation, besides being of direct advantage to Britain. The revolt in the French West Indian Islands, which broke out a few months previous to the commencement of the war, seemed to offer a golden opportunity for applying this policy with rapidity and effect, and the main strength of the British regular army was therefore despatched with all possible speed to that sphere of operations. At the same time our interests in the Low Countries could not be entirely neglected, and it was decided also to send a contingent to co-operate with the Allied armies in that theatre.

Such was Pitt's initial plan. As we shall see, it was considerably modified during the course of the next few campaigns. Various small expeditions were despatched against other distant overseas objectives; home defence became more and more a matter of pressing concern; and a series of attempts were made to foment or assist by armed force risings against the Revolutionary Government in the disaffected coastal districts of France. Under these conditions our military operations tended to become incoherent and wasteful, and all the more difficult to describe clearly and succinctly because of the non-existence of any consistent and logical general plan underlying the whole.[1] However, for our purposes we may divide the narrative into five phases: (1) The Campaign in the Low Countries, 1793-1795; (2) the West Indies Operations, 1793-1800; (3) Minor Operations in Europe and elsewhere (the Mediterranean, the French coasts, Ireland, the Cape, etc.), 1793-1798; (4) the Expedition to North Holland, 1799; (5) the Egyptian Expedition, 1800.

---

1. A previous historian of the army has appropriately headed his chapter describing the operations of this period "The Army at Sea".

2. The Campaign in the Low Countries
1793-1795

The various powers composing the First Coalition were, when England added herself to their number, anything but a happy family. The two greatest, Austria and Prussia, were consumed by mutual distrust and jealousy over the question of the fate of Poland; Spain, Sardinia and the minor German states were weak and corrupt; and Holland was apathetic, one might almost say disaffected towards the common cause. At the opening of the campaign of 1793 the Allied armies in the Netherlands, comprising in all some 60,000 men, were drawn up along the southern frontier, with their main strength north of Valenciennes, in face of that of the enemy entrenched in a position covering that fortress. The French army, weaker in numbers and under a divided command, was widely dispersed along a line from the Sambre on the right to Dunkirk on the left in an attempt to cover every possible avenue of invasion open to the Allies, who, on their part, were little less scattered. The latter possessed a fighting machine undoubtedly superior to that of their adversaries, but the methods of making war held in honour among them were such as to preclude any serious attempt to exploit this advantage; their leaders could conceive of nothing beyond a steady and methodical advance through the fortress barrier guarding the approaches to the heart of France, and a strict limitation of the objectives of each successive step. This strategy played into the hands of their adversaries by granting them the needed respite to restore their armies to the high standard of efficiency attained before the Revolution came to ruin discipline and undermine morale.

The forces in British pay, numbering in all 27,000, of whom at the outset some 20,000 were German mercenaries, arrived at Tournai in April, the Duke of York being in chief command. Coburg, the Austrian generalissimo, had already drawn up his plan of campaign, which involved an advance of the main army against the French entrenched camp before Valenciennes, the flanking of the fortress barrier at that point, and the capture of the strong places to the east of it. Once these preliminaries had been accomplished a decisive advance on Paris might be safely undertaken, and in any case the Allies would have gained real advantages. Unfortunately, the British Government felt the need of acquiring some tangible gain which it might present to its people as an early and adequate result of our military effort in the Netherlands, and in an evil hour it was agreed that after the capture of Valenciennes, the British contingent should be permitted to possess itself of Dunkirk.

This ill-advised decision went far to ruin what might well have been the decisive campaign of 1793. The first part of the programme was carried out without a hitch; the French entrenched camp was carried by storm, the fortress of Valenciennes invested and compelled to capitulate, and the hostile army forced back across the upper Scheldt. Then, with some four months of good campaigning weather still before them the Allies divided their forces and went their several ways as arranged— Coburg to besiege Maubeuge, York to secure Dunkirk. The latter found the task too great for his resources: the necessary naval cooperation was unduly delayed, his siege artillery was inadequate, and his forces were too small even to permit of a complete investment of the place. The French thus had ample time to despatch an army to its rescue; advancing from the south, it defeated and drove off at Hondschoote the troops detailed to cover the siege, and compelled York to abandon his heavy guns and fall back in haste for fear of being cut off from his base at Ostend. He effected his retreat in safety, largely because his enemies had turned their attention to Coburg, who was in his turn compelled by the French victory of Wattignies to raise the siege of Maubeuge. York was not only too far away to be able to arrive in time to be of use, but his eastward march was interrupted by the news of a French diversion which caused anxiety for the security of Flanders and compelled him to retrace his steps. The operations thus came to an end with the apparent advantage indeed on the side of the Allies; but in actual fact they had by their dilatoriness and divided counsels lost their best chance of decisively defeating their adversaries while still weak.

For by the beginning of next year there was no prospect of the Allies being able successfully to execute their proposed plan for an advance on Paris. Their mutual mistrust was becoming more rather than less acute with the lapse of time; the condition of their troops was going from bad to worse, and their effectives were gradually diminishing, so that to the 240,000 French under Pichegru and Jourdan who stood arrayed between the Moselle and the sea, they could oppose barely half that number, though these were still superior to their enemies in all military qualities. The main army, with which was the Duke of York's British contingent of 22,000 men, was again assembled around Valenciennes, preparing to advance against the centre of the French host, which on its side was planning a double enveloping movement against both the Allied flanks by way of Ghent and Liege. In April, however, Coburg took the initiative, attacking Pichegru in his fortified position between Cambrai and Le Cateau and forcing him to retire towards Guise. Siege was then laid to Landrecies, and the French attempts at relief were beaten off in two brilliant little actions in which the British cavalry covered themselves with glory. Accordingly Pichegru determined to try the effect of a diversion in Flanders, where his progress rapidly became so menacing that York was sent hurriedly to the rescue, to be followed soon after by the main body of the army. In the two days' battle of Tourcoing lack of cohesion and bad staff work threw away the results of the first successful British advance and exposed the victorious troops to annihilating attacks on both flanks, from which they were only extricated after heavy losses. Following his success, Pichegru once more assailed the right of the Allied line, while Jourdan in the Sambre valley pressed back their left, thus forcing Coburg in his anxiety for his communications to hasten eastwards, leaving York at Tournai to make what head he could against the very superior numbers of the enemy. British reinforcements arrived at Ostend only to become involved in the general retreat, which led the Allied troops in two months back by way of the Scheldt valley, Malines and Antwerp to the Dutch frontier, while Coburg, defeated at Fleurus, was compelled to retire down the Meuse and sever his connection with his Allies.

The Duke of York was thus left to secure the inviolability of Holland with 25,000 ill-trained, ill-equipped and ill-clothed troops whose officers were inferior and whose morale was declining. No assistance could be expected from the Dutch, and there was no prospect that the defensive front of close on 100 miles on the north bank of the Meuse between Venloo and the head of the estuary could be held against any serious attack. The continued retirement of the Austrians uncovered the Duke's left, and Pichegru, by a combined front and flank attack, compelled him to fall back behind the Waal. Winter had now set in; operations came to an end and the British commander left for England, handing over the charge of the army to the Hanoverian, Walmoden. But the intense cold quickly froze the waters of the river which separated the opposing forces, and Pichegru seized his opportunity to force the passage, first of the Waal, and then of the Leek, overrun Holland, and seize the Dutch fleet lying helpless in the Texel. The British army, falling back north-eastwards to the Yssel and the Ems under conditions which were a foretaste, on a smaller scale, of those of the retreat from Moscow, was for all practical purposes dissolved as a fighting force before, in April 1795, it finally reached its transports at Bremen.

So ended in utter disaster one of the few really discreditable episodes in our army's history. None the less, though the Duke of York had conclusively proved himself unequal to a high command in the field; though among both officers and troops almost every military quality was conspicuous by its absence, and the sole redeeming feature throughout remained the fighting value of the troops in battle, the main responsibility for the disaster must lie on the shoulders of the Government and people of England, who sent overseas an army unfitted for its work, neglected to provide it with the first essentials for success, and finally left it to starve and freeze for want of the bare necessities of existence. Not for the first time nor for the last had the luckless British army to serve as a scapegoat for the country's lack of preparedness and military inefficiency.

3. The Campaign in the West Indies
1793-1800

As we have seen, the occupation of the French West Indian Islands was in Pitt's mind the mainspring of the plan of operations by which he expected, in a short space of time, to reduce France to submission. Not only would the conquest be a popular and showy one, but it would bring solid financial and commercial advantage to Great Britain, while exercising a correspondingly disastrous effect on the foreign trade and internal stability of her adversary. In addition, prudence demanded that the British islands, which depended for their prosperity on slave labour, should not be exposed to the risk of infection from the revolt among the servile population in the French possessions. All these considerations combined to convince Pitt that the bulk of the British regular army could not be more advantageously employed than in conquering and garrisoning these enemy possessions, the chief of which were from west (or leeward) to east (or windward) the western portion of the large island of San Domingo, Guadeloupe, Marie Galante, Martinique, St. Lucia and Tobago. Their occupation, indeed, presented in almost every case no very difficult problem. With their retention it was far otherwise, and, as we shall see, the acts of God and of the King's enemies together were to render the task of garrisoning the French West Indies one of the most ruinously expensive ever undertaken by our army.

The first blow was to be struck in the windward sphere; and in the early summer of 1793 a tiny force from Barbados took possession of Tobago, but failed in a *coup de main* on Martinique. This was, however, but a prelude to the main attack, to be carried out by an expedition of 7,000 men under Grey, transported and escorted by a squadron under Jervis and directed against Martinique, St. Lucia and Guadeloupe. A series of vexatious and apparently quite avoidable delays prevented the flotilla leaving England till late in the year, and postponed the opening of the campaign till February 1794. Then a series of brilliant successes crowned the exemplary cooperation of army and fleet and the skill and energy of both commanders. A landing was effected at three points on the coast of Martinique, the enemy's defence rapidly overrun, a junction of the British columns effected before Fort Royal, the capital and main centre of resistance, and its surrender secured after a campaign of less than seven weeks. St. Lucia was next taken by somewhat similar methods, and the island of Guadeloupe was next assailed. This being divided into two distinct portions, Grande Terre on the east and Guadeloupe proper on the west, proved a harder nut to crack—not too hard, however, for Grey and his gallant troops. He was to find it more difficult, however, to retain the conquests of his brilliant little three months' campaign, in face of strong French reinforcements which the British Government had failed to prevent crossing the Atlantic—a task rendered none the easier by his orders to send all his surplus troops to San Domingo. The French, in fact, recovered Grande Terre, beat off a British counter-attack with heavy loss, closely invested the British garrison and finally forced it to capitulate, largely owing to the fact that its strength had been reduced by yellow fever from 1,800 to 125 men. This new army, more formidable than any human foe, had taken the field against the British, and was in the next few years to prove the real conqueror in the West Indian campaign.

Similar promising but deceptive successes had also been gained in the leeward sphere, where a small British force of 700 men from Jamaica under Whitelocke landed on San Domingo with the ostensible object of taking peaceful possession of the island, which had been handed over by treaty by the white population, lest worse should befall them at the hands of the revolted black slaves. The latter, who had been proclaimed free men by the doctrinaire Government of Paris, retired into the mountains; the mulattos, or half-castes, unable to get the British to confirm them in their liberties long enjoyed under French rule, held sullenly aloof, and the whites proved themselves, with few exceptions, greedy, corrupt and incompetent. Consequently, as soon as the tiny British force was well dispersed in an attempt to occupy all the important towns, the blacks commenced a series of fierce surprise attacks on their posts. The situation grew rapidly more critical, and remained so even after the arrival of 1,600 reinforcements under Whyte, from Grey's force to windward. The local corps, which were now raised in considerable numbers to supply the pressing need for troops^, exasperated the inhabitants by plundering and outrage, and in some places the mulattos broke into rebellion; and meanwhile, the fever was taking its toll of the scanty British force, and from home could be obtained nothing but vain promises of reinforcements. At the end of 1794 the insurgents, in a series of skilful and daring *coups de main,* recovered all the southern coast of the island, and the commanders on the spot realised that only permission to raise large bodies of negro troops under British officers could compensate for the weakness of their own forces, which had now sunk to less than 1,100 men.

Pitt, however, preferred to send out reinforcements from home, and these had barely arrived when there arose a new peril in Jamaica, where the maroons, a mountain people descended from runaway slaves, defied the Government and had to be suppressed by force. This was only effected after considerable time and difficulty. Owing to this preoccupation, operations in San Domingo were practically at a standstill throughout 1795; Toussaint l'Ouverture, the able leader of the blacks, was left ample leisure to consolidate and strengthen his position in the interior, and the campaign of conquest had to be postponed for another year. For this date troops in large numbers were once more promised, but Pitt at the same time foolishly forbade the raising of black troops locally except on impossible terms. It was May 1796 before the first reinforcements arrived, only to be so weakened by sickness that no serious operations could be undertaken; between July 1796 and February 1797 the effectives of the San Domingo garrison sank from 9,000 to 1,400, and these mostly sick.

Meanwhile affairs to windward between 1795 and 1797 had taken on a more serious turn. In March 1795 a whirlwind of insurrection swept the whole of the British islands and whipped up the negro population into armed rebellion, which the French from Guadeloupe, of course, did not fail to foment and support to the best of their power. The British were driven from St. Lucia and could maintain only a precarious foothold on the coast of Grenada. In St. Vincent, after a series of fluctuating operations in which some of the regiments can hardly be said to have added to their reputations, the garrison was finally driven back to and shut up in Kingston; while only in Dominica and Martinique were the risings taken firmly and effectively in hand and the French, parties despatched to encourage the rebels rounded up and destroyed.

Accordingly, as will be well understood, the British Government now found a more important use for its forces available for service in the West Indies than the rescue of the handful of men in San Domingo. Yet, owing to mismanagement of the first order, the sailing of Abercromby's expedition of 17,000 men to restore the situation to windward was delayed till the winter of 1795; it was then blown back or dispersed by contrary gales no less than three times, and finally not more than 5,000 were concentrated at Barbados in March 1796. There Abercromby split up his forces, one column being sent to effect the recovery of Grenada—which was done without mishap—while he himself, with the main body, disembarked on the shore of St. Lucia, and, after a severe and prolonged struggle, compelled the rebels to lay down their arms. Sailing thence southwards he next restored order in St. Vincent, but his losses had been so great and the behaviour of the troops so uneven that he felt himself in no position even to attempt to expel the French from their main stronghold of Guadeloupe. Accordingly, the British remained in occupation of their gains, and day by day their graves grew more numerous; by the end of the year they had already lost more than fifty-six per cent of their strength from yellow fever and other diseases. None the less, operations were renewed early in 1797. With the few reinforcements brought by him from home, Abercromby managed to effect the capture of Trinidad, but failed in an attempt on Porto Rico; thereafter he received orders to refrain from further offensive operations and commence the raising of black troops to replace the whites in the West Indian garrisons. This, apart from the seizure of the Dutch West Indian possessions which was effected peacefully in 1799 and 1800, marked the end of active operations in the windward spheres.

At the same time the Government at last made up its mind to refrain from further effort and expenditure in San Domingo, but Simcoe, the new commander, was bent on making one more attempt to reduce the island. This proved in the main unsuccessful, and the Government thereupon resolved to withdraw all its troops save the garrisons of two points on the coast. At this juncture the negro leader, Toussaint, assumed a general offensive, and when Maitland arrived to take control he found the situation rapidly becoming impossible. He thereupon decided, without any authority from home and entirely on his own initiative, to come to terms with Toussaint, and maintained his purpose, despite the knowledge that in so acting he was going directly contrary to the views of the Government, his superiors and all the white population of the West Indies. Accordingly, in October 1798, San Domingo was finally evacuated, and the West Indian campaign, which for close on five years had drained like a horse-leech the best life-blood of the British army, came to an end. For the islands of Tobago, St. Lucia and Martinique England had paid, it is computed, a toll of 50,000 dead and 50,000 incapacitated for life; while there must also be set in the balance her enormous financial expenditure and heavy loss resulting from the devastation of St. Vincent and Grenada in the servile insurrection.

Thus closed in disappointment and wreckage this gloomy and ill-starred campaign, of which the main result had been the fertilisation of these tropical islands with the best blood of England's army. The pity and the disgrace of it again lies less on the troops, whose conduct, however, left, on more than one occasion, much to be desired, than on the home authorities, who, despite the known deadliness of the West Indian climate for white men, nevertheless embarked recklessly and light-heartedly on this fatal enterprise. Only the *camaraderie* and cooperation of army and fleet under Grey and Jervis, Abercromby's able conduct of his difficult tasks in 1796 and 1797, and the remarkable initiative and moral courage of Maitland stand out as episodes worthy to rescue from oblivion the sordid story of these wearisome operations.

4. Minor Operations and Expeditions, 1793-1798

We have dealt above with the two theatres of military activity which absorbed, during the first period of the war, the bulk of our armed forces, and have seen how unsatisfactory and disastrous were the results of our efforts in either case. There remains to be considered yet a third series of enterprises from which much was hoped, by which much might have been achieved, but which also in the outcome brought to the army and the country little save defeat and humiliation.

At the outbreak of the war in 1793 France was in a critical condition both externally and internally, and had to reckon not merely with invasion at the hands of her foes, but with serious disaffection in her western and southern provinces. Scarcely had hostilities been declared than the district round the estuary of the Loire, known as La Vendee, took up arms for the Royalist cause against the Revolutionary Government of Paris, and defeated the Republican armies sent to subdue it; while a few months later the south also flamed up in open rebellion, and the city of Toulon invited France's enemies in as trustees for the Bourbons. Both of these movements seemed to the British Government worth aiding by every possible means: Hood, the naval Commander-in-Chief in the Mediterranean, having taken Toulon at its word, it was decided to send troops to secure the place, and an expedition under Moira (formerly Rawdon, of Carolina fame) was fitted out to unite with and assist the Vendéans. But so scanty were the available resources in men and material of every sort that Moira was unable to sail until too late; and before he could arrive to their assistance the rebels had been decisively defeated. No better fate befell the enterprise at Toulon, where an Allied garrison of very miscellaneous composition and not very good quality was speedily invested by a far superior French force, among whom was the future Emperor Napoleon, now undergoing his baptism of fire. Nevertheless, the place held out for close on four months and might well have endured a longer siege had more British troops been sent, or the other Allied contingents been of the same military value; and eventually the evacuation was successfully carried out with less difficulty and loss than might have been expected. None the less a second great opportunity of seriously embarrassing the enemy was lost at Toulon for want of adequate forces to exploit the initial advantage.

The next British enterprise in the Mediterranean was more successful. The islanders of Corsica having revolted against their French masters, appealed for aid to Hood; the latter accordingly appeared with his fleet off the northern coast, and a landing in force was successfully effected by the troops under the command of David Dundas. Despite serious disagreements between the admiral and the general, which eventually led to the resignation of the latter, the two fortified towns of San Fiorenzo and Bastia were blockaded and forced to surrender; and Charles Stuart, one of the best officers of his day, signalised his accession to command by a brilliant and successful little operation against Calvi which completed the occupation of the whole island in August 1794—the first solid success gained by Great Britain up to that date.

Meanwhile, as we know, events elsewhere had gone ill for the Allies, and worse was to come. The French successes on the Continent and their own mutual disagreements over Poland were already weakening and were soon to disrupt the Coalition altogether. In April 1795 Prussia signed a separate peace; three months later Spain followed suit, and Holland, overrun, became an ally of France, leaving Great Britain and Austria for all practical purposes alone to face the exultant enemy, who was now setting his house in order at home and abandoning terrorism in favour of milder and more conciliatory methods of government. The accession of Russia to the Coalition at the end of 1795, however, did something to restore the balance, and while the Austrian armies were making head against the French on the Rhine and in Italy, the British Government decided to employ its available forces in endeavouring once more to foment disorder in the west of France by way of a diversion. Lack of preparation made the attempt not merely a failure, but almost a disaster, and the unfortunate Royalists who rose in arms on the faith of British promises were once and for all dispersed to the four winds. It was the worst managed of these petty and futile enterprises, but, happily, it was also the last. Better fortune attended another expedition, which sailed in March 1795 to secure the Dutch colony at the Cape of Good Hope, and successfully effected its task despite the natural difficulties and the bitter opposition of the Boers. The occupation of the other Dutch possessions in the East Indies has already been mentioned in the previous chapter.

The year 1796, however, saw affairs on the Continent take a definite turn for the worse. Napoleon Bonaparte's brilliant campaign in Italy brought Austria to her knees, and in the spring of 1797 a cessation of hostilities was arranged which soon crystallised into a definite peace. In the summer of 1796 Spain was added to the number of England's enemies, and so overwhelming was the force of the combined French and Spanish fleets that Corsica was evacuated and the British squadron withdrawn from the Mediterranean. Meanwhile the internal state of England gave rise to the gravest anxiety; bad harvests led to rioting and sabotage; dissatisfaction with the conduct of the war and the meagre results accruing from so many sacrifices was widespread; and Pitt felt himself compelled to open peace discussions. Ireland, however, where religious and political feelings united both north and south against the Government, was the hotbed of disaffection and the Achilles heel of Great Britain ; armed rebellion was known to be in preparation and only to be awaiting external encouragement and aid to break forth on a formidable scale. The Government's political handling of the situation left much to be desired; troops in adequate numbers to meet the demands of the authorities on the spot were simply not available, and the quality and discipline of such as could be sent were at an alarmingly low level. To crown all, in April 1797 the crews of the ships in home waters mutinied and left the country apparently helpless before its enemies, who were known to be planning an invasion covered by the Dutch fleet. It was the darkest hour.

Luckily all these perils came to a head only in succession, not simultaneously. Discipline was restored in the navy in time to allow of the Dutch fleet being encountered and defeated, while another victory restored the situation in the Mediterranean. The elements ruined the only serious attempt made by the French to send armed support to the Irish malcontents, and when in 1798 these latter broke into open rebellion they were rigorously and mercilessly repressed by the troops in garrison in the country without any intervention being attempted by Britain's external enemies. A small French expedition did, indeed, manage to land somewhat later, but after some initial success was compelled to surrender. And, meanwhile, the main danger of invasion had passed with the decision of the French Government to send the bulk of their army under Napoleon to the conquest of Egypt.

The expedition sailed in May 1798 and effected its landing safely, but all chance of real success was destroyed by Nelson's victory of the Nile, which cut it off from any hope of return to France and left it to carry on the campaign with its own resources alone. Shortly after this great triumph a British force under Charles Stuart effected the capture of Minorca, a valuable base for operations in the western Mediterranean, and from there the bulk of the troops were shipped over to Sicily in order to secure that island against occupation by the French, who had immediately, on the unwise declaration of war against them by the King of Naples, overrun the whole of that monarch's territories on the mainland of Italy.

The aggressive policy of the French Government had, in fact, once more united the Continental powers in arms. Prussia stood aside, but England, Austria, Russia and Turkey, together with the unhappy Naples, had by the beginning of 1799 formed themselves into the Second Coalition and were preparing to undertake operations on the Rhine, in Switzerland and in Italy. These campaigns opened in March with a series of brilliant initial victories, the fruits of which were, however, not fully gathered owing to dissensions among the Allied commanders. None the less the French had by the summer been driven back to the Rhine and cleared out of all Italy, a few closely besieged fortresses alone remaining in their hands. The tables had thus been completely turned, and Great Britain, but a year since confined to a strict defensive, was once more in a position to take aggressive action against her formidable enemy.

5. The North Holland Expedition
1799

The British Government had during the early part of the year taken steps to strengthen and reinforce the army by the enlistment of large numbers of militiamen (the need for whose services had become less pressing now that invasion no longer threatened) into the regular forces; and this, combined with the enrolment of a number of militia and fencible units who had also volunteered as such for service overseas, enabled them to assemble by the summer a respectably strong, though as yet somewhat ill-trained, striking force, of which, for the first time, the reorganised artillery and the new transport service formed part. It was decided, on grounds which seem to have been less military than political, to despatch it with a Russian contingent to re-conquer north Holland, the bulk of the population of which was believed to sympathise with the Allies. How this was to be accomplished was probably not clear to ministers themselves, and was certainly not made clear by them to their chosen general, Abercromby, who was finally sent to sea in August with 10,000 men and with orders which practically amounted to permission to land anywhere on the Dutch coast from the mouth of the Ems to that of the Meuse, at whatever point might seem to him and his naval colleague most suitable for his purpose. Abercromby eventually decided for the Helder, on the south shore of the mouth of the Zuider Zee, where he might hope to capture the Dutch fleet. The landing was safely effected there, despite unfavourable sea conditions and a stiff hostile resistance; the French at once evacuated the Helder peninsula and withdrew to a position covering Alkmaar; and the surrender of the fleet completed the success of a brilliant initial operation which augured well—but, alas! falsely—for the further course of the campaign.

Lack of reinforcements and supply difficulties now unfortunately reduced Abercromby for the moment to the defensive, thus allowing his opponent, Brune, leisure to consolidate his positions and even to pass to the attack. In this, however, the French were repulsed all along the lines, and shortly afterwards the Duke of York arrived to take supreme command, while British reinforcements and the promised contingent of Russians brought the total force available to close on 50,000 men. Many of these, however, were of poor quality; all were inadequately clothed and equipped; the transport question was to grow rather than diminish in difficulty as time went on; and the terrain was one of the most unsuitable conceivable for an offensive action.

It was not, therefore, for some weeks that the attack on Brune's position could be undertaken. It failed of its object with heavy loss, largely owing to the misconduct and indiscipline of the Russians; and the moral effects of the set-hack were at least as serious as the material. The opportune arrival of fresh troop's, however, enabled the offensive to be renewed, this time with better success; and Brune, seeing his left centre forced back, was compelled to evacuate Alkmaar, and withdraw to a new line half-way between there and Haarlem. Before this the Allied advance came to an abrupt end; and after a scrambling and fruitless action, which seems in have been brought on by a misunderstanding of orders, the Duke decided that the situation left him no alternative hut to retire. He had already lost twenty per cent of his total strength; his supplies were almost at an end, and the weather in a few weeks' time would, in any case, render further operations impracticable. The retreat to the Allies' old lines north of Haarlem completed the exhaustion of the supplies, and the army was fortunate to be able to re-embark in safety under the terms of a convention signed with the triumphant French. The absence of a definite plan of operations and the complete breakdown of the administrative services may fairly be said to have foredoomed the operations to failure; but the new material that had been drafted into the army had shown itself to be good, and there was every reason for expecting that it would in the next campaign acquit itself with credit.

6. THE CAMPAIGN IN EGYPT
1799-1800

Unfortunately the ill-fortune that had pursued the Allies in Holland also attended their efforts in other theatres of war. The French, though they were unable to recover Italy, managed, thanks to dissensions among the Allies, to retrieve their disasters in Switzerland and Germany; suspicion and ill-will first between Russia and Austria, then between Russia and England, widened into positive alienation and finally into a definite breach. Before the campaign of 1800 opened the Second Coalition had been dissolved, and England and Austria were left alone in face of France, now being reorganised and strengthened under the firm and masterly leadership of Napoleon Bonaparte, who had returned from Egypt to effect a *coup d'état,* and assume supreme control of the country with the title of First Consul. He at once took the field in person, and in the decisive campaign of Marengo compelled Austria to relinquish her hold of the whole of southern and the greater part of northern Italy. By October she had been compelled to ask for a cessation of hostilities, while Russia, now become an active foe to Britain, was striving to combine the northern Powers of Europe against her former ally.

Meanwhile, the English army, which might have been advantageously utilised in the Mediterranean to assist its ally's operations in Italy, was wasting its energies in a series of petty and futile expeditions. The first of these, directed against Belleisle, off the French coast, was still-born; and it was not till the middle of June, when the fate of Italy had already been decided at Marengo, that the British Government were in a position effectively to operate in the Mediterranean. Then a policy of raiding Spanish ports found favour in the eyes of ministers, and was only abandoned after two fiascos at Ferrol and Cadiz; so that at the end of the year they had on the credit side nothing to show for all their efforts but the capture of Malta.

A new plan of operations, however, had now been adopted by the Government, which decided to use its Mediterranean army in conjunction with the Turks for the reconquest of Egypt. The forces left in that country by Napoleon, though believed to be in a bad state of morale, were numerically respectable, amounting in all to some 25,000. To deal with these Abercromby was given only 16,000, deficient as usual of many of the essentials of life in the field, and to make up the shortage reliance was placed on a Turkish contingent and a force to be sent from India to the Red Sea, both of which only arrived after the work was practically done. Fortunately for the British, they found powerful allies in the incapacity of the French commander, Menou, and the half-heartedness and lack of staying power of his army. The French general, though he had ample warning of the British approach to the Egyptian coast about Aboukir Bay, allowed his adversary to reconnoitre his point of disembarkation at his leisure, make thorough-going and lengthy preparations for this very difficult operation, and finally set on shore on an open beach forces which sufficed to drive back the small detachment left alone and unsupported to oppose them. Even so the disembarkation was a daring enterprise which only succeeded thanks to the care and skill of Abercromby and his officers in planning and rehearsing it, and the courage and dash of the troops. Three days later the army moved on Alexandria, driving the still unsupported enemy detachment before it, but halted in face of the hostile main line of resistance, just east of Alexandria, where it proceeded to take up position. Here it had to undergo the counter offensive of the main French army, which Menou had at last brought up from the interior of the country; but he still for some reason neglected to concentrate the whole of the forces at his disposal, so that the disparity of numbers between the adversaries was negligible. All his attacks, which took place mainly against the British right and right centre, were steadfastly met and repulsed, and towards evening he drew off his defeated army to Alexandria. Unhappily Abercromby, the honourable and competent commander, who had been the soul of the campaign, was severely wounded on the field and died a few days later. Hutchinson, who succeeded him, found that so well had the work been begun there was little left for him to do but to reap the fruits of victory.

The French army was dispersed and disheartened; a Turkish column had come to strengthen their enemies, and was moving on Cairo from the north-east, while a force from India under Baird was about to land on the western shore of the Red Sea with the same objective. Thither also Hutchinson, after investing Alexandria, marched with the main body of his army; weak detachments only opposed him, and by the end of June he had effected a junction with the Turks before the walls of the city, and the French commander was induced to sign a convention under which his troops were to evacuate the country and be transported home to France. Two months later Menou in Alexandria capitulated on the same terms. Baird's force, after a difficult and toilsome march across the whole breadth of the country, arrived just too late for the final operations, which rounded off with brilliance and completeness the victorious Egyptian campaign of 1801.

Events elsewhere were predisposing the new ruler of France to peace, which was already being informally discussed by British envoys in Paris. Both belligerents were exhausted by ten years of war; both had serious internal problems which pressed for settlement; and neither had succeeded in gaining any decisive advantage over the other. In October 1801, therefore, the preliminaries were signed; France retained practically all her Continental conquests, while England kept only Trinidad and Ceylon. The final treaty of Amiens, concluded in March 1802, therefore marked an interlude—but an interlude only—in the titanic struggle with France.

It has always been customary among historians to compare the war administration of the younger Pitt with that of his famous father, Chatham—very much to the disadvantage of the former. We have previously given our grounds for believing that the merits of Chatham as a War Minister have been considerably overrated, and it would seem that his unfortunate son, on the other hand, has had something less than justice done him in this respect.

The main features of Pitt's military policy were laid down in complete accordance with historical precedent, and were in fact probably modelled on the lines of Chatham's own practice in the Seven Years' War. Pitt fully realised that the true function of the army was to serve as a projectile for the fleet, and that its main effort was best directed against outlying enemy possessions, which could be first isolated by sea-power and then reduced to submission at leisure. As subsidiary undertakings there remained cooperation with Britain's allies in any suitable European theatre—Flanders for choice—and small enterprises against the coastline of France by way of diversions. This had been the essence of Chatham's policy, and his son no doubt considered he could hardly do better than apply it *mutatis mutandis* to the conditions of his own time. Yet it brought him in the event nothing but disappointment and disaster, not so much because it was in itself erroneous, but owing to negligence and blundering in its execution.

Pitt's first and greatest mistake was in the raising of the army that was to carry out his policy. It cannot be too often repeated that as the British army in peace time is reduced practically to a cadre, fresh forces in large numbers must be raised at every fresh outbreak of hostilities; and to provide himself swiftly and economically with an effective new army is the first duty of every British minister who has to conduct a European war on a large scale. In this task Pitt egregiously failed; and his error was that he studied economy before efficiency, and thus succeeded only in purchasing inefficiency at a maximum price. This parsimony sent the British troops into the field deficient of practically everything which was necessary not merely for success but for their continued existence for any length of time under war-time conditions, so that they were in the nature of things bound to melt away in a few months, whatever good or ill-fortune attended their arms. After six years of disastrous war Pitt at length hit on a rational system of recruitment for the regular forces; but the value of thorough and adequate preparation for a campaign he never learned, and the conclusion of hostilities in 1801 left his administration in this respect as open to criticism as in 1793, before a shot had been fired. The same parsimony, it may be noted, came within an ace of ruining the navy also, and that at the most critical period of the war.

For the rest it was unfortunate from the point of view of Pitt's cherished policy that France possessed but few overseas territories which could usefully serve as objectives for British military expeditions, and that in the West Indies, otherwise a favourable field, the contest became one against the climate and the inhabitants rather than against a regular enemy. It is arguable that it was therefore foolish to persist in these campaigns, and that the forces thus wastefully sacrificed might have been more profitably employed elsewhere, either in Flanders, beside the allies of Britain, or in affording assistance to the disaffected elements in France itself. With regard to the first point, the experiences of the British contingent under the Duke of York in the Low Countries were hardly such as to encourage ministers to sacrifice larger forces in the same cause; while, as regards the second, all history goes to prove how illusory are the prospects of an expedition based on hope of support from the inhabitants of the country invaded.

Thus it came about that by 1797 the First Coalition against France had been smashed to powder and England was left—for the first time since the Hundred Years' War—alone in face of her hereditary enemy, with the result that for two years her army and fleet were paralysed by the menace of invasion and had no time to think of anything beyond self-defence. It was not till the blunder of Napoleon's Egyptian expedition freed them from this menace that they could resume the offensive, and not till Europe had once more ranged itself in arms against France that the opportunity for a telling blow once more arose—only to be wasted by the launching of the army in an eccentric attack, as ill managed as it was purposeless. Thus when a really favourable opportunity offered itself for using the army in close cooperation with our allies in Italy, we were in no position to seize it; and even the expedition to Egypt, which in a sense paid for all by covering with a fitful blaze of glory the conclusion of a disastrous war, owed its success almost entirely to a combination of favourable chances on which the planners of it had no right to reckon.

As regards the army itself, its eight years' contest with Revolutionary France added to its story a few glorious but forgotten episodes, and a dreary catalogue of half successes and disastrous failures redeemed by hardly a single fruitful achievement. But the difficulties with which it had throughout to contend were such as to be almost prohibitive of success. In Flanders the jealousy and self-seeking of our allies; in the West Indies the deadly climate and the flames of social and racial antagonism; in the Mediterranean the intransigence of naval colleagues and the fatal indecision of ministers; in Holland the incredibly difficult terrain and the folly of the Russians—all these might well have baffled the ablest of generals and the best of troops; and British generals and troops were both of but average quality throughout the period. Consequently the tale of the war from 1793 to 1801 is hardly one on which either the historian or his reader can dwell with any satisfaction, though it must be remembered that during this period we were training, often in the school of adversity, those renowned leaders, and building up those famous regiments, who were soon to acquit themselves so magnificently on the battle-fields of the Peninsula and Waterloo.

CHAPTER 9

England Against Napoleon: the Last War With France
1803-1814

1. Six Indecisive Years
1803-1808

The unstable equilibrium established by the Peace of Amiens could not long endure before the constant pressure of Napoleon's restless attempts to extend the dominion of France and the counter measures of self-preservation taken by England, and in May 1803 hostilities broke out afresh. Once more the predominant power on land and the mistress of the sea joined issue, as in the old contest of the elephant against the whale. The objectives and plans of campaign on either side were clearly laid down by the very conditions of the struggle. Napoleon, soon to become Emperor of the French, sought to transport across the Channel his unrivalled army and strike a mortal blow at his adversary's heart; England's policy was to hold him at arm's length with her fleet, snap up the few overseas possessions remaining to him, and endeavour to embroil him once more with the Continental powers, who, despite their recent defeats, were all ready and willing, should favourable occasion offer, to rise once more against their feared and hated conqueror. In the West Indies, where a French army was vainly endeavouring to recover the possessions lost prior to the Peace of Amiens, the British found opportunity to open the new war with a striking initial success. The enemy troops in St. Domingo, hard pressed by the revolted population and wasted with disease, laid down their arms on finding that they were blockaded by sea and cut off alike from their supplies and from all hope of escape, while the British garrison in the Caribbean theatre, being in sufficient strength to spare considerable forces for the offensive, rapidly secured possession first of St. Lucia and Tobago, and later on the accession of Holland to the number of our enemies, of all the Dutch West-Indian colonies as well. Thus by the end of 1803 we were in undisturbed possession of all the islands, and were in a position to despatch an expedition to Dutch Guiana, which, after some fighting near Surinam, completed the conquest of that territory also. Unhappily these solid and substantial gains were somewhat diminished in military value owing to the excessive forces locked up in garrisoning them.

And, indeed, England at this time had few troops to spare for any purpose save that of defending her own territory in face of the ever-present menace of invasion. During the first few months of the war Napoleon had assembled on the French coast the so-called "Grand Army" of 160,000 of his finest troops and a flotilla of boats to ferry them over to England. At first he hoped to be able to effect this without the help of a fleet, but soon realised that command of the Channel, even if only temporary, was an essential preliminary to the success of this perilous and lengthy operation, and devoted all his ingenuity to securing such command. "Let us be masters of the Channel for six hours", he wrote, "and we shall be masters of the world". Aligned against him for the defence of England's shores were first and foremost the British fleet, "those far-distant, storm-beaten ships on which the Grand Army never looked"—but which, none the less, "stood between it and the dominion of the world", and secondly, the armed forces of the country, which, numbering at the beginning of the war less than 40,000 regular troops (out of a total of over 100,000) and about 50,000 militia, were inadequate for their task as regards both numbers and quality.

Efforts were therefore made to increase these figures; the so-called Army of Reserve was instituted to fill up gaps in the regular units, while recruiting for the militia and volunteers was pressed forward with vigour. For the two first-named forces men were to be obtained by ballot, each parish having to provide a certain quota of men, to the number of 100,000 in all, while it was hoped to enrol volunteers to a total of 300,000 men. By the end of 1804 these measures had been so far effective that they had secured for purposes of home defence a grand total of 460,000 men, for the most part unhappily deficient in organisation and discipline, and, in some cases, absolutely without arms of any kind. The Army of Reserve had entirely failed to materialise; the militia were below strength and at a lamentably low level of efficiency; and the volunteer corps, though numerous, were in a state of chaos, and many of them discontented and disaffected. In a word, none of these improvised forces could have afforded very serious or prolonged resistance to Napoleon's veteran legions had the latter once succeeded in setting foot on our shores.

Pitt, who had fallen from power shortly before the Peace of Amiens, returned to office in May 1804, and at once endeavoured to remedy this unhappy and perilous state of affairs. His measures, though hardly as successful as he had hoped, did at any rate produce some effective results; his scheme was to raise by means of parish quotas 80,000 militiamen, who were to form a permanent reserve for the regular army, and eventually to be organised into second battalions of the line regiments. Other defensive measures were also taken, such as the erection of fortifications at strategic points and the organisation of local resources in transport; but Pitt's main policy was directed from the first to the formation of a new alliance of the European powers, which should find employment for Napoleon and his Grand Army elsewhere than on the Channel coast. Early in 1805 Russia and Austria had joined with England to form the Third Coalition, to which it was hoped Prussia would also adhere, and preparations for the attack on France were at once set on foot.

Meanwhile Napoleon, seeing the storm-clouds gathering fast, redoubled his efforts to draw off or evade the British squadrons, which held his navy closely blockaded in the French ports and rendered impossible of accomplishment his projected invasion of England. More than once a small naval force did in fact succeed in slipping out from one harbour or another and causing alarm in the West Indies, but all his schemes for concentrating an adequate covering fleet in the Channel finally broke down before the vigilance of the British admirals—partly, also, no doubt owing to the lack of enterprise on the part of the executants. At length the Emperor resigned himself to the inevitable, and swinging his army eastward from the Straits of Dover found ample consolation for his disappointment in the magnificent campaign which compelled the capitulation of one enemy army at Ulm, gave him possession of Vienna, and finally overthrew in irretrievable ruin the combined hosts of Austria and Russia on the fateful morning of Austerlitz. The Third Coalition was blown to fragments, and Napoleon reigned undisputed master in Europe, though Nelson's victory of Trafalgar had established on a sure basis England's undisputed supremacy at sea.

Pitt, the artificer of the Coalition, did not survive the destruction of the machine at which he had so diligently laboured, and early in 1806 sickened and died. It is as impossible to deny his political ability and high personal character as to praise him as a minister of war, and, as will be seen, the last two military enterprises initiated by him were, as regards vagueness of purpose and wastefulness of force, of a piece with all those he had undertaken in the past.

The first of these was the despatch of an expedition to the Elbe in the autumn of 1805, with the purpose of recovering Hanover from the French. There were eventually assembled on the line of the Weser some 26,000 men (of whom about half were Hanoverian and German troops enlisted in the British army, and known as the King's German Legion), absolutely nothing was accomplished, and the army remained there inactive until re-embarked on the news that both Austria and Prussia had come to terms with France.

The other expedition was equally purposeless. A force of 7,000 under Craig was sent to south Italy to co-operate with a Russian force and the Neapolitan army, with the ultimate purpose of assisting the Austrians in their struggle with the French in north Italy. Here, again, the same fiasco was repeated; the Allies took up a position on the northern frontier of Naples, where they remained until Austria was defeated and compelled to sue for terms, and thereupon hurriedly marched off to the coast and sailed away—the British, however, only as far as Sicily, which they thus managed to save from the wreck of the kingdom of Naples. As it happened, however, Napoleon's uncertainty as to the exact object of this expedition was the determining cause of his strict orders to Villeneuve to leave Cadiz and intercept it—orders which sent the fleets of France and Spain to their final disaster at Trafalgar.

Meanwhile a new ministry had assumed office at home, and the War Minister, Windham, at once set to work to increase the strength of the army by new methods. He reverted to the system of voluntary short service for overseas; took measures to raise by ballot a contingent of 200,000 militiamen, whom he intended later to draft into regular battalions, carried out a drastic reduction of the volunteers, and took some preliminary measures for a *levée en masse* in case of invasion. The strength of the regular army at home amounted early in 1806 to some 90,000 men, and one effect of Windham's measures was to liberate a large part of this force for offensive operations. Unhappily in the matters of the choice of objectives and the general conduct of the war, the new Government followed all too faithfully in the footsteps of its predecessors.

The British army in Sicily, having evacuated the mainland of Naples before the advance of a French army of invasion in June 1806, embarked on an enterprise for its recovery. Although much hampered throughout his operations by the vanity and incapacity of his naval colleague Sidney Smith, Stuart, who had replaced Craig, effected a landing on the Calabrian coast, and, moving inland, met and defeated the French, who were superior to him in numbers, in a brilliant little action at Maida. The moral effect of this victory throughout Europe, though great and widespread, was somewhat diminished by Stuart's failure to follow up his success, and his return to Sicily consequent on a violent quarrel with the admiral; the French were thus enabled to reoccupy the lost territory at their leisure, and such damage as their prestige had suffered was more than repaired by the rapid and complete overthrow of Prussia, who had at last mustered up courage to defy Napoleon, at Jena, and the occupation of her territory by the victorious Grand Army. From Berlin Napoleon issued the famous Decrees, the first step in his attempt to cripple England by closing against her commerce all the ports of continental Europe.

Meanwhile the latter was left to reap what comfort she might from the success of a little expedition under Baird, which for the second time in ten years conquered the Dutch colony of the Cape of Good Hope. This led directly to perhaps the most ill conceived and criminally foolish military enterprise ever undertaken by British arms—the South American adventure.

This design of crippling Spain by raising a revolution in her American colonies with the help of a joint expedition originated in the fertile brain of Home Popham, the commander of the fleet which had escorted Baird to the Cape, and he persuaded that officer to allow him a battalion under

Beresford for the purpose of a descent on Buenos Ayres. As it turned out, the operation was carried out successfully, and for close on two months the tiny force actually remained in possession of the city. The Spaniards then recovered themselves, surrounded it on all sides and forced it to lay down its arms, but not before exaggerated reports of the initial advantage gained had induced the Government not only to despatch reinforcements under Auchmuty for the further prosecution of the campaign, but also to send out another force under Craufurd to take possession of the whole of Chile and connect with Beresford across the whole 900 miles breadth of the continent—a megalomaniac scheme worthy of Chatham at his worst. However, it was later found necessary to use the whole force, now placed under Whitelocke's command, for the recovery of Buenos Ayres, and accordingly after Auchmuty had brilliantly got possession of Monte Video the army was concentrated there, ferried up the Rio de la Plata and landed some thirty miles east of its objective. A difficult and toilsome march, where food and water were scarce and the administrative arrangements to the last degree faulty, brought it before the west face of the city, and next day it was plunged headlong into the streets in a number of weak columns, unable to see or assist one another. Disaster ensued, several units surrounded on all sides laid down their arms, and Whitelocke was fortunate to be allowed to evacuate the country in safety under the terms of a convention with the enemy. He was, of course, made the scapegoat for the failure, and cashiered for having failed in an impossible task and chosen the only means left him to extricate his army from a position from which no other escape was possible.

While the British were thus wasting their energies in futile and eccentric directions, Napoleon at the end of 1806 had found his triumphant career in Europe checked by the mud of Poland. Fortunately for him Russia at the same time became embroiled in hostilities against Turkey, and this new factor in the situation led directly to a new experiment in futility undertaken by the British Government, which decided to send a fleet through the Dardanelles and a military force to deny Egypt to the French by occupying and holding Alexandria. Both enterprises proved disastrous failures. 6,000 men under Fraser succeeded, indeed, in securing Alexandria, but, pushing farther eastward to consolidate their position by occupying Rosetta, were twice beaten off with loss. An attempt was then made to effect by negotiation what could not be accomplished by arms, and terms were finally signed which in fact secured the object of the expedition—if it can be said to have had one, since the French had apparently not the least intention of actually attacking Egypt. The forces thus foolishly wasted might well have found more profitable employment in Sicily, where the British garrison, none too large, was neutralised throughout the whole of 1807 and 1808 as regards offensive action, first by an outbreak of mutiny in Malta and then by continued and irreconcilable dissensions between its commanders and the corrupt rulers of Naples, while the French established themselves at leisure on the mainland, and late in 1808 succeeded in securing Capri by a *coup de main* under the noses of the British fleet.

Meanwhile the British Government in the summer of 1807 decided, six months too late, to assist their allies Russia and Sweden; but, before the new expedition could sail, news came of Napoleon's decisive victory of Friedland, the formation of a Franco-Russian alliance at Tilsit, and the imminent danger that the fleets of all northern Europe might fall into French hands for use against England. Accordingly, with a promptitude and decision worthy of high praise, a fleet and a force of 25.000 men under Gambier and Cathcart was despatched to secure the surrender of the Danish squadron, which was only effected after Copenhagen had been invested and bombarded and the Danish Government forced to sue for terms. Though the action was a high-handed one which could only be justified on the plea of life and death necessity, its initiation and conduct were creditable both from the military and the political point of view. The same could hardly be said of another enterprise, intended to assist Sweden against her enemies, who were now beginning to press on her from every side. A force of 12,000 men under Moore was detained for some six weeks off the Swedish coast while its commander vainly tried to come to an understanding with the mad King Gustavus as to how it should be employed, and then returned to England having accomplished nothing. Thus six years after the war had commenced the Government had still not succeeded in devising a reasonable and coherent policy for the use of the British army.

That army, however, had at least been brought by Castlereagh, the new Minister for War, to a high standard of numbers and efficiency. The system of recruiting the regular forces from the militia had been placed on a sound basis; while home defence had been provided for by the raising of a new force, the local militia, which in June 1808 was 65,000 strong. At the same date the regular army numbered 220,000, of which half were at home and available for service in Europe. Moreover, just at this juncture Napoleon's unprovoked attack on Spain, the greatest blunder of his career, afforded Britain an ideal opportunity for sustained and effective military action against him.

2. The Peninsular War:
the Defence of Portugal
1808-1810

It being a vital part of Napoleon's campaign against England to close all the ports of the Continent against her commerce, he proceeded at the end of 1807 to take measures to force Portugal into his system. At the same time he conceived designs upon the independence of Spain, France's ostensible but reluctant ally in the dragooning of Portugal—designs which her corrupt and effete rulers were too stupid to fathom or too pusillanimous to resist. 80,000 French troops moved into Spanish territory, ostensibly to act as support to the force under Junot, which, flanked by Spanish armies, pushed forward at breakneck pace to Lisbon, drove the Government to seek refuge on board the British fleet, and secured the whole country without firing a shot. Meanwhile the criminal folly and insane dissensions of the Spanish royal family led Napoleon to believe that he might safely expel them from the throne, and, by setting up in their stead his brother Joseph, reduce Spain to the position of a vassal state of France. The whole of northern and eastern Spain, from the Pyrenees to Madrid, was occupied by French armies; the strong places in that area were seized by force or fraud by the French commanders; and the miserable Bourbons proved, as had been anticipated, no serious obstacle to the Emperor's designs. Yet, despite the apparent absence of any real spirit of patriotism in Spain, the inefficiency and corruption of her upper and governing classes, and the weakness of her armed forces, the whole country, on the first news of the *coup d'état,* flared up into insurrection. Provincial juntas or assemblies were set up, local levies were raised and armed, the army was swollen by a flood of recruits, and war to the knife was proclaimed on all sides against the violators of the country. Moreover, the early operations of these newly raised armies against the French, who were of inferior quality and led by mediocre Generals, and suffered from lack of unity of direction, met with unexpected and important successes; the invaders were held in check in Catalonia and repulsed before the walls of Valencia and Saragossa, while in Andalusia a whole corps was compelled to lay down its arms on very discreditable conditions at Baylen. Only north-west of Madrid in the plains of Leon were the French arms victorious, and so tremendous was the cumulative effect, both material and moral, of these disasters that by the end of August the new King saw himself compelled to flee from his capital after a month's residence and take refuge with his armies behind the Ebro.

Meanwhile emissaries both from Spain and from Portugal, which in its turn had risen against the French, had sought for and obtained promises of substantial assistance from Great Britain. Pursuant to this resolve, an expeditionary force of 14,000 men was prepared and the command of it given in die first place to Sir Arthur Wellesley, a general who had already to his credit a brilliant series of achievements in India, and whom it will be simpler to denote from now onwards by his better-known title of Wellington. His mission was to repel the French from Portugal, and on August 1 he commenced the disembarkation of his force in Mondego Bay, 100 miles north of Lisbon. To oppose him Junot had 25,000 men, but these were much scattered, and in order to gain time for their assembly he threw forward a detachment, which encountered and was driven back by the British in the first action of the war at Roliça. Even with the respite thus secured, the French commander could only get together 13,000 of his troop; with these he moved out from Lisbon, and on August 21 assailed Wellington, who had taken up a position at Vimeiro to cover the landing of further reinforcements. His attacks, delivered against the British centre and left, were disjointed and ill-prepared, and were beaten off in succession; had a counter-offensive been undertaken, as Wellington intended, he must have been thrown off his line of retreat to Lisbon, but at the critical moment two newly appointed British generals-in-chief arrived to take over command in turn and temporarily paralysed the victorious army, and left the French leisure to make their escape. None the less, their situation was so precarious that Junot was glad to negotiate for and secure the honourable withdrawal of his army from Portugal under the terms of the Convention of Cintra. Public opinion at home was so enraged at what seemed an impotent conclusion to a brilliant campaign that an inquiry was held, from which Wellington alone of the three commanders concerned emerged with enhanced fame.

While Portugal was thus being lost to Napoleon—never, as it turned out, to be regained—the other French armies remained strictly on the defensive behind the Ebro, leaving the Spanish to muster unmolested in their front. By the end of the summer these numbered close on 150,000 men, with 60,000 more in reserve in the interior, but they were unhappily as inferior in quality as they were formidable numerically. Their discipline, armament and leadership left everything to be desired; they had no general-in-chief, nor indeed did there exist any united direction of the war as a whole, for the central junta which had been set up at Madrid was not only incapable but was supreme only in name. None the less, plans for a general offensive, in which the British were asked to cooperate, were drawn up by the various commanders, but were still only in the stage of discussion when the face of the war underwent a sudden and entire change owing to the arrival of the French Emperor in person at the head of 200,000 of his veterans.

Napoleon had decided once and for all to finish with the war in Spain before the troubles which he knew to be brewing in Germany and Austria should call for his undivided attention ; and his coming heralded the opening of an immediate and irresistible offensive. Early in November he burst through the hostile centre on the Vitoria—Madrid road, and dealing fierce blows to either flank hurled the Spanish left back into the Asturian mountains, broke their right into fragments, and forcing his way over the Guadarrama passes entered Madrid in triumph after less than a month of fighting. The Spanish armies were dispersed to the four winds; all resistance seemed at an end, and the victor was planning a further advance westwards for the conquest of Portugal and southwards into Andalusia when the unexpected appearance of a British army on the flank of his line of communications with France gave an entirely new turn to the whole situation.

The British Government immediately after the recovery of Portugal had decided to send forward into Spain, as requested by their Allies, a force of some 36,000 men under Moore, of which 20,000 were to be detached from the army in Portugal, while the remainder under Baird were to be sent from England by sea to Coruna. Moore was further induced, owing to reports of the bad state of the roads in his zone of operations, to divide his own force into two and send his artillery and guns under Hope by way of Madrid, while he himself moved by Salamanca. The army was thus separated into three columns, with their area of concentration fixed around Burgos, where they would be well placed to co-operate with the Spanish armies on the Ebro. Moore's difficulties, owing to lack of money, supplies and transport, and, above all, the complete absence of any reliable information as to either his allies or adversaries, were such that, although he began his march in the middle of October, it was not till the end of November that he himself reached Salamanca, with Hope and Baird 100 miles away on either flank. Here he first heard of the utter rout of the Spanish armies and the French advance on Madrid, and realising the peril of his position resolved to retire while he might. A few days later, however, as the French appeared to be moving not directly westward against him but southward across his front, he determined to venture on a bold stroke at their communications, which were protected only by Soult's isolated corps in the vicinity of Sahagun. He rightly considered that this move, by bringing the whole French army upon himself, would give an all-important breathing space to his allies, and hoped that he himself might manage to evade Napoleon's enveloping toils. He accordingly concentrated his army against Soult, and was about to attack the latter on Christmas Eve when he heard that Napoleon was on the move from Madrid against his flank and rear. Instantly he drew off, and successfully got clear across the Esla at Benavente just before the arrival of the leading cavalry of the Emperor's column, which had moved at breakneck speed through atrocious weather and over bad mountain roads to intercept him. From now on the French had no recourse but to a direct pursuit, which Napoleon soon decided could safely be entrusted to the reinforced corps of Soult. The British rearguard successfully held off the enemy throughout the whole of the ensuing retreat to Coruna, but the rigours of the winter, the shortage of supplies, and, above all, the fierce pace at which Moore conducted the march, all but broke up his army into a disorganised mob. A few days' respite at Coruna, however, restored morale and discipline, and when Soult endeavoured to interrupt the embarkation he was heavily repulsed. This success was marred by the untimely death of Moore himself, who was carried off the field mortally hurt in the moment of victory and buried to the sound of French guns a few hours before the last of his army departed.

No character and career in British military history has been more fiercely discussed than Moore's, and it is no easy task to arrive at a satisfactory verdict on either. He was perhaps the greatest trainer of troops in the history of the British army, on which he left an undying mark for good; but as a leader in the field his promise was—perhaps mainly through ill-fortune—greater than his performance. Prior to his last campaign all his tasks had been thankless and difficult and left him little chance for spectacular work ; and though the skill and daring of his stroke against Napoleon's communications are deserving of high praise, and the respite thereby gained for Spain invaluable, his ensuing operations were marred by serious blemishes. On the whole, it seems that Moore's abilities and achievements have of recent years been as unduly exaggerated as they had previously been unfairly depreciated, and that his qualities as a man have tended to inspire in his biographers an excessive admiration for his military talents.

The value of the three months' respite gained by Moore's

diversion lay not so much in the reorganisation of the Spanish armies effected during that time as in the uprising throughout both Spain and Portugal of those guerilla bands which, embodying the true spirit of popular resistance to the invasion, were to render impossibly difficult the task of the French commanders and troops, by preventing intercommunication, hampering movement, impeding supply, and inflicting a ceaseless and steady drain of casualties. For the moment, however, the tide of conquest was hardly checked. During the first months of 1809 the situation in Catalonia was restored and the Spaniards driven back to Tarragona; Saragossa fell after an epic defence; Victor, in the Tagus valley, overthrew the Spanish centre under Cuesta at Medellin, and overran Northern Estremadura; and Soult, leaving Ney to complete the conquest of Galicia, moved south from Coruna, invaded Northern Portugal and stormed the city of Oporto. Meanwhile the British troops around Lisbon, now under Cradock, remained inactive, largely because the home Government were hesitating between a continuance of operations in that theatre and the opening of a new campaign in the south of Spain, and only decided for the former because of the unwillingness of the Junta to permit the landing of British troops at Cadiz.

Thus it was not till May that Wellesley, who had superseded Cradock, found himself ready to commence operations with a force of 25,000 British and some 16,000 Portuguese, who had been rapidly reorganised and made ready for service by Beresford, their new Commander-in-Chief. Faced with the choice of striking either at Soult in Northern Portugal or Victor in Estremadura, he resolved to deal first with the nearest and most dangerous foe. While Beresford moved to threaten Soult's left in the mountains the main army marched due northward on Oporto along the coast, and, driving in the hostile advanced troops, appeared before the city on May 12. Soult's forces were widely scattered, and he could assemble in face of Wellesley no more than 13,000 men, which should, however, have been able to put up a good resistance; but the British by a daring stroke surprised the passage of the Douro under the noses of their adversaries, and compelled them to a hurried withdrawal. Soult's main line of retreat having been successfully cut by the Portuguese, he was compelled to abandon his artillery and baggage and throw himself into the mountains, through which, after a series of hair-breadth escapes, and at the cost of severe privations and heavy losses, he at length succeeded in making his escape to Galicia.

Portugal thus liberated, Wellesley turned south and east to attack Victor in conjunction with the Spanish armies under Cuesta in Estremadura, and in La Mancha under Venegas. This cooperation, owing to the intractable and jealous disposition of Cuesta, took long to arrange, but it was at length agreed that he and the British, who together could put into line over 60,000 men against Victor's 20,000, should move on Madrid by the Tagus valley, while Venegas should assist by containing or driving back the enemy forces south of the capital. Grave supply and transport difficulties caused the commencement of operations to be delayed till mid-July, and when the Allied armies at length arrived before Victor's chosen position at Talavera, the favourable opportunity of attacking his isolated corps was lost by Cuesta's dilatoriness. Venegas having completely failed to fulfil his mission, the French were enabled to reinforce Victor, oppose 46,000 men to Cuesta—who had alone resumed the advance on Madrid, the British having been brought to a standstill by lack of supplies—and drive him back in disorder to Talavera. Here on July 27 and 28 there took place one of the most fiercely contested battles of the war, in which the 20,000 British bore the shock of more than double their numbers and victoriously repulsed their repeated assaults, both by night and by day, though at a cost of close on twenty-five per cent of their strength.

The tactical victory remained with the Allies, and next day the French fell back, having been compelled to detach troops to deal with Venegas, who had at last and too late decided to advance on Madrid. While he was being chased back to the south, Wellesley and Cuesta were also withdrawing by reason of a new and unexpected turn in the situation. A French force of 50,000 men, under Soult, having assembled at Salamanca, was moving south against their left rear and threatened to pin them in between the Tagus and the mountains. To escape this peril they were compelled to fall back in haste and take up a position on the south bank of the river near Almaraz, which Soult felt himself unable to attack. From there at the end of August, Wellesley, once more straitened for supplies, retired to the vicinity of Badajoz, firmly resolved that never again would he be inveigled into joint operations with Spanish armies.

This determination remained unchanged, although on both the British flanks—in Leon and in La Mancha—the Spaniards during the last months of 1809 ventured once more upon an offensive in the open field, with the usual results. The army of La Mancha once more marching rashly on Madrid suffered an utter defeat at Oçana, while the Spanish force in Leon, after some initial success, was also repulsed with loss at Alba de Tormes. Only in Catalonia, where Alvarez' magnificent defence of Gerona held the French armies fast before its walls for seven long months, did success smile on the Spanish arms. Moreover, Napoleon, having overthrown Austria and compelled her not only to make peace but to give him a wife from the Imperial House, was now free to reinforce his armies in the Peninsula to almost any extent, and in fact by the beginning of 1810 the French troops in Spain had been increased to close on 300,000 men. By that time Wellington, in expectation that the enemy's next attack would be against Portugal, had transferred his army northwards from Badajoz to a line running from the Tagus at Abrantes to the Mondego valley west of Ciudad Rodrigo.

The hostile offensive, however, was not to develop for some months yet, and the early part of the year 1810 was devoted to a French attack in force on Andalusia. In a rapid campaign Soult overran the whole province to the gates of Cadiz, where the remnants of, the Spanish forces, assisted by a British contingent under Graham and the Allied fleets succeeded in maintaining themselves. Here, as elsewhere, invaders were constantly worried by guerilla bands and partisan leaders. In the north and east of Spain the operations during the course of 1810 resulted less favourably for the French arms. Suchet held down Aragon, but was unable till the autumn to undertake anything outside the borders of that province; while the Catalonian rising was maintained in full flame and kept busy a large army, first under Augereau and then under Macdonald, which was not in a position to undertake any important operation till the end of the year, when siege was at length laid to Tortosa.

Meanwhile the three army corps of the Army of Portugal, 86,000 strong, under Massena, one of the ablest and most experienced of Napoleon's Marshals, began to assemble on the north-eastern frontier of Portugal from March onwards. It was not till June, however, that they were ready to commence active operations, and Wellington utilised to the full the breathing space thus granted him to perfect his measures for the defence of the country. The militia, numbering some 45,000 men, as well as the popular *levée en masse,* was called out; arrangements were made for the systematic evacuation of the whole area over which the enemy were likely to advance; and the construction of a vast entrenched camp covering Lisbon was completed. This camp, known as the lines of Torres Vedras, comprised two lines of works on a front of twenty-five miles from the Lower Tagus to the sea, and about twenty-five miles north of Lisbon, together with a third line close to that city intended to cover the embarkation of the army should this be necessary. The fortifications were as complete as time and labour could make them and their existence remained to the last entirely unsuspected by the French. Meanwhile the

Allied army of 60,000 men, of whom about half were British, were held ready in the upper Mondego valley. Hill's Second Division was detached in the Tagus valley to watch for any hostile advance in that quarter, while Craufurd's Light Division, east of the Coa, covered the front of the main body.

In June, Massena laid siege to the frontier fortress of Ciudad Rodrigo, and on its surrender, after a gallant defence of five weeks, assailed Craufurd on the Coa, forced him back over that river after a smart combat, and invested Almeida. The resistance of that place was cut short owing to the explosion of the magazine, which wrecked the town and left the governor with no choice but to capitulate, and after a further three weeks had been passed by the French in collecting supplies all was at last ready for the great offensive. Wellington, relieved of his fears of a simultaneous advance north and south of the Tagus, now drew in Hill to the main army, and was soon notified that Massena had chosen for the march of his 65,000 men what he described as "the worst road in Portugal"—that along the north bank of the Mondego to Coimbra. He at once concentrated his forces to fight, and on September 27 the French found their progress blocked by the whole British army arrayed for battle on the ridge of Bussaco. Their attacks, delivered in succession at two different points two miles apart, were beaten back with considerable loss, and the French Marshal realised that the enemy must be manoeuvred out of his position. He accordingly moved his whole army across a mountain path beyond the left flank of Wellington, who thereupon executed a deliberate and unhurried retirement, by Coimbra, to the lines of Torres Vedras. Massena followed under great difficulties; supplies were short, and hostile militia and guerilla bands infested his flanks and rear, cut his communications and captured his hospital and depot at Coimbra as soon as he had left that place. Finally, on October 10, he was brought up short before the lines, which, after careful reconnaissance, he declined to attack. In this he was wise, for Wellington could have opposed to his 55,000 men not only the 20,000 second line troops garrisoning the works, but also 58,000 of the field army, ready to deal with any force which should have broken its way through the defences. The French Marshal, with a stubborn resolution exceeding his adversary's expectations, maintained his position under ever-increasing difficulties for a whole month, and then only fell back some twenty-five miles to a strong position around Santarem, which Wellington in his turn felt but dared not attack.

In this situation of apparent stalemate the campaign of 1810 closed. But the true advantage lay with the British; the French had made their last and greatest effort against Portugal and had failed to achieve their object, and Wellington and his armies had set out on the first stage of that advance which, after many vicissitudes, several checks and more than one setback, was in the end to carry them forward into France to attend the final obsequies of Napoleon's Empire.

3. THE PENINSULAR WAR:
THE PERIOD OF TENSION
1811-1812

The new phase of the war, that opened with Massena's withdrawal from Portugal, was in its actual results indecisive, leaving the two contending armies at the end in much the same position as at the beginning of the period. None the less the initiative had passed to Wellington, and his adversaries were, for practically the whole of the two years, reduced to a defensive attitude, and compelled to await and parry blows in place of themselves delivering them. On the whole—at least to outward seeming—they were successful in maintaining their positions intact, but the resulting attrition of their armies was so great, and the strain on their resources so increasingly intense, as to leave them in no situation to withstand the powerful British offensive of 1813 and 1814.

The general situation in the Peninsula at the beginning of 1811 was as follows: In Catalonia, Suchet had captured Tortosa and was about to besiege Tarragona, the only fortress still holding out in that province. Soult had more or less subdued Andalusia, but was still held up before the walls of Cadiz; while the north and centre of Spain, with the exception of Galicia and part of the northern coast, though still disturbed by irregular bands, might be regarded as French occupied territory. In January, Soult, feeling himself strong enough to carry out his orders to cooperate with Massena, who was still at Santarem, by an advance against the south-eastern frontier of Portugal, moved up to the Guadiana, routed a Spanish army outside Badajoz and secured possession of that important fortress. Even had he been able to push his victorious career farther he would have been too late to assist Massena ; but immediately after the fall of the fortress he was forced to retrace his steps by serious news from Andalusia, where the Spaniards were undertaking an advance on Seville—which eventually came to nothing—and a combined force was attempting to raise the siege of Cadiz.

This expedition of 15,000 men, commanded by the Spanish General La Rena, and including 5000 British under Graham, was sent by sea from Cadiz to disembark at Algesiras and Tarifa, and move against the rear of the investing force under Victor. The unnecessary slowness of its advance, however, gave the latter time to draw off the bulk of his troops and fall unexpectedly on the Allied right flank and rear at Barrosa. Graham's men, though caught at a disadvantage, succeeded in beating off the French attack and inflicting serious loss on their enemies; but the failure of the Spaniards to cooperate in or exploit the victory destroyed all confidence between the Allies, who confined themselves to returning tamely to Cadiz at the very moment when Victor was preparing in despair to raze his works and abandon the siege. Soult, therefore, on his return found the situation restored in this quarter also.

In Portugal, however, fortune had turned decisively against the French. Early in March, Massena, whose army, despite the arrival of strong reinforcements, had sunk to less than 50,000 men, and had completely drained the country round Santarem of supplies and foodstuffs, commenced his retirement. He succeeded in slipping away unknown to Wellington and in gaining several marches on him; and even when his adversary realised what was toward he was unable, having only some 46,000 of all ranks at his disposal, to do more than harass the French rearguard under Ney, who conducted a series of brilliant delaying actions between Santarem and the Mondego. Finding the passages of that river blocked by the Portuguese irregulars, Massena turned eastwards short of Coimbra, and, falling back along the south bank of the river, assembled his army at the end of March in the Celorico-Guarda area, intending to move south to the Tagus valley and menace Portugal on a new line of invasion. Shortage of supplies, however, quickly brought his army to a halt, and Wellington, striking at his left flank, headed him off at Sabugal—one of the most brilliant actions fought by the British in the whole course of the war—and compelled him to fall back, uncovering the fortresses of Almeida and Ciudad Rodrigo, and seek safety and rest for his exhausted and discontented army in the Salamanca area.

In less than three weeks, however, the tenacious stubbornness of the old Marshal brought his troops once more forward to the offensive, for the purpose of raising the investment of Almeida, to cover which Wellington took up a position at Fuentes de Onoro with some 37,000 men, against his adversary's 48,000. After a vain attempt to storm the British centre, Massena succeeded in turning and forcing back their right wing, but only to find himself faced with a new battle-front too strong for him to assail. He therefore fell back once more, but his failure was offset by the daring escape of the Almeida garrison, which succeeded, thanks to culpable negligence on the part of its adversaries, in making its way through the line of investment to its own army, after destroying its guns and stores.

Meanwhile important events were taking place in Estremadura. As soon as Wellington was assured of Massena's retreat, he had despatched Beresford with 18,000 men to rescue Badajoz. That general, too late to accomplish this, none the less defeated at Campo Mayor and drove back over the Guadiana the weak hostile force left behind by Soult to cover the fortress, and began the siege. Unavoidable delays in opening the investment, and avoidable blunders in its conduct, gave Soult time to collect a force of 24,000 men for the relief of the place. Beresford, with his own troops and a reinforcement of 14,000 Spaniards under Blake, delivered at Albuera a battle which, despite Soult's superiority of generalship, was turned into a victory by the magnificent fighting of the British infantry, who left on the field close on 50 per cent of their effective strength. The shattered French army drew back, and Wellington, who, having left in Beira 30,000 men to watch the Army of Portugal, had hastened to Beresford's assistance with 10,000 men, was enabled to resume the siege.

Although the British commander fully realised that he had at his disposal only a short space before the French assembled in superior numbers before him, his conduct of operations against the fortress followed the same lines as, and met with no better fortune than, the earlier ones. Marmont, who had replaced Massena after Fuentes de Onoro, hurried with great promptitude to join Soult in the raising of the siege, and though Wellington also drew down his own forces from Beira, he even so found himself able to muster only 54,000 men against his adversaries' 60,000. He therefore drew off to a strong position between Elvas and Campo Mayor, and, when the Marshals were once more compelled to separate by want of food and risings in their rear, brought back his army to a rest area extending from north of the Tagus to the Guadiana, from which he could at need assail either Ciudad Rodrigo or Badajoz.

In August he moved once more to Beira, and took up a position to menace the former place. Marmont and Dorsenne, commanding the French Army of the North, which had all the summer been engaged in a vain attempt to subdue the Galician insurgents, advanced rapidly, caught him for once at a disadvantage, and forced him to fall back in haste to Sabugal, where they once more declined to accept the offered battle, and fell back to disperse in due course for subsistence. The British also took up winter quarters extending from Celorico to south of Ciudad Rodrigo, and a brilliant little exploit by Hill's detachment south of the Tagus at Arroyo Molinos put an end to the British operations of 1811.

In the east of Spain, although Macdonald in Catalonia was engaged for the greater part of the year in the recovery of the fortress of Figueras, which, surprised by the guerillas in April, held out till August, Suchet, going from success to success, reduced Tarragona, and moving into Valencia defeated Blake at Saguntum, and in January 1812 captured Valencia city and the remnants of the Spanish army. In Andalusia, however, the French suffered a set-back, Victor's expedition against Tarifa at the end of the year being unable to overcome the sturdy resistance of its Anglo-Spanish garrison.

The campaign of 1812 was to see a face put upon events far other from that of the previous year. It opened with two brilliant strokes by the British army against the fortresses of Ciudad Rodrigo and Badajoz, the twin French sally ports on the frontier between Portugal and Spain, which during the past two years had so greatly facilitated the attack of the one country and the defence of the other. Circumstances in June 1812 were favourable for the attack on Rodrigo, before which Wellington had assembled some 50,000 men and a fairly adequate siege train; Marmont's Army of Portugal, which was responsible for its safeguard, had been weakened by a strong detachment despatched by the Emperor's order to assist Suchet in Valencia, and was scattered in widespread cantonments from the Galician border to La Mancha; while the reorganisation of all the French armies in Spain, then in progress, consequent on the growing menace of war with Russia, was bound to militate against any speedy attempt to succour the fortress. When, therefore, the British army, assembled on the Agueda, advanced and completed the investment on January 8, the siege was carried through undisturbed to the final assault, which took place on the twelfth day and was completely successful, though at the cost of somewhat severe losses; indeed news of the opening of the attack on the fortress only reached Marmont four days before its fall, and he so clearly realised the hopelessness of trying to relieve it that he made no attempt even to concentrate his army for that purpose—and that although his whole siege train was within the place and fell into British hands with it.

After some weeks spent in refitting and re-provisioning his new prize, Wellington, at the end of February, moved south against Badajoz; his siege train was sent round by sea, and the whole of the army marched off with him, the care of the frontier of Beira against Marmont being left entirely to the Spanish and Portuguese. Soult from Andalusia was hardly likely to be able to collect sufficient forces to relieve the place in face of the 60,000 British now assailing it unless he were joined by Marmont; nevertheless, two detachments under Graham and Hill were pushed out to east and south-east, and drove back the French corps of observation in Estremadura towards the Sierra Morena, and the operations against the fortress itself were pressed with all possible vigour from March 16 onwards. The works were formidable and the defence resolute and skilful; none the less, the storm could be ordered for April 6. The two main British assaults were beaten off with ghastly loss, but the subsidiary columns broke into the place, and compelled its surrender. The greatness of the achievement was marred by the disgraceful scenes of crime and disorder that took place within the city after its fall.

The efforts of the French Marshals to interrupt the siege were half-hearted and failed of all effect. Soult advanced with a weak force, but, finding himself opposed by the covering detachments of Hill and Graham, and seeing no sign of Marmont, who had earlier promised to come to his aid but had since been forbidden to do so by orders from Paris, fell back to restore the situation in Andalusia, which had, as usual, become menacing after his departure. Marmont on his side had raided Beira, scattered the weak forces in his front, and penetrated to Castello Branco, but, being unable to operate against the fortresses owing to the loss of his siege train, was eventually compelled by the advance of the British army from Badajoz against his left flank and rear to retire hurriedly to the Salamanca area, where his army occupied its former cantonments. Wellington also dispersed his forces for rest and refitment over a broad space from the Douro to beyond the Guadiana, but ordered Hill in Estremadura to attack Almaraz on the Tagus. The successful surprise and destruction of the bridge at that point severed all direct communication between Soult and Marmont, while the simultaneous restoration of the passage at Alcantara shortened by 100 miles the British lateral route across that river, and greatly facilitated their future operations on either side of it.

Meanwhile, Napoleon, having left Paris to take command of his forces against Russia, had entrusted to Joseph, assisted by Jourdan, the task of controlling and coordinating the operations of his various mutually jealous and insubordinate commanders in the Peninsula. But before the new commander-in-chief had fairly assumed the reins Wellington was on the move against Marmont. He had arranged for a series of diversions to assist the main operation by distracting the attention of all the French commanders who might be able to assist him; the Army of the North under Caffarelli was to be amused by the Galicians and the guerilla of Cantabria, aided by a British fleet under Popham operating off the northern coast of Spain; Hill and the Spaniards would give Soult ample employment; and a force was to be sent from Sicily (where, as will be remembered, there was a strong British contingent in garrison, now under Lord William Bentinck) to land on the east coast of Spain and alarm Suchet for the safety of his new conquests. In mid-June Wellington commenced his advance against Marmont's widely scattered army, but instead of pushing forward to defeat it before it could assemble, sat down to invest the forts of Salamanca, the resistance of which delayed him for ten days and caused him to lose a second excellent chance of attacking his enemy, who had rashly pushed forward with part of his army, with superior numbers and at an advantage. The French Marshal then fell back, followed by his adversary, to the north bank of the Douro between Toro and Valladolid, where a deadlock of a fortnight took place, Marmont awaiting reinforcements from the Army of the North, which, thanks to the successful operations of Popham and his Spanish allies, failed to materialise, Wellington looking vainly for the arrival of the Galicians on the French right and rear, and disturbed to hear that the Sicilian expedition was also hanging fire. At length Marmont assumed the offensive in his turn, and manoeuvring always to turn his enemy's right, forced him to fall back rapidly to the Tormes at Salamanca. Here, on July 22, while striving to extend his left and intensify his menace to the British line of retreat on Ciudad Rodrigo, he spread his army out on so wide a front as to expose it to a counter-stroke by Wellington; the battle, which only commenced at 4 p.m., ended by nightfall in the utter defeat of the French. Clausel, who succeeded the wounded Marshal in command of the beaten remnants, fell back at his utmost speed to the Douro, being unable even to effect a junction with the reinforcements brought up, just too late, from Madrid by Joseph in person. Wellington, following up his victory with less energy than might have been expected, on hearing that his beaten foes were in safety behind the Douro, turned his main body in the direction of the capital, which Joseph, retiring hurriedly before him, was compelled to evacuate without fighting. On August 12 the British effected their triumphal entry amid immense popular enthusiasm.

The consequences of this success were felt from end to end of the Peninsula. Soult saw himself at last compelled, with death in his heart, to raise the siege of Cadiz and abandon his cherished possession of Andalusia; this he safely effected, and by September had united in Valencia with Suchet, who had also been rallied by Joseph and his army. Here, then, was assembled a very strong force which it was determined to use for a counter-stroke against Wellington. Suchet, alarmed by the presence in his front not only of strong Spanish forces but of the 8000 British from Sicily who had at last effected their landing at Alicante, was unable to spare any troops from his own army, but a force of 60,000 men was finally set in motion in the direction of Madrid. This was now guarded only by Hill with some 30,000 men, for Wellington with the other half of his army had moved north against Clausel, and having forced him back from the line of Douro to beyond Burgos, was engaged in the siege of that petty fortress with hopelessly inadequate means. Its resistance was most gallant, and after five assaults had been repulsed the British commander, finding that Clausel had been reinforced by part of the Army of the North and was advancing against him with 50,000 men against his own 35,000, saw himself compelled to raise the blockade and fall back on the road by which he had come. Unable even to hold the line of the Douro in face of the menace to his rear, he sent orders to Hill to leave Madrid and join him on the Tormes, and himself withdrew to that river, where he assembled his whole force of 70,000 men in his old positions around Salamanca. The massed French armies—the Army of Portugal, which had followed him from Burgos, and Soult's and Joseph's troops, who had reoccupied Madrid and pressed on after Hill —numbered 90,000, but, fearing a repetition of Marmont's disaster, they lost the chance of bringing Wellington to battle and allowed him to draw off before their eyes towards Ciudad Rodrigo. The last stages of the British retreat, though unmolested by the enemy, were attended by widespread indiscipline and disorder comparable to those of the retreat to Coruna— and as little excusable. At length, however, the army was dispersed in winter quarters in Central Portugal between the Mondego and the Tagus.

Elsewhere in Spain throughout the year the guerilla activity had continued unchecked ; but the British contingent in Valencia had remained immobile, paralysed by frequent changes of command and quarrels with its allies.

In appearance, then, the campaign of 1812, as that of 1811, had been indecisive, and its close saw the British back in their old quarters in Portugal. None the less great things had in reality been achieved. The French power in Spain had been undermined to its foundations; their hold on Andalusia and the south had been irretrievably lost, and their tenure of all the central parts of the country rendered insecure; while the British army had proved itself not only a defensive but an offensive weapon of the first order, which its commander was fully capable of wielding in either form of war to the fullest possible effect. In a word, the future was for the British arms full of a promise which the next two years were splendidly to redeem.

4. THE PENINSULAR WAR:
THE BRITISH COUNTER-OFFENSIVE
1813-1814

Napoleon's expedition to Moscow, undertaken with the largest army he had hitherto led into the field, ended, thanks to the stubbornness of the Russian resistance and the rigours of the Russian winter, in one of the most stupendous catastrophes known in the history of modern times, and at the end of the year he was back in Paris, having left the whole of his mighty army dead or captive behind him, and all Central Europe, so long held beneath his heel, simmering with revolt against his dominion. While he was exerting himself in the spring of 1813 to raise another Grand Army, no longer for offence, but for the maintenance of his far-flung Empire, and ordering large contingents to be sent back from the Peninsula to help form the nucleus of the new levies, Prussia had joined Russia in arms against him, and Austria and Sweden were only awaiting a favourable moment to declare themselves on the same side. A new Coalition, more formidable than any of its predecessors, because founded on a widespread revolt of the peoples rather than on the wills of sovereigns and cabinets, now threatened as never before the whole fabric of the Napoleonic system.

For the moment, however, affairs were quiet in the Peninsula, for the Allied armies, fatigued by the exertions and hardships of the Burgos retreat, and much reduced in strength, were in urgent need of a long period of repose. The French, therefore, whose forces had taken up new cantonments from Le Mancha in the south to Leon in the north, were left at leisure to undertake an operation which had long been called for by the obvious necessities of their situation and by reiterated instructions from Paris,—the clearing of the area on either side of the Bayonne—Madrid high road, their main line of communications with France, from the guerilla bands infesting it on either flank. The task, however, was infinitely more lengthy and necessitated the employment of far larger forces than had been calculated either at Paris or at Madrid, and eventually all the Army of the North, under Clausel, was at work in Navarre, on the southern side of the road, and the greater part of the Army of Portugal, under Foy, in Biscay, on the northern side. Their operations continued from February to June 1813, and at the end of these four months, though the irregulars had been harried and had lost much ground, they were still at large and unsubdued, while their adversaries were even more worn out by hard marching and fighting with little tangible result to show for it all.

Meanwhile the remaining French armies—those of the Centre (D'Erlon) and South (Gazan) and part of the Army of Portugal (Reille)—were resting quietly in their cantonments, and Wellington was drawing up his plan of campaign, which was to be put into execution in the middle of May. His force of 80,000 men was to advance in two masses, the one from Ciudad Rodrigo on Salamanca, the other from Tras-os-Montes north of the Douro against the line of the Esla. When the French advanced detachments had been driven back from both these areas the whole Allied force was to reunite north of the Douro and move against the French line of communications, the Burgos—Madrid road, opening for itself as it advanced new bases and lines of supply on the northern coast of Spain, and abandoning those with Portugal. These preliminary movements of the southern force were successfully carried out in accordance with the programme; but a delay in the passage of the Esla by the northern force gave time for the French to assemble some 57,000 men north of Valladolid to oppose any further Allied advance eastwards. Wellington, however, adhered to his original plan of advancing northeastwards by his left, his army moving in four columns, Giron's Spaniards on the left, Graham and the main body of the army under his own command in the centre, and Hill on the right, by way of Medina de Rio Seco, Palencia and north of Burgos to the upper Ebro. The French, in view of this constant threat to their right and rear, abandoned in succession Valladolid, Burgos and the line of the Ebro, and fell back along the Madrid—Bayonne main road in the hope of rallying Clausel and Foy before standing to deliver battle. On June 21, however, they were forced to stand and fight in a disadvantageous position at Vitoria, in order to secure time for the withdrawal of their huge convoy of impedimenta. Wellington planned to envelop both their wings with Hill's and Graham's columns, but the latter failed to press his attack home on the decisive flank in time to prevent the escape of the enemy after a creditable resistance. The material results of the day were, however, immense; all the French artillery, 150 guns, and the whole of their baggage and material were taken, and the beaten army, thrown off its main line of retreat, fell back in great disorder and much demoralised to Pamplona. The two French detached forces which had failed to arrive in time for the battle were fortunate in being able to make their escape and rejoin the main army behind the Bidassoa; Foy skilfully made his way past the northern flank of the British army to Bayonne, and Clausel withdrew by a very roundabout route down the Ebro to Saragossa and thence back into France by Jaca. Wellington, who had made little attempt to exploit his victory, confined himself to driving back the French rearguards from the Pyrenees passes and establishing his main army on and in rear of that range to cover the sieges of the petty fortresses, San Sebastian and Pamplona, the capture of which he regarded as an essential preliminary to any advance into France. And indeed he might well remain content for the present with his masterly operations of the past six weeks, the results of which had been even beyond his highest hopes; not only had they freed the whole of Northern and Central Spain, and hurled down King Joseph's power in ruins, but they had decided Austria, hitherto wavering at the sight of Napoleon's victories over Russia and Prussia in Germany, to throw her sword into the scale on the Allied side.

A painful contrast to the triumphant British campaign in the north of Spain was afforded by the futile series of operations conducted by Murray in the east, against Suchet. After the latter had assumed the offensive in April and been smartly repulsed at Castalla, Wellington instructed his subordinate to undertake an expedition against the French rear in Catalonia, with the double object of favouring an advance by the

Spaniards against Valencia, and preventing Suchet from sending any assistance to Joseph. The latter purpose was certainly achieved, but Murray's hesitation and folly led to a shameful fiasco before Tarragona, and ruined excellent chances of obtaining a valuable local success. After hovering off the Catalonian coast for three weeks and accomplishing nothing, the expedition returned in disgrace to Alicante, where the Spaniards also had failed to take any advantage of the favourable situation resultant on the despatch of large hostile forces to rescue Tarragona, and it was the news of the disasters in the north rather than any activity on the part of the Allies on his own front that eventually caused Suchet in July to commence his withdrawal from the province of Valencia.

Napoleon who, after his victory at Bautzen, at the end of May had concluded a two months' armistice with his adversaries in Germany, had sent Soult to take command against Wellington as soon as he heard of the fatal battle of Vitoria. The Marshal on his arrival set vigorously to work to rearm and refit his broken troops and restore their discipline and morale, and in a fortnight he considered himself in a position to assume the offensive. During this period Graham, who was conducting the siege of San Sebastian, had been beaten off in a first attempt to storm the place, thanks to the gallant defence of the French garrison under Rey, and to the defective arrangements for the assault; and Soult, having no news of Pamplona and fearing it might be in danger, decided to raise the siege by an attack on the British right wing. Of the four corps in which his army was organised, two under Reille and Clausel were to drive the British from Roncesvalles, another, under D'Erlon, to force the Maya Pass, and both columns were then to converge on Pamplona. The fourth corps, Villatte's, was left on the Lower Bidassoa to cover Bayonne against a possible counter-offensive by the Allied left.

On July 25 the British advanced troops were forced back after fierce fighting both from Roncesvalles and from Maya, but whereas D'Erlon's column was unable to make much progress in the Bastan valley beyond the latter pass, the British right retreated with unnecessary precipitation to within 2 miles of Pamplona, where it finally turned to stand at Sorauren. The French followed up more slowly, and Wellington, who had received tardy information of the danger on this flank, was thus enabled to assemble a force which, though considerably inferior to that of his adversary, proved sufficient to inflict on him a bloody repulse. Soult then planned to withdraw his left wing from before Sorauren, and unite it with D'Erlon's corps for a fresh operation against the Allied centre, but counter-attacked while in the act of executing this perilous manoeuvre, Reille and Clausel were defeated and driven northwards in disorder; part made their escape to St. Jean Pied de Port, the greater part fell back upon D'Erlon, who was compelled to abandon his attack on the British centre and seek safety by the route along the upper Bidassoa. Although harried by the British divisions of the centre and left, and suffering considerable losses in the process, the French main body made its escape to rallying positions on the heights of Vera, only to be unceremoniously hurled from them by the first arriving troops of their pursuers, and compelled to fall back to its old lines in the lower Bidassoa and Nive valleys. Once more, however, Wellington, ignorant of the state of affairs in Germany and unwilling to undertake such an operation as the invasion of France without thorough preparation, refrained from pressing his advantage, and recommenced the two sieges which had been interrupted by Soult's advance, his army being disposed in its former covering line on the crest of the mountains.

While the French were resting and fortifying a defensive position on a long front of twenty miles from the mouth of the Bidassoa by way of Vera and Sarre to Ainhoa, the siege of San Sebastian was being pressed with renewed vigour, and by the end of August all was ready for the delivery of the second assault. It was little better managed, and seemed likely to meet with little better success than the preceding one, when a lucky explosion allowed the stormers to force an entry amid the resulting confusion; and while Rey retired to the castle, which only capitulated after renewed battering a week later, the victorious assailants gave themselves up to an orgy of violence and drunkenness that surpassed even the similar disgraceful scenes at Ciudad Rodrigo and Badajoz. On the very day of the assault Soult made an attempt to break the investment by pushing his right wing forward over the Bidassoa between Vera and the sea, but his attack was not vigorously pressed and was easily beaten off, the Spaniards bearing the brunt of the combat and acquitting themselves with great credit. Relieved by the fall of San Sebastian of one of his preoccupations, and of another by the news that Austria had joined the Coalition against Napoleon, who would now be prevented by the renewal of hostilities in Germany from detaching any troops to the front in South France, Wellington now determined in his turn to attempt the passage of the Bidassoa. More skilful and more fortunate than his adversary, he successfully established his left wing under Hope on the eastern bank near the mouth of the river, while his left centre under Alten drove back the French from Vera to the Rhune mountain. Soult's generalship and the fighting spirit of his troops on this day were alike of inferior quality, but once more the British general refrained from pursuing his advance until the fall of Pamplona, which did not take place till the end of October, finally secured his rear. The French had made good use of the opportunity thus afforded them of strengthening their new positions southwest and south of St. Jean de Luz and on the Rhune by the time the Allies attacked on November 10, but their labour was wasted. In the so-called Battle of the Nivelle, where the Allies' 90,000 men were opposed to Soult's 57,000, Wellington demonstrated against the French wings with Hope's and Hill's corps, while his centre under Beresford broke through their centre on the Rhune, and the defenders, abandoning their positions all along the line, retreated to the line of the Nive on either side of Bayonne. Wellington, following them up, threw Hill's corps over the upper course of that river with a view to turning Soult's left, and by this division of his forces gave the Marshal an opportunity—which he was not slow to seize—of throwing himself with all his forces on a half of the Allied army. However, he profited little in the end from his attacks, which were delivered first against Hope's wing between the lower Nive and the sea and then against Hill on the heights of St. Pierre beyond the river, where the French were with difficulty repulsed in one of the hardest fought encounters of the war.

Bad weather now enforced a pause in the operations, lasting till the end of 1813, during which period both combatants were reduced in numbers, the French by the urgent demands of the Emperor's armies for reinforcements of trained men, the Allies by the refusal of Wellington, who was well aware of the importance, from the point of view of the security of his troops and the success of his future operations, of the necessity of not arousing the hostility of the population, to take with him into France any Spanish troops with a tendency to plunder. Thus, by January 1814, Soult, who could dispose of no more than 48,000 men against his opponent's 80,000, was preparing to abandon Bayonne to its own resources, and to draw off his army to a new line facing south-west behind the Adour and the Gave d'Oloron.

In the east of Spain, Bentinck, who had replaced Murray and was soon in his turn to give way to Clinton, had since July been following up Suchet in his leisurely withdrawal along the coast from Valencia by Tortosa and Tarragona to Barcelona, his advance against the latter city being sharply checked at Ordal. His successor made no further attempt to press his adversary, who by the end of the year had assembled his forces around Gerona, and there halted to await the result of a new diplomatic move by Napoleon. The latter, having suffered a complete defeat at the hands of embattled Europe at Leipzig, had withdrawn the remnants of his army into France, and was there preparing for that magnificent defensive campaign of 1814 which Wellington and many good judges after him considered to be perhaps the finest example of his genius for war. Meanwhile, he had devised a scheme for freeing himself from the menace of Wellington's armies on his southern frontier, and recovering the use of his own troops in that theatre by the signature of the Treaty of Valençay with his prisoner Ferdinand VII., in accordance with the terms of which the latter, in exchange for his restoration to the Spanish throne, engaged to effect the withdrawal of all the contending forces from Spanish territory. This, however, the Cortes, the actual government of Spain, refused to ratify, and, accordingly, Suchet remained in possession of Northern Catalonia until the conclusion of hostilities.

Meanwhile the Allies were preparing to invade France from the east, and Wellington set to work to force Soult's new defensive line. While Hope on the left with the help of the fleet crossed the Adour below Bayonne, and circling round to north and east of that place completed its investment, the main body of the Allies drove the French in succession from the Gave d'Oloron and the Gave de Pau, and attacked them in their chosen battle position at Orthez. After some vicissitudes the hostile right and centre were beaten from their ground, and the whole forced to retreat hurriedly behind the upper Adour at Aire. From this town Soult determined to effect his further retirement eastwards and south-eastwards along the foot of the Pyrenees so as to divert the Allies from a direct invasion of France, and approach nearer to Suchet's army, which he hoped might thus be induced to come to his assistance. Wellington, after detaching a force to occupy Bordeaux, where the population were eager to revolt against Napoleon and to raise the white flag of the Bourbons, followed up the retreating French army towards Toulouse. At the beginning of April the Marshal halted once more on the line of the Garonne, and stood to fight around that city. The battle that ensued was decided after several premature and partial efforts by the advance of the main column of attack under Beresford, along the foot of the hills occupied by the French right, and the storming of those heights, and Soult, menaced with investment within the walls, made haste to withdraw his army before it was too late. The battle was needless waste of life on both sides, as was a fruitless sortie by the garrison of Bayonne a few days later; for the armies of the Coalition had already, after many set-backs, forced their way into Paris, compelled Napoleon to abdicate the Imperial throne, and put an end alike to the war and to French supremacy in Europe.

Thus the Peninsular War, the mightiest conflict hitherto fought by the British army, ended in a blaze of glory. During its course, to use Napier's words, England "expended more than one hundred million sterling on her own operations; she subsidised both Spain and Portugal, and with her supplies of clothing, arms and ammunition, maintained the armies of each, even to the guerillas. From 30,000 to 70,000 British troops were employed by her; and while her naval forces harassed the French with descents upon the coasts, and supplied the Spaniards with arms and stores and money after every defeat, her land forces fought and won nineteen pitched battles and innumerable combats, made or sustained ten sieges, twice expelled the French from Portugal, preserved Alicante, Cartagena, Tarifa, Cadiz, Lisbon; they killed, wounded and took 200,000 enemies, and the bones of 40,000 British soldiers lie scattered on the plains and mountains of the Peninsula. For Portugal she reorganised a native army and supplied officers who led it to victory; and to the whole Peninsula she gave a General whose like has seldom gone forth to conquer."

5. The Battle in Wellington's Day

As a pendant to the above narrative of the Peninsular campaigns let us try to picture to ourselves a typical battle scene of these times, as we have already done for the epochs of Cromwell and Marlborough.

From a point somewhere in rear of the British front we see the ground sloping gently up before us to a crest forming a skyline—bare of features to our immediate front, crowned to right with a small coppice, to the left with a larger wood. In a slight hollow close by, and about a hundred yards from the crest, sheltered from view and fire there is resting a battalion of British infantry, their packs thrown off and their arms piled; the men lying or sitting about in small groups; the officers in front forming a cluster round their colonel. The uniforms of the rank and file are without exception war-worn and much faded by exposure to weather, and a good proportion are attired in heterogeneous and obviously improvised articles of kit; the majority, however, are wearing the red coat, with its horizontal white stripes across the front, and the two white belts for bayonet and cartridge pouch crossing over the chest, grey trousers and boots, and black shako with crest and plume, which is the regulation dress of the line regiments. The officers' attires are equally variegated, but, it would seem, more from individual choice than from necessity; tunics are blue, brown, grey or red; short-coated or tailed according to the wearer's taste; while one or two cocked hats are to be seen among the shakos. The general effect is that of a body of men which has more important matters to consider than insistence on strict uniformity in clothing and equipment ; for men and officers alike bear the look of veterans inured to war and imbued with a well-founded confidence in themselves and their comrades.

On either flank of this unit which has attracted our particular attention, as far as the eye can reach along the ridge, lie at ease other similar units waiting for the time for action; while far off to the right beyond the coppice the sun gleaming on steel betrays the presence of a strong body of mounted troops, covering the flank of the line of battle. To the front, as we have said, our view is limited by the crest; but, from beyond, a continuous crackle of small-arm fire intermingled at moments with the deeper thud of guns, and an occasional bullet whining over our heads, warns us that an engagement of some importance is toward.

On moving forward to the skyline we see before us a level glacis-like slope stretching forward and downward for some 500 yards to a stream running in the bottom of the valley. Beyond this the ground rises once more, but more abruptly, to a second ridge, on which can be distinguished dark masses of hostile troops and a long line of enemy guns periodically veiled in the clouds of smoke from their discharge. Along the lower slopes of the valley on either side of the stream there is incessant bickering of rifle fire, where our own riflemen, who in their dark green uniforms can barely be distinguished amid the trees and scrub, are warmly engaged with the French skirmishers and appear to be holding their own successfully, at any rate for the moment. Along the crest of the ridge on which we stand there are none of our own troops to be seen, with the exception of two batteries, the one concealed near the edge of the coppice to our right, the other in a more prominent and exposed position on a knoll to our left; and quite near to us a mounted officer—to judge from his cocked hat and frock coat, and the numerous staff following him, a general of considerable rank, probably the divisional commander in charge of this sector of the front.

As we turn our eyes once more in the direction of the enemy we see that his columns are already in motion. To right and left of the line of his guns the dark masses emerge from the billowing smoke and descend at a rapid pace towards the stream. We fix our gaze on one particular column which appears to be making straight for the point on the ridge where the general and his staff are standing; this column appears to consist of about a battalion, formed on a depth of twelve men and a front of sixty[1]—a formation which is pretty general throughout the attacking force, though here and there may be seen deeper and narrower columns, with about half the frontage and twice the depth of their neighbours.[2] As we watch our chosen column it is seen crossing the brook and slowly ascending the slope of the British ridge, pressing' back before it our scattered riflemen. The latter, however, retire coolly and at their leisure, frequently halting and turning to fire at the advancing enemy, while one or two daring spirits even march level with and on the flanks of the attacking mass, galling them with bullets to which no reply is possible. Nevertheless, the French progress continues unchecked and presently brings them to within a short distance of the crest, from which can plainly be distinguished the shakos, blue coats and white trousers of a French line regiment, and the cocked hats and trailing scabbards of the officers at the head of their men.

Suddenly from behind us is heard, above the crack of the rifles and the redoubled thunder of the guns, both our own and the enemy's, the measured tramp of marching men, and turning we see the long red lines of our own troops, with bayonets fixed and arms at the shoulder steadily approaching the crest. A few seconds, and they are halted by a sharp word of command, full in view of the enemy. The latter, less than 100 yards now from their goal, halt at the sight, and the rear companies begin to double out to extend the front. But scarcely has the movement been begun, when the long line

---

1. A battalion in column of divisions (*i.e.* on a front of two companies, each front-line company followed by three other companies, each company being deployed in three ranks).
2. Battalions in columns of deployed companies one behind the other.

of British muskets, far overlapping the hostile mass on either flank, comes up to the "Present"; there is the crash of a volley, and the French column is veiled from sight in a cloud of smoke, which is ripped and torn and flung into fantastic whirls and billows by two more discharges. For some minutes nothing can be distinguished; then as the air clears the hostile column, sadly diminished in numbers and disordered in array, is seen hastily falling back down the hill, a heap of motionless and prostrate figures marking the spot where its progress was stayed. Meanwhile the victorious defenders of the ridge .closing up the few gaps in their ranks, are reloading and making ready to follow up their defeated adversaries; but an *aide-de-camp* from the general galloping up points to the strong bodies of enemy troops looming ominous on the far ridge, and the line, leisurely turning about, retires to its sheltering hollow, and lies down once more under cover. Only the riflemen make their way down the slope, galling the retreating French mass with their fire, and resume their former position in the valley bottom on the banks of the stream, beyond which fresh enemy troops, undeterred by the repulse of their comrades, are massing preparatory to a renewal of the assault.

6. Minor Operations in Europe and Elsewhere 1809-1814

The great drama of the Peninsular War, and the glorious achievements of Wellington and his armies, have naturally monopolised the attention of historians to the exclusion of almost everything else between 1809 and 1814. None the less, the British army was concerned in more than one minor enterprise during this period, and these must now be briefly noticed.

The most important was the joint expedition to the Low Countries in 1809, involving the largest army that had ever yet sailed from our shores. Intended to assist Austria in her contest with Napoleon by striking at the vulnerable northern flank of the French Empire, it was carried out by a force of 40,000 men under Chatham and a powerful fleet under Strachan, the first objective being the fortified city of Antwerp. A series of misfortunes dogged the enterprise from the start; bad weather delayed the disembarkation, and confined operations to the north bank of the Scheldt; the resistance of Flushing on Walcheren Island delayed the advance at a time when speed was all important; dissensions between the admiral and the general finally brought operations to a standstill; and an outbreak of malignant fever, which laid low a third of the force, completed the tale of mishaps and caused the abandonment of the expedition as a disastrous failure.

In Sicily, where we left Stuart in garrison with some 15,000 men, little of moment was accomplished. Some minor conquests were made in the Ionian Islands, off the west coast of Greece, and an attack on Sicily by the troops of Murat, who had been raised by Napoleon to the throne of Naples, was successfully repulsed. For the rest, interminable quarrels with the exiled Bourbon Court in Sicily and the indecision of the British Government effectually paralysed the energies of our force, until, as we have seen, the time came for the despatch of a large proportion of it to the Peninsula. The remainder, reinforced by the beginning of 1814 to some 14,000 men, were then engaged in a military promenade against the French possessions in Northern Italy, which had led them from Leghorn, by way of Spezia, to Genoa, when the news of Napoleon's abdication put an end to hostilities.

In the West Indies the British, despite the usual serious drain of disease, secured their position by the capture, in a series of well-conducted operations, of the French strongholds of Martinique and Guadeloupe and of the Dutch islands, thus establishing their supremacy throughout the Caribbean Sea. In the East an attempt was made in 1803 to complete the occupation of the island of Ceylon, the coastal parts of which, as has been narrated, had been conquered from the Dutch during the war with the French Revolution. The interior of the island was overrun with little resistance, and the Cingalese capital of Kandy was garrisoned by a small force of troops; some months later, however, these were beleaguered and induced to capitulate and treacherously massacred, and no attempt was made for the time, being to avenge them. As some compensation for this disaster in the East Indies, Mauritius and Bourbon fell into the hands of a British expedition from India in the course of the year 1810, and in the following year a force of 12,000 men under Auchmuty landed on the Dutch island of Java, garrisoned by 20,000 good troops, stormed the enemy's strong and well-fortified entrenched camp in the face of a two to one superiority, and compelled a capitulation after a six weeks' campaign—one of the most brilliant little affairs of its kind in the history of the British army.

One more minor expedition only remains to be mentioned—that sent in December 1813 under Graham to support the revolt of the adherents of the House of Orange against the French in Holland; 6,000 troops were landed west of Bergen-op-Zoom, and arrangements made with a Prussian force which had entered the country from the east, for a joint attack on Antwerp. The Prussian failure to do their part caused the enterprise to miscarry, but a month later Graham, on his own initiative, attempted to surprise Bergen-op-Zoom. His columns forced an entry at several points, but were driven out by a rally of the garrison, and with such heavy casualties that their commander had no choice but to remain inactive during the few remaining weeks of the war.

CHAPTER 10

The American War and the Waterloo Campaign
1812-1815

1. THE WAR WITH THE UNITED STATES
1812-1815

Simultaneously with the Titanic struggle with Napoleonic France, Great Britain became involved in the summer of 1812 in a second conflict with a great Power—one which in less strenuous days would have absorbed all her energies, but was regarded apparently by contemporaries, and certainly by posterity, as merely a "side show" to the greater events of the time in Europe.

The causes of dispute which finally arrayed England and the United States against each other had been long outstanding, in fact, ever since the former Power's declaration of war with France in 1803, and were the result of the strenuous commercial conflict in which England was engaged and our infringement of what Americans considered to be their rights as neutrals. It was most unfortunate, however, for the States that they only resolved—owing largely to skilful French diplomacy— to appeal to arms when the Napoleonic Empire, long past its zenith, was about to take its first plunge into disaster, and when affairs in the Peninsula had turned decidedly in favour of Great Britain.

When war finally broke out in July 1812, the first and most obvious objective for the armies and fleets of the United States was Canada, and it was confidently expected by all Americans that the conquest of this, the most valuable of their enemy's overseas possessions, would be only a military promenade. Indeed it seemed unlikely that Canada, with her weak armed forces, under command of Prevost, numbering barely 22,000, of which only four battalions were British regulars, her sparse population of 400,000, and her undefended frontier of 1,400 miles between Lake Superior and the Atlantic coast, could for long make head against the eight millions of her adversary, who could place in the field 36,000 trained and close on 100,000 partly trained men. Nevertheless, the seemingly impossible was accomplished; and the story of this remarkable but forgotten feat of arms must now be briefly narrated.

As about half of the long frontier between the contending armies is formed by the water of the great lakes, the command of these lakes was realised by both sides to be of the highest importance, and was bitterly contested throughout the war. In the earlier stages this command was in the hands of the Canadians, but in view of the superior shipbuilding resources of their adversaries it was at best precarious, and, in fact, was always menaced, and more than once—though never permanently—lost.

The American plan of campaign for 1812 comprised three widely separated attacks, one against Amherstburg, a fortified post on the isthmus between Lakes Huron and Erie; a second against the frontier on the Niagara River, between Lakes Erie and Ontario, and a third by the time-honoured route up Lake Champlain and the Richelieu River against the line of the St. Lawrence between Quebec and Montreal. All three were disastrous failures. The force engaged in the first was defeated and compelled to capitulate in the open field, and though the attack was renewed in January 1813 it met with no better success; while in this sector of the front, more to the north-west, the Canadians scored a subsidiary but important point by the seizure of Fort Mackinac at the north end of Lake Huron, which they held till the close of the war against all efforts to retake it. The American column operating in the Niagara sector, after establishing itself on the west bank of that river, was thrust back by the local British commander, Brock, who unhappily fell in the moment of victory; while the third expedition in the Richelieu dwindled away to nothing but a futile demonstration. Only at sea, where the American frigates, in a series of single combats with hostile ships, gained a series of striking and unexpected victories, did any success attend the arms of the United States during this year.

Nevertheless, the main lines of operation for 1813 were as in the previous year, except that the various attacks were to be carried out in greater strength and to be more carefully combined. Moreover, the American flotillas on the lakes were now in a position to render valuable assistance to the land forces. Early in the year the naval control of Lake Ontario was temporarily wrested from the Canadians; an American force was shipped across to raid and burn York (now Toronto), the capital of Upper Canada, and thence sailed to open the campaign on the Niagara front. The Canadians were driven from their fortified posts there and forced to retire westward, and their situation was not improved by the miscarriage of a diversion against the American naval base opposite Kingston. Meanwhile matters had gone even worse on Lake Erie, where the Canadian flotilla had been completely defeated and destroyed, and control of the lake permanently secured by the enemy; this in turn compelled the force holding Amherstburg to evacuate that place and fall back eastwards along the northern shore, during which movement it was caught and completely dispersed.

The situation of Upper Canada was, at this moment, serious, but fortunately, prior to the disaster on Lake Erie, the lost command of Ontario had been regained, and the Americans forced back once more to the Niagara. Nor were they allowed even there to rest in peace; for at the end of the year Drummond, assuming command of the Canadian troops, in a vigorous little campaign first of all swept them from the west bank, and then, crossing over, took and destroyed all their fortifications on the farther shore. Meanwhile, the American offensive against Lower Canada, carried out concentrically by two columns advancing from Lake Champlain and down the St. Lawrence, had also failed, their forces being defeated before they could effect their junction.

1813 had thus brought a real but not decisive advantage to the United States, and this it was intended to exploit and extend in 1814 by a large-scale effort on the Niagara front, combined with subsidiary operations on the flanks against Fort Mackinac and in the Richelieu valley. But meanwhile the British fleet had definitely asserted its supremacy and tightened its blockade of the Atlantic coast, and reinforcements in considerable numbers were on their way to Canada, though the first batch (four battalions) only arrived in July. The Canadians opened the campaign with a successful raid on Oswego on Lake Ontario, while far away in the north-west the American attack on Mackinac was repulsed. At length, after many delays, the United States forces commenced their offensive in the Niagara sector, but their progress was checked in the hard-fought little action of Lundy's Lane, and they were compelled to retire to their fortifications once more. Drummond, advancing to invest them, was in turn checked, and it was not till the end of the campaigning season that the Americans had to admit failure and withdraw over the river. As some set-off to this a British counter-offensive undertaken by Prevost in person against the hostile forces in Lake Champlain ended, owing to an unfortunate misunderstanding between the sailors and the soldiers, in a humiliating fiasco at Plattsburg; the flotilla was defeated with heavy loss, and the army compelled to withdraw hurriedly to its starting-point.

During the latter course of this year the British had assembled in American waters sufficient armed forces to enable them to take the initiative and open offensive operations against the mainland of the United States. One detachment from Halifax occupied Eastern Maine as far as the Penobscot, and retained it till the peace. Another force of 4,000 men under Ross sailed boldly into Chesapeake Bay, marched on Washington and, driving off at Bladensburg the militia who attempted to oppose its advance, occupied the city, and only retired after burning all the public buildings, as a reprisal for the American destruction of York in the previous year. Re-embarking, it next assailed Baltimore, but was compelled to withdraw owing to the inability of the fleet to cooperate in the attack on that city. Reinforced to a strength of some 6,000, and under a new commander, Pakenham, the little army now undertook a more difficult enterprise against New Orleans, at the mouth of the Mississippi, and with infinite labour was transported by boat to within striking distance of the fortified lines which had been constructed by the Governor of the place, Andrew Jackson, who was later to become President of the United States; but the assault failed with the loss of the British commander and many men, and the force was with difficulty got away, only to be set to undertake a new enterprise against Mobile.

Peace had in actual fact been signed between Great Britain and the United States at Ghent before the disaster at New Orleans, and the news of it reached America just after the forts of Mobile had surrendered. Its terms left the main questions in dispute unsettled, and the futile bloodshed on the Mississippi was a fitting termination to a foolish war which should never have taken place, and of which the main result was to render both belligerents—more especially the United States, the aggressors—weaker and more embittered than before its commencement. Indeed the only people to emerge from it with enhanced credit were the Canadians, who had vindicated their right to national existence by a noteworthy display in arms.

2. The Waterloo Campaign
1815

While the greater part of the British army, which had fought and endured and triumphed in the Peninsula, was being despatched overseas to America, and many units were being disbanded, the Allies had drawn up in broad outline the terms of the peace settlement, and assembled a Congress at Vienna to settle the details. The British acquisitions under the treaty were the islands of Malta, Tobago, St. Lucia and Mauritius, while we also purchased from Holland the former Dutch colonies at the Cape of Good Hope and in the West Indies, which were actually held by us at the conclusion of hostilities. Graham's troops, together with most of the King's German Legion, formed an army of occupation in Belgium under the Prince of Orange, and the Allies sat down to bicker and wrangle over their spoils at Vienna. In this congenial task they were interrupted in March 1815 by the news that Napoleon had returned from Elba and re-assumed his crown, expelling the Bourbons, who, having during their long exile "learnt nothing and forgotten nothing", had quickly rendered themselves odious to their subjects. The Allies' work was thus to do all over again, and they quickly set about raising the necessary forces. To Wellington was naturally given the command of the British troops in Belgium, reinforced, with considerable difficulty, to a strength, inclusive of the King's German Legion, of some 36,000 men; there were also added contingents from the Netherlands, Brunswick and Nassau, bringing the total up to 93,000 men, with 192 guns. The quality even of the British regiments, who were young and inexperienced, was much inferior to that of the old Peninsular army, while the rest of the troops were not only raw, but also half-hearted in the cause for which they were about to fight.

Quartered in the Low Countries there was, in addition to Wellington's host, a Prussian army which, by June 1815, comprised 120,000 men, with 312 guns. The commander was Blücher, a "hussar General" of mediocre capacity but much energy, and a loyal colleague; 50 per cent of his troops were militia, who had seen little or no service.

Napoleon, who soon realised that he would have shortly to contend with all Europe in arms, and was by no means inclined to renew the experience of 1814 by awaiting an overwhelming attack within his own frontiers, determined to seize the chance to strike at Wellington and Blücher before the other Allies were ready. For this purpose he could dispose of a striking force of 124,000 men, with 370 guns—a scratch army of men trained indeed and inured to war, but knowing neither their comrades nor their officers, and therefore lacking in cohesion and discipline. He succeeded in assembling them on the northern frontier of France between Philippeville and Beaumont, by June 14, without the Allies becoming aware of it. At this time Wellington's and Blücher's armies were spread over an area of 100 miles by 50 between the Scheldt and the Meuse, the former to the west, the latter to the east, of the Charleroi—Brussels high road. The Emperor's plan was to strike at the inner flanks of his adversaries, believing that the impetuous Blücher, whose army could be assembled in two days, would afford him an opportunity of a battle before Wellington, whose forces would take a day longer to collect, and whose caution and prudence were well known, should come to the assistance of his ally; while if both British and Prussians refused battle they would be bound to retire in divergent directions towards their respective bases, Ostend and Aix-la-Chapelle, leaving the French to occupy Brussels and overrun Belgium—in themselves achievements of great moral and political importance.

On June 15 the French army crossed the frontier and attacked the Prussian outposts on the Sambre. Bad staff work, resulting in a late start, and skilful rearguard fighting on the part of the enemy delayed its progress, and by nightfall a considerable portion was still south of the river. Nevertheless, the right wing had forced the Prussians back to Ligny, while the left, under Ney, was approaching Quatre Bras, an important point on the shortest lateral road between the Allied armies. Blücher, on hearing of the hostile offensive, at once issued orders for his army to concentrate at Ligny, but Wellington, who only got definite news late in the evening, and suspected that the move might be a mere feint covering a real attack against his right—for which he felt extremely nervous throughout the campaign—delayed issuing instructions for the assembly of his force in the vicinity of the Brussels—Charleroi road till early on the 16th.

The morning of that day was spent by the French in closing up their columns to the front, and while Ney was ordered to occupy Quatre Bras, Napoleon prepared to assail the Prussians, who by midday had collected three of their four corps at Ligny. His plan of enveloping the hostile right by means of a corps detached from Ney's command failed to materialise, but by nightfall he had heavily defeated Blücher and driven him from the field. The beaten army fell back northward, abandoning its direct line of communications with its base in order to keep in touch with its allies, who during the day had been heavily engaged with Ney at Quatre Bras. The French left wing delayed too long its attack on the weak Netherlands detachment holding that place; the latter was gradually reinforced during the progress of the fight, and at length Wellington, who commanded in person on the battle-field, was able to assume the offensive in his turn and drive Ney back to his starting-point. The tactical defeat here suffered by the French was of minor importance from a strategical point of view, inasmuch as they had prevented any assistance reaching the Prussians from their allies.

The morning of June 17 saw the French army halted in its positions of the previous evening, while Napoleon awaited information as to the results of the action at Quatre Bras and the direction of the Prussian retreat. On receipt of this he despatched Grouchy with two corps and a strong force of cavalry to follow up and contain Blücher, while he himself moved against Wellington. The latter, however, had already effected, unmolested, the retirement of the greater part of his force, leaving behind only a rearguard which successfully kept the pursuit at a distance, and by nightfall had concentrated for battle at Waterloo in a position which he had himself previously selected and reconnoitred. Meanwhile Grouchy, trailing in Blücher's wake, got no farther than Gembloux, while the latter had collected his force at Wavre and notified Wellington that he would march to his support next day with his whole army.

Early dawn on the 18th revealed to Napoleon the Anglo-Netherlands army standing to fight on a gently sloping ridge south of Mont St. Jean, with forward detachments in the farms of Hougoumont in front of its right and La Haye Sainte in front of its centre. The necessity of closing up his army, which had been much strung out by the previous day's pursuit, and of waiting till the ground, sodden by hours of incessant rain on the previous day, had dried sufficiently to allow of movement of cavalry and guns, caused Napoleon to delay the opening of the attack till 11.35 a.m. The French left was held up and remained involved all day in a fierce struggle for the possession of Hougoumont, and a massed attack on the hostile right centre, clumsily executed, was beaten off by a brilliant counter-stroke of the British cavalry. The French cavalry were now put in and executed a series of desperate but useless attacks on the Allied left centre, and while they were so engaged the leading corps of the Prussian army, after much delay from bad staff work, accidents and bad roads, deployed against Napoleon's right, which had to be thrown back to meet it. While the struggle here, increasing in intensity, gradually absorbed more and more French troops, the attack on Wellington raged with unabated fury, and for a time after the loss of La Haye Sainte the Allied centre was in grave danger of collapse. But the critical moment passed; a last attack by the veterans of Napoleon's Guard was repulsed; a fresh Prussian corps assailed and broke in the angle between the French right and centre, while Wellington ordered his whole line forward to the counter-stroke; and the French army wavered and dissolved into a panic-stricken mob of broken fugitives. The Prussians pressed the pursuit with furious energy, hounding their routed foes to well beyond the Sambre, and only halting on the banks of that river. The victory was complete and Napoleon's army had ceased to exist. Only Grouchy, who, misconceiving the situation and the nature and importance of his mission, had spent the fateful 18th in an objectless battle at Wavre, succeeded in eluding the columns sent to round him up, and effected a skilful retreat into France by way of Namur and the Meuse valley.

In less than three weeks after the battle the Allies, whose march had been practically unopposed, appeared before Paris, which was surrendered into their hands by the newly established Provisional Government. A few days later the fallen Emperor surrendered himself to the British fleet, to be eventually relegated to safe captivity in the island of St. Helena. Thus ended at once the career of Wellington as a commander in the field, the reign of the greatest soldier and statesman who ever bore rule in France or contended with the amphibious might of England, and the briefest and most famous campaign in the history of the British army.

3. Wellington and his campaigns

Although Wellington's early career in India and his period of office as commander-in-chief in England still remain to be chronicled in the further course of this book, the victorious end of his last and greatest campaign seems a suitable point for us to pause and consider what sort of man he was who, in seven short years, had raised the military reputation of his country from perhaps the lowest depths to which it has ever fallen to a level little, if at all, inferior to that of Napoleonic France, and won for himself an undisputed place in the trinity of Britain's commanders of genius.

Posterity's idea of the Great Duke, as has been well said, has been rose-coloured by the memory of the later years of his life, when he had become a national institution, the very faults and excrescences of which were venerable, and was thought of only as the last survivor of a heroic age. Tennyson's immortal phrases about "the good gray head", "great in council and great in war", "the tower of strength which stood four-square to all the winds that blew" have perpetuated for all time this somewhat misleading view. For, in fact, Wellington as a man was in his period of active command in the field—whatever he may have become under the mellowing influence of old age— the reverse of admirable or lovable. Few men with such an undeniable claim to greatness can have united in themselves so many unpleasant personal characteristics. His amours were promiscuous and sordid; gratitude, courtesy, good fellowship were all foreign to his repellent nature; and his behaviour towards certain individuals who were unfortunate enough to fall out of his good graces gives one to believe that his own verdict on Napoleon—that he was "no gentleman"—might with even greater appositeness have been self-applied. But we are not here concerned with the Duke as a man, but rather as a general, and in this respect, it seems to us, no one not wilfully and of set purpose blind can deny his pre-eminent greatness. It remains to be seen in what exactly that greatness consisted.

It must be remembered first and foremost that he was a British general, and that, like all British generals, he was working throughout within very definite limitations. He had at his disposal an army which, for its size, was as good a fighting machine as any of its time, but it was constructed on miniature lines, and it was irreplaceable. He was answerable for its safety to his masters in the Government, who in their turn were answerable to the nation. Therefore he had to utilise this formidable but fragile machine with the utmost care and circumspection. Whether in the strategical or the tactical sphere, unreasonable risks had, at all costs, to be avoided; better to lose a minute than to lose a battle;[1] better to lose a chance than to lose the army. And yet, as in all war, complete inaction was forbidden Wellington; he had to use his machine with due care, but he could not let it lie idle or rust in fruitless inactivity. In a word, he was sent to the Peninsula with a mission to do the utmost possible harm to the enemy, while himself taking the minimum of risk.

Now the Spanish Peninsula in 1808 was, as it happened, a theatre uniquely suited to the nature and methods of a British military effort against Napoleon. An expeditionary force assisted by sea-power could be landed at any point on either the southern, western or northern coasts as the situation demanded, and once landed could establish itself solidly in highly defensible country, from which it could only be expelled by greatly superior forces. Such forces could, however, be collected by the French only with great difficulty, and remain concentrated only for a short space of time, for the whole French system of war rested on the power of their armies to live on the country; "scatter to feed and concentrate to fight" was the essence of their methods, and in Spain scattered armies could not fight and concentrated armies could not be fed. Moreover, the French being an army of occupation, their forces were dispersed far and wide in small posts and garrisons, whose time and energies were fully employed in holding down the insurgent inhabitants all round them, so that the assembly of a force of any size for operations in the field always meant that a large area of country was, for the time being, lost to them.

---

1. In contradistinction to Napoleon's dictum, "I may lose a battle, but I will never lose a minute".

Meanwhile the British army, based on the sea, could draw on the resources of the whole world, and need go short of nothing, which wealth could buy. England's financial resources indeed were such that, broadly speaking, she was able throughout the war to arm, equip and maintain not only her own but the Portuguese and Spanish armies as well; and the organisation of the British supply service was—despite certain temporary breakdowns, due usually to undue reliance on local resources—so highly perfected that the army subsisted equally well whether concentrated or dispersed, whether in movement or in quarters, whether advancing or retreating. In a word, the British system of war, with its dependence on base magazines and on organised lines of communications from these magazines to the army in the field, worked better in the Peninsula than the French system of living on the country, the results of which were inadequate to support large field armies for any length of time; and Wellington's army possessed under Spanish conditions more flexibility, a higher power of manoeuvre and greater staying power than its adversaries.

How he exploited these advantages can be read in the story of his campaigns. By seizing every opportunity to fall on detached forces of his enemy before they could receive assistance; by declining battle when the French had assembled superior forces in his front, content to wait patiently till they dispersed again for subsistence; by fighting only in good defensive positions where all chances were in his favour, and the enemy would be bound to purchase success at prohibitive cost, he gradually and by steady, if slow, degrees wore down his numerically superior foes while still retaining his own precious army intact. Then when the time came for him to take the offensive he was able to utilise the superior power of manoeuvre conferred on him by his flexible supply system, and the possibility of changing his base at will to any port on the coast of Spain, to force his adversaries to battle at his will, and ensure to himself all the strategical conditions necessary for victory.

Tactically, too, the Duke was successful in finding the answer to the French methods of war which had placed them first among the armies of Europe. The generals of Austria, Prussia and Russia, drawing up their armies for battle according to eighteenth-century ideas in deployed lines, had seen their troops first harassed and blinded by clouds of wasp-like skirmishers, then shattered into fragments by overwhelming masses of cannon, and finally shivered into a routed mob of fugitives by the irresistible shock of massed columns and thundering squadrons. But Wellington realised from the first that the Napoleonic *coup de grâce* was more moral than material in its effect, and might safely be defied by intact troops who had not, previous to its delivery, suffered heavy loss from musketry and artillery fire ; and that in itself the deployed line which allowed of the maximum development of fire power had always been and still remained—despite all apparent recent experience to the contrary—superior as an order of battle to the column. And so it proved in the actual event. By choosing his fighting ground in such a manner as to allow of his deployed lines being kept under cover from artillery fire till the latest possible moment, by screening his battle front with skirmishers in numbers and training equal or superior to those of his enemy, he brought about an equal combat on a fair field between the line and the column which, as he foresaw, was bound to end nine times out of ten in favour of the former.

In the field of strategy as of tactics, then, the Peninsular War may be regarded as a contest between the old and tried methods of the eighteenth century—of William III. and Marlborough, of Amherst and Wolfe—modernised and adapted to existing conditions by a master of war second to none of his predecessors, and the new war of masses born of the French Revolution, and brought to perfection by the great Emperor. And the result of the contest was overwhelmingly and decisively in favour of the old as against the new. Even allowing for the fact that the new methods were put into practice only by the master's pupils and never by the master himself, and that the course of events elsewhere in Europe, during the later years of hostilities, exercised an influence so favourable to Wellington as to rob the result of the war, considered as a trial between his system and that of the French, of much of its value for purposes of final judgement, the fact remains that the traditional methods of British warfare had shown themselves fully equal, under suitable conditions, to a contest with those of Napoleon.

The same holds true, broadly considered, of the campaign of Waterloo. In these fateful four days Wellington found himself, for the first time, face to face with the master of the new war, and that on a field of operations which, unlike the Peninsula, permitted the Napoleonic methods full and unhampered play; and in the opening exchanges he had decidedly the worst of the deal. But once in actual fighting contact with his formidable foe he recovered his balance and realised that, bewildering as was the Emperor's rapidity of movement and fertile as were his combinations, strategical advantages can only be pushed home by tactical success, and that victory on the field of battle pays for all. If the Duke had no longer the power to choose his theatre of operations to suit his strategy, he could at least select his own position for fighting, and as the result proved, he was right in his belief that on favourable ground his tactical methods were still capable of ensuring him victory.

Wellington has always been considered by Continental writers on war as inferior to the great master whom he so decisively defeated at Waterloo. No doubt from their point of view they are right, for with Napoleon was born the modern war of masses which aligns for the decisive conflict the whole manhood of the nation, and decides the fate of that nation for a generation; while Wellington was, as we have seen, but a supremely competent exponent of a system of war based on the methods of the eighteenth century and adapted by him to modern needs. But the fact that Continental writers have passed the Duke by with faint praises is no reason why the study of his career should equally be neglected by his countrymen; for he seems to us to have been the outstanding master of a kind of war as essentially British as the art of Turner or the drama of Shakespeare—and as well worthy of study. For the task that fell to Wellington is one that will often fall to his successors in the future: that, namely, of utilising to the fullest advantage against a Continental enemy, overwhelmingly superior in numbers and military resources, a British army, small indeed, but in quality equal to or better than its opponents, and backed by the might of a supreme navy ; and the lines on which he worked in the past may serve to indicate in the future also the best possible solution to the problem.

For Wellington's character as a General—though not, it is to be hoped, as a man—was essentially English. In his lucid common sense, his grasp of realities, his wide statesmanlike outlook, his power of seeing and seizing the fleeting opportunity, his timely caution and his equally timely daring—above all in what the French call his "phlegm", which means in essence the power of rising superior to, rather than being controlled by, fortune, whether smiling or adverse—he remains without superior and with but few equals among the great commanders of history. Above all the lesser men who surrounded him his genius towers, cold and awe-inspiring indeed, but shining and magnificent, like an Alpine peak in the clear light of morning.

THE DUKE OF WELLINGTON

Fuentes d'Onoro

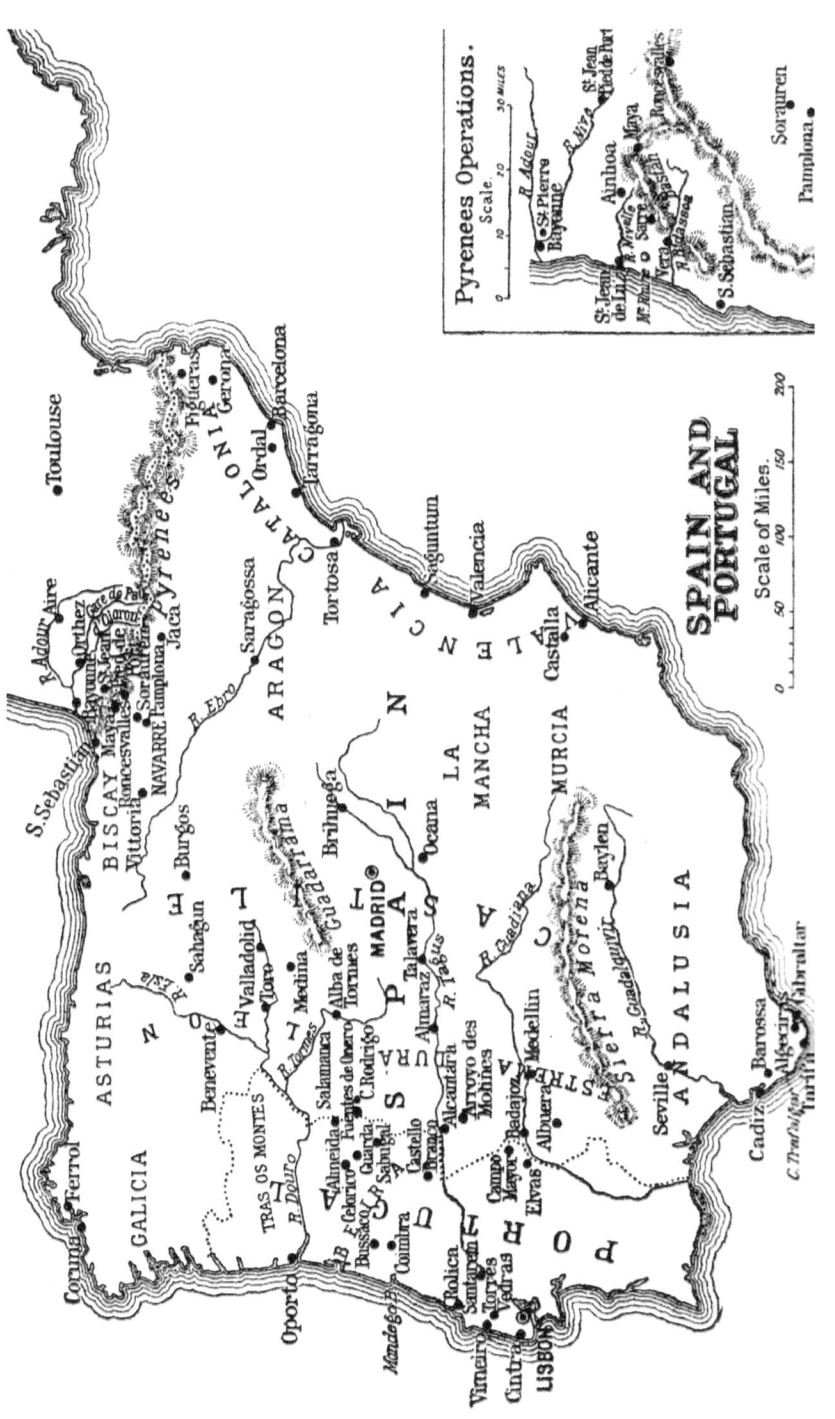

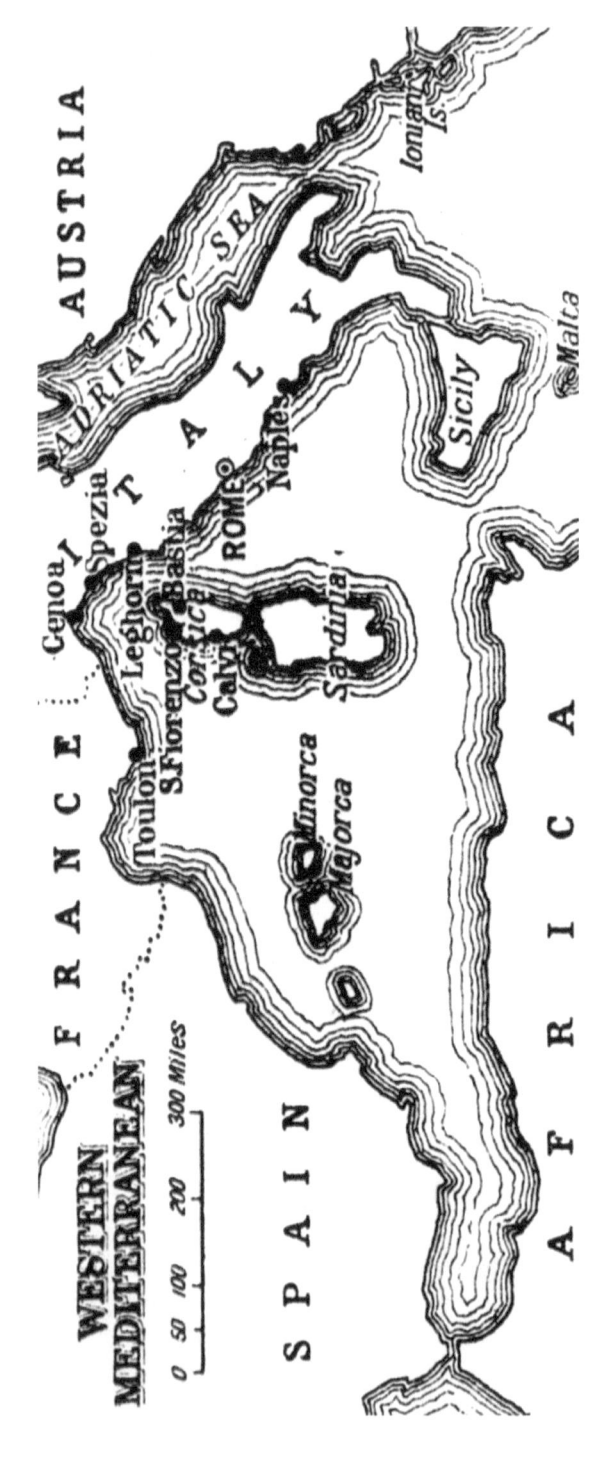

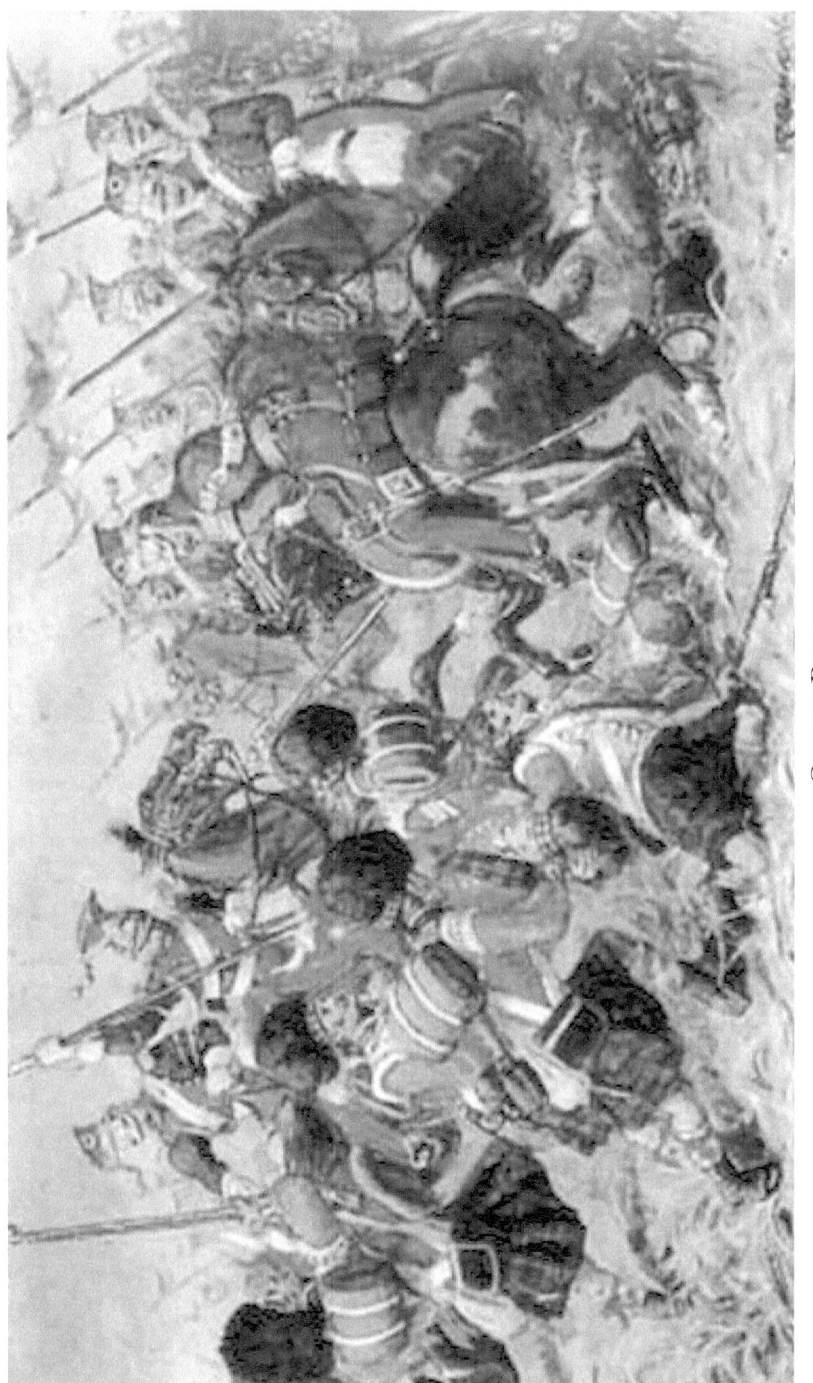

Quatre Bras

The capture & burning of Washington, 1814

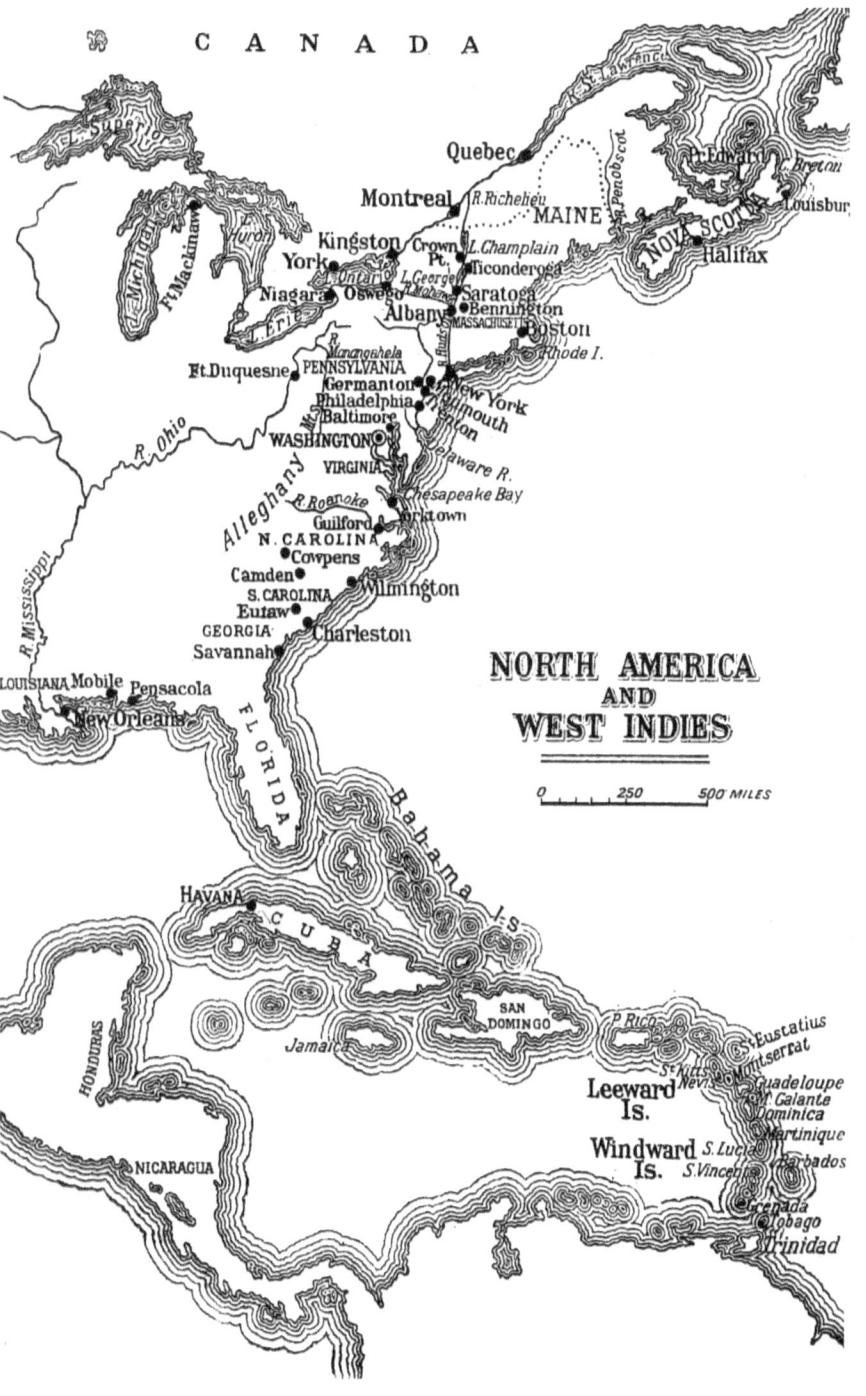

CHAPTER 11

The British Conquest of India: 2
1801-1837

1. THE SECOND MAHRATTA WAR
1803-1806

We must now, after having followed to its victorious end the struggle of giants between Great Britain and Revolutionary and Imperial France in the West, return to India, where British armies were also, during the earlier stages of the war against Napoleon, engaged in a life-and-death contest with a formidable and gallant enemy. The overthrow of the power of Mysore in 1800, already narrated, left the East India Company, supreme in the south and east of the Peninsula, face to face with the extensive domain of the Mahratta Confederacy, extending over the whole of Central and Northern India, from the Himalayas south and beyond the Kistna, and from Cuttack on the shores of the Bay of Bengal westwards to Gujerat. A fierce and warlike people, whose roving horsemen had spread the terror of their name far beyond their own boundaries, they bade fair to be worthy foemen even for the victors of Buxar and Porto Novo, while their possession of Delhi and its impotent puppet ruler, who still personified for the mass of the Indian people the legendary empire of the Moguls, seemed to give them a prescriptive legal right to inherit the power which they in fact exercised in his name. Fortunately for the British, neither to Shah Alam nor to any supreme chief even of their own race did the Mahrattas owe any but nominal allegiance; they were in fact no more than a loose confederacy of independent chieftains, incapable of long pursuing any coherent policy, divided by mutual jealousies and inherited rivalries, formidable when united in arms, but seldom so united for long. Blind to their own true interests, they had, as we have already seen, neglected to take advantage of England's difficulties and perils during her long struggle with Mysore, and so lost their best chance of crushing at birth the growing power of the intruders; and when they were themselves in turn assailed by the conquerors of Hyder and Tippoo, they refused to sink their mutual differences even before the prime necessity of opposing a united front to the common enemy.

In fact, while Lord Wellesley and his Generals were methodically completing the overthrow of Tippoo, the Mahrattas were wasting their energies in a fierce internecine strife. The death in 1793 of Mahadaji Sindia removed from the scene the one statesman who had fully realised the extent of the British menace, and consistently striven to unite the whole confederacy to meet it; his successor, the incapable Daulat Rao, fell out with two of his brother chieftains, Baji Rao, the Peshwa who aimed at the recovery of the supremacy which had always been exercised by his house, in theory at least, over all the Mahratta dominions, and Jeswant Rao Holkar, who played now and throughout his life simply for his own hand. Fighting broke out and continued with many vicissitudes of fortune until in 1802 fortune turned decisively against the Peshwa, who in desperation sought refuge in Bombay territory and implored British aid in the recovery of his dominions. This he obtained, and was triumphantly escorted back to his capital of Poona, under the terms of the Treaty of Bassein—a signal diplomatic triumph for the British, who by it accentuated the split in the Mahratta camp, and secured without fighting, not only an entry into the Peshwa's territory, but a right to interfere in the internal affairs of the confederacy. Now, at length, the warring chiefs realised to the full the danger which so nearly menaced them. Daulat Rao Sindia, the ruler of the whole vast belt of land from the northern frontier of Hyderabad on the Godavery northward to Delhi and the Himalayan foothills, began to make ready his army for war against the British, and summoned to his aid Ragoji Bhonsla of Berar, whose territories extended from Nagpore on the west to Cuttack on the Bay of Bengal. The forces which those two chiefs could put into the field amounted in all to close on 100,000 men, among whom, in addition to the famous cavalry, there were a number of battalions and batteries armed and trained on European lines and led by French soldiers of fortune. Jeswant Rao Holkar, however, in an evil hour for his race and himself, resolved to pursue his traditional policy of selfish isolation and refused for the present to declare against the British.

During the period of long-drawn-out and insincere negotiations which extended from May to August 1803, the British armies were mustered for the war that the Governor-General saw to be inevitable. The plan of campaign consisted of a double attack on Sindia in the north and the south, combined with subsidiary operations against Bundelcund, Cuttack and Gujerat on the left flank of each of these main offensives. Of the northern operations, including those against Bundelcund and Cuttack, Lord Lake, the Commander-in-Chief, was in personal charge, with a force of 21,000 men, of whom 6,000 were allotted to the former attack and 5,000 to the latter theatre, leaving 10,000 for the main army. Arthur Wellesley, the governor-general's brother, whose later career in Europe we have recently followed to its apotheosis at Waterloo, was in command in the south, having general control of the operations of his own army of 11,000 men, the Hyderabad contingent of 9,000 under Stevenson, which was to cooperate with him in the main offensive, and Murray's 4,000, whose mission it was to occupy Gujerat—and who, it may here be said, to save further reference to this force, succeeded in doing so with little difficulty.

In August 1803, Arthur Wellesley, realising that nothing was to be hoped for from further conversations with Sindia and the Bhonsla, exercised the discretionary power given him and moved forward from his area of concentration east of Poona against the strongly fortified little place of Ahmednagar, which he at once stormed out of hand and made his advanced base. Stevenson had meanwhile crossed the Hyderabad frontier, and the two armies effected their junction at Aurungabad. The enemy, who, to the strength of some 50,000 men, had been assembling north of the Ajunta hills, now in their turn took the offensive in the direction of Hyderabad territory, but being headed off by Wellesley, fell back slowly northwards, and were overtaken and brought to battle at Assaye. The British general, though his forces were so split up that he could only bring some 6,000 men on to the field, boldly assailed the hostile left, and after fierce fighting drove them from their ground with heavy loss, practically all Sindia's infantry being destroyed; the remnant fled in disorder beyond the Tapti, followed by Stevenson, who had taken no part in the battle. While the latter was besieging and taking the fortress of Asirgarh, Wellesley, who was refitting his army and collecting supplies at Aurungabad for a renewed offensive, was once more called on to deal with incursions by the Mahratta cavalry, who endeavoured to sweep round his left and rear to harry the country south of the Godavery. Before long, however, he was ready to resume his advance, which was directed against the Bhonsla's capital of Nagpore; Ragoji, attempting to oppose his progress, was swept aside at Argaum, and the capture by storm of the hill fortress of Gawilgarh left his territory at the mercy of the British. But before Wellesley could crown his brilliant campaign by the occupation of his opponent's capital, the latter, his spirit broken by the evil news from the north, sued humbly for terms

Lake's campaign had been even more rapid and decisive than that of his famous lieutenant. Assembling his army of 10,000 men at Cawnpore, he set out up the Ganges and the Kali at the end of July, invested Aligarh, reputed to be one of the strongest fortresses in India, broke his way in through a series of strongly defended gates and practically annihilated the garrison. Thence he pursued his way towards Delhi, outside which city he came upon Sindia's main army, close on 20,000 men, entrenched for battle, whereas he himself had less than 5,000 available. Drawing the enemy from their positions by a feigned retirement of his cavalry, he drove them from the field by one deadly volley and a bayonet charge, and pushing on entered Shah Alam's capital city, to be hailed as a deliverer by the aged and blinded Emperor. Crossing to the west bank of the Jumna, he then marched south to Agra, where he came on part of the beaten Mahratta army standing to fight on the glacis of the place. Having attacked and driven them off to the west, he delayed a few days to get possession of the fort, and then set off once more on the trail of his adversaries, who had now been reduced by losses and desertion to a residue of some 14,000 men only. A march of portentous length and rapidity brought the British up with their foes at Laswari, and there was fought out on November 1 the most hotly contested and desperate battle hitherto recorded in the history of our army in India. For some time the fate of the day hung by a thread, but at length the Mahratta right was turned and broken, and their host completely destroyed or dispersed. It needed only the loss of Sindia's capital of Gwalior to complete the ruin of his fortunes, and he too was not slow to follow the example of his ally and sue for peace, which was concluded in December 1803. The British gains by the treaty were great and important, including as they did the territories of Bundelcund and Cuttack, which had fallen into their hands with little resistance soon after the outbreak of war, and all Sindia's and the Bhonsla's lands east of the Jumna and south of the Tapti.

But the task of the British, though well begun, was little more than half done as yet. Scarcely four months had passed before Jeswant Rao Holkar, resolved to try his fortune where his rivals had failed, threw down the gage in his turn, and in April 1804 Lake and his troops took the field once more against this new enemy. Holkar had learnt at least one lesson from the Mahratta defeats of the previous year, and resolved to rely for his own part no longer on artillery and infantry, who could too easily be brought to battle and beaten, but on the mobility of his masses of horsemen. Driven by Lake's advance from his first position near Jaipur, he withdrew southwards across the Chambal, leaving the fortified town of Rampura to be invested and taken by his enemies. The hot weather being now well come, the British General deemed it impracticable to keep all his forces in the field and withdrew his main body to Agra, entrusting the observation and pursuit of Holkar to a force of 4,000 men under Monson, with whom Murray from Gujerat in the south was to cooperate by an advance on Indore. The latter, however, whose military incapacity we have already learnt to know at Tarragona, failed to perform his part in the combined scheme, thus leaving all the Mahratta army free to deal with Monson, who was compelled by the pressure of immensely superior forces to a disastrous retreat of 250 miles over flooded rivers and swampy plains; all his guns and baggage had to be abandoned, and less than half his detachment eventually escaped to Agra in the last stages of exhaustion and demoralisation.

Holkar's triumph, though great and resounding, was short-lived; for the indefatigable Lake was at once at hand to restore the situation. While half the Mahratta army swung north to recover Delhi and the remainder menaced Agra to cover their movement, the British forces were being assembled for the counter-offensive at Muttra. As soon as Lake realised the situation, he pushed from his path the enemy detachment in his immediate front and hurried northward to Delhi. The garrison of that city, under the able direction of Ochterlony, though only 2,500 strong, successfully held their tenfold superior assailants at bay until the sound of Lake's guns on his rear compelled Holkar hurriedly to raise the siege and flee up the west bank of the Jumna. The British horse followed hard after him, having dropped their infantry under Fraser to deal with the Mahratta force which had remained before Agra. The Mahratta chief, turning sharp to east and south near Meerut, made his way at full speed down the Kali, reached the Ganges valley at Farrukabad and, knowing Lake to be well in rear, halted for a breathing space. But he had underestimated the energy and driving power of his pursuer; covering seventy miles in 24 hours, the British burst into his camp at dawn and scattered its occupants to the four winds. Holkar himself with a few followers alone escaped from the massacre.

Fraser's operations had been equally successful, and the enemy force in his front encountered in a strong position, backed on the fortress of Deig, had been driven to seek refuge within its walls. Lake, returning from his chase of Holkar, ordered the place to be invested and stormed, which was accordingly done; and the army, flushed with victory, proceeded to lay siege to the capital of the Jat Rajah of Bhurtpore, a former friend of the British, who had turned against them after Monson's disaster. Here, however, its victorious career received a decided setback. The fortress was large and immensely strong; Lake's artillery was hopelessly inadequate to deal with its defences; and Holkar, with the remnant of his rallied troops, was hovering in the vicinity to harry and distract the attention of the besiegers. No less than four large-scale assaults were delivered during the course of the siege, which lasted from January to April 1815, and were beaten off with severe loss, and at length Lake was compelled to draw off his baffled troops. The blow to British prestige was more important than the immediate results of the failure, for the Rajah at once made his peace with Lake and set the latter free once more to deal with Holkar. Part of the Mahratta Horse, detached to raid Lake's line of communications during the siege, had been driven eastward into Rohilcund and there defeated and dispersed, so that the residue amounted to barely 8,000 men, and their leader's efforts to induce Sindia to unite with him for a final effort against the British failed before the menace of Lake's renewed advance. He therefore retreated to Ajmeer and thence northward to the Sutlej, hoping in vain to get help from the Sikhs. Lake followed him up and drove him to seek refuge in Punjab territory, where, in December 1805, the last shots of the war were fired.

Unhappily the fruits of this decisive shattering of the Mahratta power by the overthrow in succession of all their greatest chieftains were sacrificed at the conclusion of peace in January 1806. The Directors of the East India Company, alarmed at the peril and cost of Lord Wellesley's aggressive policy, had sent out Cornwallis to replace him; and on the latter's death after a few weeks in the country Barlow was appointed Governor-General with instructions to end the war at all costs and refrain from further acquisitions of territory. Accordingly Holkar found to his astonishment all his former possessions restored to him, and, what was worse, liberty to wreak his vengeance on many of his vassals who had adhered to the British cause during the war. The Mahratta power was thus scotched indeed, but not killed; for that another and even greater war was to be necessary.

None the less, the major part of the work had been accomplished by Arthur Wellesley and Lake. Of the former, whose character and career we have already discussed, it is enough to say here that he had shown himself as much a master of Eastern as later of Western warfare. His colleague and commander in these campaigns displayed qualities at least as pre-eminent— brilliant leadership in battle, tireless and all-conquering energy in advance and pursuit, an unsurpassed power of getting the best out of his officers and men. and a complete and chivalrous loyalty to inferiors and superiors alike. Of all the galaxy of great leaders who gained their fame on Indian fields, Lake's is one of the outstanding and most attractive figures.

2. The Nepal Campaign and the Overthrow of the Mahratta Confederacy 1807-1825

For some years after the sacrifice of Lord Wellesley's gains at the behest of the East India Company's directors at home, Barlow and his successor, Lord Minto, were able to carry out the policy laid down for them by their masters, to abstain from conquest and ensure economy. But their period of rule was not without trouble, both internal and external, and indeed it must have early become clear to any thinking observer of Indian affairs that England's sword would soon have to be drawn from its scabbard once more.

No sooner had the army marched back to its peace stations after the close of Lake's campaign against Holkar than it broke out into serious disaffection. The native troops in garrison at Vellore mutinied as a result of an injudicious change in their uniform, which was construed by them into an attack on their religion, and the movement was prevented from spreading only by the vigorous and timely intervention of Gillespie and his British dragoons from Arcot. Soon after the old question of reduction of the field allowance caused a renewed attempt at organised resistance among the commissioned ranks; the affair was not well handled by Minto, and sporadic outbreaks of disorder occurred in various places before a satisfactory settlement was arrived at.

Apart from these anxieties, the situation both within and

without the territory nominally subject to the British was heavy with menace. The reduction of the Mahratta armies forced upon the various chieftains of the confederacy by Lord Wellesley had let loose upon Central India a host of lawless and masterless men, who all their lives had subsisted by their swords, and now devoted themselves to preying on their peaceful neighbours. These men, formed into organised bands under elected leaders and known as Pindaris, soon became the terror of the countryside, and spread their ravages far and wide, burning, plundering, raping, destroying and creating a veritable reign of terror throughout the wide regions subjected to their depredations. Secretly or openly in league with these miscreants were the various Mahratta chieftains, afraid for the present to tempt once more the fortune of open war against the powerful enemy who had so recently and so signally overwhelmed them and their armies, but only too eager to seize any chance of covertly discrediting British authority and undermining British prestige, and biding their time for revenge. Farther afield, beyond the frontiers of our territory, new and formidable states were arising, which might soon become our rivals or enemies. On the north the Gurkhas of Nepal, whose power had during the last half-century been spreading steadily westward, had extended their frontiers to the Sutlej, and were adopting a provocative policy of raids and incursions from the Himalayan foot-hills into British territory, of parts of which they in 1813 proceeded to take violent possession. Beyond that river, in the plains of the Punjab, Ranjit Singh was engaged in laying firm the foundations of an ominously powerful military state, with which in 1809 the British were within a hair's-breadth of becoming engaged in hostilities, while far to the north-west there was now arising for the first time that cloud which has ever since overhung that distant horizon—the possibility of a Russian invasion, which might at this time, in accordance with the terms of the Treaty of Tilsit, have the assistance of a French expeditionary corps. To this last menace Minto strove to oppose a coalition of barrier states—the Punjab, Sind, Afghanistan and Persia, with all of which he opened up friendly relations; while in the interior of India he exerted himself to keep the peace, at all events in his own time. In this, despite an occasional crisis such as that caused by the incursion of one of Holkar's lieutenants into Berar and the turbulence of a gang of minor chiefs in Bundelcund, he was on the whole successful, and if by reason of this policy he handed over to his successor, Lord Moira, whose earlier military achievements as Lord Rawdon in the War of American Independence we have already had occasion to notice, a heritage of thorny problems, he at least kept his military forces free to undertake those expeditions against the French and Dutch possessions in the East Indies which form a minor but highly creditable episode in the history of the Napoleonic Wars.

Moira, soon after his arrival at Calcutta in the autumn of 1813, realised that among the questions that most pressingly called for solution, that of the future relations between British India and Nepal was of primary importance. In April 1814 he therefore sent an ultimatum, calling for the instant evacuation of the lands recently occupied by the Gurkhas, and on the latter's refusal to comply, proceeded to enforce his demands by armed action. The military task to which he had set his hand promised to be no easy one, for his adversaries, though they could dispose of but 12,000 men, were a brave and wily race of hillmen, fighting in a country well known to them, capable of rapid movement and skilled at the speedy erection of formidable stockades; while the British, whose troops were neither equipped nor trained for mountain warfare, would have to seek their foes in a region into which few white men had ever penetrated, and of which almost all that was known was that the difficulty of ensuring adequate transport and supply would be unprecedented.

A force of 34,000 men was assembled for the campaign

and divided into four columns. Of these the two westernmost under Ochterlony and Gillespie, the hero of Vellore and Java, were to move north from their area of concentration between the upper Ganges and the Sutlej against the flanks and rear of the main Gurkha army, which was known to be on the left bank of the latter river west of Simla; a third from Benares was to cut the enemy line of communications with Katmandu, their capital, 100 miles west of that place, which was simultaneously to be attacked by the fourth column from Patna. This ambitious scheme of operations broke down from the very start; the two right-hand columns, timidly led, were sharply checked; Gillespie lost his life in an unsuccessful attack on a hill fort near Dehra Dun; and only Ochterlony, whose skilful operations stand out all the more strongly by reason of the ineptitude of his colleagues, pursued his advance against the Gurkha army, which he at length, after six months' methodical operations, brought to battle in a strong position at Malaon, and completely defeated. This success redeemed all our other failures, and Kumaon having meantime been overrun by another British force, the Gurkhas were reduced to asking for terms, which, however, on receiving they refused to accept. Accordingly operations were renewed; Ochterlony was placed in chief command of an army of 20,000 men, and moved from Patna direct on Katmandu ; all the formidable enemy fortifications were one by one turned and abandoned to the invaders, who had reached a point within thirty miles of the capital when the Gurkhas once more, and this time in earnest, sued for peace, which was duly concluded in March 1816. By its terms the British gained an area of valuable territory to the west and south of Nepal, within which were to be situated the hill stations of the Government and the army—and later acquired, what was of still greater importance, the friendship of a gallant people who have since furnished the Indian army with some of its best regiments, and its most desirable recruits.

During the course of the Gurkha War another minor campaign had been taken in hand at the opposite extremity of India for the subjection of the native kingdom in the interior of Ceylon, which twelve years before had, as will be remembered, successfully repulsed invasion. Little effective resistance was now encountered by the various small columns, numbering some 4000 men in all, which converged upon Kandy from all sides in the spring of 1815; but various insurrectionary movements in the outlying districts kept the British troops, whose losses from disease were severe, fully occupied for some three years before the island could be said to be finally subdued.

No sooner had the dispute with Nepal been settled by force of arms than the governor-general was compelled to turn his attention to the problem of Central India, where the activity of the Pindaris was growing from a scandal to a menace. In 1815 and again in the following year they made a number of serious incursions into British territory, carrying fire and sword southwards beyond the Kistna, and eastwards and westwards as far as the Carnatic coast, and the shores of the Indian Ocean south of Bombay. Accordingly Moira decided to take the field and put an end to the pest once for all, but his task was complicated by the necessity of simultaneously keeping a close watch on the Mahratta chiefs, who were with justice suspected of intriguing against the paramount power. Whereas the Pindaris were estimated to number little more that 30,000 all told, and were known to be of little value as fighting men, the various Mahratta states could put into the field some 180,000 troops of all arms, whose military reputation was considerable. The governor-general therefore assembled for the forthcoming campaign a mass of 113,000 men with over 300 guns—the largest British army yet seen in India. In the north the Grand Army, under his own personal command, 43,000 men in all, assembled on the line of the Ganges between Delhi and Allahabad, and was destined to advance from north and east on the Pindaris' line in Malwa, north of the Nerbudda, while the Army of the Deccan, numbering 70,000 men, under Sir Thomas Hislop, concentrating on the line of that river, from Hoshangabad to Gujerat, drove the enemy northwards into the arms of their comrades. Hislop's reserve divisions, posted in Khandesh, to the west of Berar, and in the north-west corner of Hyderabad, were to support the main advance and keep an eye on the Mahrattas, while a defensive cordon of posts, still farther to the south along the line of the Kistna from sea to sea, were to guard the frontier of British territory against any predatory bands which might escape the net drawn around them.

The preparations for these widespread operations were prolonged, largely by reason of unfavourable weather, throughout the whole of the spring and summer of 1817, and it was not till well on into November that all was ready for the combined advance. Then, at the moment assigned for its commencement, the grand scheme was disarranged by an outbreak of hostilities on the part of the Mahrattas in rear of the Army of the Deccan. Baji Rao, the Peshwa, and Apa Sahib, the Bhonsla, both suddenly assailed the British detachments guarding the Residencies at Poona and at Nagpur with overwhelming forces; both were heroically repulsed, but Hislop felt himself compelled to despatch a large proportion of his troops to deal with the rebels, and was only prevented by direct and precise orders from Moira from abandoning altogether the advance against the Pindaris. At the same time a serious epidemic of cholera devastated the ranks of the Grand Army, and the joint operations thus commenced under the most unfavourable auspices. None the less, they were executed according to programme and with satisfactory enough results. The first marches of Moira's divisions placed Sindia, whose artillery was collected in his capital at Gwalior while the remainder of his army was stationed far to the west and southwest of that city, in such a position that he had no choice but to conclude the treaty of alliance tendered him by the British, who thus disposed of one potential enemy. Shortly afterwards the advance of Hislop's columns, by driving the Pindaris back from the Nerbudda into the arms of Holkar's army north of Ujjein, compelled that prince also to show his hand; choosing to ally himself with the outlaws, he was brought to action at Mehidpur, and although his 35,000 men, strongly posted, far outnumbered the British, who fought their battle with more courage than skill, suffered complete defeat. The treaty concluded some weeks later inflicted on him as the price of his treachery the loss of all his territory south of the Nerbudda.

Meanwhile in the south the Peshwa had abandoned Poona on the approach of the British relieving columns and taken to the open country, while Apa Sahib had been overawed and reduced to abject submission, and was practically a state prisoner in his own capital. Thus the campaign both here and in the north resolved itself into the chase of an active and elusive but no longer formidable foe. Baji Rao, retreating rapidly first to the south and then to the east, outdistanced his pursuers, and, doubling back towards Poona, encountered a detachment of 500 sepoys under Staunton, who took refuge in the village of Koregaon, and held out for a day and a night against the repeated attacks of 28,000 enemies. This heroic feat blasted all the Peshwa's hopes of recovering his capital and left him no resource but renewed flight. For the next few weeks he moved rapidly to and fro between the Kistna and Godavery, until Moira, in February 1818, realising that continual direct pursuit of him would be a lengthy and profitless task, decided to entrust the chase to a number of light columns of mounted troops, and to bring him to terms by the reduction of his fortresses and the complete occupation of his country. Some days later, as luck would have it, one of these light columns encountered Baji Rao at Ashti and dispersed the greater part of his following, and in June he himself was rounded up near Asirgarh and compelled to capitulate unconditionally.

He was deposed from his throne and became a pensionary of the British; but the occupation of his territory proceeded but slowly, and it was not till March 1819 that Asirgarh, the last of his fortresses to hold out, was battered into surrender.

The extermination of the Pindaris had all this time been proceeding methodically, and by February 1818 they were no longer a force to be seriously reckoned with, such as survived being reduced to a few skulking bands, too few in numbers and too cowed even to face the villagers upon whom they had formerly preyed. While these fugitive bodies were being hunted and exterminated by small mobile columns, the greater part of the British divisions were broken up, the units composing them returning to their peace stations. By the end of 1818 peace had been completely restored, and the few Pindari chiefs who survived the dispersal of their followers—including the Bhonsla Apa Sahib, who had escaped from his British captors but had been unable to collect any troops to help him to regain his throne—were living with a few companions the harried life of outlaws.

Thus the British had asserted beyond dispute their sway over Central India, and had added to the vast dominion already owning direct or indirect allegiance to them the wide expanse of territory formerly ruled by the Mahratta Confederacy. In truth the Mahratta troops had shown themselves, in this last war at any rate, as contemptible in battle as any that had ever fled before our arms, and Moira's main difficulty had been not to defeat them but to find an opportunity for doing so. None the less, this task too—and how toilsome and thankless a task it is has been shown within living experience by the guerilla warfare in South Africa, in 1899-1902, to which the campaign just described bears many points of resemblance—had been admirably accomplished, thanks mainly to the foresight, industry and painstaking thoroughness of the governor-general, who, by his conduct of this campaign, proved himself well worthy to a place in history beside the greatest of our organisers of victory, Amherst and Kitchener. It is one of the ironies of fate that Moira's operations in 1817-1819, which are perhaps, for the lessons which may be learned from them and their applicability to the present day, better worth study than anything in our Indian military annals prior to the Mutiny, should, by reason of the very completeness of their success, and the absence of any dramatic achievement in battle, be an unknown chapter even to well-informed students and soldiers.

It will be convenient here to deal with two episodes which, though somewhat out of place as regards chronology, form a necessary epilogue to the story of the subjugation of Central India. Five years after the last of the Pindaris had been driven into the jungle, and when the military energies of British India were deeply involved, as we shall see, in a heart-breaking campaign in Burma, a disputed succession in Bhurtpore necessitated our armed intervention. To deal with this fortress, which had gained a somewhat fictitious reputation from Lake's repeated failures before its walls twenty years before, the Commander-in-Chief, Lord Combermere, assembled an army of 27,000 men, equipped with what Lake had lacked, an adequate siege train of over 100 guns. After less than a month's investment the place, though held by a garrison as strong or stronger than the besieging force, was stormed at little cost, and its defenders for all practical purposes exterminated or taken; and thus bloodily and effectively was British prestige, shaken by causes both remote and recent, restored to its former height.

The second episode took place nearly twenty years later, at a time when the military fame of Great Britain, after having once more fallen to a low ebb by reason of the serious disaster which had befallen the army in the First Afghan War, had been only partially restored by her successes in the latter part of that war and in Sind, while the political horizon was clouded by the critical state of her relations with the Sikhs of the Punjab. The house of Sindia, the only member of the Mahratta Confederacy who had not felt the weight of British arms in the field in 1817, owing to its enforced surrender to our demands, narrated above, now became embroiled with us by reason of a disputed succession to the throne in 1843, and the seizure of power by an anti-British candidate. Sindia's army, numbering 22,000 good troops, was a formidable menace which required to be instantly dealt with, and an equal British force was assembled in two bodies, the one under Sir H. Gough, the Commander-in-Chief, south-west of Agra, the other under Grey, near Jhansi, with orders to converge on Gwalior. The campaign, which lasted only forty-eight hours, was the briefest and one of the most decisive in our history. The Mahrattas, who fought unevenly, were hopelessly defeated in a double battle on the same day, by Gough at Maharajpore and by Grey at Punniar, though in the former engagement they outnumbered their adversaries by nearly two to one, and were compelled to accept the treaty imposed upon them, the main clause being the drastic reduction of their army and the incorporation into it of a contingent of British sepoy troops. During the Mutiny this contingent was destined to give us more trouble than the conquered Mahrattas, whose pretensions to ascendancy in Central India were finally shattered by the campaign of 1843 and who henceforward disappear from history as an independent power. With their overthrow was finally accomplished the third stage in the British conquest of India.

3. The Conquest of Lower Burma
1824-1826

Barely five years had elapsed since the victorious conclusion of the Pindari War before the Indian Government was forced to enter upon a campaign against an enemy whose military character and methods were totally unlike those of either the stubborn mountaineers of Nepal or the elusive Mahratta horsemen. Relations with the Burmese kingdom of

Ava had for some considerable time been strained, owing to a series of raids on the borders of the newly conquered Burmese provinces of Arakan, Manipur, Cachar and Assam, carried out by exiles from these areas who had taken refuge in British territory and made it the base for their sporadic activities; the consequent reprisals frequently led the Burmese across our frontier, and an attempt to come to an understanding with them in 1818 merely led to their putting forward extravagant claims to portions of the Bengal Presidency, which, however, they were not so foolish as to try and enforce. In the winter of 1823 matters came to a head by reason of two deliberate attacks in force on our garrisons in Sylhet and on an island off the coast of Chittagong, and on redress for these being refused by the Court of Ava, the Governor-General, Amherst, declared war in February 1824.

The plan of campaign, as drawn up by the Commander-in-Chief, Sir E. Paget, involved two main operations, the expulsion of the enemy from Assam, and an expedition which was to land at the mouth of the Irrawaddy and advance up that river on Ava, while the troops in Sylhet and Chittagong were for the time being to remain on the defensive. The scheme seems to have been based on an inadequate knowledge of the peculiarities alike of the country and of the enemy. Lower Burma was then swampy, covered with thick jungle and highly unhealthy for troops; while the Burmese, who were well armed, especially with artillery, skilled in the rapid erection of stockades and rifle-pits for shelter against the hostile fire and to impede his progress, practised in the handling of their war-canoes and fire-boats, and supremely confident in their own prowess, were no despicable foemen.

The major operation on the Irrawaddy was entrusted to Sir A. Campbell, with a force of 10,000 men, practically all of them from the Madras army, as the Bengal sepoys felt intense aversion to overseas expeditions—an aversion clearly shown some months later by the mutiny at Barrackpore of one regiment, which was only quelled at great cost of life. The expeditionary force, to which was attached a strong naval flotilla, rendezvoused in the Andaman Islands, and early in May set sail for Rangoon, at the mouth of the Irrawaddy, which was occupied without resistance, the inhabitants having all fled to the jungle. Two detachments sent to secure the islands of Negrais, off the coast of Bassein, and Cheduba, west of Arakan, were similarly fortunate, though the former place was later abandoned. For some weeks the British, who had neither transport nor supplies for a further advance, remained inactive in Rangoon, where disease took such toll of them that in a few weeks less than one-third of the force was left fit for duty; meanwhile the enemy began to close in and entrench themselves close to the outskirts of the city, and Campbell was compelled to undertake a series of petty sallies in order to prevent himself being completely invested. These enterprises, thanks to the bravery of the troops and the effective assistance rendered by the flotilla, were almost invariably successful, at any rate in their immediate objects. So the situation remained until the end of November, the British proving time and again their fighting superiority over their enemies but without sufficient strength to pursue their tactical advantage. Meanwhile the operations in Assam had been quickly interrupted by the coming of the rains, while in Chittagong the Burmese, taking the offensive, had inflicted on the garrison a serious disaster, which caused great alarm in Bengal, and necessitated the deflection of considerable bodies of troops to succour the menaced territory.

Finally, at the beginning of December matters came to a crisis at Rangoon. Bundoola, the best of the enemy generals, having assembled a host of 60,000 men, moved down river against the city, took up a position surrounding it on three sides, and delivered a series of assaults which were stubbornly repulsed. After six days of fighting, Campbell, in his turn assumed the offensive with complete success, and by the 15th the enemy had fled from before Rangoon, never to return.

His retreat up the Irrawaddy to an entrenched camp at Donobyu marked the definite termination of the campaign of 1824 and of the first phase of the war.

For 1825 the British command now prepared a most ambitious and, as it turned out, impracticable plan for a combined advance against Ava, from three directions. While Campbell with his main army advanced up the Irrawaddy, in accordance with his previous instructions, a force of 10,000 men under Morrison was to assemble in Chittagong, occupy Arakan, and, crossing the mountains between that province and Ava, fall upon the latter place from the west, and a smaller force was to push southwards from Sylhet by way of Manipur upon the same objective. These subsidiary operations ended, the one in failure, the other in disaster. The Sylhet column found the ground before it impassable for regular troops and confined itself to taking possession of Manipur with its auxiliary forces. Morrison, after successfully completing the occupation of Arakan, pushed a detachment over the mountains eastward, which was practically wiped out in a few weeks by malaria ; with the coming of the rains the remainder of his force fell victims to the same deadly disease and perished in such numbers that the remnant had eventually to be withdrawn home. As against these setbacks the conquest of Assam was at length completed and Campbell's campaign was ultimately carried to complete success.

That general commenced his advance in February, his force being divided into two main columns; the one, 2,700 strong, under his personal command, to move up the Hlaing River, and strike the Irrawaddy in rear of Bundoola's entrenched camp at Donobyu, which would be menaced in front by the second column of 1,200 men under Cotton, pushing up the main river. A detachment was sent off to the west to take possession of Bassein, the rest of the army being held in reserve at Rangoon. Cotton was unable to force the enemy's position in his front, and as Bundoola still persisted in holding his ground despite Campbell's appearance at Henzada in his rear, the British general was compelled by shortage of supplies to move downstream and regain connection with Cotton and his base. The Burmese were invested, and shortly afterwards the fall of their general induced them to disperse, leaving open to the invaders the road to Prome, which was peacefully occupied at the end of April.

Here Campbell, compelled to pause in his advance by the coming of the rains, opened abortive negotiations for peace with the Court of Ava, who after some discussion agreed to a cessation of hostilities till November 1, and made use of the breathing space thus afforded them to collect a new army of 40,000 men. These on the termination of the armistice took up positions north and east of Prome on either bank of the river, where they were at once assailed and utterly defeated. The British advanced, meeting no further resistance, some eighty miles farther upstream to Melloon, and there made yet another effort to induce the Court of Ava to come to terms. The latter, completely disheartened not only by their ill success in the main theatre but also by the failure of an attempt to recapture Pegu and alarm their adversaries for their communications and base, agreed to the preliminaries of a very disadvantageous peace, but hesitated to sign a definite treaty until the invaders, having stormed the Burmese entrenchments at Melloon, had approached to within sixty miles of the capital.

The terms of the peace deprived the Burmese of all their territory in Assam, Cachar and Manipur, and all their coastal districts from the southern border of Chittagong to the southern point of Tenasserim, except the Irrawaddy delta itself, which was left to them. That these valuable provinces were thus annexed to British India was due entirely to the adaptability and tenacity of the troops, the valuable assistance of the naval contingent, and the persistence and resolution of the leaders, who, despite the initial difficulties afforded both by nature and by the enemy, had thus conducted this curious amphibious campaign to final success.

CHAPTER 12

The British Conquest of India: 3
1838-1856

1. THE FIRST INVASION OF AFGHANISTAN
1838-1842

We now come to one of the darkest chapters in our history—one of the few, indeed almost the only one, which has to tell not only of defeat but of disgrace, of shame as well as of sorrow. For once our arms were employed in a cause which has met with universal condemnation at the hands of posterity, and in the course of an unjust aggression met with condign defeat; and though our ruined prestige was later in some measure repaired, the objects for which we took up arms were in the ultimate outcome left unattained. This ill-conceived and ill-starred campaign is known to history as the First Afghan War.

In 1838 the British Government of India, which had hitherto never resorted to arms, except in self-defence or upon extreme provocation, suddenly took upon themselves, in defiance of the dictates of reason and justice, to commit an unprovoked assault on a harmless neighbour. This course of action must be attributed primarily to a motive which had as early as the first decade of the nineteenth century begun to exercise the minds of our Indian statesmen and soldiers, and has since that date been ever present with them—the fear of an invasion of India by Russia across the north-west frontier. This fear had at this time become acute, chiefly by reason of a Persian attack, believed to be instigated by Russia, against the Afghan city of Herat, and reported intrigues by Russian emissaries at Cabul. The internal state of Afghanistan itself, which for years had been in a chronic state of internecine strife over the succession to the throne, also seemed to call for some British action to erect a firm barrier to any further Russian enterprise in the direction of India. The immediate danger was in fact absurdly exaggerated, and diplomacy might safely have been left to deal with it. No serious attempt, however, appears to have been made in this direction, and the alarmist views of irresponsible and ignorant men led the Governor-General, Lord Auckland, to adopt another course of action, the wrong-headedness of which was only equalled by its unrighteousness. The existing Amir at Cabul, Dost Mahomed, having declined to accede to our first tentative overtures for alliance, it was decided to supplant him by another claimant to the throne, one Shah Sooja, who had previously held and lost it, and had since proved in several unsuccessful attempts his inability to regain it without outside assistance. He was therefore a convenient tool in our hands ; the Sikhs of the Punjab, inveterate foes of the Afghans, were persuaded to join us in the iniquitous attempt to force a discredited prince on a reluctant people; and the original design, which had at first involved merely the assistance of Shah Sooja with money, arms and officers to train his levies, had swollen by the autumn of 1838 to a large-scale invasion of Afghanistan by British and Sikh forces, on grounds which, even as stated by the aggressors, could only be regarded as of the flimsiest order.

The plan of campaign, as finally drawn up, involved the advance of a large British force, drawn from the Bengal and Bombay armies, and concentrated on the lower Indus, in the nominally friendly territory of the Ameers of Sind, via the Bolan Pass and Quetta, on Candahar and Cabul, while a Sikh contingent was to force the Khyber Pass and cooperate against the Afghan capital. Shah Sooja's corps was to move with the British, who, as soon as they had set him upon the throne and effected the relief of Herat, were to evacuate the country and leave him to fend for himself. While the concentration of the "Army of the Indus" was still in process of completion, however, news arrived that the Persians had raised the siege of Herat and were retiring to their own country, thus removing every shred of real justification from the expedition. The governor-general, however, felt that matters had gone too far to allow of its abandonment, and confined himself to reducing by about one-third the force originally destined to take part in it. By the end of 1838 the Bengal contingent, numbering, with Shah Sooja's motley army, 15,000 men, were assembled around Shikarpore, on the west bank of the Indus, while the Bombay troops, 5,000 strong, had effected their landing at the mouth of that river; but further delays were still to occur before the campaign could be opened, owing to the hostility of the Ameers of Sind, who objected—with good reason—to our troops battening on their country, as being contrary to a treaty concluded with them some years before, and by obstructive tactics and even by open opposition strove to throw every possible obstacle in our way. They were eventually overawed by a display of force, and by February 1839, although the Bombay troops had not yet effected their junction with their comrades, Sir John Keane decided to commence his advance with the force at Shikarpore only.

His difficulties sprang not so much from hostile resistance, for as far as Candahar none, and beyond that little more, was met with, as from the inadequate provision of transport and of the supply service for his army, which it must be remembered included two followers and three camels for every fighting man in its ranks. Consequently he only reached Candahar at the end of May, and was compelled there to make a long halt of two months to complete the concentration of his army and replenish his magazines. The march was then resumed; the fortress of Ghazni was surprised and captured despite the absence of the siege train, which had been unwisely left behind at Candahar; and the levies collected by Dost Mahomed for a last gambler's throw lost heart and melted away before the inexorable progress of the invaders. The unhappy Amir fled for refuge to the Hindu Kush mountains, and early in August Shah Sooja was enthroned in his stead on the British entry into Cabul. The bulk of the Afghan forces had in fact been detained far from the decisive point by the menace of a Sikh invasion by way of the Khyber Pass, and dissolved into fragments at the news of the loss of their capital.

Thus an almost bloodless triumph had been won and a large part of Keane's army was forthwith despatched home, Elphinstone with 5,000 men being left in garrison at Cabul, Nott with a similar number at Candahar, and smaller detachments at various places in the centre and east of Afghanistan. But the disturbed state of the country gave ominous proof that our task was as yet but half fulfilled, and that Shah Sooja's power, resting as it did only on British bayonets, must collapse if deprived of that support. The dethroned Amir collected his forces in the heart of his mountain fortress, and made more than one bold attempt to retrieve his lost fortunes; the tribes between Cabul and Candahar rose *en masse,* and an insurrection of the Baluchis menaced our communications by way of Quetta with the Indus. Full employment was afforded the British flying columns throughout the spring and summer of 1840 in dealing with those various centres of unrest, but in November the surrender of Dost Mahomed, at the very moment when his affairs were apparently taking a turn for the better, seemed to presage a speedy end to our troubles. Although many of the tribes still remained in the field during the early part of 1841, by the autumn the state of the country seemed to be approximating to its normal degree of quietude—never very great,—the relief of part of the army of occupation was ordered, administrative economies were enforced, and the British subsidies to the tribal chiefs were drastically cut down. Dread of Russian designs in Central Asia was, however, still lively, and this, and the realisation in Government circles that Shah Sooja was still too weak to stand alone, combined to forbid for the present the complete withdrawal of the British army from Afghan territory. But a fearful Nemesis was now hard at hand.

In October, with a suddenness and simultaneity which pointed clearly to pre-arrangement, the whole of the occupied area flamed up in rebellion. Sale's brigade, marching back from Cabul to India on relief, was vigorously assailed in the passes, and compelled to throw itself for safety into Jellalabad. Nott in Candahar was closely beset by hordes of tribesmen and had to fight hard and frequently to rid himself of them; an attempt to bring supplies to him from Quetta was beaten back, and the garrison of Ghazni was rapidly and effectively invested and driven into the citadel of the place. It was at Cabul, however, that the hapless tools of an iniquitous policy requited to the full the sins of their rulers. Elphinstone, who was physically and temperamentally unequal to the demands of his difficult position, did nothing effective to deal with the rising in the city. He let himself be deprived of his stores and shut up in indefensible cantonments, and refused to sally forth from them either to revenge the murder of his political officers, or to redeem his own army from destruction by the only honourable and possible means. Akbar, the favourite son of Dost Mahomed, had now assumed chief control of the insurgents, and with him there was at length concluded a disgraceful treaty, by which the British signed away everything they still held and agreed to withdraw from the country at the bare price of their lives. The terms were not and perhaps were never meant to be observed, and barely a week after Elphinstone's demoralised and half-starved regiments had set out on their Via Dolorosa, a solitary survivor arrived at Jellalabad to tell of the utter destruction of the whole British army.

So staggered were the Government by this unexpected catastrophe, which shed a lurid and baleful light over the last days of Auckland's term of office, that for a while no serious attempt was made to retrieve them. The fate of the Ghazni garrison, who in March 1842 surrendered on terms and were at once massacred, was all but shared by that of Jellalabad, the commander of which, a premature attempt at his relief having miscarried, was only withheld from asking for terms by the vigorous opposition of the junior member of his council of war, Broadfoot. And in fact the new Governor-General, Lord Ellenborough, had at first no design beyond the safe withdrawal of the "illustrious garrison" and the force at Candahar, leaving British men and women prisoners in Afghan hands and British honour trailed in the dust. Fortunately George Pollock, the cool-headed and resolute commander of the relieving army now collecting at Peshawar, had other and less timid views. Owing to the low morale of many of his regiments, and the difficulty of collecting sufficient supplies, it was April before he could force his way through the Khyber Pass and effect his junction with Sale at Jellalabad. Akbar's investment of the latter place had been neither incessant nor vigorous, the greatest danger to the garrison having been from an earthquake which overthrew all their defences, and a few days before Pollock's arrival the Afghan besieging army had been totally defeated by a sortie. A long pause of four months now ensued, while the Governor-General was debating in his own mind and discussing with his generals the alternative policies of advance to Cabul to restore British prestige, and evacuation of the country. In the end he left the choice to Pollock and

Nott as to whether they would retire "by way of Cabul", which they eagerly decided to do. Accordingly this strange "retreat" was commenced both from Jellalabad and Candahar in August. The hostile forces who endeavoured to oppose Pollock were handsomely beaten at Tezin, and Nott in his turn defeated his immediate adversaries south-west of Ghazni. On September 15 Pollock, anticipating his colleague by a few hours, took possession of the capital city, which thus fell for the second time in three years into our hands; and suitable vengeance was taken for our previous humiliations and disasters. Ellenborough was in no way inclined to repeat the errors of his predecessor by sanctioning any prolonged stay in Afghanistan, and by the end of 1842 the victorious armies were back once more in British territory. The hapless Shah Sooja having been assassinated some time before, there seemed no better solution to the question of the succession to the throne than the restoration of the deposed Dost Mahomed. To him was therefore generously given back what we should never have taken from him.

The disasters of the first Afghan War dealt to our arms a blow the echo of which resounded throughout India and the East; but that they were at all possible must be attributed rather to the faults of the political authorities and the higher command than to any decline in the fighting value of the troops, who nobly redeemed their tarnished reputation under Pollock, Nott and Sale. The political objects of the war, however, remained even in the end unachieved, and indeed its result was on the whole rather disadvantageous to us than otherwise. The Russian menace, such as it was, remained as potent a bogey as ever; the ruler and people of Afghanistan were left willing to wound if afraid to strike; and our enemies in the East suddenly realised with wonder and hope that the hitherto irresistible might of Britain had, like Achilles, a vulnerable heel.

2. THE SUBJUGATION OF SIND
1843

As a corollary and pendant to the first Afghan campaign there followed the reduction of the power of the Baluchi Ameers of Sind and the annexation of their country to British India.

It has already been seen how these chiefs had been compelled, by a show of overwhelming force, to permit the assembling of the Army of the Indus in their territory, although our treaty with them expressly excluded them from any such obligation. This high-handed action on our part, which did not drive them into hostility even during the worst period of our Afghan disasters, was merely a prelude to further aggression. The handling of our relations with the Ameers was in 1842 entrusted to Sir Charles Napier, who, believing that no country could have a better fate than to come under the sway of Britain, adopted a line of conduct which soon reduced the chiefs to desperation. In order to force upon them a humiliating revision of the treaty, which struck a fatal blow at their independence, Napier assembled his forces, some 3,000 men, in Upper Sind, about Sukkur, and though no war had been declared, sent out a small flying column to destroy the fort of Emaum Ghur, the heart of the desert. He followed up this blow by taking military possession of all Upper Sind, and moving down the Indus to within fifty miles of the capital of the country, Hyderabad. A popular uprising in the city against Outram, the envoy sent to secure the signature of the new treaty, gave Napier the pretext he desired for opening active hostilities, and on February 17, 1843, his tiny force attacked and utterly defeated a host of 35,000 well-armed and brave Beluchis at Meeanee. Hyderabad fell into his hands without further resistance, and here he established himself in an entrenched camp beside the Indus, and received the submission of the majority of the principal Ameers. One, however, Shere Mahomed, of Khyrpoor, known as the Lion, the ablest and most powerful of all, still kept the field, and advanced with 25,000 men to recover the capital. Napier succeeded in bringing up under the nose of his enemy reinforcements which brought his army up to a strength of 5,000 men; with these he marched out, and on March 24 stormed the hostile position at Dubba. The remnant of the Lion's forces fled into the desert, where they were pursued, and, after their strong places had been captured, finally brought to action and dispersed after a mere show of resistance. By the end of June 1843 the operations were at an end; Sind was annexed to the British dominions, and Napier's able and upright paternal government soon reconciled the Baluchis to the loss of their independence.

Whatever may be thought of the policy which led to the conquest of the country—few, except Sir Charles Napier's brother William, have even attempted to defend it—the actual campaign was one of the most workmanlike and brilliant in our records, and its conception and execution by the British commander worthy of the high praise bestowed on it by all good judges. Napier's fame as a General, which deservedly stands high, may well be left to rest on this little masterpiece of war; and his title to grateful memory among all Englishmen on the fact that he was the first to mention in his public despatches the names of humble private soldiers who had distinguished themselves in action under his command.

3. THE SIKH WARS
1845-1849

The time was now at hand when the British power in India was to encounter its last and most powerful antagonist. The Sikh state of the Punjab, founded on a religious basis among the Hindu population of the territory between the Indus and the Sutlej as long ago as the fifteenth century, had recently been consolidated and brought to a high state of efficiency under the enlightened and far-seeing rule of Ranjit

Singh. Despite various disagreements with the British, this chief, who feared their strength and foresaw that in the future "all would become red", desired to postpone the inevitable clash between them, and pursuing a settled policy of conciliation, succeeded in keeping the peace until his death in 1839. His alarm, but not his foreboding, was shared by his subjects and his successors in power, and indeed the efficiency of the army of the Khalsa—the saved or elect who held the tenets of the Sikh faith—was such that it might hope for success even in an encounter with the foes who had proved irresistible to all other Indian troops. Recruited from a fine fighting stock, well equipped, especially in the artillery arm, and disciplined by French officers who had learnt their trade under Napoleon, it was, as its achievements in the field were to prove, a fighting machine of a high order, and burned with zeal to measure itself against the only adversary worthy of its steel. In the period of anarchy that followed Ranjit Singh's death, it soon imposed its masterful will upon the scheming intriguers and impotent puppets who in succession possessed themselves of the nominal control of the Punjab. The blow to British prestige given by our disasters in Afghanistan and the suspicion of our good faith engendered by the high-handed annexation of Sind seemed to show that the occasion for action had come and might not easily return; and in December 1845 the Sikh army took the bit between its teeth, and 50,000 men and 100 guns crossed the Sutlej into British territory.

The fear of precipitating the crisis which was recognised to be sooner or later inevitable had so far withheld the Indian Government from concentrating large forces on the frontier, which was guarded at the moment of the Sikh offensive by no more than 32,000 men and fifty-eight guns, the nearest reserves being far back at Ambala, 150 miles east of the Sutlej. Sir H. Gough, the Commander-in-Chief, would have preferred to have had these last nearer the front, but had been overruled by the Governor-General, Sir H. Hardinge, on the above-mentioned political grounds: He had made all preparations for a rapid concentration of his forces on the news of any hostile advance, and leaving Ambala at the head of 10,000 men, marched for Ferozepore, where the garrison of 7,000 men had already been invested by the enemy. The British army on reaching Mudki was attacked in the late afternoon, as it was already preparing to bivouac for the night, by a Sikh detachment of little more than its own strength, which was roughly handled and beaten off with loss. After a pause to await the arrival of reinforcements it moved forward against the strong entrenched camp of Ferozeshah, where half the army of the Khalsa had taken up position to cover the investment of Ferozepore. This last operation, however, had been so slackly conducted that the garrison was able to slip away and effect a junction with Gough. The latter, impatient to attack the enemy entrenchments before the rest of their army could come up, was only withheld from this course by the direct intervention of Hardinge, who accompanied the army as second in command, but took upon himself to decide the question in his political capacity as governor-general. The assault, thus postponed till late in the day, degenerated into a confused and costly battle which lasted throughout the night and after many vicissitudes ended next morning in the retirement of the Sikhs, a few hours only before the belated arrival on the field of the corps which had been blockading Ferozepore. Their army thus united fell back across the Sutlej, and Gough decided to refit and await further reinforcements before attempting to force the passage of that river.

This inaction emboldened his adversaries, who shortly afterwards re-established themselves on the south bank and began to construct fortified lines near the village of Sobraon, at the same time detaching a force to move eastwards against the British line of communications by way of Ludiana. Sir H. Smith's division was sent off to deal with this menace and relieve the garrison of that town, which, after a series of rapid marches and skilful manoeuvres, he succeeded in doing at the cost of the loss of his baggage. He then, turning against his enemies, defeated them in a brilliant little action at Aliwal, driving them over or into the Sutlej, and freeing the rear of the main army. Meanwhile Gough, justifiably confident of his ability to carry the hostile entrenchments whenever it pleased him to do so, was maturing his plans for the decisive battle, which was fought on February 10, 1846, at Sobraon. Fifteen thousand British troops stormed the Sikh entrenchments, held by 20,000 gallant foes, and after fierce fighting carried them all along the line; the cavalry, pouring through, completed the rout of the beaten enemy, numbers of whom were drowned in attempting to recross the river in their rear. Unable to oppose any further resistance to the advance of the victorious British, the Lahore Government laid down its arms, and accepted a treaty which effected sweeping reductions in the Khalsa army, and placed on our shoulders the responsibility for the future administration of the Punjab, without effective power to enforce our will save by a renewal of hostilities.

For close on two years, however, the new regime worked with, at any rate, outward smoothness, and the Sikh Durbar at Lahore co-operated readily and whole-heartedly with their British colleagues and advisers in the administration of the country. In reality discontent was smouldering, not extinguished; the spirit of the Khalsa army, far from being broken, had only been inflamed by its recent defeats, and everywhere there were menacing underground fires of revolt, which in the spring of 1848 burst out into open flame. The occasion was an isolated outbreak of disorder at Multan, where the Governor, Mulraj, quarrelled with the Durbar, murdered two British officers sent to treat with him, and once more raised the national standard. A young British subaltern, Herbert Edwardes, who was political officer in the Derajat territory, west of the middle Indus, on his own initiative took the offensive against the rebels, defeated them in the open field, and with the assistance of the troops of the friendly chief of Bahawalpur, from south of the Sutlej, shut them up within the walls of Multan. The revolt thus seemed for the present to be localised, and Edwardes was sanguine of his ability to suppress it entirely if some assistance could be sent him. Unhappily the fidelity of the Sikh forces which had been put in motion by the authorities at Lahore, as soon as news of the outbreak reached them, was with only too good reason suspect, and both the Governor-General, Lord Dalhousie, who had just succeeded Hardinge, and Lord Gough, the Commander-in-Chief, were agreed on the unwisdom of sending British troops at the present juncture.

Drastic reductions in the strength of the Indian army, after the victorious termination of the Sutlej campaign, had left available barely enough men to keep order in the occupied territories. Gough, therefore believing that Mulraj's fiery cross would find ready response elsewhere in the Punjab, considered it wiser to let the rebellion come to a head, and perfect his preparations, during the short respite allowed him, for a large-scale campaign which would finish the war with one decisive blow. Accordingly the hot weather months were devoted to collecting troops and transport, a process which was unduly prolonged owing to Dalhousie's unwillingness to give immediate effect to his commander-in-chief's requirements. It was not till November that the 16,000 men whom Gough considered necessary for the forthcoming offensive were assembled at Ferozepore, and meanwhile his worst fears as to the intentions of the Sikh rulers had been realised. All the Punjab was ablaze. In Hazara, the mountainous area between Kashmir and the Upper Indus, Chattar Singh had raised the countryside, invested the British and their levies in Attock, and called upon the Afghans to assist him; Peshawar and Bannu were also in revolt. But worse was to come. The arrival before Multan of a British force of some 8,000 men, under Whish, which had been sent by the Resident at Lahore on his own initiative to assist Edwardes, decided one of the Sikh commanders, Shere Singh, the son of the rebel chief, Chattar Singh of Hazara, to follow his father's example. The junction of his forces with those of Mulraj compelled Whish to raise the siege and revert to a defensive attitude; and Shere Singh, leaving a strong garrison in the city, at once moved off north-eastwards with 30,000 men and took up a position behind the Chenab, where he proposed to await the arrival of the northern rebels.

Gough, therefore, although his preparations were as yet incomplete, resolved to attack this enemy without delay and force him to leave his present ground, where supplies were plentiful, for the barren country south of the Jhelum. The Sikh advanced troops were driven from the southern bank of the Chenab in a costly and ill-managed cavalry action at Ramnuggur, and a few days later the main army reached that river and halted, facing the hostile entrenchments on the far side. The despatch of a strong turning column to cross beyond Shere Singh's left flank, and turn his position, compelled him to retire hurriedly to the Jhelum, where he took up and fortified new ground near the village of Chillianwala. This he was permitted to do at leisure, as the British commander was inclined to pursue his advance no farther until he should be reinforced by Whish's force from Multan, the fall of which he believed to be imminent. The news, however, that Chattar Singh, with 27,000 troops, was on his way southwards indicated the necessity of defeating the enemy before this reinforcement could reach him. Accordingly there ensued on January 13, 1849, the bloody and indecisive battle of Chillianwala, in which the British attack was disorganised by the Sikhs advancing out of their entrenchments to meet them in thick jungle, which prevented any proper artillery preparation; and at the end of the day both armies abandoned the field with heavy loss.

The news of this set-back, for as such it was represented to be, caused a storm of indignation both in India and at home, and led to a public outcry for Gough's supersession. The Government yielded to the clamour and despatched Sir Charles Napier to take over the command, but before he could arrive the fame of British arms had been brilliantly vindicated and the Second Sikh War had been brought to a victorious conclusion. Soon after Chillianwala both the combatants had been reinforced, Shere Singh by the Hazara troops, Gough by Whish's force. The latter, whose operations had been seriously hampered by the delay in the arrival of a promised contingent from Bombay, had stormed Multan and forced Mulraj to capitulate on January 22, 1849, and at once marched to join the main army on the Jhelum. Meanwhile the Sikhs, striving to tempt Gough to deliver a premature battle, had moved past his right towards the Chenab and taken up position at Gujerat. Here, on February 13, their army, numbering 60,000 men, was attacked after a careful and thorough artillery preparation and utterly dispersed by barely a third of their numbers. The remnant which held together were hotly pursued, rounded up, and forced to lay down their arms at Rawal Pindi; the Afghans who had come to their assistance were hurled back from Attock across the Indus to their own territory; and the Punjab henceforward became part—and by no means the least valuable or loyal part—of British India.

The victorious commander, Lord Gough, has hardly even yet received from posterity the just meed of praise which was' denied him by a large proportion, at all events, of his contemporaries. No leader whose campaigns were so fruitful of results has ever been more hardly treated by commentators, most of whom have voted him a blundering, hot-headed butcher, a hussar general of the Blücher genus, who was never fortunate enough to find his Gneisenau. Close and impartial investigation of his career and campaigns affords little support for this judgement. It is clear that the causes of his ill-successes lay mainly in circumstances over which he had little or no control, and of which he was too loyal to make complaint. Chief among these were political interference with his plans, errors by his subordinates, a definite decline in the military value of his sepoy regiments, and above all, the fine qualities of his adversaries, victory over whom would have taxed the powers and enhanced the fame of even the greatest of our Indian military commanders.

4. The Second War with Burma
1852-1853

Scarcely had the formidable Sikh power to the north-west of British India been laid low in the dust than Lord Dalhousie was compelled to turn our arms against a foe in quite another quarter. The First Burmese War had indeed resulted in the defeat of the Court of Ava, but had by no means put an end to its self-esteem or its arrogance in its dealings with foreigners. The British envoys, which it had been forced to receive, had from the first been treated with half-veiled disdain, so much so that they had finally been withdrawn for fear that some unpardonable insult should provoke a rupture. Next, a series of harsh and oppressive measures against the merchants, who, confiding in Burmese good faith, had settled at Rangoon for purposes of trade, called forth an appeal to the governor-general for protection. The frigate despatched in response was fired upon before any attempt at opening negotiations could be set on foot, and though the action of its commander in reprisal was perhaps unduly precipitate and high-handed, Dalhousie conceived he had no alternative but to back up his representative by an ultimatum to the Court of Ava. No answer having been received, war was therefore declared in February 1852, and preparations were at once commenced for the despatch of an overseas expedition to Lower Burma.

The governor-general, determined not to repeat the error which had rendered the previous campaigns in the same theatre so lengthy and costly, himself supervised the execution of the extensive and well-thought-out measures for the organisation, commissariat and transport of the force, and no expense was spared amply to provide for every possible contingency. Early in April the little army of 5,700 men under General Godwin sailed in two portions from Madras and Calcutta and concentrated punctually in accordance with programme at the mouth of the Rangoon River, and after a small detachment sent eastwards to Martaban and Moulmein had effected the capture of both these places with practically no opposition, the attack on Rangoon was proceeded with. The Burmese, numbering some 20,000, were well prepared to resist the landing, and had fortified all the ground as far as the Shwe Dagon pagoda, which formed their headquarters and citadel; but the British troops quickly swept them from all their positions. A few days later a brilliant little enterprise, in which a force of barely 1,000 men were transported sixty miles up river and defeated and drove back an enemy seven times their own strength, all in one day, placed us in possession of Bassein, and with the solid establishment of the force on the sea coast of Lower Burma the advance for the present came to a stand.

For the moment, in fact, Godwin was content with what he had achieved. The repulse of a hostile effort to recapture Martaban seemed to show that our gains could easily be held; the unresisted occupation of Pegu and Prome by small detachments sent forward to reconnoitre these places, that there would be little difficulty in extending them if desired. It was not, however, until the arrival of Dalhousie at Rangoon in July that the definite decision to push the advance farther was arrived at. Godwin, one of whose motives for inaction had been anxiety as to the possibility of maintaining a lengthy line of communications up the Irrawaddy, devoted two months to the accumulation of supplies, and then once more took possession of Prome early in October with ridiculous ease. The detachment sent to occupy Pegu, however, had a stiff little fight before it could penetrate into the place, and then, the bulk of it having been unwisely withdrawn, the small garrison left behind was closely invested by the enemy. For over three weeks 500 British troops held out undismayed against some 11,000 Burmese until they were opportunely relieved by a force sent from Rangoon, which defeated and drove off the besiegers.

Apart from some minor operations partaking rather of the nature of guerilla warfare, in the Donabyu area, to the east of Bassein, and around Beeling, east of Pegu, which revolted and was brilliantly recaptured in April 1853, the campaign was now at an end. The Court of Ava, though it could not be induced definitely to agree to the cession of the Pegu province, covenanted not to molest us in our occupation of it; accordingly in December 1852 it was annexed to British India, and the whole of the Burmese coast-line passed into British possession. The restoration of order and peace, however, was to prove a lengthy and tedious process, fully occupying all the energies of the able administrators entrusted with it. The final settlement with the Court of Ava was, as it turned out, not to take place for thirty years.

This little campaign, though barren of decisive actions and therefore to some extent of interest, reflected great credit both on the governor-general, who planned and prepared for it, and on Godwin and his troops, who executed it, it seems, with judgement, skill and courage. So careful and thorough were the initial measures, and so nicely were ends proportioned to means, that, whereas the First Burmese War, which was certainly no more fruitful in result than the second, cost the Indian Government over twelve million pounds, the expenditure on the latter amounted to well under one million.

5. THE ENGLISH IN INDIA

The story of the English conquest of India is perhaps the grandest epic in all the annals of mankind, finer than the Spanish acquisition of Mexico and Peru, more lasting in its results than the Crusades, more unified in achievement than the opening up of the New World by the nations of Europe. Yet, for want of a Prescott or a Parkman to tell in fitting terms this stupendous story, it has failed to win due recognition, even among us, the fellow-countrymen and descendants of its heroes —among the men of British race who have most cause for pride in it. And indeed, where the history and fortunes of our Indian Empire are concerned, some draught of "poppy or mandragora" seems ever to dull the senses and stupefy the minds of Englishmen, so that they forget their own greatest achievement and become unconscious of their most imminent responsibilities. Of all the giants who wrought for us the fabric of our Indian Empire, but two, Clive and Wellington, can be said to be in any sense household names today; but Clive, as we have had occasion to show, was but *primus inter pares* among his fellow-workers, and the hero of Assaye, had he been nothing more, must long since have been forgotten. Yet among the long list of generals who led our armies to victory beneath the Indian sky, some—such as Coote, Lake, Hastings and Charles Napier—may rank with all but the greatest of our great commanders; and such men as Forde, Munro, Cornwallis, Pollock, Nott and Gough—to mention but a few—would, could they have fallen on the Heights of Abraham or been present at the battle of Waterloo, have been accorded at least the doubtful honour of a two-volume biography. The great men of the Mutiny were in this respect more fortunate than they; yet these but recovered for us what we had almost lost, while those who in the first place set the brightest gem in our Imperial Crown have passed into almost complete oblivion with the armies who followed them to victory.

Consider for a moment the bald statement of the facts, moving from their very sobriety, of this mighty achievement. A little island race, poor in numbers and resources but rich in valour and inspiration, sends its sons over 10,000 miles of sea to an alien land close on a hundred times its own size, and containing within its borders a vast population, one-sixth of all the inhabitants of the globe. This little handful of Englishmen —which even on the eve of the Mutiny numbered less than 50,000 men under arms, and during the greater part of the heroic era of the conquest counted less than half that strength —fought turn by turn and subdued on the battlefield men of every faith and race that India could array against them, and turned them from fierce and crafty foes to submissive subjects or faithful allies—nay, even used them, once subdued, to fight their battles against other enemies. So an army was built up from the peoples of India themselves, which in the end brought its own country under the sway of its masters. And then when that army itself, misconceiving the source of its own victories, endeavoured to shake off the grasp of those who had used it so effectively and so well, the little band of white men proved once more, by its utter destruction, that they remained still the masters alike of their tool and of their destiny.

Put thus the thing seems incredible—and only one thing could perhaps be conceived more incredible, that it should still seem to nine out of every ten Englishmen a matter calling for no explanation and arousing no interest in their minds. It is true that the armies encountered by the heroes of this epic all exhibited in their turn varied but glaring military defects. The mere mobs in arms that scattered in tumultuary rout before Clive and Munro; the hybrid Mysore armies who had lost their native virtues in an ill-judged attempt to acquire those of Europe; the Mahrattas whose abilities were most noticeably displayed in running away; the Sikhs whose very stubbornness in defence fitted them only for the unhappy role of anvil to the British hammer—some of these were contemptible, all of them vulnerable foes. Yet, when numbers were so invariably on their side, armament and equipment so equal as between the belligerents, pride of race and national sentiment so nicely balanced on either hand, and conditions of climate and terrain so inimical to our own men, it seems that only some portentous supremacy in fighting calibre and spiritual strength could account for such an unbroken career of British victories. Nor is the wonder lessened but rather increased when we remember that this same white handful could not only themselves drive in rout before them overwhelming hosts of Asiatic warriors, but could fill these same warriors, once brought under their control, with the same inexplicable power and lead them to emulate their own deeds on other fields. What is this potent talisman that can so inflame the hearts and inspire the minds of an alien soldiery and make the sepoys worthy comrades-in-arms of the heroes of Flanders and America, of the Peninsula and Waterloo? None can define it, save as the spirit which breathes life into an army, and without which even the bravest, the best armed and the most numerous host marches forth only to defeat and disgrace.

CHAPTER 13

From Waterloo to the Boer War
1816-1898

1. THE ARMY DURING THE LONG PEACE
1816-1853

The British military machine which, organised and administered by the able and conscientious tutelage of the Duke of York and led to decisive victory by the calculating genius of the Duke of Wellington, had throughout the long contest with Napoleonic France done such yeoman service to its country and to Europe was dissolved shortly after the conclusion of the Treaty of Paris, but a shadow surviving. In 1816 it was drastically cut down to 225,000 men (35,000 forming the army of occupation in France), and suffered successive thoroughgoing reductions in the ensuing five years, till by 1821 it touched rock-bottom at a figure of 100,000 of all ranks, of which 30,000 were distributed among the various Colonial garrisons, 20,000 in India and the remaining 50,000 at home. This handful of men was exiguous indeed for the needs of the times, when Great Britain had not only to provide for the security of an overseas empire vastly increased by her acquisitions during the Great War, but also to contend with political ferment and social disorder at home. As a second line behind it there stood nothing but an even smaller number (less than 60,000) of yeomanry and volunteers, the militia having been abolished soon after the peace. The yeomanry were mainly responsible during these perilous years for the maintenance of order throughout the country, an invidious task from which they were partially relieved only in 1829, on the formation of a civilian police force. Nor was the smallness of the army's numbers made good by its high state of efficiency. The abolition of the Staff Corps and the Wagon Train, two corps whose value had been fully proved by the experience of the past, and was to be so again in the near future, practically crippled it for campaigning purposes. The central administration was chaotic and cumbersome to the last degree. Responsibility was divided in 1815 between four principal and eight subordinate offices of government, of whom all but three were still in active existence twenty-two years later, when a Royal Commission met to consider the whole question; its labours, however, were in vain, all its recommendations being incontinently shelved, and matters remained *in statu quo* until the Crimean War brought the vital necessity for reform vividly before the Government and the country. Finally, the internal condition of the army itself left much to be desired. Officers and men alike were ill paid, and the expenses of the former at least were out of all proportion to their remuneration. Conditions of life in barracks were still such as to give point to Dr. Johnson's dictum that "no man will go for a soldier who has contrivance enough to get himself into a gaol". Regiments on foreign service were hidden away—to shelter them, it is said, from the Argus eye of the economist—in fever-haunted or disease-ridden stations for what in too many cases amounted to a lifelong exile. Discipline was savagely enforced by the lash, considered, and too often with justice, as the only means of appeal to the class of men of whom the army was normally composed. Training hardly existed, and, thanks largely to the baneful conservatism of

Wellington, no attempt was made to modify or improve the armament, equipment and methods which were considered to have proved their eternal value at Salamanca and Waterloo. Enlistment was for life, discharge being granted only for exceptionally good or exceptionally bad conduct, and only in 1847 was a term of service of ten years introduced, and a better class of recruit thereby attracted to the colours. During these depressing thirty years, in a word, the British army as regards its quality and efficiency suffered a disastrous reversion to the standard of its worst days.

From 1824 onwards, however, it underwent a gradual change for the better in a slow but steady increase in its numbers, till by 1854 it had obtained a total strength of 140,000 men, half being stationed at home, 30,000 in India and the remaining 40,000 in the Colonies. Moreover, in 1852 the militia was revived, on a voluntary enlistment basis, so that an effective second line was reconstituted in time for the Crimean War. No provision was made, however, for drafting into regular units, and though bounties attracted many recruits from the militia into the line, such enlistments were strictly illegal and often treated as such. The only recognised reserve in 1854, in fact, consisted of 10,000 pensioners, who were permitted in case of emergency to volunteer for garrison duty at home. To such a degree of impotence had forty years of "peace, retrenchment and reform" reduced what had once been the finest army in Europe.

2. MINOR CAMPAIGNS
1816-1853

Such active service (exclusive, of course, of our Indian wars) as was seen by British regiments between Waterloo and the Crimea may be very briefly summarised.

In Asia the occupation of Aden was carried out in 1838 by a force from India, in consequence of the menace to our communications with that country caused by the Persian attack instigated by Russia against Afghanistan, and the occupation of Syria by France's protégée, Mehemet Ali, the Pasha of Egypt.

In the following year a commercial dispute with China caused the despatch of an overseas expedition against her coasts. Four thousand men occupied Chusan island in Hang-chow Bay, while the navy forced the outer defences of Canton River. Prolonged but inconclusive negotiations followed, during which the British withdrew from Chusan and took possession of Hong-Kong; finally hostilities were resumed and Sir H. Gough, who had assumed charge of the operations, stormed Canton in May 1841, and Amoy, farther north along the coast, some months later. The scene of operations was then transferred once more to Hangchow Bay; a landing was effected on the southern shore and the city of Ningpo captured and held till the spring of 1842, when the Chinese made a gallant but fruitless effort to retake it, and were later counter-attacked and dispersed. Shortly afterwards the British force, now reinforced to a strength of 7000 men, once more shifted northwards to the mouth of the Yang-tse-Kiang; Shanghai was occupied, and Nanking closely invested and on the point of surrender when the Chinese Government agreed to a suspension of hostilities. The treaty, concluded in August 1842, gave Hong-Kong to Great Britain and opened a number of Chinese ports to the ships of all nations.

In Africa there took place between 1824 and 1826 an unimportant little war with the Ashanti tribes, living in the hinterland of our Gold Coast settlements, where the only British troops were the so-called "penal battalions". The campaign opened with a crushing disaster which the tribesmen fortunately failed fully to exploit, and after a series of desultory but destructive raids and incursions they were finally defeated north of Accra. Peace, however, was not finally concluded till 1831.

A more interesting series of operations took place in South Africa, where, it will be remembered, we had in 1806 conquered the Dutch Colony at the Cape of Good Hope, and retained it at the termination of the war. During the immediately succeeding years we became embroiled in hostilities with the Kaffirs, our neighbours on the eastern frontier of the Colony, which then ran along the Great Fish River, 450 miles east of Cape Town. Relations with this people remained constantly in a state of tension till December 1834, when they suddenly invaded British territory in great force and spread panic along all the border districts. Sir H. Smith, hurrying up from the capital, at once assumed control of affairs, restored confidence among the panic-stricken settlers, and assuming the offensive, succeeded in less than a month in driving the invaders back to their own side of the frontier. D'Urban, the Governor, however, decided that signal punishment must be inflicted, and collecting a force of 3000 men, marched into Kaffraria in April. His plan was to force back the enemy and reduce him to terms by destroying his cattle, which formed at once his chief source of wealth and his main means of subsistence. By May 1835 all the Kaffir territory up to and even beyond the Kei had been swept clear of the tribesmen, and vast quantities of cattle rounded up or otherwise accounted for, and in September a treaty was concluded which annexed to Cape Colony all the lands between the Great Fish and Kei rivers. The home authorities, however, now intervened and the British frontier was brought back to the Keiskamma—a decision which was to prove a fruitful source of trouble for all concerned.

Not only were the Kaffirs themselves so filled with self-confidence and a belief in British weakness that they felt little hesitation in once more taking up arms when it suited their convenience to do so, but the Dutch elements in the white population, despairing of finding any protection from the British Government, resolved to seek out new territory and rely for defence on themselves alone. Ten thousand of them between the years 1835 and 1842 emigrated north and east, some to Natal, some to the area between the Orange and the Vaal, some to the north of the latter river. Over them the Cape Town Government still claimed sovereignty, and when in 1848 a new northward movement took place, Sir Harry Smith, the Governor, resolved to prevent it by force. Pursuing the main body of the emigrants with a mobile column of some 1200 men, he overtook and dispersed them at Boomplaats, and, after reducing to order the territory between Orange and Vaal, returned to Cape Colony in triumph. So peaceful indeed was the outlook that he was able, in response to urgent appeals from the Government, to reduce the garrison.

Hardly had he done so than the Kaffirs, who had unsuccessfully risen in arms in 1846, once more rebelled in December 1850, raiding the whole British border from their fastness in the Amatola range between the middle courses of the Fish and Kei rivers. Smith's plan for dealing with them by a movement of converging columns from King William's Town and Beaufort could not at first be carried out: he had less than 8,000 men at his disposal; an alarming rising of the Hottentot population in his rear distracted his attention and energies, and the white farmers failed to render any effective assistance. It was only in June 1851 that the arrival of fresh troops enabled active operations to be undertaken, and not till October was any effective result achieved. The home Government, unable or unwilling to understand Smith's difficulties, recalled him in January 1852, just when his campaign was nearing a successful conclusion; but the retiring Governor had at least the satisfaction of being able to inform his successor that the war was, for all practical purposes, at an end. Though South Africa therefore sank for a space into an unquiet peace, its great problems remained still as acute as ever to trouble successive British Governments, the heirs of their predecessors' impatience and blunderings, and to afford work to British generals and armies right down to our own day.

3. The War with Russia
1854-1856

In 1854 the British military machine, rusted by forty years of peace and neglect, was once more set in motion against a Continental enemy. The process by which England, in alliance for the first time in modern history with her hereditary enemy, France, drifted into war with the Russia of Nicholas II. is too lengthy and obscure to call for detailed description. The Czar, in pursuance of his predecessors' traditional designs on the integrity and independence of the Turkish Empire, which by its situation controlled Russia's shortest sea communications with the outside world by way of the Bosphorus and the Dardanelles, seized the occasion of a petty religious quarrel with the newly established French Emperor, Napoleon III., to claim the protectorate of the Greek Orthodox Church in the Ottoman dominions. The powers of Europe, rightly seeing in this a menace to Turkey's continued existence as an independent State, intervened, but in vain, and in October 1853 Russia declared war and took armed possession of the Turkish territory lying north of the Danube. France and England then sent warships to take post in the Bosphorus, and when the Russian Black Sea squadron, undeterred by their presence, attacked and destroyed the Turkish fleet, followed up this move by a definite declaration of war in May 1854. Before they could complete the assembly of their expeditionary forces to assist the Turkish defence of the Danube line, Russia, in obedience to Austrian pressure, drew off her army and abandoned the provinces, the seizure of which had been the occasion of offence. But the tide of warlike enthusiasm, now running high on either side of the Channel, precluded any possibility of the Allies consenting to abandon the conflict without a serious attempt to draw the teeth of their adversary and put it out of his power to commit further aggression for some time to come. It was accordingly decided to seize Sebastopol, his fortified naval base in the Black Sea, and destroy the fleet which had taken refuge in that harbour.

Accordingly in the middle of September a force of 63,000 men was transported to the western shore of the Crimean peninsula, and effected its landing unopposed at a point some 30 miles north of Sebastopol. The British contingent, 27,000 strong, was organised in one cavalry division and five infantry divisions, under the command of Lord Raglan, one of Wellington's most trusted officers and steeped in the Wellingtonian tradition;[1] 28,000 French under St. Arnaud and 7,000 Turks comprised the remainder of the army. To oppose them the Russian leader, Menschikoff, could put into line only some 37,000 men on the heights overlooking the Alma stream. The battle, ill conducted on all sides, ended, despite the French failure to bring all their strength to bear, in a decided victory for the Allies. The Russian positions were vigorously stormed by the British regiments, in numbers but little superior to those of the defenders, and Menschikoff, conceiving himself unable to conduct an active defence of Sebastopol, abandoned the care of the fortress to a mixed garrison of some 36,000 men, more than half of them sailors from the fleet, and withdrew with his field army to the interior of the Crimea. His adversaries, shrinking from the costly process of an assault on the northern defences, moved round to the east of the place, and passing *en route,* without realising it, close to the rear of the retiring Russian host, took up position before the south front, on the plateau known as the Chersonese Upland. The necessary interval of time which elapsed before they could disembark and bring forward their siege artillery was put to excellent use by the garrison, who, under the energetic direction of Todleben, so strengthened their defences that when the besiegers' guns finally opened their bombard-

---

1. So much so that he frequently, throughout the campaign, referred to his enemy as "the French".

ment, the results achieved, though in themselves satisfactory, were insufficient to warrant the delivery of an assault. A few days before this St. Arnaud had died of disease, and was replaced at the head of the French army by Canrobert.

Meanwhile Menschikoff was preparing a counter-offensive. His first blow was delivered on October 25 by a corps of 25,000 men, which advanced from the Tchernaya valley against the right flank of the British and their communications, with their base in Balaclava cove. After some initial success he was checked by a fine counter-attack by the British heavy cavalry, and finally brought to a standstill by the gallant if ill-conceived charge of the Light Brigade—a feat which, for literary rather than military reasons, has become enshrined as an imperishable episode in the history of our army. Eleven days later, on November 5, a second blow was struck, this time at the British right wing on Mount Inkerman. Here, though some 72,000 Russians were from first to last brought into action against less than a fourth that number of British and French, the victory, after ten hours' desperate fighting, lay with the latter, who at the end of the day held all their positions intact. Henceforward Menschikoff confined himself to feeding the garrison of Sebastopol with constant reinforcements, and desisted from all attempts to measure himself against the Allies in the open field.

The latter, however, were for the next few months too preoccupied with their own internal troubles to be able seriously to prosecute the siege. With the coming of winter's rain and snow there ensued a time of fearful suffering and privation for the soldiery encamped on the bleak slopes of the Upland. The service of the trenches was carried on under conditions made by a greater war all too familiar to the youth of our own generation, who, however, had seldom to endure the shortage of food, of fuel, of warm clothing and of all the other necessaries of life in a winter campaign endured bravely and uncomplainingly by our ill-fated Crimean army. The complete inadequacy of the transport service crippled all attempts to ameliorate its fearful lot, and in a few weeks over fifty per cent of its effective strength had been rendered unfit for service. Nor had the residue that remained at duty any reason to envy their crippled comrades. The hospitals at Scutari, even when reached after a lengthy and painful journey by land and sea, proved merely a breeding ground of further suffering and death until purged and remodelled by the medical authorities under the urge of an enraged public opinion in England, and the vigorous and unceasing pressure of the head of a band of nurses, Florence Nightingale—with all her domineering asperity, the one heroic figure of the campaign, if indeed it be permissible to except those thousands of nameless men who paid in suffering and death for their countrymen's resolve to wage war without preparing for it.

Not till the coming of the spring, and with it a lavish supply of all necessaries from home, was the plague stayed and the army once more rendered fit for action. Even during the worst of the winter weather, indeed, sporadic operations had gone on incessantly; mining and countermining, bombardment and sortie had been always in progress, and the disgraceful failure of a Russian attempt to drive into the sea a Turkish detachment entrenched at Eupatoria, on the coast, had brought to a welcome grave the broken heart of the once proud sovereign of All the Russias.

With the coming of finer weather in the spring of 1855 the besiegers pressed their preparations for the final intensive bombardment which was to precede and prepare the assault on Sebastopol. Five hundred siege guns were placed in position, and early in April fire was opened and continued unintermitted for ten days. The resulting destruction and slaughter in the city attained appalling proportions, but no infantry attack ensued. The reason for this was that the French Emperor was toying with another plan of campaign, which involved the suspension of the siege of the fortress for the time being, pending the result of active operations in the open field by a new army then in process of assembly around Constantinople. Of this army he proposed to take command in person, and hoped that its success would of itself lead to the voluntary evacuation of Sebastopol by the Russians. Strenuous opposition was raised to this design both by the British Government and by the French commanders in the Crimea, but the resulting repercussion on the operations actually in train continued until its final abandonment late in the summer. A secondary result was the replacement of Canrobert, whom recent events had proved to be unequal to the supreme command of the French army, by a man of far stronger calibre, Pelissier. Under his vigorous impulsion the task of reducing Sebastopol was soon in a fair way to accomplishment. An important success was achieved at the end of May by the capture of Kertch, the Russian base in the eastern portion of the peninsula, by a joint expedition of 15,000 men, and the destruction of the stores and shipping collected there; and June 18, the anniversary of Waterloo, was fixed on for the assault which should seal the fate of the fortress. But despite an effective preparation by the Allied artillery, the infantry, both French and British, failed to effect any lodgement in the Russian works. The set-back dealt the final blow to the failing spirit of Lord Raglan, who died some ten days later, and was succeeded in his command by General Simpson. Some compensation, however, was to be found in the fact that Todleben, the soul of the Russian defence, had been incapacitated in the course of the assault.

Gortschakoff, who had some time since replaced Menschikoff in chief command in the Crimea, was under no delusions as to the temporary nature of the respite afforded by the failure of this attack, and determined to make a final effort to relieve the fortress before it was too late. His offensive in the Tchernaya valley was, however, beaten off with crushing loss by the French troops holding the right of the Allied line, assisted by a contingent from Piedmont, which had joined the alliance early in the year. Yet though it was clear to every one from the Russian commander-in-chief downwards that all was now lost save honour, Sebastopol was left to stand the final assault, which took place on September 8. Along the greater part of the line, including the British sector before the Redan, no permanent success was achieved, but the surprise and capture of the key position of the Malakoff by the French put an end to all hope of further resistance, and the long agony of the city was ended by the withdrawal of the remnant of the garrison. Its defence had bled Russia white; apart from the casualties in battle and by disease within its walls, the losses among the raw, half-starved and sickly recruits sent from the interior attained the appalling proportion of two men out of every three; and it was computed by Allied statisticians that the enemy's defeat had cost him little less than 500,000 men.

The Allies now had such a preponderance in the Crimea as to be easily able to detach forces for other purposes. Kinburn, an important Russian base on the Black Sea coast, west of the peninsula, was captured, and the loss of this harbour, the destruction of the works and dockyard of Sebastopol, and the obvious hopelessness of further continuance of the struggle, predisposed Czar Alexander II. to ask for terms. France and England felt no inclination to face another Crimean winter, and hostilities therefore came to an end. The Treaty of Paris, signed in February 1856, by excluding Russian warships from the Black Sea, gave a check, though a temporary one only, to her onward progress in the direction of Constantinople; but though her losses may be said to have crippled her for a generation, it is doubtful if this result was in any way commensurate with the efforts put forward and the sacrifices endured by the victorious Allied powers.

The Crimean War, apart from the heroism and endurance of the lower ranks of the contending armies, reflected little glory on any of the participants. It is a dreary story of divided counsels, administrative short-sightedness and incompetence, and uninspired leadership. Its course and result, however, afford to the historian one of the most striking examples on record of the immense range and potency of an army based on sea power. A composite expeditionary force numbering at no time more than 200,000 men was enabled, despite glaring defects in composition and conduct, to establish itself on the territory of an adversary immeasurably its superior in military resources, men and material; to wrest from him a strong place the maintenance of which was of vital importance to the pursuit of his most cherished national ambition; and to inflict on him, in the course of his unsuccessful struggle to keep possession of his own, casualties amounting to more than double its own strength. And yet this European power, which thus displayed to the world its inability to defend its own frontiers against the attack of a numerically insignificant enemy, was for many years after the Crimean War, and even down to our own time, believed by sane and experienced observers to be competent successfully to solve the colossal military and administrative problem involved in an offensive through Afghanistan against India.

4. THE BIRTH OF THE MODERN ARMY
1855–1882

The radical defects in our military system revealed by the war in the Crimea, and to a less extent in the Indian Mutiny, awakened Parliament and the public to the urgent need for a thoroughgoing and speedy reorganisation. Yet so great were the forces of inertia, and so spasmodic the interest taken in army affairs by the governing classes and the mass of the electorate, that close on thirty years had passed before we had fashioned our "New Model" army to our satisfaction. Accordingly the period between the close of the Crimean War and the Egyptian campaign of 1882—the first waged by the new army—was one of slow but complete transition.

The first and indeed only immediate effect of our Crimean experiences took the form of a remodelling of the higher administrative system, which, as then constituted, involved a division of responsibility between nine independent and often mutually conflicting offices. These were in 1855 reduced to two; of the four principal authorities the Secretary of War and the Ordnance Board were swept away, leaving the Secretary of State for War at the War Office responsible for the civil, and the commander-in-chief at the Horse Guards for the military departments connected with the army. This system, which was at all events less anomalous than that which had preceded it, endured for fifteen years.

The three years, 1858-1860, were epoch-making in the history of our military organisation—only less important than the vital period ten years later, when our modern British army was born. The establishment of the present Staff College in 1858 was followed next year by two very far-reaching changes. The first of these, the reconstitution of the Indian army, was of course a direct result of the great Mutiny which had just been suppressed at a heavy cost of blood and treasure. The events of the Mutiny itself will be dealt with in a subsequent chapter; but its effects on the organisation of the army fall naturally into their place here. Briefly it was a question whether, now that the responsibility for the government of India had been definitely assumed by the Crown, the proportion of white troops necessary for the defence of the country should be provided by the British army or should form a separate force raised and equipped specially for that purpose. After prolonged discussion, and in the face of no little opposition from many whom long residence in India and honourable service under "John Company" rendered perhaps more mindful of past glories than of present necessities, the former course was adopted. The nine white battalions maintained by the East India Company were incorporated in the British army, and the contingent to be maintained in the country and charged to the revenues of the Indian Government was fixed at a round figure of 80,000 of all arms. The native army, much of which had disappeared during the turmoil of the revolt, was completely reorganised. The number of infantry battalions was reduced by amalgamation or disbandment to 142, and that of the cavalry regiments to 42; and the native artillery was for all practical purposes abolished. This process took much time, not being completed till 1865, and even then much had still to be done before the Indian army system could be said to have reached a reasonably high standard of administrative efficiency.

The second great change brought about in this period in the military sphere was the formation of the Volunteer Force. Born in a moment of spontaneous popular enthusiasm engendered by a recrudescence of Anglophobia in France, the movement in a few weeks assumed national proportions, and by the summer of 1860 no less than 180,000 volunteers had been enrolled. The War Office did its best to foster and encourage it by every means short of the assumption of direct control; and though the military value of the force was somewhat discounted by the absence of such control, and the lack of any unified system in the recruitment, equipment and terms of service of the various units, which depended mainly on private and voluntary effort, the moral accompaniments of an enhancement of popular interest in and knowledge of military affairs were to prove incalculable benefits alike to army and to nation.

The triumph of the admirably organised and scientifically trained armies of Prussia over her two enemies, Austria and France, who had relied to an undue extent on traditional and out-of-date methods, gave irresistible point and weight to the arguments for radical military reform in this country; and in 1868 there came into office as Secretary of State for War one whose name deserves to be held in high honour as the father of the present-day British army—Mr. Edward (later Lord) Cardwell. Under his able and patient direction there was carried through, between the years 1868 and 1872, a series of measures which had the effect of remodelling the whole of our military system from top to bottom. The higher command was once more centralised and unified by placing the commander-in-chief and his staff at the Horse Guards in direct subordination to the Secretary of State for War, who thus became the supreme head of the army, responsible to Parliament and the country. The unfair and anomalous purchase system, by which the moneyed officer could buy promotion over the heads of his more experienced but impecunious comrades, was, despite the vested interests involved and the consequent outcry at the first suggestion of its abolition, swept away root and branch, and all holders of the Queen's commission were placed henceforward on an equal footing for all purposes throughout the service. The introduction of a uniform term of service for twelve years, apportioned between colour and reserve service in accordance with the needs of the arm or branch concerned and with the exigencies of the recruiting and industrial situation, tended to attract a better class of men to the ranks, and automatically provided for the maintenance of an adequate reserve of trained men who could be called up if and when need arose. Further, the Regular Army and the separate reserve forces, such as the Militia and Volunteers, who were liable for home service only, were welded into one homogeneous army by the establishment throughout the country of regimental districts, in which units of all these forces were brought into direct and intimate conjunction; each district normally comprised two line battalions (of which one would be on service abroad), a regular depot feeding both in peace time, two militia battalions, which it was hoped would supply recruits in war, and a proportionate number of volunteer units. Each pair of regular battalions, at first merely linked, were later formed into one regiment and renamed accordingly; the militia and volunteer corps also received the new names, and with this measure the unification of the component parts of the regimental district was completed. Finally, the reduction of certain colonial garrisons rendered possible the equalisation of the number of units at home and abroad, thus facilitating a system of regular reliefs at short intervals, a constant and ample supply of drafts from the units at home to those on foreign service, and the provision of a force in the British Isles adequate either for home defence purposes or for despatch overseas at need.

This last change was not carried out till 1882, some time after Lord Cardwell had retired from office. His work had, as was only natural, caused considerable heartburning, and aroused much determined opposition in many quarters, even the highest, and to achieve his aims he had perforce trampled on many a cherished tradition and done violence to much legitimate and honourable sentiment. Nevertheless, none will now dispute that the end in this case justified the means. The man who, in place of a heterogeneous concourse of military atoms and an outworn and antiquated system, gave us a unified army raised and trained on up-to-date lines, yet eminently adapted to our peculiar domestic and Imperial needs, deserves a high place among British statesmen and in the grateful memory of all soldiers who since his time have entered into his labours and proved the sterling value of the foundations thus truly and diligently laid.

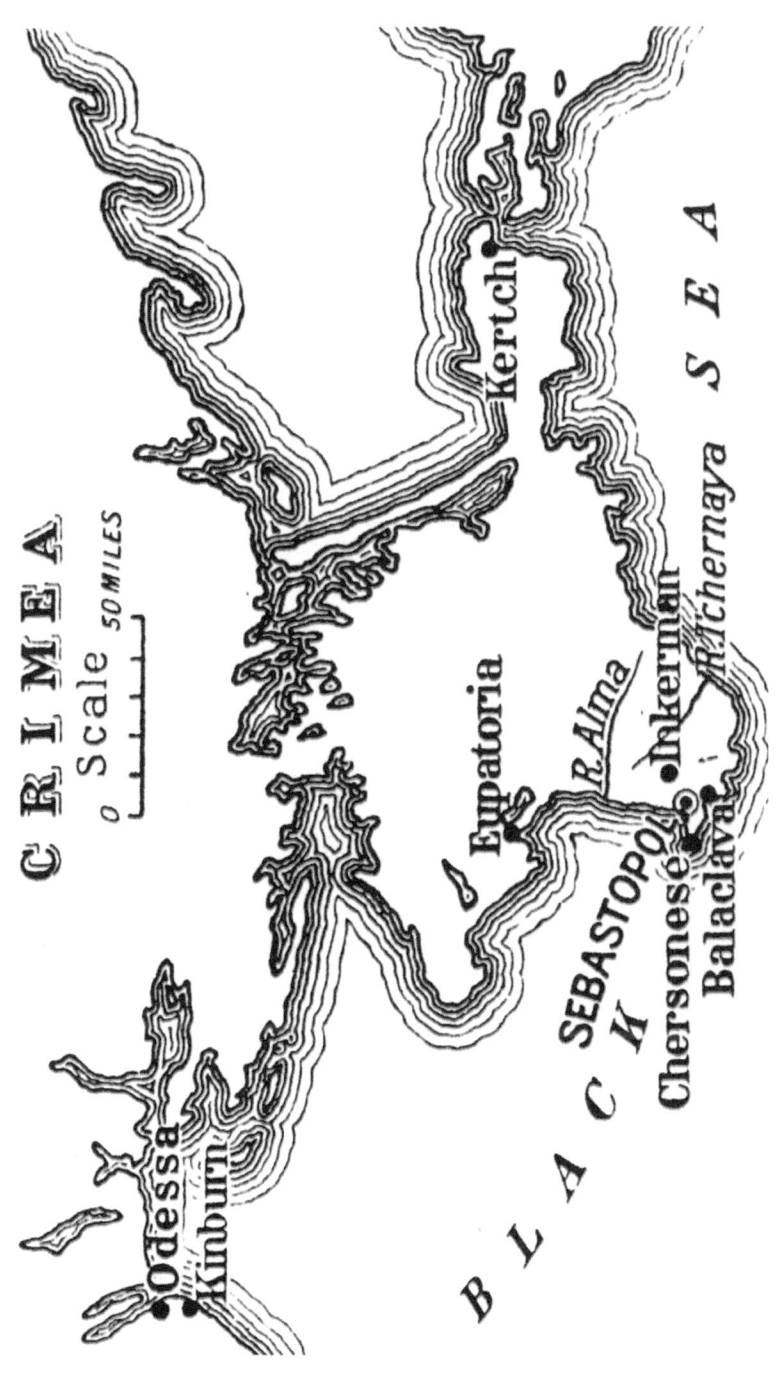

British infantry in the Crimea

Charge of the Highlanders before Cawnpore under General Havelock

Gurkhas at Tirah

CHAPTER 14

The Mutiny and Our Later Indian Wars
1857-1913

1. The Sepoy Revolt
1857-1859

In the summer of 1857 there burst out, with the appalling suddenness of a convulsion of nature, a catastrophe which shook the edifice of our rule in India to its foundations, and all but brought it crashing down in irremediable ruin.

The causes of this disaster have since been widely discussed with all the wisdom that comes after the event, but only a very brief summary of them is necessary here. From the political point of view there was general dissatisfaction and unsettlement consequent on the forceful government of Dalhousie, with its vigorous assertion of the rights of the paramount power as evinced particularly in the annexation of Oude, and the enforcement of the doctrine of lapse in the cases of Nana Sahib, the adopted heir of the last Peshwa, and the Rani of Jhansi. Allied and interdependent with this was the widespread fear, among Hindu and Moslem alike, of a deliberate and far-reaching attack on their faiths and customs in the name of Christianity. All this, however, could only prepare the ground for a revolt which was essentially military in origin and found little support outside the lowest elements of the people. Even among the sepoy regiments in British service those of the Madras and Bombay armies were hardly affected, and indeed took a creditable share in the suppression of the mutiny engineered and carried out almost entirely by their comrades of Bengal. Among these, discipline had been undermined, and vanity and arrogance increased beyond measure by much pampering, while at the same time many of their most cherished religious and military prejudices had been thoughtlessly offended or harshly overridden. Out of touch with their officers, whose general level of efficiency was not high, and knowing nothing of the real power of England, they believed themselves able to remedy their grievances by force of arms, and set themselves up in the place of the handful of their white masters, whose soldiers numbered barely 38,000 in all India as against 200,000 sepoys, and were unsuitably disposed for the purpose of dealing with internal disorder. The issue of the famous greased cartridges, abhorrent to men of both the great Indian faiths, was accepted as a sign that the time for action had come ; but if any plans had been concocted for simultaneous and universal action, they were forestalled by the outbreak at Meerut on May 15, 1857—the first act in the great Mutiny, which, but for the lamentable inaction of the local commanders, might well have been also the last. But the rebels were allowed to make their way unmolested to Delhi, where they raised the garrison, restored to his throne Bahador Shah, the last of the Moguls, massacred the hated Europeans, and sent forth the fiery cross to the thousands of their waiting comrades throughout the length and breadth of the land. In six weeks their example had been followed in countless stations, great and small, where there were white men and women to be butchered and wealth and property to be had for the taking. From Behar to the Punjab and Rajputana borders, from the Himalayan foothills to the banks of the Tapti, all the countryside was furiously aflame. Along every road leading west and north bands of triumphant mutineers were streaming towards their new capital; and the white garrison which held India for England heard in one and the same breath of private grief and public catastrophe, of the loss of their dear ones, and of the tottering of their empire.

Within our present limits it is of course impossible to do anything like justice to the epic of the great Mutiny and its suppression; we can only deal briefly with the broad lines of the story—shorn, it is to be feared, with all of its splendour, of much of its interest—and must perforce concentrate our attention on the main foci of the rebellion and the main theatres of operations, in Rohilkhand, in Oude and in Central India. Beyond the borders of these territories there were only sporadic and isolated incidents which need not long detain us. The recently conquered Sikhs of the Punjab, which was under the rule of John Lawrence, one of the outstanding figures of his time, and a band of subordinates in every way worthy of their chief, not only remained loyal, but later sent many troops and much material assistance to the British forces operating against Delhi and in Oude and Rohilkhand. Rajputana, though more disturbed, was on the whole kept well in hand by another Lawrence, George. The simmering discontent in Behar was also long prevented from coming to a head; and though military operations became ultimately necessary for the restoration of complete order, they were on nothing like the same scale as elsewhere. There was a brilliant little episode at Arrah, where a garrison consisting mainly of civilians defended themselves heroically in a fortified house for a considerable period of time, and were finally relieved by an equally creditable operation conducted by Vincent Eyre. The able guerilla rebel, Koer Singh, kept a number of British columns, in aggregate many times his own strength, busy in the angle between the Gogra and the Sone from August 1857 till May 1858; and it was not till the end of the latter year that his followers were completely dispersed and the province at peace once again.

All this, however, was but subsidiary to the main campaign, which for four months after the first outbreak of the Mutiny centred round Delhi. Here the rebels had their titular chief, their headquarters, their strongest forces, and—despite the blowing up of the magazine by a handful of heroes in the first day of the rising—immense reserves of guns and ammunition. On the ancient city the gaze of all India, as of all England, was focussed, and with its fate was bound up by universal admission the whole future of the rebellion. With a sure instinct then, and by a wise policy, was its recapture made our first objective.

A force of some 4,000 men, made up of troops from Meerut and Ambala, was assembled before the city by the second week in June; the rebel detachments which attempted to prevent their concentration were defeated and forced to fall back within the walls, and the besiegers took post on the historic Ridge facing the northern front. Although its right flank was weak, the position, was on the whole a strong one, and there for two months we maintained ourselves against a series of gallant attacks delivered at the average rate of one every other day. The enemy's defence was as active and his resources of men and material so overwhelmingly superior that during this period the occupants of the Ridge were only in name the assailants, and had all their work cut out to hold their ground. It was only on the arrival of the Punjab movable column under John Nicholson, the most vivid and heroic personality among the galaxy of giants brought into prominence by the stress and strain of the Mutiny time, who had just done yeoman service in the reduction of the disorderly elements in the Punjab, that an attack on the city could be even thought of; it was not till the coming of the siege train, the way for which had been cleared by his dashing little victory at Najafgarh, some miles west of the city, that it could be seriously taken in hand. Although Wilson's besieging army still only numbered under 10,000 as against the 30,000 of his enemies, batteries were at once constructed, and after three days' effective bombardment an assault was delivered by four columns at dawn on September 14. All but one penetrated by breaches or gate, and effected a firm lodgement within the walls; but so stubborn was the resistance that it was not till the seventh day of fighting that Bahadur Shah's palace was stormed, the fall of Delhi an accomplished fact, and the last of the Moguls a prisoner in our hands.

Thus was achieved the first, the finest and the most costly of our Mutiny triumphs. More than forty per cent of the victors, including the great Nicholson, were struck down during the three months of the siege—a loss numerically exceeding that incurred in all the other major operations of the war put together, and proportionately as high as that in any British campaign prior to this date. Even from these bald figures can be gathered some idea of the suffering and sacrifice, of the toil and blood so lavishly paid for Delhi; but the gain was worth the price, for it was, and was universally recognised as, the turning point of the war and an earnest of assured victory.

Meanwhile, farther to the east, Oude, ruled by Henry Lawrence, the third and noblest of the famous brotherhood, was from end to end in arms against us, and anarchy was temporarily triumphant. In Lucknow its outbreak had for the time been forestalled, but at Cawnpore, Allahabad and Benares the white men were shut in by hordes of enemies, and the resources at the disposal of the Government were hopelessly inadequate to deal with the crisis. However, Neill led a small column by rail and river up country, and succeeded in succouring the two last-named places. But at Cawnpore the tragedy was played out to its poignant *dénouement.* Eight hundred souls, of whom half were women and children, ensconced in an indefensible entrenchment, suffered for three weeks the terrors of bombardment and assault before surrendering themselves on promise of their lives to the good faith of Nana Sahib, and all—the men at once, the rest a few weeks later—paid for their trust in the only coin left for them to pay.

The fires of racial hatred henceforth flamed unchecked; the war became for England a crusade for vengeance, and to this day the memory of the crime remains, to the obliteration of everything else, as the chief legacy of those unhappy times.

With the blood of their captives still fresh on their arms a body of the rebels moved against Lucknow, and Lawrence, unwisely leading forth his few troops to meet them outside the walls, was defeated and closely invested in the Residency. Here with a heroism equal to, but a better fortune than, that of the garrison of Cawnpore, the English maintained themselves—3,000 souls, of whom only 1,700 could bear arms— for a long twelve weeks against repeated assault, an incessant bombardment, and mining, assiduously carried on by an overwhelming hostile force. Lawrence was killed early, and his mantle fell on the worthy shoulders of Inglis. It was early July when their fiery trial began, and in addition to all the other evils that afflicted them they had to suffer that of hope deferred; for less than fifty miles from them a tiny force of less than 2,000 men under Havelock was fighting victoriously, but for many a long day in vain, to succour them.

Havelock, setting out from Allahabad at the beginning of July, had executed a victorious advance to Cawnpore, which he had reached and reoccupied in less than a fortnight, after scattering the Nana's troops in rout before him, only to find that the latter had consummated his crime the day before, leaving nothing but a heap of blood-stained corpses of women and children to be mourned over and buried. The British commander was steadfast to push on to Lucknow, but so wasted was his force by daily casualties and the ravages of disease that, though he made two separate attempts to break through, and in three weeks fought five successful actions, the hostile forces were impenetrable, and he had enough to do to maintain his ground. At last, however, in mid-September, reinforcements, bringing his strength up to its original exiguous figure, reached him and enabled him to renew his attempt at succour; Outram, who had brought them, and was destined to supersede Havelock, generously refrained from doing so until he should have completed his glorious task. Driving the rebels before them into Lucknow, the British made their way along the outskirts of the city as far as the north-eastern corner, and then breaking by sheer hard fighting and at heavy cost into and through the maze of defensible buildings separating them from the Residency, joined hands on the evening of September 25 with the little band they had come to save. But so weak in numbers were they that they were a reinforcing rather than a relieving force, and seeing the hopelessness of any attempt even to withdraw the garrison, Outram, who was now in command, decided that he could for the present do no more than remain where he was.

Meanwhile, the fall of Delhi having released some British troops for other operations, a column had been sent to the relief of Agra, which was menaced by the revolted contingent of sepoys in the service of Sindia of Gwalior. The operation was unskilfully conducted, but was carried through to a successful conclusion, thanks to the fine fighting qualities of the troops, who redeemed the errors of their commanders.

Such, then, was the situation when the new Commander-in-Chief, Sir Colin Campbell, an able, methodical and cautious soldier, whose wide experience of war included service in three continents, arrived at Cawnpore to assume charge of the operations in the field. Delhi, the main centre of the revolt, had been retaken, and its titular head was a captive about to stand his trial, but both to the north and south of the middle Ganges vast tracts of country still remained to be reconquered, and the rebel forces still in the field were formidable both numerically and morally. To the north the garrison of Lucknow was still in great peril, surrounded and beset as it was by a host of enemies; to the south the Gwalior contingent, with all Central India at its back, hovered awaiting its opportunity to strike. Campbell, undeterred by this menace to his rear, resolved to deliver his first blow at Lucknow with the main force at his disposal—a paltry 4,000 men—leaving a detachment to guard his base at Cawnpore. The calculations of time and space were so nice as to leave no margin for error or ill fortune, but success deservedly rewarded his courage and vigour. Seven days of rapid marching and well-directed and stubborn fighting brought him to the gates of the Residency. The available time and force was insufficient to allow of anything more than the withdrawal of the beleaguered garrison with its long convoy of non-combatants, whose safety was for the moment the general's first care, and by skilful staff work this was successfully secured. Hardly was the whole clear of the city than urgent news of imminent disaster at Cawnpore summoned Campbell hurriedly to retrace his steps. The Gwalior contingent, under the able leadership of Tantia Topi, had some days before fallen on the detachment left behind, and driven it back in disorder to the banks of the Ganges. By forced marches the main army sped to its rescue, and in a well-fought little action drove the enemy off in disorder northwards and westwards. The game of interior lines had been admirably and successfully played to its conclusion, and it now remained to reap its full fruits. Accordingly Campbell set to work to reconquer the Doab between the Ganges and the Jumna as a base for further operations. Three converging columns from Delhi, Cawnpore and Allahabad moved concentrically on Fatehgarh, encountering little resistance, and by the early weeks of 1858 had completed their junction and fulfilled their missions as laid down. The rebels to the south were too cowed to interfere, and Outram, who had been left to observe Lucknow, effectually prevented any hostile counter-offensive from Oude.

Campbell's plans now envisaged as the next move the restoration of British rule in Rohilkhand, but for political reasons the Governor-General, Canning, preferred as a preliminary the recapture of Lucknow, the loss of which he considered would be an irreparable blow to the Oude rebels. Against his own wish, but with complete loyalty, the commander-in-chief therefore set to work to prepare with conscientious thoroughness for this new task. Reinforcements in great numbers were now arriving by every ship from home, and when in early March he finally set forth it was with a magnificent army of close on 25,000 men, including a Gurkha contingent from Nepal, at his back. After a junction with Outram, who with less than 4,000 men had held his ground with consummate resolution and skill against a rebel host of over 100,000 men within Lucknow, a comprehensive scheme for the reduction of the hostile stronghold was drawn up and methodically carried to a victorious conclusion, after nearly three weeks of continuous fighting amid the maze of streets and houses. Owing, however, partly to the mistakes of his subordinates, and partly to Campbell's own reluctance to incur heavy loss of life, a large part of the garrison managed to make their escape, and survived to prolong the struggle in the open country for many months.

That they were allowed a respite to recover their morale and organise a new resistance was not Campbell's fault, for he was now directed, once more against his own desire, to attempt what had before been forbidden him—the reconquest of Rohilkhand. His plan of operations was on similar lines to that which had worked out so successfully in the Doab four months before—a concentric advance in three columns from north-west, south and south-east, with the capital of the province, Bareilly, as their appointed place of meeting. After some fighting on the way thither, the junction was duly effected early in May; the rebel force, in all some 30,000 strong, which stood to give battle and acquitted itself admirably, was defeated and dispersed, and though some further clearing-up operations were necessary before the full fruits of the victory could be reaped, Rohilkhand from end to end was once more in our hands by mid-June.

The way was thus cleared for the final enterprise against Oude, where 150,000 armed men were still defying our arms in open rebellion. By the commencement of the cold weather all Campbell's preparations for this last of his campaigns had been completed. The insurgents were first driven by the carefully combined operations of a number of mobile columns from the area between the Ganges and the Gogra; this part of the scheme took some two and a half months in fulfilment, and was not finally accomplished till mid-December. The next and last stage was short and decisive; in a fortnight the remnant of the rebels, including the infamous Nana, were seeking refuge in the inhospitable mountains of Nepal, and the victorious army was returning to the plains prior to being dispersed.

Our lost dominion in northern India had thus after eighteen months of campaigning been finally regained. This triumphant result was due first and foremost to the indomitable endurance and valour of the British soldier, then to the daring, enterprise and constancy of a host of brilliant leaders such as Outram, Havelock and Nicholson, and last but not least to the solid and patient generalship of the commander-in-chief, who, if his military qualities can hardly be said to qualify him for a place among the masters of war, deserves to be put beside Amherst and Hastings as an outstanding organiser of victory. To him, more than to any other single man of the time, was it due that our dominion in India survived the awful convulsion of 1857 and emerged from its fiery trial more firmly founded than before.

Meanwhile equally important and equally successful operations had been in progress during the year to the south of the Ganges, amid the hills and jungles of Central India. Here the chief figure on the rebel side was the Rani of Jhansi, a masterful woman whose passionate sense of wrong had led her in the first days of the revolt to commit a massacre less well known but not less treacherous and horrible than that of Cawnpore. The reigning Mahratta princes, Sindia and Holkar, fortunately for themselves and us, remained staunch to their faith, but were unable to restrain their followers from joining forces with the insurgents. Of the fortunes of the Gwalior contingent we have already seen something; the Indore troops cooperated with those of the Rani and of the lesser Central Indian chiefs and the revolted sepoys to raise the standard of rebellion in Bundelcund and Malwa. By July 1857 the area between the Jumna and the Tapti had passed entirely from our control; nor for the moment could any effective steps be taken to reconquer it. A small force under Stuart was indeed assembled with great difficulty and after much delay for operations in Malwa, but so formidable was the strength of its opponents, and so vast the territory to be dealt with, that by the end of the year it had effected little more than the reoccupation of the country round Mhow and Indore. This, however, formed an excellent base for further operations, for which there were now available not only a small but excellent body of reinforcements, but also a commander of remarkable energy and ability, Sir Hugh Rose.

The general plan was that the Central India Field Force, as this little army was called, should advance by way of Jhansi to Kalpi, restoring order as it went, and driving the insurgents across the Jumna into the arms of the main British force operating north of that river. Two flanking columns on either side, one of Madras troops under Whitlock advancing from the neighbourhood of Jubbulpore on Banda, the other of Bombay regiments under Roberts along the eastern border of Rajputana, were to assist and cooperate with Rose. The scheme, however, had to be modified from the outset owing to the urgent necessity for succouring Saugor, which was invested by a large body of rebels; accordingly Rose moved in person in that direction with half his troops, leaving the remainder under Stuart to follow the original line of advance. Both forces were successful in their enterprises; the commander-in-chief defeated and dispersed the enemy in his front, while his subordinate stormed Chanderi and drove his immediate adversaries back on Jhansi. Before the walls of this city the army rapidly concentrated, opened its trenches and commenced the bombardment; but before the time was ripe for assault, Tantia Topi, with 22,000 men of the Gwalior contingent, appeared to the rescue. With a handful of men, less than one-twentieth of his enemy's numbers—all that could be spared from the work of prosecuting the siege—Rose fell upon him and utterly defeated him all along the line, and this brilliant feat was at once followed up by the storming of the city. By April 3 Jhansi was in our hands and the Rani a landless fugitive. The hostile field army, however, formidable at least in numbers, still remained to be dealt with, and under the deadly rays of the Indian sun Rose followed remorselessly and tirelessly on its heels. Before Kalpi he effected his junction with a detachment of Campbell's army from the Doab, and thus reinforced brought his enemies to battle and defeated and dispersed them. The campaign appeared to be at an end; Whitlock, though his operations had been distinguished by little vigour or ability, and Roberts also, in their respective areas had effectively fulfilled their allotted tasks, and the orders for the dispersal of the Central India Field Force were actually in process of execution when news came that Tantia and the Rani had moved with a handful of men on Gwalior, corrupted Sindia's troops, and taken possession of the city.

Their triumph was but short-lived. Rose gathered together everything within reach—under 5,000 men in all—and directed them from all sides upon Gwalior. In a series of engagements lasting for four days the enemy's forces were enveloped, defeated and driven from the city. The Rani found the soldier's death to which her courage entitled her; the fort fell into our hands by a daring *coup de main*; and the remnant of the rebels, fleeing to the westward, were overtaken on the east bank of the Chambal by a mobile column and scattered to the four winds.

Tantia Topi, however, still remained at large with a small band of faithful followers, and before Central India could be considered pacified it was necessary to hunt him down. But he showed more talent and resource in his flight than ever he had done in his battles, and for many long and weary months eluded every wile of his pursuers. To and fro, doubling and twisting and turning, he ranged swiftly from Gwalior southwest to Udaipur, thence east to beyond the Betwa, and south to beyond the Nerbudda; then swinging north and east between Indore and Gwalior, he doubled north once more as far as the Bikanir border, then south again to Udaipur, and so to the jungles near Sironj. But fast and far as he fled, the avengers followed remorseless and relentless on his heels; time and again he was brought to action and defeated, until at long last, by losses and weariness, his small force had sunk to a handful of retainers, and from the leader of a forlorn hope he had become a mere fugitive criminal. At last in April 1859, after nine months of wandering, he was betrayed into our hands and expiated on the scaffold his share in the horror of Cawnpore. Thus the word "*Finis*" could at last be written to the long story of the Indian Mutiny.

Long ere this, on November 1, 1858, the East India Company, once the protagonist in the mightiest conquest of modern times, but long since shorn of all trace of its former glories, had passed into the limbo of forgotten things, and Queen Victoria had assumed the direct sovereignty of India. With the consequent changes in the status and organisation of the native army we have already dealt elsewhere.

The heroic yet tragic events of the Mutiny, in their terror and their grandeur a fitting pendant to all the preceding history of the British in India, proved that the men who had succeeded to the mighty heritage of their fathers were worthy to have and to hold what had been so well and hardly won. In essence it was on the British side a war of small columns, all highly mobile, brilliantly organised and led and directed by a master mind for the swift and effective reconquest of a vast tract of country defended by a gallant and disciplined enemy, vastly superior in numbers, but inadequately officered and without any effective superior direction. From first to last it was leaders that the rebels lacked, and that we, fortunately for England and for India, had in ample quantity and surpassing quality. The result of the Mutiny thus remains for all time a standing example of the superiority of mind over matter, of the triumph of the intellectual and moral military qualities over the purely physical.

2. The Second War with Afghanistan
1878-1881

It was not till twenty years after the last embers of the Mutiny had been stamped out that the newly constituted Indian Army received its first blooding in a large-scale war. The causes of this second conflict with Afghanistan bear a striking resemblance to those of the first. In each case the policy pursued by the British was motived by their fear of Russian aggression through the Amir's territory against India's north-west frontier, and was pushed on at headlong pace by a tempestuous Viceroy. Lytton, however, had more excuse for his actions than Auckland by reason of the greater proximity of Russia, whose territory now marched with the northern frontier of Afghanistan, and whose relations with England had become noticeably strained at the end of the Russo-Turkish War in 1878. For some years Afghanistan had been rent by a series of murderous conflicts for the succession to Dost Mahomed's throne, and when the successful candidate, Sher Ali, met with a blunt refusal to his request for British support against his internal and external foes, he naturally turned to Russia for aid, even going so far as to receive a mission at Cabul. Lytton at once demanded that a similar favour should be accorded to a British envoy, sent it in spite of Sher Ali's dissuasion, and saw it turned back at the frontier. This insult formed the occasion of the war which broke out in November 1878.

The British at once invaded Afghan territory at three points. A force of 12,000 men under Stewart, starting from Quetta, was directed by the Bolan Pass on Candahar; 6,000 men under Roberts entered the Kurram valley; and a strong right wing of 15,000 men under Browne moved west from Peshawar into the Khyber. To these forces, which with reserves totalled 43,000 men and 181 guns, the Afghans could oppose on paper 50,000 with 300 guns; but in actual fact their resistance was feeble and ineffective. Browne's part was a limited one, and according to his instructions, after he had driven the enemy from the mouth of the Khyber Pass, he halted at Jelalabad, where he remained from Christmas 1878 to the termination of the campaign by the Treaty of Gandamak in May 1879, with no more serious task than the guarding of his flanks and rear against the inroads of the turbulent tribesmen around him. Stewart's progress on the opposite wing was also attended with little serious fighting; early in January 1879 he arrived at Candahar, after a march which had been rendered arduous only by reason of the severe weather and the immense natural difficulties of the route, and pushed out detachments north and west to Khelat-i-Ghilzai and Girishk. The main Afghan effort was put forth against Roberts' small force in the Kurram, which, after overrunning the whole length of the valley, found itself faced by a threefold superior enemy in a strong position on the Peiwar Kotal; from this he was driven by an enveloping movement round his left, and the British success was exploited by a penetration into the Khost valley and the permanent subjection and occupation of the Kurram. The cession of this latter territory, of the Khyber Pass and of the Sibia-Pishin area were the main conditions of the Treaty of Gandamak, which after prolonged negotiations was signed with Yakub Khan, Sher Ali's successor, in May 1879. He also agreed to receive a British mission at Cabul and admit British control of his foreign policy. Pending the taking of effective steps by the Amir to give effect to the agreement, the British forces remained in their positions.

Events were not slow in justifying the fears of those who considered this peace to be premature and unlikely to endure. Less than four months after Cavagnari, the new envoy at Cabul, had taken up his residence there, he and his escort lost their lives in an armed insurrection which Yakub Khan made no effective attempt to repress, and an avenging army was at once started off for the treacherous city. Roberts and the Kurram column were entrusted with this task, and after dispersing with heavy loss a hostile force which endeavoured to block their progress near Charasia, entered the capital in mid-October. The Amir, despairing of his throne, had already surrendered his person into British hands, and shortly afterwards his abdication, and the lack of any candidate who was either suitable or immediately available, left the British no choice but to assume the temporary government of the country.

Before very long they had to assert this supremacy by force of arms. The rapidity of Roberts' advance and the swift completeness of his success had for a moment stunned the Afghans into acceptance of the *fait accompli*; but his enforced halt at Cabul, and the known weakness of his force, which rendered impossible any extended occupation of territory, soon emboldened them once more to try the fortune of battle. Early in December strong masses converged on Cabul from north, south and west, far outnumbering the scanty British garrison; the latter in a series of brilliant and daring manoeuvres succeeded for some days in holding them at arms' length, but finally its commander, considering the risks incurred by keeping the open field to be increasing beyond measure, prudently withdrew it into the fortified camp of Sherpur, north of the city. Here for ten days it was closely invested and cut off from the world. Two days before Christmas

100,000 Afghans sprang from their trenches to the assault, and in less than six hours' fighting were hurled back with such loss that on the morrow not a sign of them was to be seen. Cabul was peaceably reoccupied and communication with India restored, and by the end of the year not an enemy was abroad in northern Afghanistan.

None the less, to avert the danger of any fresh outbreak, and to render possible the occupation of a wider area than the mere vicinity of Cabul, it was decided that Roberts' troops should be reinforced from Candahar as soon as the weather permitted. At the end of March 1880 Stewart in person set out at the head of 7,000 men, moving in two columns by Khelat-i-Ghilzai and Ghazni. Two marches south of the latter place he had a sharp skirmish at Ahmed Khel, and the detachment sent out by Roberts to bring him in was also attacked *en route*. None the less, the junction was safely effected at the end of May, Stewart, by virtue of his seniority, assuming chief command of the united forces.

Meanwhile steps had been taken to put an end to the impossible political situation in Afghanistan by opening negotiations with Abdur Rahman, a nephew of Sher Ali, and the best of the claimants to the Amir's throne. This prince, though at the moment an exile in Russian territory, was regarded as an acceptable candidate, and after lengthy *pourparlers,* lasting from April to the end of July, agreed to ratify the terms of the Gandamak treaty in exchange for recognition as ruler of Cabul and as much of the rest of the country as he could conquer for himself. Accordingly he was proclaimed Amir, and the British, relieved at this happy termination of their labours, were preparing to leave Cabul when disastrous news from the south compelled them to postpone their departure. Ayub Khan, a brother of Yakub, and Abdur Rahman's most formidable rival, had appeared in arms on the Helmand; the Afghan regiments opposed to him had deserted to his standard, a British brigade sent west from Candahar to cooperate with them had been practically wiped out in a disastrous action at Maiwand, and the troops left in the city were now closely invested by the triumphant rebels.

Stewart, summing up the situation with cool resolution, declined to interrupt the British evacuation of northern Afghanistan, and considered that the new crisis could be dealt with by the despatch of a relieving force from Cabul. At the same time a second column was preparing to move up to the rescue from Quetta. Roberts, who had been given charge of the former enterprise, after making careful and thorough preparations for his supply and transport *en route,* set out with 10,000 men early in August, and for the second time in less than nine months disappeared from the sight of the world for the space of three weeks. At the end of that time he was reported at Candahar, having covered 300 miles without encountering any resistance, relieved the beleaguered garrison, and scattered Ayub's army, drawn up for battle on the precipitous hills west of the city, to the four winds. Thus ingloriously terminated the last Afghan' effort in arms.*

Meanwhile the British troops from Cabul and the Kurram had been streaming steadily eastward, and by the end of October Abdur Rahman was left to the undisturbed possession of his new kingdom. It was, however, decided that we should remain at Candahar for the present till he should be ready to take it over; and accordingly it was not till April 1881 that the last white soldier was clear of Afghan soil. The new Amir proved himself to be not only possessed of unusual capacity, but a good friend of the British, and for forty years the relations between the late enemies left little to be desired.

Whatever may be thought of the morality or the wisdom of our policy before and during the second Afghan War, the military conduct of the campaign was entirely admirable and affords no ground for criticism; and the results achieved were as brilliant

---

* At the time of writing, 1914.

as the victories by which they were secured. The series of difficult administrative tasks on which the whole fate of the war turned were successfully dealt with; the troops invariably fought admirably against a brave and numerically superior enemy; and one of their commanders, Roberts, though perhaps favoured by a fortune which set him time and again in the forefront of the stage, displayed military qualities which placed him last but by no means least on the illustrious list of British sepoy generals.

3. The Conquest of Upper Burma and the Subsequent Campaigns on the North-east Frontier
1885-1898

Ever since the successful conclusion of the second war with Burma it had been evident that our final conquest and complete occupation of that country must sooner or later follow as an inevitable consequence of previous events, and the Court of Ava, with insane blindness to its own interests, did nothing to avert or even postpone the sealing of its fate. On the contrary, King Theebaw, the last occupant: of the Burmese throne, from his accession in 1878, repeated all the errors of his predecessors, insulting British representatives, dealing in tyrannical and high-handed fashion with our merchants, and misgoverning his unhappy country in so brutal a fashion that on humanitarian grounds alone our interference soon became necessary. His manifest desire to adopt a foreign policy hostile to British interests, and to place himself in close relations with France, whose territories closely adjoined his own eastern frontier, gave us further cause for complaint; but it was the infliction of a peculiarly outrageous fine on a British trading company which finally in November 1885 led the Viceroy, Lord Dufferin, to issue an ultimatum, and follow it up by a declaration of war.

The plan of campaign was at once simple and daring. Twelve

thousand men assembled at Rangoon under the command of Prendergast were to embark on a river flotilla o fifty-five craft, make a dash up the Irrawaddy on Mandalay Theebaw's new capital, and dethrone that monarch without more ado. It was anticipated that the Burmese army, the total strength of which was little if at all superior to that of the expeditionary force, would make no great resistance, nor did it in fact do so; while the well-known difficulties of climate and terrain were effectively overcome by the choice of the time and method of the advance. On November 15 the army crossed the enemy frontier at Thayetmyo, and in less than a fortnight had passed up the 300 miles of river separating it from its objective and entered Mandalay. Theebaw surrendered his person and family and was carried off as a State prisoner. The occupation a few weeks later of Bhamo, some 200 odd miles upstream from the capital, completed the operations, and on January 1, 1886, Upper Burma became a province of India, and the independent existence of the Burmese people came to an end.

The work of the British troops, on the other hand, had only just begun; and its difficulties were tremendous. The climate was extremely unhealthy, the country a tangle of swamp, sand, jungle and mountains, in places absolutely impenetrable, and everywhere passable only with extreme difficulty and labour. The Burmese troops had dispersed far and wide, and from them, and the more lawless elements of the population, various leaders had recruited the robber bands, known as dacoits, who early in 1886 appeared in great numbers, infested the whole land, terrorised and plundered the peaceful inhabitants, and spread petty war, confusion and anarchy everywhere. Their repression could only be a matter of time and infinite labour. The procedure for dealing with them had perforce to be, of course, the time-honoured and well-tried one of garrisoning the country with small fortified posts, operating with small flying columns, usually some 200 strong, against any band that showed itself, and gradually extending the boundaries of the occupied area as circumstances and resources permitted. The fulfilment of this toilsome and thankless task absorbed large numbers of troops, which had perforce to be dispersed over an enormous area, and were kept day in and day out constantly on the alert or on the move for weeks and months on end. So small in scale and multitudinous in number were the resulting marches and engagements, that they defy all attempt at detailed chronicle in a work such as this. All that can be essayed here is to describe in the broadest possible outline the general progress of the pacification to its successful conclusion.

In April 1886 the army, now under White, was ready to enter upon its Sisyphean task. The base of solid occupation from which further conquest was to be undertaken was formed by the southern frontier districts between the Irrawaddy and the Sittang, and the course of the former river by way of Mandalay to Bhamo. A railway along the valley of the latter stream, from Toungoo at its mouth to Mandalay, was taken in hand, and the communications by road and track through swamp and jungle were gradually extended and improved. Meanwhile the small flying columns operating north, east and west from their bases began to thread the country in all directions. During the five months to the end of August there were fought throughout the length and breadth of Upper Burma no less than one hundred little combats, all uniformly successful; the losses in action were insignificant, but disease took a far heavier toll, the hospital cases amounting to some twenty per cent of the effectives. At the end of the period in question some 25,000 troops in all were on the strength of the Upper Burma Field Force, while some thousands of military police, picked men from all over India, were being made ready to assist the army and take over its work as soon as the main dacoit bands had been satisfactorily dealt with. Many of these had in fact already been crushed or dispersed, but there were still a sufficient number at large to necessitate the undertaking of an even more elaborate and far-reaching campaign in the winter of 1886-1887, with the purpose both of consolidating our authority where it was already in existence and extending it yet further into the territories beyond.

Accordingly, as soon as the advent of suitable weather conditions permitted of the resumption of extended operations, the British were once more on the move. Small columns, each numbering anything from 200 to 1,000 men, were pushed outwards from the Irrawaddy on either side, up its various tributary streams and into the hills to north, east and west of the great river basin. By rapid and prolonged marches, and a series of sharp engagements, the various dacoit gangs still at large were overtaken, defeated and dispersed, and their leaders compelled to surrender or take to the hills as fugitives. Even so, complete success was not in sight till the end of 1888; and some idea of the immense nature of the task and the number of troops necessary to carry it out may be gathered from the fact that at this date garrisons had to be found by the Upper Burma Field Force for 141 separate posts. White, now that the fulfilment of his mission was all but accomplished, handed over his command in April 1889; but local outbreaks of disorder continued at intervals throughout the next two years, and culminated in the spring of 1891 in a serious rising at Wuntho, 150 miles north of Mandalay, which necessitated the despatch of a considerable force for its repression. With its successful termination the conquest of Upper Burma may be said to have been completed—five years after the *coup de main* which had hurled from his throne the last Burmese king: so great is the difference between defeating an enemy and pacifying his country. This new acquisition of territory brought with it a new frontier problem—that of our relations with the various tribes inhabiting the high lands to the west, north and east of Upper Burma. Of these the most turbulent were the Chins, who held the tangle of mountains separating Burma from the provinces of Chittagong and Manipur; but the difficulty of dealing with them arose rather from the nature of their country than from the inhabitants. A number of Burmese dacoit leaders had escaped into these hills on being driven from Burma, and stirred up the Chins to raid and burn and plunder in the plains; so that by 1889 some attempt to curb their aggression had become imperative. A considerable expedition, numbering some 3,500 men in all, was accordingly despatched against them in the winter of that year, a smaller force cooperating from Chittagong; but though the tribes were several times defeated in the field and reduced to submission for the moment, three smaller columns had to take the field next year against various refractory sections, or against the Chins' northern neighbours, the Lushais, who proved equally troublesome. Two further expeditions were necessary in the spring of 1892, and in the autumn a general rebellion on a large scale took place, which gave us considerable trouble before it could be repressed. From this time on the country became gradually more settled, and by the end of 1894 normal conditions of peace had been completely restored.

In the extreme northern part of the country, around the head waters of the Irrawaddy, lies a series of north and south mountain ranges inhabited by the Kachin tribes. Though capable of fighting well behind stockades, their usual form of fighting took the form of desultory raids. Our first appearance in their country at the end of 1885 aroused no hostility, and it was not till some six months later that they began to be troublesome. From this time on to the beginning of 1893 a series of annual punitive expeditions had to be undertaken in reprisal for some outrage or to reduce to order some refractory district or chief, and in 1898, after a long period of peace, there was a recurrence of local disorder which had to be forcibly repressed. The operations of these punitive columns, which rarely numbered as many as 1,000 of all ranks, were uniformly successful, though on more than one occasion determined resistance was encountered.

The Shan States, as they are called, are situated in the basin of the Salween River and the mountain ranges, extending thence westwards to the Irrawaddy valley, and eastwards up to and beyond the frontiers of French Indo-China and Siam. Formerly subject to Burmese rule, they fell into disorder when this disappeared, and at the end of 1886 certain elements in the southern Shan territory begged the British for their support. The expedition sent in compliance with their request early in 1887 had no fighting worthy the name, and in some six months this part of the country had been pacified. The northern States gave more trouble, small columns having to be sent out in 1887, and again in 1888, to deal with local disturbances. Generally speaking, however, it may be said that the Shan States, alone of the various peoples comprised within the limits of Upper Burma, accepted British authority practically without resistance, and since then have given no real trouble.

4. The North-West Frontier Campaigns 1852-1913

We come now to that phase of our military activity in India which has for the past fifty years filled the public eye more than any other—the series of campaigns on the northwest frontier. Our annexation of the Punjab and Sind, and the consequent extension of our boundary up to and beyond the Indus between 1840 and 1850, brought us into immediate contact, along a belt of mountainous territory extending from north and east of Peshawar right down to the Arabian Sea at the Indus delta, with the turbulent and uncivilised tribes inhabiting that inhospitable land. To the south of a line drawn roughly from Dera Ghazi Khan to Quetta dwelt the Baluchis, and with these our dealings were for the most part of a peaceful character up till the second Afghan war, when the hostility shown by the inhabitants of the Zhob Valley necessitated the taking of steps to tighten our control over this district. Thanks to the able and conciliatory policy of Sandeman, this was done without any expenditure of military effort beyond a small expedition of 1,600 men under White, which executed a military promenade through the country and met with no resistance. By 1891 the country was being administered right up to the Durand line, the delimited frontier between India and Afghanistan; it had been opened up to trade, the task of maintaining order was being carried out by the tribes themselves in exchange for money payments, and the British writ ran unchecked from the sea to the Gomal valley. Since that date Baluchistan has been as peaceful and orderly as any other part of India.

Far other was it with the territory to the north. Here the inhabitants were of the Pathan race, hereditary fighters and robbers—a people of magnificent virtues and vices; brave indeed, independent, hospitable and manly, but also treacherous, bloodthirsty, cruel and superstitious.

Rent by tribal, clan and individual feuds, the pursuit of which forms their favourite occupation, they may be relied on none the less to unite against a common invader, and to fight fiercely for the defence of their native valleys; while the first sign of weakness or withdrawal on his part is the signal for every tribe for miles round to flock to the scene of possible plunder and revenge. With this formidable and unconquerable race the British army in India was from 1847 onwards, up to, during, and after the Great War, incessantly at strife.

Our relations with the Pathans were from the first governed by what is known as the "close border policy," officially defined as "a stationary one where circumstances permit, and a forward one only when necessity compels". In other words, our military forces were held back within the territory directly administered by us, the western boundary of which ran roughly by way and inclusive of Muzaffarabad, Abbottabad, Peshawar, Kohat, Bannu and Tank; the tribes to the west of this line being normally left to their own devices, one of which was periodically to raid and plunder the plains beneath them. When this had been going on for some time, strong measures had to be taken against the offenders; fines were imposed, and if not paid were exacted by means of a blockade, or in extreme cases by a punitive expedition. After the second Afghan war, under the influence of Sandeman and the success of his "forward policy" in Baluchistan, some attempt was made to deal with the Pathans on similar lines, but the results were not considered satisfactory, and in 1898 the "close border" policy was reverted to, and continued in force till the outbreak of the Great War. Of the British posts established west of the administrative frontier, and between it and the Durand line prior to 1898, only Chitral was still retained, the posts in the Khyber Pass and in Waziristan being handed over to the care of units raised locally from the tribes and paid by us.

Into the various advantages and disadvantages of the "close border" as opposed to the forward policy, as regards which discussion was long, and indeed still is, vehement, it seems needless here to enter. The former is no doubt the more economical both militarily and financially; but it is arguable that lasting economy and military security in the event of war on or beyond the frontier can only be ensured by penetration of the territory of these turbulent tribesmen, and by turning their energies, at present directed towards strife and bloodshed, into the paths of peace, and that only a "forward" policy on our part can contribute to this desirable but possibly Utopian end.

We are here concerned, however, not with the merits or demerits of any future policy, but with the military results of that actually adopted in the past. It cannot be denied that the cost of the maintenance of our north-west frontier between 1847 and 1913 was, from the point of view of the British army, a very high one. During this period there took place in all sixty-six punitive expeditions—on an average one every year—carried out by forces ranging from a few hundred men to many thousands. On six occasions the rough equivalent of a modern division took the field, and in the greatest expedition of all—the Tirah campaign of 1897—practically an army corps was mobilised. Most of the infantry regiments in both British and Indian armies, not to speak of cavalry regiments and batteries, have at some time or other gone on active service on the north-west frontier; and in the aggregate, throughout the whole period, well over 300,000 men have been employed in these campaigns, which have cost us over 4,500 casualties.

It will readily be realised that it is impossible within the limits of a brief work such as this to retell in any detail the stories of all these little wars, in the course of which practically every one of the Pathan tribes on the frontier was visited and punished. We can only deal with those of major importance, in which forces of some magnitude—close on or exceeding 10,000 men—were employed.

The histories of these campaigns, of course, vary much in detail, but little in their broad outlines. After the provocation on the part of the tribe concerned had become too extreme for further endurance, or the fines for robberies and other outrages committed by it had reached so high a figure as to render them worth while collecting by force, a mixed detachment of all arms would be assembled at some suitable point adjoining the territory to be dealt with and a punitive raid carried out. If submission were not made on the terms offered, villages would be burnt, crops destroyed, and all possible material damage done to tribal property during the period of the stay within the offending territory, such period varying from a few hours to several weeks. At times the advance would be opposed by the tribesmen from a chosen position behind natural or artificial defences, where resistance would continue till put an end to by shell, bullet or bayonet. Usually, however, hostile action would take the form of sniping and surprise attacks against the outposts, or the flanks and rear of the column, or of night attacks with the *arme blanche* on entrenched camps or piquets ; while the retirement of the invaders would be a signal for a series of daring and persistent attempts to hustle or drive in its rearguard, destroy and plunder the baggage, and cause confusion and loss among the animals or the carriers accompanying the force. From about 1890 onwards, when the tribesmen first began to secure modern rifles in any number, frequent and effective sniping replaced hand-to-hand fighting as their normal tactics. The activity, local knowledge and resource with which these new methods were put into practice made our task of dealing with them more difficult and costly as time went on, necessitating ever more careful preparation and execution of every military enterprise and the employment of increasing numbers of troops, till our punitive expeditions became wars in miniature and the forces engaged in them little self-contained armies. This constant and increasing strain on our military resources had, however, its compensating advantages, for the North-West Frontier proved invaluable to us as a training ground, alike for the troops and their subordinate leaders, as also for the personnel of the administrative services.

During the period from 1847 to 1863 twenty-one expeditions were undertaken by us against various frontier tribes; the numbers engaged were in every case small, and though the natural difficulties encountered were often considerable, no serious fighting occurred. The chief interest, indeed, of this period lies in the appearance, at the head of one or other of these small expeditions, of such well-known figures as Colin Campbell, John Nicholson, and Neville Chamberlain, who here served their apprenticeship in independent command.

The Ambeyla expedition of 1863 first claims more extended notice. A small body of troops under Chamberlain was sent to rout out a troublesome band of Hindustani fanatics from their lair on the banks of the Indus, west of the Black Mountain. The Buner tribes lying to the north of our line of advance, between the Upper Swat and the Indus, who were expected to remain neutral, suddenly turned on the column after it had crossed the Ambeyla Pass and assailed it so fiercely that the advance was held up for six weeks before the arrival of British reinforcements, together with their own losses and ill success, induced the revolted tribe to come to terms. Our own casualties were also abnormally heavy, amounting to ten per cent of the whole force engaged.

The next five years saw only two small enterprises, but in 1868 the recalcitrance of the Black Mountain tribes necessitated the despatch against them of 12,000 men under Wilde, who traversed their territory from end to end, covering eighty miles of difficult and partly unexplored country in twenty-one days; little resistance was, however, met with.

The next twenty years, to 1888, were fruitful in frontier fighting, much of it arising from the passage through the tribal territory of British forces during the second Afghan war. None of it, however, was on a sufficiently important scale to call for detailed description here, till we come to the second Black Mountain campaign of 1888. Once again this turbulent area was the scene of extensive operations by a considerable force, 7,000 men under M'Queen converging in several columns, after several smart actions, on the crest of the mountain, whence all parts of the country, including some where no white man had yet set his foot, were visited and thoroughly opened up. Two more expeditions, in 1891 and 1892, were, however, necessary for the complete reduction to order of the Black Mountain area.

The first of these years also saw a campaign which, from brilliancy of conception and execution rather than from the forces engaged, deserves a mention at least. It was directed against the twin states of Hunza and Nagar nestling in the recesses of the Pamirs far to the north of Kashmir, whence a tiny force, less than 1,000 men, forcing its way through a series of rugged and seemingly invulnerable defiles, and storming several strong hill forts *en route,* forced its way to the capital of the state and dictated terms to its rulers.

Three years later, in 1894, an unprovoked attack by the Wazirs on the commission engaged in delimiting the Indo-Afghan boundary within their territory caused the despatch of a strong punitive force of 11,000 men under Turner and Lockhart. Their progress was a mere military promenade through the country, and the submission of the tribesmen was quickly enforced.

In 1895 a succession quarrel in the little state of Chitral far to the north beyond the lands of Swat and Bajaur, and the interference in the dispute of the ambitious chief of Jandol, led to the destruction of several British detachments then within or on the borders of the country and the investment of Chitral fort, which was held by a small British garrison. The siege was closely pressed for six weeks, until a division 15,000 strong under Low, collected at Peshawar for its relief, traversed the Swat and Dir valleys, scattering all opposition before it, and carried the war into the land of Jandol, whose chief had been the root of all the trouble. The siege was actually raised, however, by a small column under Kelly, who forced his way thither from Gilgit, north of Kashmir, over snow-covered mountain passes and in face of determined hostile resistance. Chitral from now onwards became a permanent station for British troops.

Two years later, in 1897, there burst out along the whole frontier from Swat and Buner in the north, by way of the Mohmand country, the Khyber Pass, and the territory of the Afridis to Tirah and the Tochi valley, a great tribal insurrection. The causes of this are in part still obscure, but the chief of them were undoubtedly the general belief that the demarcation of the frontier between India and Afghanistan would shortly be followed by the loss of tribal independence, and the unceasing efforts of the tribal Mullahs to stir up a religious war in defence of that independence. The garrisons of Malakand and Chakdara were vigorously assailed by the Swat and Bajaur tribesmen; our posts in the Khyber were overwhelmed one by one before help could be sent to them; and those west of Kohat either suffered or went near to suffering a similar fate. Various expeditions were at once set on foot to deal with this widespread revolt. Twelve thousand men under Blood repulsed the enemy from before Malakand and Chakdara, crossed the passes northwards into Swat territory and thence westwards into Bajaur, and after considerable fighting, much of it fierce and sustained, restored order in these valleys. Thence it turned east against Buner, crushed the insurgents in one sharp action, and enforced complete submission in this area also. Meanwhile, in close conjunction with it, Elles, with 8,000 men, had been successfully operating against the Mohmands, whose country lying north of the Cabul river was overrun with no great difficulty in two weeks, after which the tribes asked for and obtained terms. The posts west of Kohat, which had been vigorously assailed by the Orakzais, were finally relieved by a column of 9,500 men under Yeatman-Biggs, which moved out from that town and drove off the besiegers in disorder. Only the Afridis still remained to be dealt with, and for this purpose there was assembled between Kohat and Thai in October a force of 30,000 men under Lockhart—far the largest ever collected for any of our minor campaigns either in India or elsewhere.

The Dargai heights, blocking the road into the Tirah valley, were stormed with considerable loss, and the column burst northwards through the passes into the virgin valley. From end to end it was traversed in the next six weeks; the enemy resistance was stubborn, and our progress was always difficult and often costly. None the less every Afridi valley was in turn visited and laid waste, before the coming of wintry weather in early December made it necessary for the British to turn their faces homewards. The withdrawal eastwards was carried out in two columns; the southern one was unmolested, but the northern one had to undergo severe privations and hold off a series of fierce and incessant attacks before it could get clear of Afridi territory, and rest and refresh itself south-west of Peshawar. The curtain was rung down on the great tribal rising of 1897 by a successful incursion into the Zakha Khel fastness in the Bazar valley, west of Peshawar, and the reoccupation of the Khyber forts, which had, as above described, been lost to us some four months previously, at the beginning of the trouble.

Unwonted peace, undisturbed save for two encounters with the Wazirs, now ensued on the frontier for a space of ten years, to be broken by an uprising among the Zakha Khels early in 1908. Willcocks, with 14,000 men, organised his advance so carefully and fell on the insurgents so quickly that they were quite unable to put up any effective resistance, and in three weeks had been reduced to sue for peace. There followed at once an outbreak of disorder farther north among the Mohmands, our main anxiety being less the actual revolt than the possibility, which at one time seemed something more, of their receiving assistance from Afghanistan. This peril was, however, averted, and though the Mohmands put up a better resistance to Willcocks and his 12,000 men than their southern compatriots, the same space of time sufficed for him to relieve the British posts which had been attacked by them, and put an end to the rising in a few brisk little actions. From that time on to the outbreak of the Great War in 1914 the peace of the frontier remained undisturbed by any outbreak of disorder necessitating the employment of armed forces.

It would be unseemly in any historian to leave the subject of our Indian frontier wars without a tribute of admiration for the high qualities alike of leaders and of troops that have made his tale one of almost unvarying success. Organisation, discipline, and armament proved themselves throughout more than a match for courage, craft, local knowledge and high tribal and religious spirit, and the Pathan tribesman, perhaps the finest natural fighter in the world, could be time and again sought out and defeated on his own chosen ground by the man of a civilised race, individually hardly his military equal, because the latter possessed material, and still more moral advantages scorned, or at least never acquired, by his enemy. The problem of the North-West Frontier is still with us, as urgent and apparently as insoluble as ever it was; but as long as the British and Indian soldier and his officer, on whom the solution, so far as such solution is military, ultimately rests, are of the same stamp as the men who held the borderline during the stormy and stressful crises of the past, that problem will exist only as a disturbance, not as a menace, to the peace of British India.

5. Other Minor Expeditions in India and the Reorganisation of the Indian Army 1861-1914

Apart from the long series of North-West Frontier campaigns, the Indian army saw little fighting from the end of the second Afghan war to the eve of the Great War; and the few occasions on which the monotony of peace-time routine was for a few months and in the case of a few units broken by active service need only be very briefly noted.

In the north of India there took place in the spring and summer of 1888 some fighting on the border of Sikkim, which had been violated by Tibetan troops. These were quickly driven back to their own territory, but returned to the attack some months later without success. Finally in September they were sought out in their entrenchments, defeated and dispersed. The total troops engaged on our side was somewhat under 2,000.

Fifteen years later, in 1903, an attempt was made to open up Tibet to trade and relations with the outer world. This hermit State, which owed a shadowy allegiance to China, had hitherto remained closed to all foreigners; and as negotiations with China had led to no practical result, a mission under Younghusband was despatched with instructions to proceed to Lhasa and there discuss matters directly with the supreme ruler of Tibet, the Dalai Lama. The mission was, however, stopped on the frontier, and was only able to proceed after a column of 3,000 men had been sent forward to escort it, so that from now on it took the form rather of a warlike than a peaceful enterprise. In April 1904, after fighting three actions, Younghusband reached Gyangtse, where a halt was made to allow of the organisation of a line of supply and the arrival of reinforcements. After a Tibetan attack early in May had been repulsed, and an ultimatum sent to the Dalai Lama had met with no reply, the advance was resumed at the end of June. Progress was of necessity slow; but early in August the little force, pushing aside the enemy who attempted a last stand before their capital, occupied the sacred city, where a satisfactory treaty was concluded. By the end of October the troops, having successfully braved the first fearful rigours of a Himalayan winter, had returned to India.

In 1911 another expedition took place in a different quarter of India against the Abors, a wild tribe dwelling on the north-east frontier of Assam, who had murdered one of our political officers and committed other outrages. Two thousand men, under Bower, were sent to exact punishment; the main difficulties encountered were due to the density of the jungles and the steepness of the hills traversed rather than from the enemy, whose weapons were poisoned arrows and whose favourite method of fighting was the launching of avalanches of rock from hills beneath which their foes were passing.

Finally, mention may be made of a small punitive expedition sent overseas to Perak in Malaya, owing to an outbreak of disorder in that country, resulting in the murder of the British Resident. The trouble was, however, successfully dealt with by the troops on the spot, the reinforcements arriving only in time to complete and maintain the military occupation of the province.

With a few words on the reorganisation, between the end of the Great Mutiny and 1914, we propose to bid farewell to the Indian army.

The disappearance of "John Company's" army consequent

on the assumption of government by the Crown in 1858 did not involve the abolition of the traditional division into three independent Presidential armies, which still remained in existence for over thirty years. There can, however, be traced throughout the period prior to the final unification of these armies in 1895 a general trend towards greater co-ordination of administrative and supply services under the control of the commander-in-chief. During this period also there was established for the first time in 1886 an Indian Army Reserve, divided into two classes—the active, called up for a month's training every year, and the garrison, which was liable for training every second year only; this basis of service remained in essentials unchanged till 1914.

It was not, however, till some time after the unification of the Indian army had officially been accomplished on paper that all traces of the old separatist spirit of the Presidential armies can be said to have disappeared; and on Kitchener's assumption of the chief command in 1908, he found that the four commands into which the army was organised were entirely separated one from the other, and exercised complete and independent control over their troops which were permanently localised within their areas. Kitchener's greatest work in India was the translation of the ideal of one single Indian army into fact.

By 1908 all the regiments had been re-numbered and re-named; the system of dual control between the commander-in-chief and the military member of the Viceroy's Council had been abolished in favour of the former; an Indian Staff College had been set up; and after several successive schemes had been tried, the whole of the British and Indian troops were organised in two armies, the one of five, the other of four divisions and some independent brigades, all ready to take the field, and distributed and trained in peace under the leaders and in the formations which would be theirs in time of war. This was a vast improvement on anything yet seen or dreamed of in India in the way of army organisation; but it had, among other disadvantages, that of excessive centralisation of responsibility for administrative matters at Headquarters. Measures to amend this and other weak points were for financial reasons long delayed, and were still in process of realisation when the war of 1914, by throwing an unparalleled and undreamed-of strain upon the machine, made its defects patent to the world. This, however, takes us beyond the limits of our story.

At the outbreak of the Great War the army in India was divided into a Field Army of 150,000 men and internal security troops numbering 80,000—a total of 230,000 in all, of which one-third were British and two-thirds Indian troops.

CHAPTER 15
Half a Century of Small Wars
1856-1913

1. MINOR CAMPAIGNS IN ASIA
1856-1901

The War with Persia, 1836—A secondary result of the Crimean War had been a breach in the friendly relations between Great Britain and Persia, and the occupation of Herat by the latter. As in 1838, the ever-present anxiety of the British Government for the north-west frontier of India led it to make this a *casus belli,* not this time, however, against Afghanistan, but against the true offender, and an expedition of 7,000 men under Stalker was despatched from Bombay to induce an evacuation of Herat by the Persians, by means of an attack on the southern coast of that country. Early in December 1856 a landing was successfully effected near Bushire, and the town occupied after a weak resistance. Six weeks later Outram arrived to take over command, bringing with him reinforcements which practically doubled the original force, and moved out to attack the enemy, who had taken position at Khushab, to the east of Bushire. The ensuing action was successful, but was followed by the return of the victors to their starting-point, and the despatch, after considerable delay, of a detachment of 5000 men to occupy Mohammera in the delta of the Tigris. After a brief bombardment the town was taken, and a body of 300 men, despatched up the Karun river to destroy the hostile magazines at Ahwaz, attacked and brilliantly defeated the whole Persian army, 8000 strong. The Shah agreed to the evacuation of Herat, and a treaty to this effect, signed in March 1857, put an end to the campaign.

The Operations against China, 1857-1860—Despite China's acceptance of British terms at the termination of Gough's campaign in 1842, their attitude remained truculent and hostile, and further causes of quarrel soon arose. In December 1857 it became necessary for the Viceroy of India, Lord Elgin, to demand redress for British grievances against the city of Canton, and on this being refused a Franco-British force of 6,000 men was sent to occupy the city and retain possession of it pending some satisfactory solution of the questions in dispute. Following on this the Allied fleets attacked and silenced the Taku forts at the mouth of the Peiho river, and sailing up stream occupied Tientsin. A new treaty in yet more stringent terms was presented to and accepted by the Emperor of China, who had, however, no real intention of carrying it out; and frequent and urgent remonstrances having no effect, further military operations became necessary.

A new naval attempt to force the Taku forts having failed with serious loss, it was decided to despatch a strong combined expedition capable of forcing its way, if necessary, to Pekin, and there dictating terms which could not be evaded.

Sir Hope Grant, with 10,000 British troops, left Hong Kong in May 1860, and leaving detachments to occupy the territory at the mouth of the Yangtse Kiang and Shanghai, formed a base near Port Arthur for his future operations. Seven thousand French were also to form part of his command, and the opening of the campaign had to be postponed till early August to permit of their arrival. The whole force then effected its landing at the mouth of the Peiho unopposed, and pushing up the river drove the Chinese forces before them, stormed the Taku forts, and reduced the local enemy commander to such straits that he was glad to sign a convention for the peaceful evacuation of Tientsin. Thence the advance was pressed towards Pekin; but while the Allies were halting some thirty miles from the city in order to allow their supplies to catch them up, negotiations were opened at the request of the Chinese. This, however, was merely a device to gain time, and as soon as this purpose had been achieved the British envoys were treacherously set upon and taken prisoners. Their treachery availed the enemy nothing, for their forces were once more beaten in a brief combat at Palikao, and on October 9 the Allies took possession of the Imperial capital. The treaty of peace, re-stating and re-emphasising the terms of that signed in 1842, was once more accepted and solemnly ratified; an indemnity was also exacted to cover part of the cost of the expedition, which was withdrawn by the end of the year, except for a garrison left at Tientsin until the completion of the payment of the indemnity. British relations with China were to continue peaceful for the next forty years.

The Suppression of the Boxer Rebellion in China 1900-1901.—In the early summer of 1900 the rise of a fanatical Chinese sect known as the Boxers suddenly developed into a national and anti-foreign movement, culminating in a series of outrages and massacres of Christians and their adherents in the Shantung and Chihli provinces. In mid-June the fanatics got control of the capital, and closely invested the foreign legations in which the European community had been collected for safety. Urgent appeals for succour were at once despatched, but an attempt to effect their relief by a composite naval brigade from Tientsin proved premature; Tientsin itself was indeed for a time in danger and had to be succoured by a force from Taku, which had been attacked and captured immediately on receipt of the news of the outbreak. A contingent from India under General Gaselee was then ordered to China, there to form part of an Allied force comprising Japanese, German, French, Russian, American, Austrian and Italian troops for the rescue of the besieged Europeans in Pekin.

The British contribution to this international army numbered 8,000 men, but half of these had to be left at Shanghai to ensure the safety of that city. The rest were collected at Tientsin by the end of July, and it was decided, after considerable discussion among the various commanders, that the advance on the capital should be taken in hand at once. Some 20,000 men were available, and proved amply sufficient to deal with the ill-organised and ill-armed enemy opposed to them. The latter were defeated just outside Tientsin, and again a few days later at the village of Yang Tsun, the leading part in this latter engagement being played by the British. By August 14 the Allies were in position before the walls of Pekin, ready for the final dash to the rescue of their fellow-countrymen in distress; and next day they broke into the city, the British being the first to effect an entry into the legations and join hands with the garrison. The fighting was heavy, and in places costly, and it was not till the evening of the next day that the Boxer resistance was completely at an end. Another small band of Europeans in a cathedral, which had had to endure even greater trials than that in the legations, was also rescued. The task of clearing the country round was now taken in hand, but though little effective resistance was met with, its completion was delayed by jealousy and friction among the various national contingents and their leaders. This was somewhat reduced on the arrival at the end of September of the German Field-Marshal von Waldersee, to act as generalissimo of the whole of the forces in North China, and henceforward the work of pacification made more rapid progress. The final act in the military operations was the despatch of two columns, including a strong force of British troops, from Pekin and Tientsin to Paotingfu, eighty miles south-west of

Pekin, whither the main body of the defeated Chinese were believed to have retired; no enemy, however, was found so the march resolved itself into a mere military promenade. By June 1901 the British forces in China, which had been strongly reinforced, numbered 18,000 men, and the remainder of the allies some 50,000; but there was nothing left for them to do, and some months later the dispersal of the army began. By the end of the year the British garrison had been cut down to some 3,500, inclusive of the legation guard.

2. Minor Campaigns in East and Central Africa 1868-1904

The Abyssinian Expedition, 1867-1868—This well-conceived and brilliantly executed little campaign was rendered necessary by the series of insults offered by Theodore, King of Abyssinia, to the Queen of England's representatives and a course of atrocities which revolted the conscience of the civilised world. The Commander, Sir Robert Napier, was an able soldier who had made his name in the Mutiny, and the preparations for the campaign undertaken under his immediate and personal guidance, though involving a heavy financial outlay, were so thorough and well thought out as to be models of their kind. 62,000 personnel and 55,000 animals were sent from various Indian ports, but of the former only 11,000 were fighting troops. The leading elements landed near Massowah late in October 1867, but owing to the need for reconnaissance of the route and other local preparations, the advance on Magdala, Theodore's fortified capital, could not be commenced for some three months. The average daily progress was some seven to ten miles; no resistance was encountered in the earlier stages, and by the first week in April the British advance guard was in sight of the Abyssinian stronghold. A preliminary action was fought at the foot of the plateau of Magdala, in which the enemy suffered heavily, and our troops but little. Theodore in despair made an appeal for terms, but was unwilling to accept these offered. On April 13 the place was stormed ; the greater part of the garrison surrendered with little resistance, the king took his own life, and the campaign was thus brilliantly terminated. The force carried out its withdrawal unmolested after seeing peace and order restored in the occupied territory, and by mid-June 1868 all the troops composing it had sailed for Abyssinia. The unchecked British advance through 300 miles of unknown and barren country, and the complete victory at the end of it, were acclaimed with great popular enthusiasm in England, and contributed in no small degree to the reawakening of interest in military matters which paved the way for the Cardwell reforms.

Operations in East Africa, Jubaland and Uganda, 1897-1901—During the last decade of the nineteenth century Great Britain consolidated the interests she had acquired in the newly opened up territory in Eastern and Central Africa by the declaration of protectorates over East Africa, Jubaland and Uganda. The five years from 1897 to 1901 saw a series of military operations in these areas by small columns which, though encountering considerable difficulties owing to the nature of the country, and meeting at times with stubborn resistance from the warlike tribes, are not of sufficient interest to be described in any detail. The forces engaged in these expeditions varied from 600 to 1,500 men, and consisted mostly of Indian troops or units raised locally.

The Somaliland Campaigns, 1890-1904—In northern Somaliland, the country lying to the south-east of the Sudan, on the southern shore of the Gulf of Aden, a protectorate had been established by us at the request of certain tribes in 1884. Apart from a small punitive expedition in 1890 against a refractory clan in the north-west corner of our sphere which had been guilty of depredations against its neighbours, no military operations were undertaken until the rise of the "Mad Mullah" in 1898. This man organised a religious movement against the British which in a year had attained formidable proportions, and owing to the South African War no troops could be spared to deal with him till 1901. In the summer of that year he was attacked in his fastness in the Nogal valley, 150 miles south-east of Berbera, and driven off into the territory of Mudug, some 150 miles more to the south. At the end of the year, however, his depredations were resumed, but it was not till May 1902 that a force was once more despatched to subdue him, and again expelled him from the Nogal; while following him up towards Mudug it was attacked, thrown into confusion, and suffered so heavily that the pursuit had to be given up.

It was now decided to undertake operations on a larger scale, expel the Mullah from Mudug, and if possible round him up by an operation to be carried out by two converging columns from Berbera on the north and Obbia on the east coast of Somaliland. The total of the forces engaged amounted to some 5,000, General Manning being in supreme control of the whole. The provision of camel transport was the main difficulty to be overcome, and the impossibility of finding enough animals was the real cause of the failure to achieve complete success. Mudug was occupied without resistance by the Obbia column and the Mullah driven westwards, while the Berbera force secured the Nogal. A small flying column sent by the Obbia force to pursue him was, however, compelled to halt for want of supplies, and when it set out to rejoin the main body its rearguard was attacked and annihilated, while a second detachment from the Berbera force was also compelled to retreat. It then became necessary to cut loose from Obbia and effect a junction of the two columns, but before this could be done the Mullah, passing in between them, had returned to his old refuge in the Nogal. Here it was possible, by reason of the arrival of fresh reinforcements from India, to strike at him in great force.

Six thousand men now took the field under command of

General Egerton, who, after a pause of four months for preparations, set them in motion against the Mullah's following in the western end of the Nogal valley, the southern exits from which were blocked by pushing forward detachments well in front of the main body advancing from Berbera. The Mullah was brought to action at Jidballi and totally defeated with heavy loss; the greater part of his levies thereupon dispersed, but he himself fled away to the north-east with a few adherents, and though a flying column of 1,500 men was despatched on his trail, they could do no more than drive him into Italian territory east of Rat. To prevent him doubling back to the south, Illig, at the mouth of the Nogal, was attacked and stormed from the sea, but the elusive chief once more escaped from the net into which he had been driven owing to the failure of the local chiefs to cooperate with the British, and survived to be a source of yet further trouble in the future. For the present, however, his power had been destroyed, and as the continuance of the campaign offered little prospect of further results being achieved, the bulk of Egerton's force was withdrawn to Berbera and there dispersed overseas, leaving the interior of Somaliland for the time being at peace.

3. Operations in West Africa
1873-1906

Wolseley's Campaign against the Ashantis, 1873-1874—The cause of the second Ashanti war was an aggression by this warlike tribe against their neighbours the Fantis, dwelling between Elmina and the lower Prah, who had lately come under British protection. During their incursion early in 1873 the invaders came into contact with our garrison at Elmina, and though repulsed, remained in observation before that post, and the situation seemed to be sufficiently serious to warrant the despatch of a force from home to secure the safety of our West African coastal possessions. Wolseley was therefore instructed to undertake an offensive campaign against Ashantiland, and this plan was persisted in despite the fact that before his preparations were even approaching completion, starvation and fever had compelled the tribesmen to fall back behind the Prah.

At last, by January 1874, all was ready for an advance of 3,500 men from Cape Coast Castle on Kumasi, the capital of the Ashanti King, Coffee Kalkalli. A road had been constructed as far as the Prah, and it was planned to enter the enemy country in four columns, but of these only the main one under Wolseley's personal command was expected to have any serious fighting to do, or play any important role in the campaign. The Prah was crossed without opposition, and King Coffee's urgent requests for a suspension of hostilities being treated with contempt, the Ashanti army was encountered drawn up for battle in dense bush at Amoaful and driven back after a confused and prolonged action. Despite his losses from both battle and disease, which were high, Wolseley continued to press on in face of a weakening enemy resistance, and finally entered Kumasi in triumph after little more than a month's campaign. After destroying the town and palace, and imposing a humiliating treaty on Coffee, the force returned to its base. Among other terms of the treaty, our frontier was advanced to the Prah.

The Fall of the Ashanti Dynasty, 1895-1896—The failure of King Prempeh, Coffee's heir, to observe the terms of the agreement signed by his predecessor, and the barbarities of his rule, necessitated the despatch of a second expedition in 1896. Following on an unanswered ultimatum 2,000 men under Scott set out in mid-December to cut their way through the jungle to Kumasi from Cape Coast Castle. Prempeh's habitual state of intoxication rendered him incapable of any resistance, so no fighting took place; the difficulties of the march were overcome by methodical and thorough organisation, and early in 1896 the British entered the capital, being greeted in friendly fashion by the inhabitants. Prempeh, unable to purchase his independence at the price of a large indemnity, was dethroned and deported, and the country became a British protectorate, governed by a Resident.

The Last War in Ashanti, 1900—Four years later, in April, there broke out a formidable rising in the country. Kumasi, with its Resident and small garrison, was closely invested, and once more military measures became necessary for the restoration of order. The capital was for a time in serious danger, from which it was only saved by the opportune arrival of reinforcements from the north, who cut their way into the place but were unable to raise the siege. The assembly of the relief column could be effected but slowly, and it was not till some three months after the first outbreak that Willcocks was able to set out from Bekwai with some 1,500 men. Prior to this the Resident, with part of the Kumasi garrison, had left the city and made his way with great peril and hardship to safety at Elmina; and those left behind were literally at the last gasp when saved by the arrival of the relief force, which, by skilful manoeuvring, had got through with little fighting. Returning to Bekwai, Willcocks now despatched flying columns in all directions to destroy the various nests of rebels, which was effected after a number of small combats with armed enemy bands. Finally, at the end of September, the Ashantis were crushed in a decisive action, and the complete pacification of the country quickly ensued. A year later Ashanti was definitely annexed by us.

Other West-African Campaigns, 1891-1906—In Gambia, which had become a Crown colony as early as 1843; in northern and southern Nigeria, which, after it had been colonised by a Chartered Company in 1886, became two separate protectorates in 1900; and in Sierra Leone, our possession of which dates from the late eighteenth century, various small expeditions, all of an exploring or punitive nature, took place between 1891 and 1906. There were two such campaigns in Gambia, in 1891-1892 and in 1901, and one in Sierra Leone in 1899. Nigeria, less explored and more turbulent, proved more troublesome to pacify, and forces had to be employed in this work almost constantly from 1899 to 1906, the full tale of these little expeditions numbering in all over forty. All were carried through by locally raised West African troops under British officers. Space forbids any detailed description of the incidents of these prolonged and laborious operations, which, after some vicissitudes, culminated by 1906 in the successful opening up of the Niger territory and its hinterland and the enforcement of British authority throughout the country.

4. Campaigns in South Africa
1877-1896

The last Kaffir War, 1877-1878—The ninth and last of the long series of our wars with the Kaffirs, who had been constantly at feud with us from the time of our first occupation of South African territory in the Napoleonic epoch, broke out in the autumn of 1877 in Transkei. Here Kreli, the chief of the Galeka tribe, raised the standard of revolt and attacked two of our outlying posts, only to be beaten off. The spread of what might well have been a serious menace to British ascendancy was checked by the prompt action of the local military authorities, who despatched two columns into Kaffraria from south and west, and beat down Kreli's resistance with little difficulty. On the completion of the occupation, the rebel chief's country was annexed by the British, whereupon a neighbouring tribe, the Gaikas, joined forces with him to help him to recover it. Indecisive fighting on the border followed and continued for several months, and in February 1878 the enemy made a serious attack on one of our camps and was beaten off with heavy loss. This severe defeat broke the back of their resistance, but it was not till the death of the Gaika chief, Sandilli, in action in May, that they gave up the unequal struggle and resigned themselves to the acceptance of British rule.

Later on in the year the suppression of native risings in Griqualand and the capture of the stronghold of a revolted band of Basutos further affirmed our claim to the predominance over the native races of South Africa, of which only one, and that the most formidable of all, the Zulus, remained unsubdued.

The Conquest of Zululand, 1879—For some years prior to 1879 the Zulus had been pursuing an aggressive policy, and it was in order to defend from their depredations the Transvaal Boers, who proved unable to defend themselves, that that country was annexed in 1878. Far from being debarred from their evil ways by this step, which in effect isolated them as against Great Britain in South Africa, the Zulus persisted in their career of outrage and murder, until at length the British were forced to demand satisfaction from their king, Cetewayo. On his neglect of this summons, the invasion of Zululand was decided on.

Lord Chelmsford, the British commander, had at his disposal 18,000 troops, and with these he planned, after leaving detachments behind to watch the enemy's northern and western frontiers, to advance upon the Zulu capital, Ulundi, in three columns: the right wing, under Pearson, from the mouth of the Tugela; the second, which he himself accompanied, from the Buffalo at Rorke's Drift; and the left wing, under Evelyn Wood, from the Transvaal border. Pearson advanced as far as Etshowe, established himself there, and was invested by the enemy; Wood penetrated with little difficulty as far as the Umvolosi, and fortified a strong position on Kambula mountain. The centre column, however, suffered a serious disaster at Isandlhwana, a detachment left behind by

Chelmsford to guard his camp, while he was pursuing a small force of the enemy, being surprised and annihilated. An even more serious peril, nothing less than the loss of his base and supplies, and the overrunning of Natal by the savage Zulu hordes, was only averted by the heroic defence of the small garrison of Rorke's Drift. The set-back was so serious as not only to cause a panic among the population, but to disarrange the whole of the British plans. Wood was ordered to stand fast at Kambula and the main column fell back hurriedly behind the Buffalo to refit and await the coming of reinforcements which were known to be on the way.

For some four months no further attempt was made to resume the general offensive against the Zulus. Chelmsford led forward a small relief force which successfully repulsed the enemy bands around Etshowe and brought Pearson's troops safely back behind the Tugela. Wood was kept fully employed in the north, and before long had the main strength of the Zulu army on his hands; but although an attempt to hold them at a distance from Kambula miscarried, he was able to beat off the attack ultimately delivered against his stronghold at that place, with serious loss to the assailants. In this unsuccessful attack the fighting power of the Zulu army suffered a blow from which it never recovered, and when, in mid-June, the interrupted British offensive was at length recommenced with augmented forces, its progress was unimpeded up to the outskirts of Ulundi itself. Here Chelmsford, who had drawn in Wood's column to join him on the Umvolosi, gained a decisive victory which shattered the military power of the Zulus. Wolseley now took over chief command, and the capture of Cetewayo finished off the war, though Zululand still continued to enjoy a simulacrum of independent existence until its formal annexation in 1886. Thus success ultimately crowned an ill-directed campaign in which the fine fighting qualities of the troops throughout counted for considerably more than the abilities of their leaders. Chelmsford, like Gough thirty years before in India, must be considered fortunate to have been allowed an opportunity of redeeming his military reputation before the general who had been sent to supersede him could arrive to take over his command.

The Disastrous Conflict with the Boers, 1881—In the war with the Dutch Boers of the Transvaal, which broke out some eighteen months later, we were not destined to have a similar opportunity of making good our early errors and disasters. When the Boers, among whom discontent had long been simmering, took steps at the end of 1880 to shake off the British yoke which had been imposed upon them against their will two years before, it was not considered that the task of dealing with them would be an unusually difficult one. But these bold and cunning riflemen proved to be the most formidable foes British arms had yet encountered in all the long tale of our little wars, and succeeded in inflicting on us a series of humiliating reverses which caused the British Government of the day to think better of its first decision to assert and maintain at all costs its supremacy over their territory.

At the time of the insurrection the British troops in the Transvaal, under the command of Colley, the High Commissioner, numbered barely 3,000 men, widely distributed in half-a-dozen small detachments on a circle with a radius of some 100 to 150 miles round Pretoria; all were at once invested by the Boers, and a detachment which at the moment happened to be moving in from Lydenburg to the capital was surprised and destroyed. Colley, who was in Natal at the moment, at once collected his few available troops, less than 1500 in all, in the northern angle of the colony, preparatory to a march to the relief of the beleaguered garrisons, but found himself opposed by a strong enemy force entrenched on Laing's Nek, from which he failed to dislodge it. Reinforcements arrived but slowly, and meanwhile a hostile raid was directed against his left and rear which necessitated the despatch of a column to free his communications. This was successfully accomplished at the combat of the Ingogo, but the losses suffered by the British were disproportionate to the result.

The fresh troops expected by Colley had now arrived and he determined to resume his offensive against the Boer positions in face of him by placing a force before dawn on the crest of Majuba Hill, which commanded their right and rear, and thus compelling them to withdraw. The first part of this programme was carried out as conceived, but instead of retreating the Boers delivered a counter-attack, which drove the British from the hill in panic rout. Colley himself was among the long list of slain, and by the time Roberts arrived to take over the vacant command, he found that the British Government had decided to accept their defeat and grant to the triumphant Boers a form of diluted self-government, which was translated three years later into complete independence.

Such a result, arrived at in such a manner, could only bear within itself the seeds of a future war, for while the British army and people, as distinct from the Government, were by no means inclined to accept it as final, it encouraged the victors in the belief that the same policy which had gained them their independence would enable them to maintain it inviolate. As regards the causes of the greatest misfortune suffered by British arms since 1842, there can be little doubt that, though Colley's conduct of the campaign was severely and not unreasonably criticised, the inferiority of the British soldier, man for man, to his opponent, was the factor which contributed more than any other to the unfortunate issue.

The Matabele War of 1896—The country known as Matabeleland, lying between the Limpopo and the Zambezi rivers, had been allotted for exploitation to a British Chartered Company as early as 1889, and a few years later the power of the Matabele king, Lobengula, was broken by the Company's troops in a series of small but hard-fought actions. No British troops took part in these operations, but early in 1896 a serious rising throughout the whole land, accompanied by a revolt of the locally-raised police and a massacre of many of the white settlers in the outlying districts, necessitated the despatch of considerable forces to the scene. The administration of the country was at this time in the hands of Rhodes, under whom Carrington exercised the chief military command. Columns were despatched in haste to the relief of Bulawayo, the capital, and Gwelo, which had been invested; the blockade was successfully raised and the rebels driven to seek refuge in the Matoppo Hills, to the south of these towns, where they fortified themselves and awaited our attack. Carrington was not long in seeking them out, and in August a force under Plumer decisively defeated them after a prolonged engagement. Rhodes seized the psychological moment to initiate negotiations for peace, at the request of the rebel chiefs, and by the end of the month the latter had agreed to lay down their arms, though desultory fighting did not definitely cease till some three months after.

5. THE BRITISH ARMY IN EGYPT AND THE SUDAN 1882-1898

The Campaign in Egypt, 1882—From the date of the opening of the Suez Canal in 1869, British interests in Egypt, always great, became vital and led her on to assume the virtual control of the country. From 1879 onwards the state of chaos into which Egyptian finances had fallen induced Britain and France to claim and secure a considerable voice in the government, which still, however, remained nominally in the hands of the Khedive. This state of tutelage provoked a military rising under the direction of an Egyptian colonel, Arabi, who in 1882 became the virtual ruler of the country; and our anxiety for the safety of the European population and for our financial interests, as well as reluctance to leave the important

Suez Canal traffic at the mercy of a self-seeking adventurer, induced the British Government to sanction armed intervention in July 1882. The first step was the bombardment of Alexandria, where a massacre of Europeans had taken place, the reduction of the forts by the guns of our fleet, and the occupation of the city by a brigade from Cyprus. In order to deceive the enemy as to the true direction of the attack, which, according to the plan of campaign adopted by the British commander, Wolseley, was to be from the canal at Ismailia by way of Tel-el-Kebir, where the main body of Arabi's army was known to be, on Cairo, this brigade was ordered to feign an advance south and eastward. By this means the enemy was in fact kept in the dark as to our true projects till it was too late for him to assemble superior forces for the defence of the capital from the east.

The forces sent from England amounted in all to two divisions and one cavalry brigade, some 20,000 men in all, with a mixed brigade from India, but it was not found possible, in view of the limitations on traffic in the canal, and of the port of Ismailia, to disembark the whole of these simultaneously or indeed with any great rapidity. By August 23 a large fraction of the army had, however, set foot on shore and pushed out a detachment westwards to prevent the destruction by the enemy of the locks on the Sweetwater Canal, the main source of water supply for the force; at the same time the Indian contingent began to land at Suez. While the remainder of the troops and stores were being disembarked and preparations being taken in hand for the next stage of the advance, our advanced force at Kassassin was twice sharply attacked and had to fight hard to hold its own. After the second of his onslaughts had been repulsed the enemy, now some 12,000 strong, fell back to his entrenched lines at Tel-el-Kebir, and there awaited our advance. The position was so formidable that Wolseley, after careful reconnaissance, resolved to approach it under cover of night and deliver his assault at dawn. The preliminary measures, on which success in such an enterprise so largely depends, were admirably elaborated; the whole affair went forward without a hitch, and with the first grey of morning on September 13 the Egyptians, who kept but a careless watch, were swept out of their defences at the bayonet's point, and utterly dispersed. Thirty-six hours later the British cavalry, appearing out of the desert before the gates of Cairo, received the surrender of the city and the 10,000 men garrisoning it, together with the sword of Arabi himself; and before the end of the month all the hostile detachments in the Nile valley had laid down their arms. The Khedive's authority was re-established under the aegis of British troops, who remained in the country pending the return of more settled conditions. This virtual occupation of Egypt was destined to last for forty years, in fact till our own day, and incidentally to involve England in the thorny question of the Sudan.

The Earlier Sudan Expeditions, 1884-1885—Control of the Sudan had been slipping from the Egyptian Government's hands ever since the rise of the Moslem prophet, known as the Mahdi, in 1881. All attempts to put down his fanatical followers by force of arms had failed, and finally his power was established on a permanent basis as the result of his annihilation of Hicks' army near El Obeid in October 1883. Shortly afterwards Osman Digna, the chief of the Arabs dwelling in the area between Suakin and Berber, declared for the Mahdi, put to the sword all the Egyptian garrisons in that district and utterly defeated an army of relief under Baker. The British Government, unwilling to tolerate Mahdism on the shores of the Red Sea, at once authorised the despatch of a force of 4,000 men under Graham to Suakin. At the same time, at the request of the Khedive's Government, the services of Gordon, who had had previous experience of the Soudan and enjoyed a high reputation as a leader of lost causes, were loaned for the purpose of withdrawing the Egyptian garrisons from the country. It is difficult to imagine a more unsuitable selection for such a task, which it is doubtful if Gordon ever made any serious attempt to execute. In any case, before the end of May 1884 he had been cut off from Egypt and shut up in Khartum and the British Government was more or less committed to an expedition for his rescue.

Meanwhile Graham's undertaking in the Suakin area had met with considerable success. Marching out to the west, he repulsed Osman Digna's first attack at El Teb, brought off the garrison of Tokar in safety, and fought a second fierce battle at Tamai. One of his squares was breached for a time, but finally beat off its assailants, who were so cowed by their heavy losses that their offensive will was completely broken, and remained so even when the British force, its mission having been accomplished, was withdrawn from Suakin, leaving only a small garrison in that town.

Meanwhile Gladstone, the Prime Minister, was fighting hard against what he regarded as a wanton attempt on Gordon's part to drag England into intervention in the troubled affairs of the Sudan, and it was not till September that the growing pressure of public opinion, and the threatened revolt of part of his Cabinet, compelled him to give a reluctant assent to the despatch of a relief force to Khartum. Six thousand men were given to Wolseley for this purpose, but much had to be done before a start could be made. Supplies had to be provided, camels and other animals to be collected in great numbers, and the whole pushed up the difficult and treacherous course of the Nile over 300 miles from Wady Haifa as far as Korti, beyond the territory of Dongola, whence the advance was eventually to commence; and this process consumed weeks and months of valuable time. It was not, in fact, till the end of 1884 that Wolseley felt himself able to take the field with reasonable hope of success. By this time reports as to the perilous condition of Khartum induced him to modify his original plan of campaign for an advance along the Nile all the way, and to send a flying column of 2,000 men under Stewart across the desert from the river at Korti to touch it again at Metemmeh, and thence make a dash to Gordon's rescue. Meanwhile the rest of the force, 3000 men under Earle, were to carry out the original programme, and regain touch with the desert column after clearing the course of the river from Korti by way of Abu Hamed and Berber to Metemmeh.

These operations however were, as it turned out, undertaken too late to achieve their main object, the rescue of Gordon. Stewart left Korti in the first week in January 1885, and repulsing two fierce enemy attacks at Abu Klea, where again the British square was penetrated for a few moments, and at Gubat, touched river again at Metemmeh, where two of Gordon's steamers were found awaiting him. Here, however, Wilson, who had succeeded Stewart on the latter being wounded, had to spend four days in clearing up the situation and preparing the steamers for their return voyage, and this delay was enough to decide Gordon's fate. When, on October 28, Wilson arrived off the city, he found that it had fallen two days before, and its gallant commandant was dead; he himself only escaped from the Mahdists with the loss of both his vessels and thanks to the opportune arrival of a rescue ship from Metemmeh. On his return to the main column he found the command had been taken over by Buller, who decided that no object was to be served by longer delay in his somewhat precarious position, and led the desert column back to Korti unmolested.

The fortunes of the column under Earle had been less chequered but equally indecisive. Leaving Korti two weeks later than Stewart, it made its laborious way up the swift-flowing river and over swirling and perilous cataracts to within fifty miles of Abu Hamed, where the enemy were met in position at Kirbekan. Their left flank was enveloped and they were soundly beaten; but the column had not reached Abu Hamed before orders recalling it arrived, and by mid-March Wolseley had his whole army once more under his own hand at Korti.

Despite the failure to achieve what had ostensibly been the only object of the expedition, the Government still did not despair of regaining what had been lost and crushing the Mahdi in an autumn campaign. A strong force of 13,000 men under Graham, including an Indian brigade and a contingent from Australia—the first time Colonial troops had been sent overseas to take part in a British expedition—was sent to Suakin to cover the construction of a railway thence to Berber, which had been chosen as the base for our future operations. Graham was ready to move in March, defeated his old enemy, Osman Digna, at Hashin, and returning to Suakin sent out a column to establish posts to cover the progress of the railway. This force was surprised at Tofrek, but succeeded in rallying and beating off the Arabs, who henceforward made no attempt to interfere with our construction. The enterprise thus fortunately begun was, however, broken off late in May when the British Government, in full accord with the men on the spot, decided to abstain from any further offensive against the Mahdi, and withdrew its troops from the Sudan. Before the end of the summer of 1885 the first phase of the Sudan campaigns had ended with the reduction of Graham's army to a weak garrison at Suakin, and the retirement of our troops in the Nile valley to the vicinity of Assuan.

The Reconquest of the Sudan, 1896-1899—Eleven years were to pass before Great Britain once more put her hand to the plough from which she had looked back after the death of Gordon, and meanwhile Mahdism in the Sudan had reached and passed its flood-tide mark. More than once during this period the Dervish hordes had swept northwards down the Nile valley and eastwards against the walls of Suakin, only to be firmly met and handsomely repulsed by the British and the newly modelled Egyptian army. This, under the careful training of Grenfell and his even more famous pupil and successor, Kitchener, with their devoted British retinue, was being rapidly converted from a menace only to the country which relied upon it for its defence, to an enthusiastic and efficient force fully capable of meeting and beating off the most formidable fanatic charge. On three separate occasions between 1885 and 1891 the Mahdist hosts in their efforts to extend their conquests in the Nile valley met their match and had to own defeat; while Osman Digna's operations around Suakin, after a transitory gleam of success in the summer of 1888, which necessitated the despatch of a British contingent under the Sirdar in person, were finally brought to an inglorious end in 1891 by an Egyptian force, fighting victoriously for the first time without British aid. Long ere this the Mahdi had passed away, and his mantle fallen on the Khalifa Abdullah, who succeeded to a troublous heritage. The tribes under his sway became more and more restless and dissatisfied as time went on and had to be dealt with by force of arms ; famine and disease stalked far and wide through his territories ; and a series of campaigns against the Abyssinians on his eastern frontier brought in their turn only disappointment and defeat. By 1891, indeed, Mahdism was a spent force in the eyes of the world, and the passing years only accentuated its visible decline. Nevertheless, it was not till the spring of 1896 that the British army once more took the field against the Dervishes. Even then the motive cause was less the internal situation in the Sudan than a desire to lend a helping hand to the Italians in Abyssinia, who had just suffered a serious disaster at Adowa and could ill afford to have another enemy on their hands, as might easily happen if the Khalifa's forces were not otherwise occupied. Kitchener was therefore instructed to undertake a campaign for the reoccupation of Dongola and at once began to take the necessary initial measures under the direction of the British agent in Egypt, Lord Cromer. While an Indian brigade was sent to Suakin to keep Osman Digna employed, the main striking force of 15,000 British and Egyptian troops was assembled at Wady Haifa preparatory to an advance up the

Nile. This route had been chosen because of the ease of water supply and the facilities for transport of provisions and necessaries afforded by the river, which was to be supplemented by the construction of a railway as the army advanced. Preparations for the campaign were both laborious and extensive, and progress could be made but slowly. It was not till June that the first engagement took place at Ferket, when an enemy advanced detachment was surprised and driven back, and then an outbreak of cholera, bad weather, and a series of mishaps to the Nile flotilla accompanying the army caused another three months' delay. Early in September, however, everything was at last ready for the decisive move; and before the end of that month the invaders were in secure possession of Dongola, the enemy having been severely chastised and driven back in headlong flight beyond Korti.

Between this, the penultimate, and the next and final stage of the offensive there came a long and somewhat inexplicable pause. The British Government seemed unable to make up its mind to complete what had been so well begun until after personal consultation with Kitchener, and much anxious deliberation. A report that a French expedition to the Upper Nile from the west was in contemplation seems to have finally ended its hesitation. However, as the Dongola province had to be restored to order, the railway pushed forward, and many other preparations to be made, the interval was put to good use. For the advance to Khartum, Kitchener decided to adopt a different line of communications by driving a railway across the Korosko Desert from Wady Haifa to Abu Hamed, pending the completion of which the troops moved up river to the latter place. Meanwhile the enemy forces, lulled into security by the long pause after the taking of Dongola, remained quiescent around Khartum, and their little detachment at Abu Hamed was easily surprised and overwhelmed in August 1897. As a result of this success, Berber was also abandoned to the British, who pushed their advanced troops forward to the junction of the Nile and Atbara rivers, less than 200 miles from the Khalifa's capital, and sent their steamers reconnoitring as far up stream as Metemmeh. Meanwhile the railway advanced rapidly, reaching Abu Hamed at the end of October, and, in order to secure our left flank, a detachment landed at Massowa took over possession of Kassala from the Italians in December, according to a previous treaty dating from 1891.

By this time the Khalifa had determined to make a last effort to ward off the danger which inexorable as fate was drawing nearer and nearer from the north; but his plans for effecting a powerful concentration of all available forces failed to materialise, and his lieutenant at Metemmeh was ordered to do his best with the 15,000 men at his disposal. He decided to move against Berber by way of the Lower Atbara, hoping thus to turn our left, but our concentration was too rapid for him, and his entrenched camp was stormed, his army dispersed, and he himself made prisoner in the action of the Atbara on April 7. Four months later the Sirdar's army, now reinforced to 26,000 men, of whom one-third, one division, were British troops, set forth on its final march to Khartum. The Khalifa had concentrated under its walls a force double that of his enemies, and as soon as they put in an appearance flew at their throats. The ensuing battle, though hardly a tactical masterpiece, sounded the knell alike of Khartum and of Mahdism. By the evening of the battle day, September 2, the city was in our hands, its former ruler a fugitive, and the memory of Gordon's death wiped out in victory. The Khalifa, though his power was for good and all broken, and his ventures in the field invariably unfortunate, maintained, with an ever-dwindling band of followers, a precarious existence for over a year, until, in November 1899, when the eyes of Great Britain and the world were all directed towards a greater and sterner struggle, he was hunted down and slain with all his warriors in Kordofan by a force under Wingate. Thus the long fever of Mahdism finally burnt itself out, and Britain, with halting tread and by devious ways, had at last completed, on the banks of the old Nile, her civilising mission, the fruits of which have endured to this day.

6. A Minor Campaign in Canada: the Red River Expedition 1870

Since the termination of the war between Great Britain and the United States, in 1815, British troops have conducted only one small campaign on the American continent. This was occasioned by trouble among the French Canadians and half-breeds following on the transfer of the North-west Territory from the Hudson Bay Company to Canada in 1867. A Provisional Government was set up, the leading spirit being one Riel, who defied the authority of the newly-appointed Governor and ended a prolonged career of misrule by the judicial murder of a British subject. Twelve hundred men under the command of Wolseley were therefore despatched from Toronto to reduce the malcontents to reason. The real problem lay in their transport over the desolate wastes of water and prairie to within striking distance of their objective, 1,200 miles from their base; and all available means of communication—railway, lake steamer, sleigh, and canoe—were utilised for this purpose, which was ultimately accomplished with triumphant success. The rebellion collapsed on the appearance of the troops, who, after eight months in the field, were back home at Toronto with their task fulfilled. Riel himself lived to cause more trouble fifteen years later, but the story of his second revolt and its suppression, which was effected entirely by the Canadians, can hardly be regarded as forming part of the history of the British army.

7. THE MAORI WARS IN NEW ZEALAND
1863-1870

The last of these manifold and wearisome little wars which have to be chronicled in telling the history of the British army in the latter half of the nineteenth century were fought against the Maoris, the aboriginal inhabitants of New Zealand. They took place entirely within the limits of the northern island, in the area lying south of Auckland; and the foes against whom we were pitted were perhaps the ablest, and certainly the most chivalrous, of all the savage races who have ever in the various quarters of the globe measured themselves against us. Their armament, consisting of spears, axes, clubs, and shotguns, was primitive, but their methods of fighting were well thought out and gave us much trouble. They awaited our attacks behind high stockades or *pahs*, so strongly built as to be practically impervious even to the artillery fire of those days, and so well sited as to necessitate a direct assault, which was always costly and often unsuccessful. Expelled from one, they would retire to another, and so weary out their enemy by enforcing on him a series of bloody and fruitless attacks until his advance was brought to a stand. Eventually their resistance was overcome by the British investing their positions and compelling them in their turn either to attack or be starved into surrender; but it was .long before this method was adopted, and the cost in money and lives of these wars eventually attained so high a figure that before the actual completion of the victory the British troops were withdrawn from the colony, leaving the final settlement with the Maoris to the New Zealand forces.

The First Maori War, 1860-1861—A petty dispute as to the ownership of certain lands in the Taranaki district in i860 brought about a general rising of the natives, who had long seen with misgiving the process of continued petty encroachments by the white man on their ancestral domains.

The first British attempt, in March 1860, to suppress the revolt was ill-conceived and worse conducted, and several bloody repulses were suffered before the Maori *pahs*, so that reinforcements from Australia had to be awaited before fresh operations could be undertaken. Before these came on the scene the enemy had disappeared into the interior, and the task of following him up was one of great labour and difficulty. Eventually the pursuers came up against his new positions, from several of which he was expelled at considerable cost, and the war thereafter degenerated into guerilla operations which were finally terminated by a truce and a treaty early in 1861.

The Second Maori War, 1863-1866—Meanwhile the Maoris in the heart of the north island, though nominally subjected to British rule, had thrown off their allegiance, set up a king of their own at Ngaruawahia, a village situated on the Waikato River, seventy-five miles south of Auckland, and commenced a series of aggressive actions against the British settlers, which brought on a second war. In July 1863 Cameron with some 1500 men set off up the Waikato to crush the revolt at its heart; but before he had got very far he was compelled to halt before the ever-stiffening hostile resistance in his front, and by a series of daring attacks on his lines of communication. It was not till November that the arrival of fresh troops enabled him to renew his advance, drive the aborigines from their *pahs*—not without serious casualties—and take possession of the Maori king's capital. This achievement not proving decisive of the campaign, he was compelled to follow them up farther into the heart of their territory, forcing his way along rivers, up mountains and through dense bush, and suffering much from shortage of supplies and lack of adequate and suitable transport. Eventually his enemies vanished before him into the mountains, whence they periodically issued in forays and raids against Cameron's detachments pushed out to observe them, on more than one occasion inflicting serious loss. The campaign had in fact trailed away into indecisiveness, and the result of our lack of success quickly made itself felt in the spread of trouble to the south-eastern and western quarters of the island. In the former area our troops suffered a costly set-back at the Gate *pah*, which delayed the final settlement with the insurgents. In the west our task was rendered one of almost insuperable difficulty by the rise of a fanatical sect known as the Hauhaus, who added religious fuel to the political flames, and by serious friction between the civil and military authorities over the policy to be followed in dealing with the Maoris. An ambitious project for converging operations in the early months of 1865 by two columns from Taranaki and Wanganui against the heart of the revolted districts came to nothing. Eventually Cameron gave way to Chute, who, resolved in future to abstain from direct assaults on the Maori *pahs*, undertook an offensive westwards from Wanganui in January 1865, which finally led him right round through the whole of the disaffected area to Taranaki, and broke the back of the hostile resistance. On the conclusion of his march the final stamping out of the revolt was quickly accomplished, after the withdrawal of the regular forces before mentioned, by the colonists themselves, and by the end of the year peace had been restored throughout the island.

The Third Maori War, 1868-1870—Two years later fresh disturbances were caused by the activities of certain outlaw chiefs and their bands, who, from their fastnesses in the mountains, began raiding and murdering in the scattered settlements along the eastern and south-western coasts. These incursions never attained the dimensions of a national rising and indeed many of the Maori chiefs and their clans cooperated with the white militia and volunteers in repressing them—a task which was only accomplished after some eighteen months of marching and fighting. By January 1870 the bandit leaders had all either been laid by the heels or driven into hiding, and the disturbed areas were once more pacified.

8. The Imperial Policeman

The work of the British army during the last half of the nineteenth century may be considered from two points of view, from either of which it appears in a highly creditable light. If we adopt the purely military standpoint, we see that, if we include in our catalogue of small wars the Indian Frontier campaigns, scarcely a year has passed between 1860 and 1908 without seeing British troops in the field in one or another of the four continents, while on many occasions we had on hand two or even more little military enterprises at once. Thus, to take a few random instances, the period from 1878 to 1881 saw us engaged in one important war and a number of incidental expeditions in Asia, and three minor campaigns in Africa. In 1896 and 1897 we had on our hands, besides the great North-West Frontier rising, campaigns in the Sudan, in Matabeleland, in East Africa, and in Ashanti. During the period of the South African War, which strained our military resources to their utmost, we were yet able to send troops to China and Somaliland, besides the North-West Frontier.

All this involved not merely a considerable military effort on the part of the army and the nation, but a high degree of readiness for the most varying kinds of war in conditions and against adversaries resembling each other in nothing but their diversity. Preparation for war, so easy for a Continental power, was under these conditions impossible for us to ensure in any perfection; the most that could be done was to render the army capable of entering upon any sort of campaign anywhere, in the shortest possible time necessary for its adaptation to the local conditions. If this point of view be steadily maintained, the marvel will be not that we often took months before being able to commence our operations, but that we were able to do so at all within reasonable time; not that victory was sometimes dearly bought and long of coming, but that it was in almost every case ultimately secured. The minor campaigns of the army in this epoch are characterised throughout by a facility of adaptation to circumstances as they arose; by a flexibility of thought among the leaders, a high range of administrative ability among the organisers, and a power of endurance, a courage and a discipline among the rank and file, which are worthy of far higher praise than they have received from historians in general and from military commentators in particular. The colonial campaigns of France in Morocco and Algeria were no more creditable achievements; those of Russia in Central Asia, of Germany in Central Africa, of Italy in Tripoli and East Africa, and of Spain in Morocco, show a far higher percentage of failures and fiascos. In the matter of these little wars other nations have nothing to teach Britain and much to learn from her.

And if we take for a moment a more lofty standpoint than that of mere military merit, and consider the work of the British army in the light of social science and world progress, here, again, we have cause for legitimate satisfaction. The British army has been, indeed, one of the foremost civilising agents in the world. It has been not unusual in the past to refer to these little wars as "nigger smashing" or "cannibal chasing", to talk of "the brave barbarian struggling to be free", of "conquest as a prelude to exploitation". The use that has been or may be made of any conquest is a matter which is altogether out of the army's province, though our country's record in this respect will certainly bear comparison with that of any other. But as to the conquest itself, if we believe, as most sane men do, that peace and order are preferable to massacre and plunder, that the cultivation of the soil is more fruitful than slave-trading, that sheep and oxen rather than human beings are meant for human food, that the rule of an enlightened, disinterested and justice-loving civilised man is more endurable than that of an irresponsible and blood-stained barbarian or a half-crazy religious fanatic—then there is no question but that conquest by a civilised power is at least a stepping-stone to those higher things. Such liberty as these savage races have lost has been usually merely the liberty of the strong and the fierce to tyrannise over their less fortunate fellows; such powers as have been taken from them have been normally used by them for evil rather than for good. To be subjected even to a stern alien government which at least respects life and liberty is better than being butchered in a private feud or sold into slavery for another's gain; and to be at peace is the first step to real freedom. It is the crowning glory of the British army that it has brought so many barbarous and uncivilised races to take perforce this essential preliminary step, and has throughout vast regions of the earth opened up the road of order and civilisation. Compared to this vast humanising achievement, all the great European wars for rectifications of frontiers or possession of provinces seem to be degraded exhibitions of barbarian savagery, their course productive only of misery to thousands, their results petty, inconsistent and inconclusive.

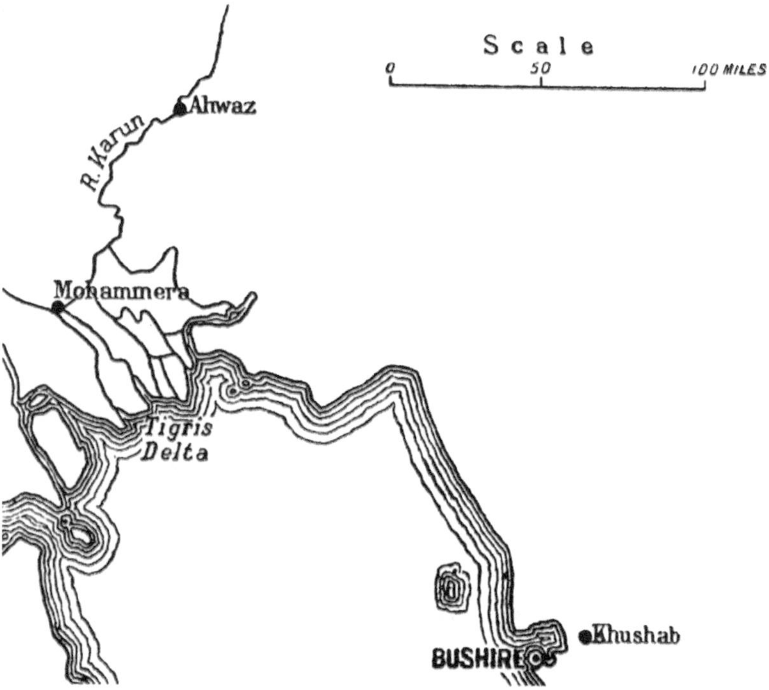

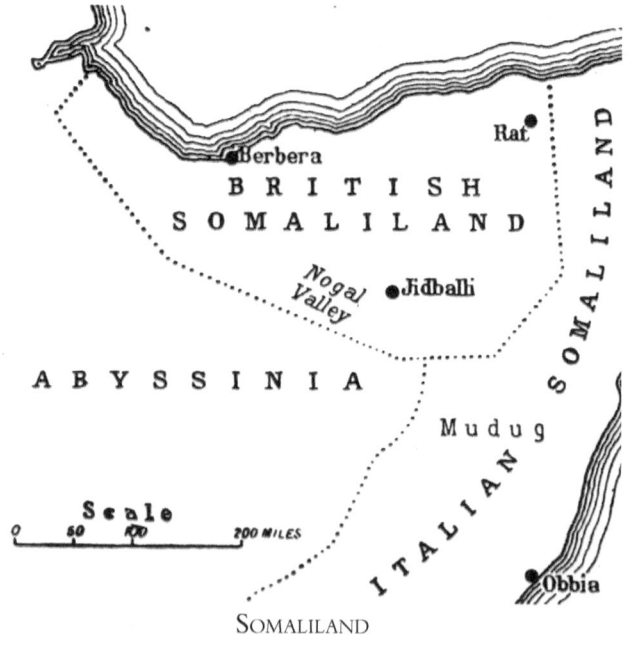

THE PERSIAN WAR

SOMALILAND

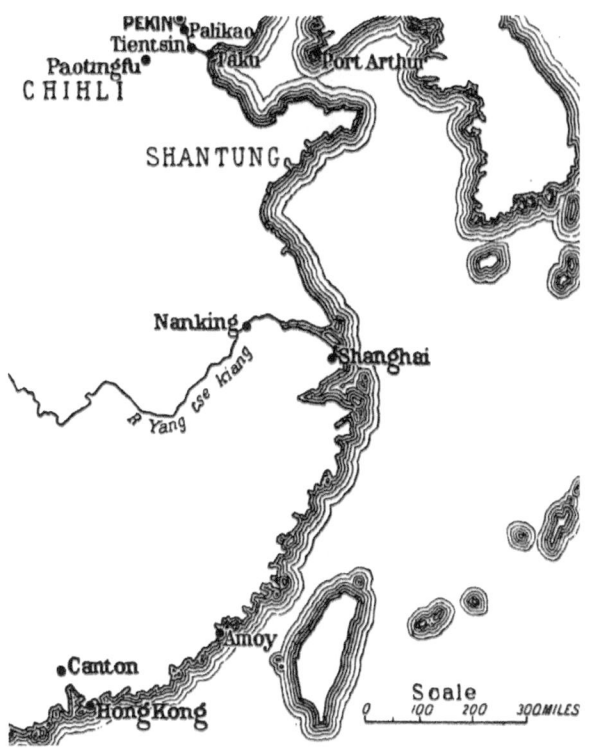

THE CHINA WARS

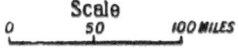

THE ABYSSINIAN WAR

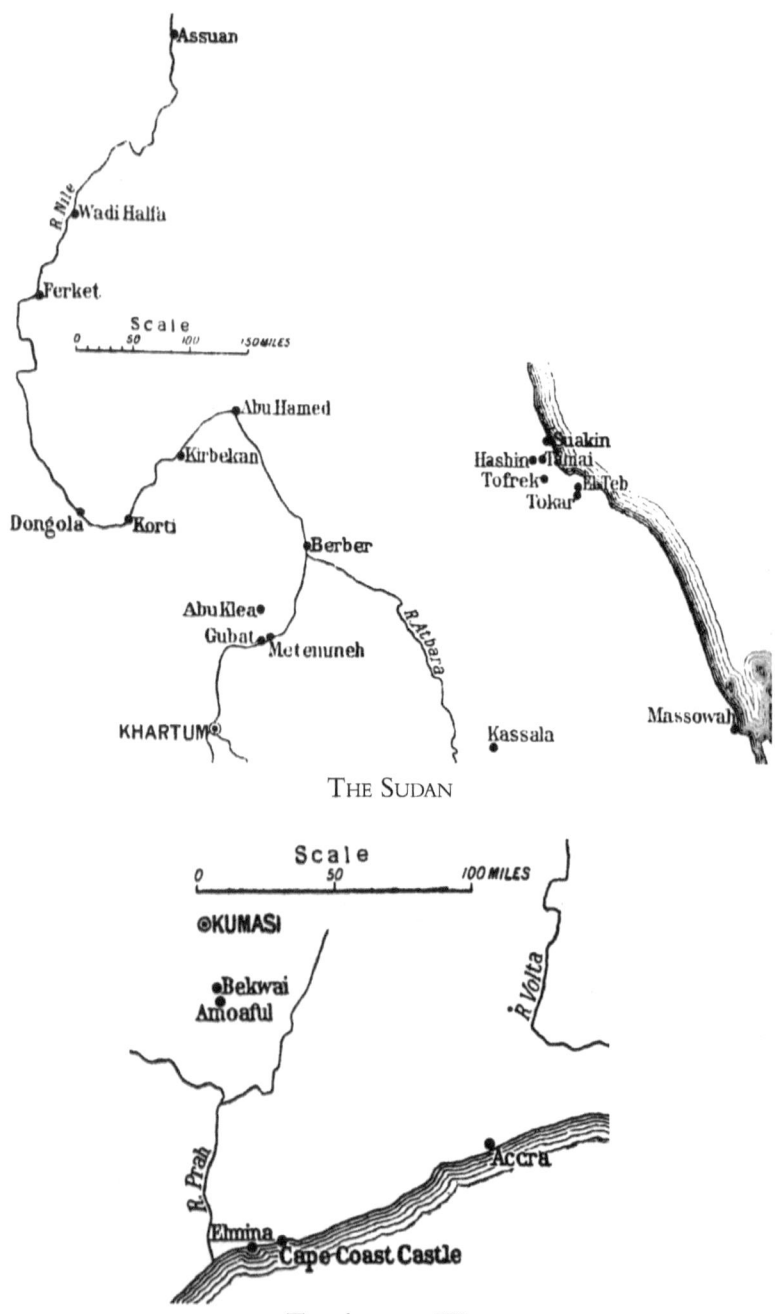

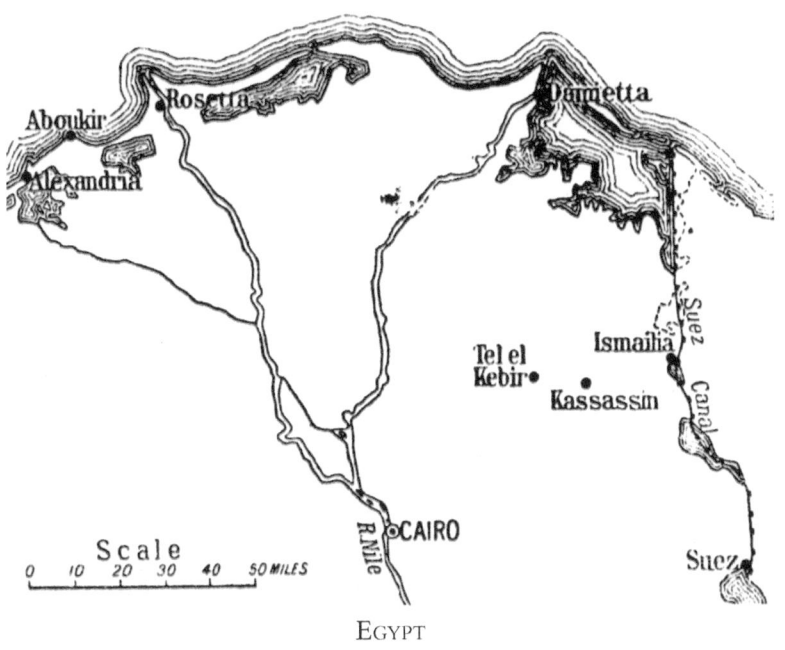

EGYPT

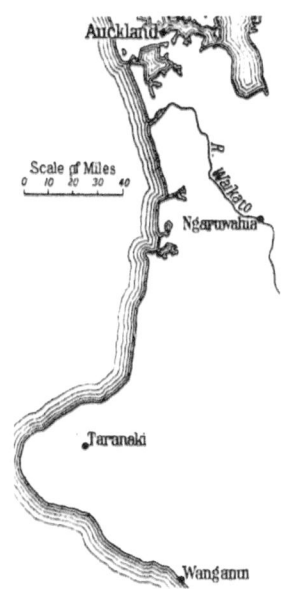

THE MAORI WAR

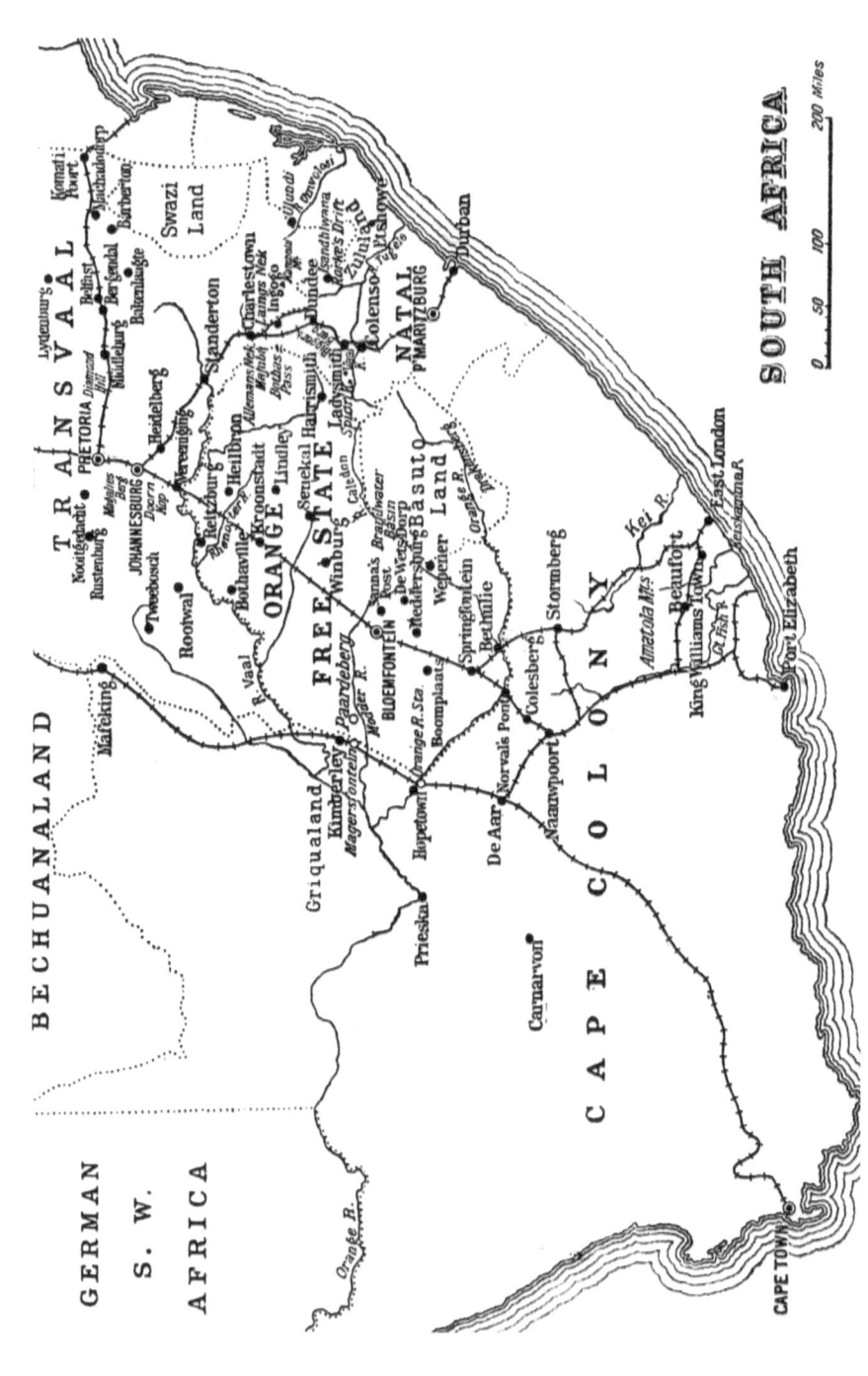

KITCHENER

A Tommy

CHAPTER 16

The South African War and After
1899-1913

1. The Early British Reverses
October-December 1899

British South Africa, extending at the end of the reign of Queen Victoria north and south for over 1,200 miles from the Zambesi to the Cape of Good Hope, and east and west for 800 miles from Durban to the South Atlantic, was still separated into two parts by the two Dutch Boer Republics, the Transvaal and the Orange Free State, which had conquered their independence less than twenty years before from the irresolution of Gladstone and his Government. Geographically and historically this was an anomaly which could hardly long continue, as the governments of the Republics were well aware; and when the discovery of large deposits of gold within their frontiers brought in its train hosts of European settlers and prospectors, it became clear that delicate international questions must soon arise as sources of potential trouble. These Uitlanders, as they were called, refused the franchise in the country of their adoption, and subjected to political and social restrictions which seemed to them unreasonable, soon began to demand better treatment, and from about 1890 onwards to plot to secure it by violence. In 1895 the fiasco of the Jameson Raid revealed their designs and Great Britain's championship of their cause to the world; and from this date the Republics began to regard as certain an ultimate war, in which their memories of 1881 encouraged them to hope for a good chance of victory. Henceforth they pressed forward their military preparations, and as soon as these were completed in 1899, hurried on the outbreak of hostilities. Great Britain, on the other hand, despite—or perhaps because of—her bitter memories of former humiliating defeats at Boer hands; despite the powerful financial and commercial interests urging her to take up the challenge, still hoped and worked for peace through all that summer, only to find herself in October presented with a completely unacceptable ultimatum, while she had yet of set purpose, lest peace should be imperilled by warlike measures, taken no real steps to prepare for a campaign.

In mid-October, when the Boer ultimatum expired, there were in South Africa, south of the Limpopo, no more than 27,000 British troops, and these widely scattered over a vast area of territory. To cover the whole of Cape Colony and Bechuanaland, lying to the west and south of the hostile republics, stood ready less than 11,000 men, close on half of which were locally raised, echeloned in small detachments along the Cape Town—Mafeking railway, the bulk in the De Aar-Orange River area with posts at Naauwport, to guard the Port Elizabeth line, and Stormberg, to guard the East London line. In Cape Colony there was known to be much sympathy with the Boer cause, and readiness in certain quarters to express that sympathy, if opportunity arose, in terms of action. In the colony of Natal, at and north of Durban, there were 16,000 men under command of White, who had assembled his main body in a central position about Ladysmith. Here he could best meet the concentric attack which the contour of the frontier of northern Natal, projecting like a wedge into enemy territory, almost imposed upon the Boers; but political pressure had induced him, against his better judgement, to push forward a detachment to protect the Dundee coal mines.

As against the tenuous array of their enemies, the Boers could place in the field close on 90,000 men, of whom, however, little more than half were employed in first line, with no guns superior to the British artillery in everything but numbers. Regular troops were few, but the Boer farmer's skill as a marksman and rider and his eye for country made him, on the defensive at any rate, a first-class individual fighting man, while the high mobility and fire power of a Boer army went far to compensate for its lack of discipline and of proper organisation for war, for the dearth of first-rate generalship, and for the absence of offensive power. If the military defects of the republics' military forces caused them to miss, in the first few weeks of the war, the chance of ending it at one blow, their qualities at all events enabled them to endure for three years against overwhelmingly superior numbers and resources, to succumb only before a military effort such as England had not been called on to put forth since the days of Napoleon.

The Republican plan of campaign involved in the west the investment of Mafeking and of Kimberley, the headquarters of the diamond industry, and the residence of the most powerful individual in South Africa, Rhodes; and an attempt to rally Cape Colony to their side by an advance over the middle Orange at Norval's Pont and Bethulie. In all these enterprises as will be seen, they were ultimately unsuccessful; but their main effort, in which half their forces were engaged, was directed against Natal, which was simultaneously invaded by 14,000 Transvaalers from east and north, and by 10,000 Free Staters from the west. The Dundee detachment seized a chance of falling upon and beating off the Boer column from the east before being compelled by pressure against its left and rear to fall back on Ladysmith, whither it successfully made its escape, thanks to White's offensive actions at Elandslaagte and

Rietfontein, in which the vanguards of the invading forces were checked. His forces thus concentrated, the British commander advanced to deliver a decisive battle at Lombard's Kop, which turned out adversely, and compelled him to seek refuge in Ladysmith. Here, by the end of October, he was invested after less than a fortnight's fighting; but the enemy fortunately failed to utilise the two critical weeks that elapsed before the first British reinforcements landed at Durban in mid-November, and made no attempt to push southwards otherwise than by a half-hearted raid by a small force, which was easily driven back to the north bank of the Tugela.

If the initial Boer successes had failed of decisive effect, they at least hopelessly disarranged the British plan of campaign as conceived by Buller, the Commander-in-Chief in South Africa, of an advance from the Norval's Pont—Bethulie area through the Orange Free State by way of Bloemfontein, the capital, to the chief Transvaal town of Pretoria. On his arrival at Cape Town at the end of October, he at once realised that the first necessity was to relieve the beleaguered garrisons of Ladysmith and Kimberley, and for this the forces now or shortly to be placed at his disposal, amounting in all to an army corps, plus one brigade for line of communication work, and a cavalry division, close on 30,000 men of all ranks, would be by no means excessive. He decided therefore to assume in person the command in Natal, leaving Methuen with 10,000 men to work up the railway from Orange River to the relief of Kimberley, which was already, thanks to the influence of Rhodes and his fellow-magnates, calling prematurely for help.

Methuen set out in the third week in November, fought three successful actions before the end of the month, and got to within twenty miles of his objective before encountering the formidable hostile position of Magersfontein. An attempt to carry this by a night march followed by an attack at dawn miscarried with heavy loss, and the British advance in this area was definitely held up for the time being. Away to the south-east an almost exactly similar attempt made by Gatacre with a small force to surprise the Boers at Stormberg met with like ill-fortune; luckily, neither here nor at Colesberg, where French by skilful manoeuvring had contrived, and for two months was to continue, to contain a superior hostile force, did the enemy attempt to exploit his advantages.

The tale of British reverses was completed in Natal by Buller's repulse at Colenso. Having collected 20,000 men to force the line of Tugela and break through to White, the British commander, after his advanced troops had been checked with loss, drew off his force before half of it had been engaged. This repulse, the last of "Black Week", had at least the beneficial effect of arousing Britain and the Empire to a full realisation of the situation. The Government determined to prosecute the war at any cost to a victorious conclusion, and the flood of recruits, both at home and overseas, ratified their decision by the voice of the people. Three more divisions, a cavalry brigade, many militia and volunteer corps, and Colonial contingents were prepared for despatch overseas; Roberts, with Kitchener as his Chief of Staff, was appointed commander-in-chief in the place of Buller, who was thus left free to devote his undivided attention to the Natal campaign; and while the British Empire thus resolutely donned its armour the Boers let their precious weeks of respite pass in inaction.

2. The Restoration of the Position in Natal and the Occupation of Bloemfontein January-March 1900

The new commander-in-chief, who with his chief of staff arrived in the theatre of war early in January 1900, now recast the original plan of campaign. While still maintaining as guiding principle an advance by way of Bloemfontein on Pretoria, he determined to execute it from the west instead of the south, and as a preliminary to relieve Kimberley, defeating or destroying the Boer army which, under Cronje, had held up Methuen on the Modder. It was two months, however, before all was ready for the opening of the new offensive, for which 30,000 men had been assembled, quite unknown to Cronje, between De Aar and Orange River stations; and during this period of preparation the condition of the garrison of Kimberley was believed—erroneously, as it turned out—to have become serious, and that of Ladysmith had become so in reality. In the first week of the new year, indeed, the besiegers had delivered a dangerous assault on White's southern defences which, if executed with more skill and vigour, would probably have decided his fate, and had it been repeated at any time within the next two months, must certainly have done so; while Buller had, as we shall see later, made two unsuccessful attempts, in January and February, to effect the relief of the town. Roberts, therefore, when he commenced his operations in mid-February, felt himself bound as a first move to throw a force into Kimberley, in the hope that this success would exercise a favourable influence on the situation in Natal. Once Cronje was defeated and Bloemfontein in his hands, it would be easy to open up a new line of communication along the railway from Colesberg and Stormberg *viâ* Springfontein, and revert to the original plan of campaign.

French's cavalry led the advance, and, moving east over the Riet and north to the Modder, in three days rode right round Cronje's left flank and entered Kimberley, the siege of which was at once raised. The infantry followed, but Cronje, at last awake to his danger, was able to make for the gap between French and the main British army, and to effect his retreat by the line of the Modder. His rearguard was pressed hard, and the cavalry from Kimberley, by a supreme effort, started off once more south-eastwards and succeeded in heading off the retreating enemy, who found himself thus caught in a trap. Cronje entrenched himself in the river-bed at Paardeberg and here beat off with loss an impetuous and ill-coordinated attempt to crush him out of hand by a concentric advance. The end, however, was only delayed; a dash by De Wet to create a diversion and enable him to cut his way out came to nothing despite its bold execution; and on February 27, the anniversary of Majuba, he and his 4,000 Boers laid down their arms after an investment of ten days and an almost incessant bombardment.

The advance on the Free State capital was forthwith resumed. De Wet, the ablest and most resolute leader produced by the Boers throughout the war, vainly strove to rally his demoralised fellow-countrymen for its defence; driven from two successive positions, he was forced to fall back to the eastwards, leaving the British army to possess itself quietly of Bloemfontein, on March 13, less than a month after the initiation of its brilliantly successful offensive. Here a long pause ensued, while the next stage of the campaign which was to seal the fate of the Transvaal capital also, and complete the overthrow of both the Republican Governments, was in preparation.

In Natal, also, the tide of war had, after many vicissitudes and at disproportionate cost, been turned at last in our favour. In mid-January, Buller, now reinforced to 26,000 men, embarked on his second attempt on the Boer lines north of the Tugela. His new scheme was to cross that river by the fords beyond their right, and by turning north-eastwards, to envelop their wing, and thus open the road to Ladysmith. The execution even of the preliminary moves, although the crossing was effected without opposition, consumed a week, so that the enemy had ample time to pierce and prepare to counter the British design by the concentration of strong forces in prolongation of their right and in face of the advancing British.

At length Warren, to whom Buller had practically given over the direction of the advance, decided to attack the Boer position frontally, and to storm Spion Kop, apparently the key of it, at night; but when morning dawned the captors of the hill found themselves a target for devastating fire from three sides, and suffered so severely that at nightfall their commander withdrew just as reinforcements and artillery were arriving to his aid and the enemy were preparing to give up the struggle. In face of this set-back Buller and Warren decided that the game was for the moment lost, and that it only remained for them to retire and renew the attempt elsewhere; and by the end of the month the army was once more back on the south bank of the Tugela. A week later a new attack was undertaken, this time against the left of the new Boer front, where only the peak of Vaal Krantz blocked the road to open country beyond. When this hill had been captured, however, it was found that guns could not be brought up, and that without their support further advance in face of flanking fire from the heights on either side of it would be too costly to risk. Thus there petered out in failure the third of Buller's attempts to relieve Ladysmith; but if he himself was inclined to despond, his troops were still ready and eager for battle; and urged on by Roberts, and by reports as to the critical condition of the beleaguered town and the departure of a proportion of the enemy forces to face the new British offensive in the Free State, he resolved to try one more throw of the dice.

This time the Boer left was the objective of his attack. This, resting as it did on a group of hills lying east of Colenso and on the south bank of the Tugela, had all along seemed to many the most promising of good results; the operations were well conceived and admirably executed, and after six days' methodical fighting the whole group was in our hands. The Tugela, however, still remained to be crossed, and the main Boer position on the hills beyond it to be dealt with; and its capture took several days of desperate attacks, all costly, and more than one unsuccessful to boot, before the storming of Pieters Hill, the northern buttress, on February 27, involved the fall of the remainder of the hostile defences and the collapse of the resistance. While Buller's cavalry joined hands with the wrecks of gallant men who had for four months so stubbornly held Ladysmith, the Boers were permitted to draw off unpursued.

Thus in less than a month from Roberts' taking the field in person the situation both in the east and in the west had undergone a decisive change. The Boers, who at the end of January 1900 stood everywhere on British territory and held three British garrisons closely invested, now retained a precarious grip on but one of these garrisons and a strip of northern Natal; one of their capitals, with half the surrounding state, had been wrenched from them, and much of their confidence in themselves and in their leaders had vanished with the change in their fortunes.

3. The Clearing of Natal and the Orange Free State, and the Capture of Pretoria
April–July 1900

Many causes combined to necessitate the British army's six weeks' halt at Bloemfontein from mid-March to early May. Not the least among these was a serious outbreak of enteric, the result of drinking foul water during the investment of Cronje, which took heavy toll of the troops and increased the already urgent need for strong reinforcements. Remounts were also required in large numbers, as also were supplies, ammunition and material, if a further advance were to be undertaken with any prospect of success. But first and foremost, in order to cope with these large demands, the railway to Bloemfontein from the south had to be reopened for traffic and secured against molestation by the numerous bands of Free Staters still at large in the eastern part of the country.

This task was entrusted to Gatacre from Stormberg and Clements, French's successor at Colesberg, who by the end of March had repaired the Orange River railway bridges and restored the line throughout. The detachments sent out by them and also by the main army to restore order to the east, however, soon found that they had run their heads into a hornet's nest. The Boers, under the able leadership of De Wet, had quickly recovered from the depression into which the fall of Bloemfontein had cast them, and were once more ripe for mischief. Roberts' detachment, sent northwards to clear the Pretoria railway as far as the Modder, had to fight hard to accomplish its task ; a cavalry brigade despatched eastwards was ambushed and suffered heavily at Sanna's Post; one of Gatacre's columns was surrounded and compelled to surrender at Reddersburg; and a second had to undergo a fortnight's siege at Wepener before being rescued by a force from the south. In fact, it was clear by the end of April that any further advance north from Bloemfontein by the British main army could only be made at considerable risk to its communications. This, however, appeared to Roberts no adequate reason for a change of plan on his part. Everything was now in readiness for an offensive against Pretoria, which he proposed to carry out with imposing forces, over 100,000 men, covering the whole breadth of the enemy's country from east to west. Before this grand movement was taken in hand, however, two subsidiary expeditions had been undertaken. The first of these was the suppression of a smouldering rebellion in north-western Cape Colony and Griqualand, in the Prieska and Carnarvon areas. Kitchener was despatched on this mission; the Boer raiders, who had been the prime cause of the trouble, were quickly driven beyond the Orange, and Warren, following them up northwards, had reduced the whole disaffected region to order by June. The second enterprise was the relief of Mafeking, which, under the resourceful and cheery guidance of Baden-Powell, had already sturdily sustained investment for more than six months, and focussed upon itself the whole of the enemy's effort on his north-west border. A tiny force under Plumer, which had moved down the Rhodesian railway to its help, had been held up a day's march north of the place; and a column under Mahon was now despatched from the south, which in mid-May, striking off to the west of Mafeking, effected its junction with Plumer, drove off the besiegers, and freed the combined forces for further service in cooperation with the main offensive.

This was now in full progress. Roberts, escorted by French and his cavalry on the left and by Ian Hamilton on the right, was moving up the Bloemfontein—Pretoria railway with 45,000 men; Methuen and Hunter with 20,000 were on his left, between him and the Free State border, while Buller with 46,000 was preparing to clear northern Natal.

Before this imposing force the enemy, under Botha, outnumbered as they were, fell back steadily with little resistance. Skirmishes took place at the crossing of the Zand and before Kroonstad, and a somewhat more serious opposition behind the line of the Vaal was overcome by the expedient of transferring Hamilton from the right to the left of the army, and from there passing him round the hostile flank. After an action at Doorn Kop, the great mining centre of Johannesburg, the source of the greater part of the country's wealth, was occupied, and on June 5, 1900, the British commander made his triumphant entry into the capital of the Transvaal, the enemy's army drawing off after its government to the east. In this direction it was further driven as the result of a two days' battle at Diamond Hill, which established the British in their possession of Pretoria and left them leisure to undertake the consolidation of their hold on the territory recently traversed by their armies.

One of the first measures to be undertaken was the establishment of connection with the right wing of the army under Buller, which had been left well to the right rear of the main force, and in fact was not yet clear of Natal. The necessity of resting and re-fitting his own troops as well as those of the Ladysmith garrison after the relief of that place, and of organising from them a force fit to take the field, had delayed the re-commencement of active operations till some days after Roberts' departure from Bloemfontein. The enemy on Buller's front had taken up a strong position on the Biggarsberg, blocking his way north from Ladysmith and resting their right on the Drakensberg; the left, however, was weak and could be enveloped, and on the British advancing by this route the Boers evacuated their stronghold and retired to the scenes of their victories twenty years before—the heights of Laing's Nek and Majuba, in the extreme northern corner of the colony. Three weeks elapsed before Buller was ready to attack this new position; he then passed a column through the Drakensberg by Botha's Pass, which came round in rear of the enemy right, storming their new front covering the Standerton road and railway at Alleman's Nek, and forcing them to withdraw in haste to the north, to avoid complete envelopment. Continuing its advance by Standerton, the Natal army in the first week in July gained touch with Roberts' extreme right, stretched south-east to Heidelberg to connect with it.

With this achievement there may be said to have terminated the major operations against the Boer republics, one of which indeed had already been annexed to the British Empire under the name of the Orange River Colony. The rulers of both these States were now homeless exiles without a capital or a government; their armies, manifestly incapable of resisting any British advance in force, were rapidly dissolving under the depression of failure ; practically two-thirds of their country had already been overrun, while British territory had been entirely freed from their grasp; and large numbers of their fighting men had already given up the apparently hopeless contest. According to all precedent and probability, a few months should have sufficed for the completion and acceptance of the British conquest. But this was not the view of the ablest and boldest of our adversaries, and so accurate was their estimate of the true military position, and so many and so well utilised the resources still left to them, that they were enabled, to the astonishment of the world, and possibly beyond their own expectations, if not their hopes, to prolong their struggle for independence for close on two years.

4. The Guerrilla Warfare to the End of Roberts' Period of Command
June–November 1900

The capture of Pretoria and the eastward flight of Kruger, his Government and his army, was followed shortly afterwards by yet another striking British success in the newly proclaimed Orange River Colony. Even while Roberts' victorious advance was in progress, De Wet was giving ample employment to the strong forces which he had left behind to guard his line of communications. A deceitful period of quiet had, in fact, caused a considerable reduction in their strength and a consequent diminution in vigilance about the end of May, and of this the elusive guerilla chief took full advantage. Pouncing on and compelling the surrender of a small force of yeomanry near Lindley, he next turned his attention to the railway between Kroonstad and Heilbron; three garrisons in rapid succession were surprised and destroyed, and the whole of the stretch of line on either side of the Rhenoster passed out of British control at a critical moment in the campaign.

The British commander-in-chief at once ordered the despatch of important forces to restore the situation. Four columns under the general direction of Hunter were assembled on the line Heidelberg—Heilbron—Lindley—Senekal, with orders to close in from north and west on De Wet and his colleagues, who had fallen back eastwards after their daring exploit. The scheme, well conceived and admirably executed, worked out to perfection—in all but one small but vitally important detail. Gradually, and at the cost of constant fighting, the enemy were driven back until they were compelled to seek refuge in the Brandwater Basin—a natural fortress ringed round with high hills and backed against the Caledon and the border of Basutoland; and here, surrounded by a largely superior hostile force which closed up every possible avenue of escape, they laid down their arms at the end of July, to the number of 4,000 men. But the main prize which would have been worth all the rest had escaped Hunter; De Wet, with President Steyn and the remnant of the Free State Government, had slipped away to the north before the closing of the net and was still at large. Another Boer leader, Olivier, had also followed his example, but he, after a month more of meteoric raiding, was run to earth near Winburg. His abler and more troublesome colleague, though dogged at every step, outstripped his pursuers and, breaking north-west across the railway, appeared once more on the far side of the Vaal, whither he had gone to convey Steyn to Kruger's headquarters at Machadodorp for consultation.

At this moment the British cause was not prospering in the western Transvaal, where the enemy, under Delarey, were active and enterprising, and had succeeded in surprising and capturing several weak detachments in the Rustenburg area and the passes of the Magaliesberg range. Our forces of occupation were kept fully employed in hurrying to and fro to repress the risings that broke out in every area not held down by one of our garrisons, and eventually Roberts resolved, much against his will, to evacuate the country for the present and utilise elsewhere the troops thus made available. This movement, however, Was still in process of completion when De Wet appeared and drew all our troops like a magnet to his orbit; and indeed he had two very narrow escapes, once on his way north, when, pressed by his pursuers and menaced on either flank, he was all but headed off from the Magaliesberg passes; and again on his return, when, having delivered Steyn to the charge of the Boers operating north of Pretoria, he had to take refuge in the mountains to escape being completely hemmed in. After his departure for the Orange River Colony in the third week in August, British influence once more permeated through the western Transvaal, where the Boers remained more or less quiescent for some months, only minor punitive expeditions being found necessary.

Operations for the subjection of the eastern Transvaal by the final dispersion of the main Boer army and the eviction of Kruger from his territory had already commenced. An advance in force astride the Pretoria—Komati Poort railway was carried out by French's cavalry, working on the right, a body of infantry from the main army on the railway itself, and Buller's Natal army, which had been called up from Charles-town to Belfast, and now took the left of the line. After a smart little action at Bergendal the wings were pushed forward, the left into the Lydenburg district, the right towards Barberton, and before the overwhelming pressure on both their flanks Botha's forces gave way and finally broke up. By the end of September Kruger had fled into Portuguese territory, the British had occupied Komati Poort, and the independence of the Transvaal had been proclaimed at an end. The sturdier elements among the enemy were, however, no more inclined to give up the struggle here than their fellows in the south and west. While some of them passed round the northern flanks of the British and carried out, during November and December, a series of incursions against the Pretoria—Komati Poort railway, one of which led to a considerable action north-west of Middelburg, others slipped off south-westwards, and, by their harassing tactics, made the journey of French from the Portuguese frontier to Heidelberg very unlike the return march of a victorious force.

Meanwhile, throughout all these months De Wet was still

very much in evidence in the Orange River Colony. In the middle of October, forsaking his own territory once more, he came north of the Vaal and invested a British force at Frederikstad, but was beaten off with loss, and on his way back was surprised at Bothaville, losing the greater part of his following. The prestige of his name, however, sufficed to raise another equally large, and his next exploit was the capture of Dewetsdorp, far away to the south in an area which the British had supposed to have been long since effectively pacified. From here he planned a dash into Cape Colony, but was headed off, driven into the angle between the flooded Caledon and Orange Rivers and almost caught; at the critical moment, however, the waters subsided and allowed him once more to escape from a seemingly hopeless position.

At the end of November 1900, Roberts, who had been appointed commander-in-chief of the British army, handed over his charge in South Africa to Kitchener and sailed for home. If there had been in his conduct of the campaign signs that his hand had lost something of its former cunning, it is impossible to deny that it is to him, more than to any other man, that England owes the position she holds in South Africa today, and that this land, where so many of her soldiers had marred or buried their military reputations, had but enhanced that of this last of our Sepoy generals. His conduct of operations had been distinguished throughout by lucidity, firmness of purpose, and energy combined with prudence. On his advent he found the fame and fortunes of British arms at the lowest ebb to which they had sunk for a hundred years; in less than a year he carried them victoriously throughout the whole of the enemy's country, broke all their armies in pieces, and left to his successor a task which, however much weariness and disappointment must attend its full accomplishment, could, if resolutely and systematically pursued, have in the ultimate resort but one termination

5. KITCHENER'S OPERATIONS TO THE CONCLUSION OF PEACE DECEMBER 1900–MAY 1902

From Kitchener's assumption of command in December 1900 to the termination of hostilities some eighteen months later, the nature of the British operations took on a form which defies brief description. It consisted of a series of attempts to round up a few bold partisan leaders who, being practically unfettered by the factors usually limiting the activities of armed bodies of men, were free to wander at their will over all the vast theatre of war. The course of the fighting is therefore as hard to summarise now as it was in those days to forecast, and the story of the last phase of the war tends to degenerate into a detailed and wearisome narrative of petty combats without any apparent interconnection and leading to no measurable result. We can only briefly describe the policy and methods of dealing with the military situation arising from the Boer adoption of guerilla tactics, and summarise the fortunes of the more prominent hostile chiefs during the period under review.

On his assumption of command Kitchener found himself faced with a potential force of some 50,000 Boers, of whom little more—probably considerably less—than one half were ever in the field at any given moment. The numbers at his own disposal were never less than four times these figures; and by May 1901, when the British recruiting effort had reached its maximum, he had close on 250,000 men under his command. Of these, however, only two-thirds were available for field service, and a good half of these again were permanently immobilised in garrison or other duties. Of the remaining 80,000, by far the greater proportion were mounted troops; but they were by no means of equal, nor all of high, military value, as a series of unhappy incidents were to show in due course.

Kitchener's methods of dealing with the situation before

him were based on two devices—the blockhouse system and the drive. Both were interdependent, and were gradually extended and developed as time went on into a very elaborate and complete system which in the end proved effective for the task in hand, though it brought us few spectacular successes such as the capture of the more famous Boer leaders in the field.

Blockhouses, which were small forts of corrugated iron and earth surrounded by barbed wire, were first erected to protect the main railway lines, but later their number was multiplied; the intervals between them were reduced to a few hundred yards and blocked by wire and continuous trenches; and a barrier was thus erected capable of preventing an enemy band not merely from cutting, but from crossing the railway line, whether in advance or retreat. A further development of the system was its extension to main roads and tracks across the plains, so that the whole country was at length parcelled up into small sub-areas within which any hostile movement could be easily localised and dealt with. By the end of the war all the main railway lines had been thus converted into defensive belts, and other blockhouse lines ran for miles across country in the north-east and east of the Orange River Colony and in the south-east and west of the Transvaal, as well as in northern and western Cape Colony. Though never quite impenetrable to small bands of determined men, they imposed severe limitations on hostile movement, and rendered possible a systematic reduction of the country by means of organised drives through the various enclosed areas.

These drives were executed by mobile forces within the limits of these areas, with the object not only of penning up and forcing the surrender or dispersal of hostile bands, but of putting pressure on the Boer will by the sweeping off of the local resources, the destruction of buildings and crops, the collection of arms and ammunition, and even in certain cases the wholesale deportation of recalcitrant populations.

The burden of the war thus began to press with increasing weight and severity on all elements of the Boer people, who, despite their native stubbornness and lack of education, at length came to realise the hopelessness of their cause, and to long for the return of peace even at the cost of their independence.

Nevertheless, as far as the actual course of the campaign went, the honours of war as between Briton and Boer hung in even balance up to the very last weeks; and if the former could point to vast spaces of occupied territory, to enemy attacks heavily repulsed, to enemy bands dispersed and enemy leaders driven to seek safety in headlong flight, the latter could claim that they had time and again broken through their adversaries' fortified lines, evaded their carefully planned *battues,* and fallen upon and annihilated their detachments under tried and trusted leaders, and that at the end all but one or two of their partisan chiefs were still at large and apparently capable of indefinite further mischief. How this occurred can best be seen by a brief glance at the course of the campaign in each of the main theatres.

In the western Transvaal Delarey, from his lair in the foothills west of the Magaliesberg, remained active and troublesome throughout the whole period. In December 1900 he inflicted a severe blow on the British at Nooitgedacht, necessitating a punitive campaign against him, which lasted till May 1901, but proved unavailing to evict him from his stronghold, though it certainly caused him to lie low for several months. In October he once more took the field but was brilliantly repulsed in an onslaught on an isolated British column under Kekewich at Moedwil; early in February 1902 he emerged again with better success, snapping up an armed convoy and defeating and capturing Methuen, who had been dispatched to deal with him, at Tweebosch. Ian Hamilton was therefore given the task of running him to earth, and the last fight of the war at Roodeval in April saw the complete defeat and disintegration of Delarey's force, at that time under the command of Kemp, who fell in the action.

Botha and Viljoen in the northern and eastern Transvaal had an equally chequered career. The former's activity in January 1901 caused the dispatch of French to deal with him, but the wily Boer refused to let himself be driven to bay either against the Swaziland border or in the south-eastern corner of the Transvaal. Simultaneous operations north of Pretoria had the effect of reducing that territory to order for some months, and when Viljoen once more became active in January 1902 his career was quickly cut short by his capture. His colleague was more fortunate. Foiled in an attempt to invade Natal, he managed to wriggle away from the net cast to snare him and return to his old haunts, where he scored a resounding success over a British force at Bakenlaagte at the end of October. After this, however, he was driven to earth by the forces of Bruce Hamilton and remained *perdu* from January 1902 till his appearance as an envoy at the peace conference in May.

Meanwhile small bands of raiding Boers had carried war into Cape Colony. Two of them, riding east and west, in December 1900, had reached both the Atlantic and the Indian Oceans, and were still hovering around when De Wet, two months later, made his third and last incursion into British territory. Crossing the Orange north-west of Colesberg he struck west for Prieska, pertinaciously hunted all the way by our mounted troops; circling round in the bend of the river, he re-passed the Capetown—Kimberley railway near Hopetown, and fled east along the south bank of the flooded river while his pursuers closed in on him from all sides. None the less he successfully effected his crossing by a ford to the west of Norval's Pont and got away untouched, after infesting Cape Colony for close on three weeks. His mantle then fell on the worthy shoulders of Smuts, who, after riding through the whole length of the Orange River Colony from north-west to south-east, crossed the Orange near its junction with the Caledon, swung south-west, and penetrated to within 100 miles of Capetown itself. Here, in the heart of enemy territory and constantly hunted but never caught by enemy columns, he maintained himself with great cunning and resolution till the end of the war.

The Orange River Colony was the scene of more than one drive in the spring and summer of 1901, under the direction of Elliott, who in July captured all the officials of the Free State Government except Steyn. Later the return of De Wet caused a new recrudescence of hostile activity, and after the failure of an attempt to round him up near Reitz he scored another success by the destruction of a small yeomanry detachment near Harrismith. Consequent on this a new series of westward drives between the blockhouse lines running east from Heilbron and Kroonstad was instituted in January 1902, and in one of these De Wet's whole force, with the unhappy exception of the arch guerilla himself and Steyn, were ringed round and forced to surrender. The last of these drives ended just before the conclusion of hostilities and left the country still a prey to sporadic disturbance.

May 1902 saw the fruition of those hopes of peace which, ever since the fall of Pretoria, had been in the air and for some months were likely to materialise. A conference of the British and Boer leaders met at Vereeniging, in which Kitchener, the triumphant organiser of victory, was able to employ his genius no less usefully as a negotiator and conciliator. On May 31, 1902, the union of the Boer Republics and the British Empire was solemnised, De Wet, the incarnation of his people's resistance, still sternly forbidding the banns. The magnanimous policy of the victors, and the grant of self-government to their late enemies within a decade of the signing of the peace, finally healed the wounds and stilled the passions of the three years' conflict, and brought the men and the descendants of the men who had then fought for their independence against Britain once more into the field, but this time to fight beside her sons and on her behalf, in the day of her fiery trial in 1914.

Thus ended in long-delayed and dearly earned but decisive and fruitful victory the last and strangest of our Imperial wars. The conquest of the vast territories of the Boer Republics, and the subjection of the stubborn centaurs inhabiting them, had cost us even more in men, money and military effort than our previous trials of strength with the France of Louis XIV. or Napoleon. It had in its course blasted many a fair military reputation, revealed to us and to the world many a weak joint in our armour, and caused our rulers and our people more than once to grieve at temporary failure and to doubt of ultimate success. But on the whole the war, which was far more complicated and difficult than was possible of realisation from a distance, proved once more the adaptability of our military machine to even the most peculiar of conditions, brought forth a host of leaders and administrators of high merit, and called out again those fine qualities both of the British soldier and of the British people which many critics had begun to believe dead rather than dormant. The result of the South African War was as valuable as a testimony to the sound foundation of our military institutions and to the survival of warlike enthusiasm and prowess in our highly civilised community as was the course of the struggle in the strategic and tactical lessons which it afforded, and the repairs and additions to our fighting machine which it proved to be necessary and induced us to undertake in the interlude between it and the Great War.

6. Towards Armageddon
1902-1914

The conclusion of the conflict in South Africa brought with it the usual crop of post-war military troubles with which this generation of soldiers is all too familiar. Among the most acute of these was the re-formation of the Reserve after its depletion by three years of high wastage, and the recruiting of the army to a sufficient strength to find drafts for foreign service. Several schemes were adopted with more or less success until the whole question came to be dealt with in the root-and-branch reorganisation of our military system under Haldane.

In 1902 there were assembled two important Royal Commissions on military matters. The Norfolk Commission dealt with the future constitution of the Militia and Volunteers, and its report, which was not acted upon, recommended the adoption of a system of universal compulsory training for home defence in one or other of these forces. The Esher Committee inquired into War Office organisation and our methods of military administration generally, both of which were as a result of its findings radically remodelled. The commander-in-chief was done away with and in his place was set up an Army Council consisting of military and civil members, while the formation of an Imperial General Staff was also undertaken. The army was redistributed into six army corps, only one of which—that stationed at Aldershot—was in fact constituted, the rest of the army remaining organised in six independent divisions. This was the situation when Haldane took office as War Minister of a Liberal Government in 1906 and introduced a series of army reform measures which for breadth of vision and fruitfulness of result can only be paralleled by those of Cardwell a generation before.

The main lines of his policy are well known. The General Staff was made a living and working entity instead of a shadowy ideal. The Regular Army at home was organised in complete readiness for war as a striking force of six infantry divisions and one cavalry division; the Militia became the Special Reserve, of which a portion was ear-marked for garrison or line of communication duty abroad in the event of war; while the rest were allotted the role of finding drafts for the regular units to which they were attached. The Yeomanry and Volunteers were reorganised from top to bottom, and emerged as the Territorial Army of fourteen infantry divisions and fourteen cavalry brigades, raised, administered and financed by local bodies known as County Associations but called out for annual training under the direction of the War Office, and organised throughout on Regular Army lines complete for war service. Behind these the Officers' Training Corps in universities and schools ensured a supply of partly-trained officers for the second line forces both in peace and in war.

A new spirit was introduced into the Regular Army by the institution of annual manoeuvres and the increase in training schools and courses in various branches of the military art, while our relations with the self-governing Dominions in matters of doctrine and defence were made more intimate and systematic by consultation and cooperation between the various branches of the Imperial General Staff. Finally the Committee of Imperial Defence, an unofficial but authoritative body meeting under the auspices of the Prime Minister, considered and made recommendations on all matters of military and naval interest, laid down lines of policy to be pursued in peace and in war, and prepared for the complete co-ordination of our preparations in the event of an outbreak of hostilities with any European Power.

It had long been evident to most men of perception that such an eventuality was not only possible but even to be expected in the near future, and that Haldane's new military machine would not have to wait long before being put to the test. Meanwhile he and his military coadjutors felt that their work had been good, that for almost the first time in her history Britain would enter upon her next war, if not fully prepared, at any rate without being from the first hopelessly surprised and outclassed. Indeed, as events were to show, the new army was, for its size, the finest fighting force in Europe, and the cooperation of the whole military power of the nation behind it had been arranged for as thoroughly and rapidly as the exigencies of peace conditions would allow.

Time passed, and in the hot early August days of 1914 the

British army was suddenly called upon to undergo its supreme trial. Into the sombre clouds of that tempest we, pursuant to the wise dictum that they who have attended, in however humble a capacity, at the making of history should leave the writing of it to others, do not purpose to follow it. The writing of this last and greatest chapter of our military history is better left to other and abler pens whose wielders stand not so near as to have shared in the sacrifices, nor too far off to be able to appraise the achievement.

CHAPTER 17
Epilogue

At the end of this brief survey of the history of the British army from its first beginnings down to the commencement of the Great War, 1914-1918, a glance back over the ground which has been traversed leads us to much the same general conclusions as those arrived at in the first chapter.

The main role of the British army in our history has been the acquisition and maintenance of the British Empire. If it is true to say that only by the constant and never-failing aid of our supreme navy has it been able to fulfil this role, it must not be forgotten that the achievement has been and must always be, in the future as in the past, a purely military one. The navy has sent the army to its field of battle, and maintained it there; and but for this purely naval achievement the army must have been left helpless to play any part in our wars beyond that of idly guarding our coasts against raids or invasion. But once it has disembarked the troops on the shore of their chosen theatre of operations the power of the navy for decisive offensive action has ceased; the rest is for the army to see to. The command of the sea has been throughout our history an essential preliminary to the winning of our Empire, and a necessary condition of its retention; but both the gaining and the holding of it have been effected and must still be effected by the land forces alone. An Empire of the Seas is a contradiction in terms : for empire to be either profitable or desirable must comprise the control of lands, the ultimate source of all wealth, and not of mere barren wastes of waters. Now a navy is powerless either to strike or to hold on land; these are the functions of an army, which a navy may facilitate or hinder, but can of itself neither forbid nor fulfil.

The truth of the whole matter seems to be as fairly enshrined as is possible in a mere simile in our previous comparison of the British army to a projectile fired by the British navy. If it be permissible to press this simile somewhat further, one may say that such a projectile may fail of its full effect for a variety of reasons. Firstly, the gun itself may be faulty. It is only due to the navy to say that military failures attributable to this cause have been the rarest of occurrences in our history; in fact, in modern times the only instance of moment occurred at the end of the American War of Independence, when the temporary eclipse of our fleet involved us in a crisis in the Madras Presidency and in the disaster of Yorktown. With this cause of defeat, the most serious and fatal of all when we consider how close has been the interdependence between all our military operations and maritime preponderance, we have seldom had to reckon, though it must not be forgotten that naval weakness or impotence has sometimes maintained our army in forced idleness or locked it up in an attitude of passive defence. More frequent, though less disastrous, have been faults of design or construction in the projectile itself—the army. Our military forces have on many occasions failed, for a variety of reasons which it is needless to specify here, to fulfil the missions on which they were dispatched. As instances of purely military failure may be quoted the Helder expedition of 1799 and the First Boer War in 1881. The final and most fertile cause of failure has been mishandling of gun and projectile by those who have been entrusted with them; that is, by various British Governments and ministers, who have, so to speak, chosen targets out of range or otherwise unsuitable, or battered at defences too strong to be overcome by the weapon in their hands; or again, have allowed the weapon or its ammunition both to become rusty, antiquated, or useless from other causes, necessitating its hasty repair or renewal at short notice, with a corresponding loss of efficiency. Instances of such mishandling will readily occur to every reader: our Southern campaigns in the War of American Independence, Pitt's West Indian enterprises, the Walcheren expedition, the First Afghan War, will serve as good examples.

Generally speaking, it may be said that our military affairs have prospered most exceedingly when we have exploited most fully the advantages which sea power has placed in our hands. The chief of these advantages are two: secrecy and speed. It has been throughout our history possible for us with our command of the sea to take our enemies by surprise by sudden landings of troops at points where they were not expected, thus securing for ourselves an initial superiority of force; and to maintain our predominance so acquired by the transport of reinforcements by sea more rapidly than they could be moved over land. The ideal exploitation of our sea power—and one frequently realised in our history—is of course the throwing of overwhelming forces, either at one blow, or in a short space of time, upon some isolated hostile force or possession which is cut off from hope of reinforcement or rescue by the very fact of our command of the sea. It is in fact in this way that the greater part of our Empire has been won; and the power possessed by us of acting thus has ever been our most potent military weapon. By going far afield for our objectives and striking at our enemies in their most distant possessions we have not only caused them irreparable damage, but have established our own overseas Empire and won a position for ourselves as a humanising and civilising influence unique in world history.

This view may seem to leave out of account a whole series of wars which are from the purely military point of view undoubtedly the most interesting and the most creditable in our annals—those waged on the Continent under William III. and Marlborough, under Ferdinand of Brunswick and Wellington. But a general view of these as a series will, we think, bear out the contention that, though we are accustomed to regard them as British wars and our successes gained in their course as British victories, they were in reality, so far as we were concerned, side-shows, subsidiary to the main issue. In nearly all we were merely auxiliaries, supplying a contingent and a general to a composite force of allies. Many of our generals were men of high military quality; two at least were among the greatest masters of war of all time ; and our troops were always a tower of strength to, and often the mainstay of, the army of which they formed part. None the less, the glory even of Blenheim and Waterloo is not solely our own, any more than were the fruits of these victories; indeed, our allies in either case had an equal share in the credit, and reaped far greater profit, if only for the reason that the battles were fought and won on soil in which their interest, in contradistinction to our own, was direct and immediate. Moreover, against these victories we must set a series of defeats and disappointments, ranging from the days of the Norman and Plantagenet kings down to quite recent times, which, considered as a whole, have involved us in immense loss incurred in a field where we, fighting our friends' battles rather than our own, stood to gain little and lose much.

It must also be remembered that the British army has never been fashioned primarily for a Continental campaign, nor has it ever carried one through to the end without drawing heavily for fresh strength on the manhood of the country. Strictly speaking, our European victories have been won by the "new armies," which were recruited and trained in Great Britain after the beginning of the war, and disbanded at the end of it.

The armies of Marlborough were renewed many times over between 1702 and 1713. Ferdinand of Brunswick's British regiments were mostly made up of war-time recruits. The regular army with which we entered the war with revolutionary and Napoleonic France had perished to a man in Flanders and the West Indies, in South America and in Egypt, long before the crowning mercies of the Peninsula and Waterloo. The small British regular army has never been able to affront a Continental foe on his own ground without drawing largely for men on the soil from which it sprang.

Whether the experience of the past and its lessons will hold good also for the future is a question which may perhaps best be left for the reader to answer for himself. It will be found on a broad view, not only of military but of all history, that the development of cause and effect is but gradual; that a sudden and complete breach with the past is seldom or never met with; and that even what at first sight seems revolution usually turns out on close examination to be merely evolution after all. One would therefore expect that, in the sphere of our military policy also, what has proved so fruitful and effective in the past may do so again and that we shall still find the true role of our little army to be the dealing of sudden and overwhelming blows at our enemy's extremities with the aid of the long arm of sea power. On the other hand, it is arguable that the complete remodelling of transportation resulting from the advent of the locomotive, the motor and the aeroplane has deprived sea power to a large extent of its greater secrecy and swiftness as compared with land power, so that an enemy who possesses a highly organised network of communications can usually discover sea power's objective and get there before it, while few parts of the globe are now so far off as to be unreachable by air. If this is so, then here we have indeed established that rarest of human phenomena—a complete breach with our past; and the guidance of history, which we were once told invariably repeated itself, must seem merely to resemble that of the Delphic oracle, usually dubious, and too often misleading.

ALSO FROM LEONAUR
AVAILABLE IN SOFTCOVER OR HARDCOVER WITH DUST JACKET

WELLINGTON AND THE PYRENEES CAMPAIGN VOLUME I: FROM VITORIA TO THE BIDASSOA by *F. C. Beatson*—The final phase of the campaign in the Iberian Peninsula.

WELLINGTON AND THE INVASION OF FRANCE VOLUME II: THE BIDASSOA TO THE BATTLE OF THE NIVELLE by *F. C. Beatson*—The second of Beatson's series on the fall of Revolutionary France published by Leonaur, the reader is once again taken into the centre of Wellington's strategic and tactical genius.

WELLINGTON AND THE FALL OF FRANCE VOLUME III: THE GAVES AND THE BATTLE OF ORTHEZ by *F. C. Beatson*—This final chapter of F. C. Beatson's brilliant trilogy shows the 'captain of the age' at his most inspired and makes all three books essential additions to any Peninsular War library.

NAVAL BATTLES OF THE NAPOLEONIC WARS by *W. H. Fitchett*—Cape St. Vincent, the Nile, Cadiz, Copenhagen, Trafalgar & Others

SERGEANT GUILLEMARD: THE MAN WHO SHOT NELSON? by *Robert Guillemard*—A Soldier of the Infantry of the French Army of Napoleon on Campaign Throughout Europe

WITH THE GUARDS ACROSS THE PYRENEES by *Robert Batty*—The Experiences of a British Officer of Wellington's Army During the Battles for the Fall of Napoleonic France, 1813.

A STAFF OFFICER IN THE PENINSULA by *E. W. Buckham*—An Officer of the British Staff Corps Cavalry During the Peninsula Campaign of the Napoleonic Wars

THE LEIPZIG CAMPAIGN: 1813—NAPOLEON AND THE "BATTLE OF THE NATIONS" by *F. N. Maude*—Colonel Maude's analysis of Napoleon's campaign of 1813.

BUGEAUD: A PACK WITH A BATON by *Thomas Robert Bugeaud*—The Early Campaigns of a Soldier of Napoleon's Army Who Would Become a Marshal of France.

TWO LEONAUR ORIGINALS

SERGEANT NICOL by *Daniel Nicol*—The Experiences of a Gordon Highlander During the Napoleonic Wars in Egypt, the Peninsula and France.

WATERLOO RECOLLECTIONS by *Frederick Llewellyn*—Rare First Hand Accounts, Letters, Reports and Retellings from the Campaign of 1815.

AVAILABLE ONLINE AT
www.leonaur.com
AND OTHER GOOD BOOK STORES

ALSO FROM LEONAUR
AVAILABLE IN SOFTCOVER OR HARDCOVER WITH DUST JACKET

CAPTAIN OF THE 95th (Rifles) by *Jonathan Leach*—An officer of Wellington's Sharpshooters during the Peninsular, South of France and Waterloo Campaigns of the Napoleonic Wars.

BUGLER AND OFFICER OF THE RIFLES by *William Green & Harry Smith* With the 95th (Rifles) during the Peninsular & Waterloo Campaigns of the Napoleonic Wars

BAYONETS, BUGLES AND BONNETS by *James 'Thomas' Todd*—Experiences of hard soldiering with the 71st Foot - the Highland Light Infantry - through many battles of the Napoleonic wars including the Peninsular & Waterloo Campaigns

THE ADVENTURES OF A LIGHT DRAGOON by *George Farmer & G.R. Gleig*—A cavalryman during the Peninsular & Waterloo Campaigns, in captivity & at the siege of Bhurtpore, India

THE COMPLEAT RIFLEMAN HARRIS by *Benjamin Harris as told to & transcribed by Captain Henry Curling*—The adventures of a soldier of the 95th (Rifles) during the Peninsular Campaign of the Napoleonic Wars

WITH WELLINGTON'S LIGHT CAVALRY by *William Tomkinson*—The Experiences of an officer of the 16th Light Dragoons in the Peninsular and Waterloo campaigns of the Napoleonic Wars.

SURTEES OF THE RIFLES by *William Surtees*—A Soldier of the 95th (Rifles) in the Peninsular campaign of the Napoleonic Wars.

ENSIGN BELL IN THE PENINSULAR WAR by *George Bell*—The Experiences of a young British Soldier of the 34th Regiment 'The Cumberland Gentlemen' in the Napoleonic wars.

WITH THE LIGHT DIVISION by *John H. Cooke*—The Experiences of an Officer of the 43rd Light Infantry in the Peninsula and South of France During the Napoleonic Wars

NAPOLEON'S IMPERIAL GUARD: FROM MARENGO TO WATERLOO by *J. T. Headley*—This is the story of Napoleon's Imperial Guard from the bearskin caps of the grenadiers to the flamboyance of their mounted chasseurs, their principal characters and the men who commanded them.

BATTLES & SIEGES OF THE PENINSULAR WAR by *W. H. Fitchett*—Corunna, Busaco, Albuera, Ciudad Rodrigo, Badajos, Salamanca, San Sebastian & Others

AVAILABLE ONLINE AT
www.leonaur.com
AND OTHER GOOD BOOK STORES

ALSO FROM LEONAUR
AVAILABLE IN SOFTCOVER OR HARDCOVER WITH DUST JACKET

A JOURNAL OF THE SECOND SIKH WAR by *Daniel A. Sandford*—The Experiences of an Ensign of the 2nd Bengal European Regiment During the Campaign in the Punjab, India, 1848-49.

LAKE'S CAMPAIGNS IN INDIA by *Hugh Pearse*—The Second Anglo Maratha War, 1803-1807. Often neglected by historians and students alike, Lake's Indian campaign was fought against a resourceful and ruthless enemy-almost always superior in numbers to his own forces.

BRITAIN IN AFGHANISTAN 1: THE FIRST AFGHAN WAR 1839-42 by *Archibald Forbes*—Following over a century of the gradual assumption of sovereignty of the Indian Sub-Continent, the British Empire, in the form of the Honourable East India Company, supported by troops of the new Queen Victoria's army, found itself inevitably at the natural boundaries that surround Afghanistan. There it set in motion a series of disastrous events-the first of which was to march into the country at all.

BRITAIN IN AFGHANISTAN 2: THE SECOND AFGHAN WAR 1878-80 by *Archibald Forbes*—This the history of the Second Afghan War-another episode of British military history typified by savagery, massacre, siege and battles.

UP AMONG THE PANDIES by *Vivian Dering Majendie*—An outstanding account of the campaign for the fall of Lucknow. This is a vital book of war as fought by the British Army of the mid-nineteenth century, but in truth it is also an essential book of war that will enthral.

BLOW THE BUGLE, DRAW THE SWORD by *W. H. G. Kingston*—The Wars, Campaigns, Regiments and Soldiers of the British & Indian Armies During the Victorian Era, 1839-1898.

INDIAN MUTINY 150th ANNIVERSARY: A LEONAUR ORIGINAL

MUTINY: 1857 by *James Humphries*—It is now 150 years since the 'Indian Mutiny' burst like an engulfing flame on the British soldiers, their families and the civilians of the Empire in North East India. The Bengal Native army arose in violent rebellion, and the once peaceful countryside became a battleground as Native sepoys and elements of the Indian population massacred their British masters and defeated them in open battle. As the tide turned, a vengeful army of British and loyal Indian troops repressed the insurgency with a savagery that knew no mercy. It was a time of fear and slaughter. James Humphries has drawn together the voices of those dreadful days for this commemorative

AVAILABLE ONLINE AT
www.leonaur.com
AND OTHER GOOD BOOK STORES

ALSO FROM LEONAUR
AVAILABLE IN SOFTCOVER OR HARDCOVER WITH DUST JACKET

WAR BEYOND THE DRAGON PAGODA by *J. J. Snodgrass*—A Personal Narrative of the First Anglo-Burmese War 1824 - 1826.

ALL FOR A SHILLING A DAY by *Donald F. Featherstone*—The story of H.M. 16th, the Queen's Lancers During the first Sikh War 1845-1846.

AT THEM WITH THE BAYONET by *Donald F. Featherstone*—The first Anglo-Sikh War 1845-1846.

A LEONAUR ORIGINAL

THE HERO OF ALIWAL by *James Humphries*—The days when young Harry Smith wore the green jacket of the 95th-Wellington's famous riflemen-campaigning in Spain against Napoleon's French with his beautiful young bride Juana have long gone. Now, Sir Harry Smith is in his fifties approaching the end of a long career. His position in the Cape colony ends with an appointment as Deputy Adjutant-General to the army in India. There he joins the staff of Sir Hugh Gough to experience an Indian battlefield in the Gwalior War of 1843 as the power of the Marathas is finally crushed. Smith has little time for his superior's 'bull at a gate' style of battlefield tactics, but independent command is denied him. Little does he realise that the greatest opportunity of his military life is close at hand.

THE GURKHA WAR by *H. T. Prinsep*—The Anglo-Nepalese Conflict in North East India 1814-1816.

SOUND ADVANCE! by *Joseph Anderson*—Experiences of an officer of HM 50th regiment in Australia, Burma & the Gwalior war.

THE CAMPAIGN OF THE INDUS by *Thomas Holdsworth*—Experiences of a British Officer of the 2nd (Queen's Royal) Regiment in the Campaign to Place Shah Shuja on the Throne of Afghanistan 1838 - 1840.

WITH THE MADRAS EUROPEAN REGIMENT IN BURMA by *John Butler*—The Experiences of an Officer of the Honourable East India Company's Army During the First Anglo-Burmese War 1824 - 1826.

BESIEGED IN LUCKNOW by *Martin Richard Gubbins*—The Experiences of the Defender of 'Gubbins Post' before & during the sige of the residency at Lucknow, Indian Mutiny, 1857.

THE STORY OF THE GUIDES by *G.J. Younghusband*—The Exploits of the famous Indian Army Regiment from the northwest frontier 1847 - 1900.

AVAILABLE ONLINE AT
www.leonaur.com
AND OTHER GOOD BOOK STORES

ALSO FROM LEONAUR
AVAILABLE IN SOFTCOVER OR HARDCOVER WITH DUST JACKET

DOING OUR 'BIT' by *Ian Hay*—Two Classic Accounts of the Men of Kitchener's 'New Army' During the Great War including *The First 100,000* & *All In It*.

AN EYE IN THE STORM by *Arthur Ruhl*—An American War Correspondent's Experiences of the First World War from the Western Front to Gallipoli and Beyond.

STAND & FALL by *Joe Cassells*—A Soldier's Recollections of the 'Contemptible Little Army' and the Retreat from Mons to the Marne, 1914.

RIFLEMAN MACGILL'S WAR by *Patrick MacGill*—A Soldier of the London Irish During the Great War in Europe including *The Amateur Army*, *The Red Horizon* & *The Great Push*.

WITH THE GUNS by *C. A. Rose & Hugh Dalton*—Two First Hand Accounts of British Gunners at War in Europe During World War 1- Three Years in France with the Guns and With the British Guns in Italy.

EAGLES OVER THE TRENCHES by *James R. McConnell & William B. Perry*—Two First Hand Accounts of the American Escadrille at War in the Air During World War 1-Flying For France: With the American Escadrille at Verdun and Our Pilots in the Air.

THE BUSH WAR DOCTOR by *Robert V. Dolbey*—The Experiences of a British Army Doctor During the East African Campaign of the First World War.

THE 9TH—THE KING'S (LIVERPOOL REGIMENT) IN THE GREAT WAR 1914 - 1918 by *Enos H. G. Roberts*—Like many large cities, Liverpool raised a number of battalions in the Great War. Notable among them were the Pals, the Liverpool Irish and Scottish, but this book concerns the wartime history of the 9th Battalion – The Kings.

THE GAMBARDIER by *Mark Severn*—The experiences of a battery of Heavy artillery on the Western Front during the First World War.

FROM MESSINES TO THIRD YPRES by *Thomas Floyd*—A personal account of the First World War on the Western front by a 2/5th Lancashire Fusilier.

THE IRISH GUARDS IN THE GREAT WAR - VOLUME 1 by *Rudyard Kipling*—Edited and Compiled from Their Diaries and Papers Volume 1 The First Battalion.

THE IRISH GUARDS IN THE GREAT WAR - VOLUME 2 by *Rudyard Kipling*—Edited and Compiled from Their Diaries and Papers Volume 2 The Second Battalion.

AVAILABLE ONLINE AT
www.leonaur.com
AND OTHER GOOD BOOK STORES

ALSO FROM LEONAUR
AVAILABLE IN SOFTCOVER OR HARDCOVER WITH DUST JACKET

THE JENA CAMPAIGN: 1806 *by F. N. Maude*—The Twin Battles of Jena & Auerstadt Between Napoleon's French and the Prussian Army.

PRIVATE O'NEIL *by Charles O'Neil*—The recollections of an Irish Rogue of H. M. 28th Regt.—The Slashers— during the Peninsula & Waterloo campaigns of the Napoleonic wars.

ROYAL HIGHLANDER *by James Anton*—A soldier of H.M 42nd (Royal) Highlanders during the Peninsular, South of France & Waterloo Campaigns of the Napoleonic Wars.

CAPTAIN BLAZE *by Elzéar Blaze*—Elzéar Blaze recounts his life and experiences in Napoleon's army in a well written, articulate and companionable style.

LEJEUNE VOLUME 1 *by Louis-François Lejeune*—The Napoleonic Wars through the Experiences of an Officer on Berthier's Staff.

LEJEUNE VOLUME 2 *by Louis-François Lejeune*—The Napoleonic Wars through the Experiences of an Officer on Berthier's Staff.

FUSILIER COOPER *by John S. Cooper*—Experiences in the 7th (Royal) Fusiliers During the Peninsular Campaign of the Napoleonic Wars and the American Campaign to New Orleans.

CAPTAIN COIGNET *by Jean-Roch Coignet*—A Soldier of Napoleon's Imperial Guard from the Italian Campaign to Russia and Waterloo.

FIGHTING NAPOLEON'S EMPIRE *by Joseph Anderson*—The Campaigns of a British Infantryman in Italy, Egypt, the Peninsular & the West Indies During the Napoleonic Wars.

CHASSEUR BARRES *by Jean-Baptiste Barres*—The experiences of a French Infantryman of the Imperial Guard at Austerlitz, Jena, Eylau, Friedland, in the Peninsular, Lutzen, Bautzen, Zinnwald and Hanau during the Napoleonic Wars.

MARINES TO 95TH (RIFLES) *by Thomas Fernyhough*—The military experiences of Robert Fernyhough during the Napoleonic Wars.

HUSSAR ROCCA *by Albert Jean Michel de Rocca*—A French cavalry officer's experiences of the Napoleonic Wars and his views on the Peninsular Campaigns against the Spanish, British And Guerilla Armies.

SERGEANT BOURGOGNE *by Adrien Bourgogne*—With Napoleon's Imperial Guard in the Russian Campaign and on the Retreat from Moscow 1812 - 13.

ALSO FROM LEONAUR
AVAILABLE IN SOFTCOVER OR HARDCOVER WITH DUST JACKET

ARMOURED CARS IN EDEN by *K. Roosevelt*—An American President's son serving in Rolls Royce armoured cars with the British in Mesopatamia & with the American Artillery in France during the First World War.

CHASSEUR OF 1914 by *Marcel Dupont*—Experiences of the twilight of the French Light Cavalry by a young officer during the early battles of the great war in Europe.

TROOP HORSE & TRENCH by *R.A. Lloyd*—The experiences of a British Lifeguardsman of the household cavalry fighting on the western front during the First World War 1914-18.

THE LONG PATROL by *George Berrie*—A Novel of Light Horsemen from Gallipoli to the Palestine campaign of the First World War.

THE EAST AFRICAN MOUNTED RIFLES by *C.J. Wilson*—Experiences of the campaign in the East African bush during the First World War

THE FIGHTING CAMELIERS by *Frank Reid*—The exploits of the Imperial Camel Corps in the desert and Palestine campaigns of the First World War.

WITH THE IMPERIAL CAMEL CORPS IN THE GREAT WAR by *Geoffrey Inchbald*—The story of a serving officer with the British 2nd battalion against the Senussi and during the Palestine campaign.

STEEL CHARIOTS IN THE DESERT by *S.C.Rolls*—The first world war experiences of a Rolls Royce armoured car driver with the Duke of Westminster in Libya and in Arabia with T.E. Lawrence.

INFANTRY BRIGADE: 1914 by *Edward Gleichen*—The Diary of a Commander of the 15th Infantry Brigade, 5th Division, British Army, During the Retreat from Mons

HEARTS & DRAGONS by *Charles R. M. F. Crutwell*—The 4th Royal Berkshire Regiment in France and Italy During the Great War, 1914-1918.

TIGERS ALONG THE TIGRIS by *E. J. Thompson*—The Leicestershire Regiment in Mesopotamia During the First World War.

DESPATCH RIDER by *W. H. L. Watson*—The Experiences of a British Army Motorcycle Despatch Rider During the Opening Battles of the Great War in Europe.

AVAILABLE ONLINE AT
www.leonaur.com
AND OTHER GOOD BOOK STORES

www.ingramcontent.com/pod-product-compliance
Lightning Source LLC
Chambersburg PA
CBHW021956160426
43197CB00007B/148